The Manhattan Directory of Private Nursery Schools

Victoria Goldman

SEVENTH EDITION

SOHO

Copyright © 1987, 1989, 1995, 1998, 2002, 2007, 2012 by Soho Press, Inc.

Published in the United States of America by
Soho Press, Inc.
853 Broadway
New York, NY 10003

Library of Congress Cataloging-in-Publication Data is available.

ISBN 978-1-61695-051-4
eISBN 978-1-61695-052-1

SEVENTH EDITION

Printed in the United States of America

www.victoriagoldman.net

10 9 8 7 6 5 4 3 2 1

I would like to acknowledge the previous authors of this directory, especially Linda Faulhaber, its originator, for they laid the groundwork on which this book rests. I also gratefully acknowledge and thank the many directors, administrators, and parents who have shared their insights and experiences, and provided the most accurate and up-to-date information about their schools. And, to my editors at Soho Press, Juliet Grames and Bronwen Hruska for their guidance and support, as well as for giving me the opportunity to write this book.

Also by Victoria Goldman

The Manhattan Family Guide to Private Schools and Selective Public Schools
The Los Angeles Guide to Private Schools

Contents

Individual school entries in this book appear
alphabetically by geographic neighborhood

Please note: tuitions listed usually increase
three to six percent annually.

PARENTS' PRESCHOOL PRIMER

This is Manhattan, home of some of the world's finest nursery schools, and at some of the top schools, the gun goes off at 7:30 A.M. roughly the day after Labor Day. Frenzied parents jam the phone and internet lines of schools they deem most desirable to request nursery school applications. There are schools that run out of applications by noon. Some parents send their babies and toddlers to parenting programs and play groups that are supposed to be "feeders to the feeders" of the schools that will, they hope, secure a place for their offspring in an Ivy League college. Such pre-preschools, like Free to Be Under Three at All Souls, Barnard Toddler Program or the Parenting Center at Central Synagogue help one- and two-year-olds learn to socialize, share, and play nicely so they can ace their nursery school interviews.

But since this is Manhattan, you need not take part in the madness unless you choose to. There are hundreds of nursery or early childhood programs available. The so-called top tier nursery schools or "Baby" Ivies have directors with over twenty years of experience, fabulous facilities, students with famous (or rich) parents, teachers with masters degrees, expertly thought out programs, and strong track records of sending their graduates to all the best public and private schools in town. Yet there are many other schools that do as well by their students and frequently are a better match for a particular family. If you want to secure a place for your child at a supposed "feeder" nursery school, one that is thought to guarantee a place at a "top" ongoing school—most of which would honestly disclaim this ability—you have to prepare a balanced list of schools to apply to of no fewer than six and no more than twelve possibilities. Some of your choices should be schools that are less competitive, so-called "safeties." And before you can draw up any list, you must decide what sort of school would be best for your child.

What kinds of schools are there?

You have half a dozen and more from which to choose:

- **Montessori**
- **Developmental** (developmental-interaction)
- **Progressive** (included in developmental)
- **Traditional**
- **Eclectic** (a term used to cover the programs that combine several approaches or are not concerned with defining themselves in terms of methodology)
- **All-Day or Day Care Center**

1

There are also such institutions as the Rudolf Steiner School (a Waldorf school), which have developed their own individual teaching approaches. Other schools are distinguished from their counterparts by strong affiliations with religious groups. So there is a lot to think about and a lot of answers to find. The first concerns are mercifully practical—like birthday cutoffs, tuitions, proximity, and school hours, for instance.

School hours for young children going into the 2s are either from about 8:30 A.M. to noon or from 1 P.M. to 4 P.M. Older children attend from 8:30 A.M. until about 3 P.M. Bringing children to school earlier than 8:30 A.M. is possible at many schools (called **early drop-off**), and many offer **extended hours** for the youngest preschool grades whereby the normal three-hour school day may be expanded to perhaps five hours, but rarely more.

There are alternatives to the traditional nursery school hours. For working parents requiring child care during normal workday hours there are **All-Day** or **Day Care centers**. These centers consider themselves preschools and some are included here. They typically take children from 8:30 A.M. to 5:30 or 6 P.M.

For parents who do not want to be separated from very young children by sending them to school there are **parent-toddler programs**. These not only permit, but actually require the presence of a parent. Some programs allow caregivers or sitters as substitutes, but the idea is to provide a preschool-like setting for parents and children not yet ready for the separation inherent in any school experience.

By law, mandatory enrollment in school only begins at 6 years of age. But not here in Manhattan where the sociocultural norms have families on a faster, earlier track.

The Law and Preschools

All schools listed in this directory are licensed by the New York City Department of Health, Bureau of Day Care. Each school must be relicensed every two years. Preschools caring for children under 2 are relicensed every year. Each facility is inspected at least twice a year.

Space. The legal requirement is 30 square feet per child. Every room in an all-day care center has an assigned maximum occupancy figure that specifies how many children may be in that room. The one variance is that all-day centers and nursery schools are allowed to enroll two children above the maximum allowance because daily attendance varies so greatly among preschoolers. Each classroom with children two years of age or older must have a minimum of one state-certified teacher.

Every classroom must have one teacher and one assistant for:

6 to 10 two-year-olds
11 to 15 three-year-olds
13 to 20 four-year-olds
16 to 25 five-year-olds

Four other regulations you should know about:

All people working in schools or centers must be fingerprinted.
School staff members are forbidden to administer any medications.
All children under the age of 3 years are required to have a yearly physical examination within 30 days prior to attendance.
Children age 4 years and older must have a medical exam within 90 days of starting school.

Each program must also receive approval from the city's Buildings and Fire departments and from the Public Health and Sanitation Department.

Many schools also voluntarily elect to be chartered by the Board of Regents of the State University of New York. Its standards are stringent for classroom size, location, and construction; eating, rest, and sanitary facilities; equipment and outdoor play space; and fire and safety requirements. Classrooms must include activities centers for block building, housekeeping play, water play, creative arts, painting, clay and collage, science and nature study, cooking, and music, as well as adequate books, pictures, puzzles, games, and small play objects. Outdoor equipment must include well-anchored climbing and dramatic play structures, plus wheel toys, tricycles, wagons, trucks, building equipment, ladders, sawhorses, and a storage shed.

The maximum number of infants in any one room is 6, the maximum number of toddlers is 10; 4s, 20; 5s, 25

Schools must show evidence of a consistent curriculum and education program adapted to the ages, interests, and needs of the children. The child must be afforded the opportunity to choose and become involved in the manipulation of various materials and objects, large motor play, discussions and games, literature, music, science, and field trips.

Schools must also show positive parent collaboration in the education of their children, including conferences, parent workshops, classes or lectures, and newsletters.

These are the standards.

The Basics

What are the different pre-school or nursery school grades?

• Infants	6 months to 1 year
• Toddlers: 2s or 3s	1½ to 3 years
• 4s or Pre-Kindergarten	4/5 years
• Kindergartners, 5s and prefirsts	5/6 years

What is an "ongoing" school?

A nursery school or preschool traditionally goes from age 2 or 3 years to age 5 or 6 years when the child is about to enter kindergarten—the first rung of most ongoing schools. An **elementary (or primary) school** goes through the 8th grade; **comprehensive schools** go all the way through high school to the 12th grade. An ongoing school refers to either one.

You will also hear teachers and administrators use such terms as "old 2s" or "young 5s" in describing children, depending on the relationship of their birth month to the school year. These terms simply mean that a child who is, say 2.1 (two years, one month) to 2.5 (meaning two years and five months) at the start of the school year is said to be a "young 2." A child who is from 2.6 (two years and six months) to 2.11 (two years and eleven months) in age would be considered an "old two." This same method of designating ages is used throughout this book.

What is the first thing to look for in a nursery school?

The first consideration is practical: How far from home is it? Other basic questions come in quick succession:

- Are the days and hours right for our needs?
- What are the age qualifications?
- When should we apply?
- Is this school in our price range?
- Must children be toilet trained by the time school starts?

4

The answers to many of these questions are given in the individual entries. Do keep in mind, however, that programs change and that tuition usually goes up by about 6 to 8 percent a year depending on the school. (The tuitions listed in this book were being charged when the book was written.)

And then, of course, there is the biggest item of all: What **type** of school is best for my child? To answer this question, you need to know what the various educational approaches are about.

Just what is a Montessori school?

It is a school based on precepts formulated by Maria Montessori, who in the early 1900s created a strict method for training young children. She held that intelligence is the ability to classify and impose order on the apparent chaos of life. That was, for her, the paramount quality to be developed. At its most faithful, a Montessori school is one in which the Montessori-designed didactic materials (e.g., frames with buttons to be buttoned, color tablets to be matched, and bead boards) are to be used only in ways that demonstrate their unique pedagogic characteristics. Creative extensions by the child may arise out of the original presentation but are to be faithful to the original intention regarding the material.

Montessori, a medical doctor working primarily with orphans, observed that young children have an innate desire to learn, and in particular, a desire to master real-life tasks and skills. To nurture that desire, she developed the "prepared environment," an orderly, secure setting in which children feel free to explore sequential materials designed to stimulate and challenge. Learning skills embedded in real-life experiences, she was convinced, inculcates a sense of genuine achievement that is crucial to children's ongoing development. Thus, in addition to traditional academic and cultural subjects, the Montessori nursery emphasizes the mastery of essential life skills, such as putting on a coat, wiping the table and preparing a snack, sweeping the floor, watering plants, putting away materials, etc.

The mood of the classroom tends to be purposeful and task-oriented. While the classroom materials are often beautifully arrayed, children's original artwork is rarely displayed on the walls or in the hallways of a strict Montessori school.

Montessori did not believe that children were able to socialize at very young ages. Consequently, her program, where strictly followed, does not encourage social interaction in the classroom except perhaps for lessons in getting along with others. Children must always put away what they are working on—returning their materials to the proper place before embarking on another project—and file the results when they are finished. They must put away their mats. They must not disturb the projects of other children without permission, nor should they interrupt them. When finished with a project, the children raise their hands and wait for the teacher to come and review it.

Socializing takes place during outdoor play, on field trips, and during lunch, but this is not part of the curriculum. Children gather in large groups for demonstrations of proper usage of work materials or to be shown nature experiments: seeds growing, colored inks being absorbed by a plant, and so forth.

There is no room for "make believe" in the curriculum. There is no art work. Nor is there dramatic play, although children are read stories and, obviously, can engage in play fantasies during their outdoor periods. Children work individually for the most part, occasionally in pairs or small groups, and their interaction must further the work. Each activity is graded according to difficulty and the children must use the materials in the prescribed sequence until they have mastered the particular skill involved and are able to move on to more difficult projects. The idea of each undertaking is to have the child gain a particular bit of knowledge or skill from, for example, a pie-shaped puzzle that demonstrates the relationship of fractions to the whole, or from a series of boxes that resonate with different tones.

Three major skill areas are defined and practiced. *Practical life tasks:* tying shoelaces, wiping surfaces properly, pouring liquids, operating a zipper or button. *Sensory:* handling three-dimensional geometric shapes, arranging color cards by tone, fitting cylindrical blocks of varying sizes into their proper holes, judging wooden tablets of different weights. *Language and math:* handling rough-textured alphabet letters and learning their sounds, tracing shapes to perfect small muscle control for writing and the development of penmanship, counting beads strung on long chains, and more.

Beyond these, there are geography materials (interesting puzzle maps of the world, three-dimensional dioramas), and science materials (natural objects, small animals, perhaps a garden patch).

Age groups are mixed in the classroom and older children teach younger ones the correct use of materials and also serve as role models. The mix can vary from school to school: at one Montessori school typically from age 2.6 to 6 years. Although other kinds of nursery schools also mix ages, the differential is usually two years at most.

The respect for the child is absolute, most child psychiatrists assert, and is a statement with which every Montessori teacher would agree. Children are seen as immensely responsible and capable, and fully able to learn at a rate of their own choosing from a wide variety of materials and projects designed to intrigue and challenge. The primary relationship is between child, the materials, and the environment, not between the child and his peers or the child and his teachers. Teachers remain in the background.

Since independence is stressed, separation from parents is expeditious. Children are brought to the school door and from there they are escorted to their classroom by staff members or by older classmates.

The degree of adherence to the Montessori method varies from school to school. One clue to the strictness is a school's affiliation with one or the other of two Montessori federations. The first is the Association Montessori Internationale, which was organized by Maria Montessori herself, succeeded by her son. This is the purist or orthodox group. A good example of a school adhering faithfully to the original principles is Resurrection Episcopal Day School.

The Montessori schools that are members of the American Montessori Society have modified the basic method. They will provide the child with the prescribed project materials and also **open-ended** play things with undefined applications: sand, water, clay, art materials, blocks. They also allow for the child's dramatic or fantasy play, and are more flexible about the separation process when a child first enters school. An excellent example of a modified use of Maria Montessori's tenets is the West Side Montessori School.

What is a "child centered" developmental-interaction approach?

Schools with a **developmental** approach follow a curriculum that adheres to what teaching professionals would refer to as the **developmental-interaction** method. (You may hear the term "The Child Development Method" or the expression "The Total Child Approach.") **Progressive** schools basically use the same methodology.

Developmental-interaction is a concept which revolutionized early childhood education when first introduced more than eighty-five years ago at about the same time Maria Montessori was developing her theories.* The basic tenet is that the child has a need to explore, and then to

---

*Reggio Emilia, like Montessori, is Italian in origin. With roots dating back to the twelfth century, the Reggio Emilia is a progressive philosophy holding that community, democracy, and citizenship are the most important components of a healthy society and should be taught to young children.

TriBeCa Community School, p. 349, *infra*, is an example of a Reggio Emilia nursery in New York City, and many schools have incorporated various elements into their programs. (*The Hundred Languages of Children—The Reggio Emilia Approach—Advanced Reflections*, 2nd Edition, Bolen, 1998.)

express his or her discoveries through a variety of channels: imaginative play, discussion, art, and the deceptively simple but central activity of block building.

Play is seen as the child's work. It is the means by which the child re-creates and re-examines, again and again, everything they have experienced and observed. Play is considered purposeful, exceedingly important, and serious. Hence activities chosen by the child are treated as important explorations. The developmental approach emphasizes the inseparability of the child's emotional life from his or her intellectual and physical development.

The child's emotional and fantasy life is indeed thought paramount— the key. Social interactions are of major importance in these schools. To learn to be aware of emotions, to identify and talk about them, to express needs and negotiate their resolution with classmates and faculty is considered vital. The idea is to encourage and facilitate interactions between the children. The teacher facilitates the forming of friendships.

Separation is seen as a part of the curriculum to which the teachers and parents devote a great deal of time, as all concerned learn and adjust to this new concept of going to school. Separation is approached as a major psychological and developmental milestone, a profound step in a child's life and not at all a minor, quick adjustment.

Developmental-interaction classrooms and progressive classrooms abound with what are called **open-ended** materials—water, sand, puzzles, fabrics, paint, clay, funnels, and lots of different size blocks. Children use the same materials at different ages in ever more elaborate ways. Free play time is generous, and even planned activities may suddenly give way to the children's spontaneous interests. Rooms may be messy or noisy. Teachers are addressed by their first names. Artwork tends to be varied, often beautiful, and sometimes rather more expressive than at other schools.

The aim of this approach is to allow the child to learn at his own pace through active play, and to facilitate constant interaction between emotional and cognitive development. There are no workbooks. There are no tests prepared for or given, and there are no prescribed points at which a child must master any skill, such as reading or arithmetic. There is no pressure to achieve prescribed levels at predetermined junctures. The teacher mediates, prepares materials, and observes. Specific learning and direct instruction are frowned upon, and hastening development through training or rote instruction is considered inappropriate, even possibly damaging.

Community is stressed, especially in the form of joint undertakings that require the continual interaction of the children. That is why so much emphasis is placed upon building with varieties of blocks. By the time children become proficient in block building, usually as 5s, they will build as teams, constantly discussing, deciding, and planning. The ambitiousness of their projects and their evident success can be truly impressive.

The Bank Street College of Education is the promulgator of this method. Established in 1914, its mission was to collect information on new teaching concepts then being developed in progressive schools such as City and Country. It resulted, four years later, in the founding of a new nursery school today known as the Bank Street School for Children. Over the intervening years it and the College trained many of the teachers and directors of developmental and progressive preschools in Manhattan, and fostered the growth of these approaches nationwide. It was and remains the hub of the innovative methods developed in City and Country School and the Little Red School House, all of which were avidly putting into practice the theories of psychologists Piaget, Anna Freud, John Dewey, and others. The philosophy and methodology that evolved profoundly influence educational approaches to this day.

As with the Montessori method, adherence varies from school to school and, in fact, many preschools in Manhattan call themselves adherents of developmental-interaction but are modified versions at best. So you cannot automatically accept labels or descriptions that schools apply to themselves. Developmental, child-centered, Bank Street, progressive—these terms may have been misappropriated or may be ill-fitting at best. The model developmental-interaction/progressive schools are quite open to inquiries and visits, Bank Street School for Children and City and Country School chief among them. They will give you an excellent idea of what a "Bank Street oriented" preschool is about.

The traditional schools are there too.

Traditional schools are often familiar, and in many instances associated with a religious institution. They have definite curriculum goals that usually will include mastery of specific skills such as numbers or phonics and the like. The programs vary quite a bit school to school but most share basic elements. They have activities centers and a consistent class format that is usually teacher directed. There is a detailed curriculum with regular units of study and specific goals for the children. These are generally based on their skills or **readiness levels**, as they are called. Reading, writing, and math are stressed, often using workbooks and worksheets.

The term **academic** is often used in connection with traditional schools because of their emphasis on performance. Their goal is to develop skills, such as speaking, listening, time measurement, problem solving, and record keeping. Each day's activities are planned and the schedule closely followed in order to ground the children in an agenda of daily events and undertakings that are consistent and predictable.

Traditional programs also employ open-ended materials which can be explored and manipulated in innumerable ways: sand, water, blocks, paint, and clay. The classrooms resemble those of developmental preschools, with their housekeeping areas and sand tables, water trays, blocks, story corner, carpentry tools, art supplies, science area, and so forth. But the approach is distinctly different. The teacher instructs, explains, and organizes projects. Workbooks and worksheets are often used, and there may be formal lessons, particularly for older children. Classroom etiquette, and readiness to pay attention and to learn from a teacher are skills being taught.

The alphabet and numbers are systematically introduced, usually in the 3s, and games and books will further encourage their use. Printed artwork or teacher-made art objects will be displayed to illustrate lessons. The teacher directs the child's focus to the learning tasks at hand, urging the preschooler to color in a particular letter of the alphabet or, perhaps, to tell the class how many dots appear in an illustration. At more traditional schools that are dedicated to this approach, there is less "free-play" time and more academic activities like formal reading and arithmetic lessons. The children gather in groups and sit in their seats while the teacher covers specific curriculum areas. Workbooks and worksheets are used to practice reading, writing, mathematics, and to master certain concepts. Colors, shapes, letters, and numbers were formerly introduced to the 2s at some schools. This is no longer the case.

Some traditional schools, such as Convent of the Sacred Heart or Temple Emanu-El Nursery School and Kindergarten, eschew the use of workbooks and similar "academic" materials and may resist such a label, but they are similar in that they, too, are performance oriented. And that, really, is the hallmark of the preschools described as traditional.

Some preschool programs are loosely described here as **eclectic**— a term coined purely for convenience—simply because they seem to have adapted a variety of methods in constructing their curriculum, or they do not promulgate any one approach. In such nursery schools you might find play and academic work, blocks and workbooks, all being utilized, and perhaps even some Montessori techniques or materials. Pieces and aspects of several theories may have been combined to create an effective hybrid.

All-day centers or **Day Care centers,** for instance, are generally more loosely structured and eclectic about the methods they employ. These schools may use a variety of teaching techniques, often combining several approaches over the course of a day. They differ from their preschool counterparts only in that they offer daylong programs from early morning until early evening, and will, therefore, allow the children more free-time activities. One director of a day care center pointed out, "We don't have to squeeze learning into two and a half or three hours. We have the whole day, and the children are learning all the time."

Unlike other nursery programs, they run year-round without a summer hiatus. Many also enroll children at much younger ages, beginning as early as six months, when the question of a particular approach is moot.

All-day centers consider themselves preschools in every way and somewhat resent the conventional preconception of their being simple caretakers. The Educational Alliance's Nursery School program is a prototypical example of the early child-care center concept.

Putting a particular school into one of these categories can be an art in itself. Even if you visit several schools before applying, you may be whisked through so quickly that you are unable to perceive the very real differences among them. Unfortunately, there is a tendency on the part of schools to be very general in briefing parents. Although the staff may be professional about teaching and extremely attentive to children, handling parents is not always their forte; sometimes vagueness is even deliberate.

Administrators worry. They may want their school to be seen as elite or desirable, but they do not want this exclusivity to be interpreted negatively. Or they may be trying to maintain and protect their image as a "child-oriented" school that emphasizes the child's development and disdains pressuring youngsters to perform especially when it comes to the touchy area of preparation for the test known as the ERB,* that most preschoolers will take and the scores of which will be used by ongoing schools to determine admission to their kindergarten/ongoing school programs.

Directors and teachers will insist, devoted as they are to the education and welfare of "the total child," that they do not coach or train youngsters for these tests, even as they try to assure you that they do, in fact, produce students who succeed on these tests and get into the best ongoing schools.

Administrators and teachers are terribly sensitive about the alleged

*See ERB, p. 393, *infra*.

coaching of children for the ERB, used by ongoing schools to evaluate candidates. Often preschool staff will criticize such practices even while showing prospective parents the tasks and other materials that, coincidentally, replicate the tasks and materials used by ERB tests. Additionally, many private test prep tutors and companies have sprung up in recent years. Hence, ERB scores have improved too. But be aware that a high score doesn't always guarantee acceptance, but low scores often result in rejection.

As a further convenience, and to make youngsters more comfortable and ostensibly help their scores, the tests may be administered in the school instead of at a testing facility. Such an advantageous arrangement may be emphasized, however subtly (and despite the testing organization's insistence that there is no statistical difference between the results of tests administered in the school and those given at its centers). Directors may even take children individually from their classrooms to familiarize them with the materials and testing procedure, insisting all the while that such is not the purpose.

An administrator may also eschew the use of workbooks and worksheets and cite their absence as evidence of a school's nonacademic orientation yet the program can be highly structured and academic in every other way. For instance, when introducing alphabet letters—let's say **W**—everything done that week from painting to cooking will involve **W** words. So even though workbooks are not being employed, the class activities may be highly structured to fulfill weekly and monthly learning units.

Other complications you may encounter: It is in the school's interest sometimes to maintain the impression that the demand for places in their class groups is far greater than the supply. You may get a lot of dire intimations about how few openings there are and how fast a decision needs to be made about accepting the school's possible offer of a place in their program. So another obvious obstacle to any probing discussion is the parents' anxiety about placing their child and the school representative's wish to depict the institution as desirable.

Finally, as often as not, tours are conducted by the parents of enrolled students who know the school as volunteers and not as teaching professionals, and report to the admissions director—so, watch what you say during your tour!

What are the admissions procedures like?

There are hundreds of nursery or early childhood programs to choose from. In all-day or day care centers for infants through five-year-olds, you will be invited to come informally, with or without your child, and spend time observing the program. This can be at any point in the calendar year. You will probably find on your visit that the all-day center is loosely structured and that the staff is used to parents visiting and being around. Most of these centers accept children on a first-come basis and receive applications all year.

Most preschools, for two- through five-year-olds, are more formal. You will be asked the birth date of your child, you may be asked how you heard of the school, and some of the more exclusive preschools may even ask for references. In a few instances you will be able to arrange for a visit when you phone. The school visit may be a one-time individual family session for the parents and the child, or a collective meeting with another family or with both sets of parents. Or it may be a large gathering for twenty families and kids, depending on the school. Mostly, you will be expected to call for an application first and then schedule a visit; occasionally you will be asked to wait for the school to call you.

The majority of ongoing schools with nursery enrollments and lower schools start with either a tour or a personal interview with the parents. However, that word—**interview**—is used discreetly by school functionaries, so when arranging a "visit," make sure of what it is you are going for:

- A tour of the facilities
- An interview for you and your spouse
- An interview by the staff or director for your child

Some schools collect all the applications before evaluating the applicants pool and making decisions. Other schools process applications in the order they are received *as* they are received and, once the vacancies are filled, the admissions are simply cut off. There are also lotteries at some schools to get an application. After that they may only accept applications provisionally for unanticipated openings.

Ask each school what their policy is.

What should you look for on your tour of the school?
- Do the children look happy and involved?
- Are they too noisy/quiet for your taste?
- Are there "boys" activities and "girls" activities?
- How formal, or casual, is the atmosphere?
- Are the teachers working on the floor with the children, or do they keep their distance?
- How clean is everything?

13

- Do the windows have guards on them?
- What are the toilet facilities like and are they separate for adults?
- Does the temperature and air circulation of the school feel comfortable for the children?
- How do you feel about the level of order/disorder?
- Do the indoor and outdoor areas seem spacious enough for children to move with ease?
- Do the teachers seem warm?
- How are the interactions among children handled?
- How on top of things are the teachers?
- If you have a chance to see classroom conflict, how is it handled?
- How comfortable are you with the staff?

What's the most revealing question you can ask?

The one question that might reveal the most about a school is how they view and handle separation. There is a real difference among schools and it can be a significant indicator as to the nature of the school's program and philosophy. The more liberal (progressive, developmental-interaction, "Bank Street-oriented," "child-centered," modified Montessori) devote a great deal of time to it. The more conservative (traditional, academic, strict Montessori) tend to de-emphasize it.

Questions about separation you might ask if not already answered in the school's literature are:

- Do teachers make home visits before the school year begins?
- Does the school allow parents in the classroom?
- Do parents wait nearby?
- How many days or weeks does the school have parents in the classroom or standing by in the school?
- At what point do teachers usually begin suggesting the parent leave?

Another question that may suggest the totality of the program and the school's style involves the children's **free time**: How much of it do they have?

The developmental and progressive programs allow for a great deal of free time; the more traditional and conservative schools limit it.

Here is a checklist of significant questions you might pose during the tour, but be sure that the answers are not already available in brochures or elsewhere, such as the school's website.

- At what age does the school introduce phonics, the alphabet, numbers, formal lessons?
- Do they use learning games?
- Are children required to join activities?
- Does the school provide lunch?
- What kinds of snacks are served?
- Are naps mandatory or can the children just rest quietly?
- How are sick children cared for?
- Are there workshops for parents?
- How often during the year are parent/teacher conferences scheduled?
- How long do parent/teacher conferences last? (They can vary from between fifteen minutes to one hour.)

Typically, after the parent tour, an interview ("visit") with the child is scheduled at the school. This is usually a group-play session with two to six children of the same age (most often all applicants), who will be observed by the director and staff, sometimes without, but most often with, parents present.

A child may be seen singly for a play session with a teacher or the director, or the standard procedure may be to invite the child into a functioning classroom to participate (or not, as he wishes).

What is the school looking for?

The staff will be looking at your child's developmental level to decide if he or she is ready for school. They are interested in seeing:

- How the child responds to suggestions or directions.
- How well he or she can be understood.
- What are the interactions between your child and the others (if in a group).
- How the parents respond. What are *your* personalities like?

To a great extent the admissions process is, as one nursery school director described it, "a numbers game." Once the school has allotted spaces for returning children, siblings, and legacies,° it must balance the

---

°Children of alumni

ages, personalities, and sexes as best it can among its remaining applicants. If 15 three-year-old boys apply and four girls, the odds are astronomically in favor of the girls being accepted.

There is no point in taking acceptance, or rejection, as a judgment of you or your child. It may be a relatively random decision based on factors having nothing to do with you or your child.

Making a decision.

- When you get home think about what you observed.
- Compare what you observed at each school.
- Reassess your feelings about each school.
- Be sure that the schools that you like meet your needs for location, hours, and cost.
- The most important thing you can ask yourself is "Do I feel comfortable leaving my child at this school?"

Certain schools will be looking at you, the parents.

A cooperative will want to know how well a prospective member may "fit in" because of the amount of time they will be spending with you in the collective work required to operate a cooperative nursery school.

Some preschools have chosen to cultivate specific populations. One institution's preeminence as a "society nursery school" was reported to be the result of a deliberate policy set years ago.

The level of privilege in a school may be a serious concern to parents. Many Upper East Side preschools, for instance, enroll extremely privileged children from this neighborhood. One nursery school director gave evidence of the wealth and sophistication of her charges by noting that even the youngest had been to Europe. Working middle-class parents, and even upwardly mobile two-career couples, have reported feeling uncomfortable with the ambience, and inconvenienced by required attendance at daytime functions and the private SUV-with-driver-lock at pick up and drop off times.

The director of a school with a more mixed population commented that children are sensitive to social differences. "By the time children are five, they know who has a townhouse, chauffeur, and cook, and who hasn't."

The attitude at some schools is actually condescending toward the less-privileged children enrolled. At one preschool, which offered several scholarships yearly to low-income children, the director commented that, "Yes. We have them, but you would hardly notice that they are in the classroom. I interview them as I interview everyone else." Other schools, like All Souls, encourage scholarship children by allowing them to bypass the school's application lottery system.

Yet another school, in its literature, congratulates its students' parents on their generosity in supporting the scholarship fund and entreats them to welcome scholarship children on an equal footing in their children's classrooms.

If your child's education is going to present a serious strain financially, you should know this: **Independent schools or centers which accept public funding offer up to half of their places to children funded by the Agency for Child Services**.*

Some independent schools that accept public funding include the Educational Alliance Nursery School and West Side Montessori.

These programs generally have a better racial and economic balance than exclusively private programs.

The director of a nursery school observed that low-income and middle-class children learned a great deal from each other: "Middle-class children frequently cannot concentrate on a task alone. They are so used to being spoiled and pressured and attended to by parents who have a hard time saying 'no' to them. On the other hand, low-income children hear 'no' a lot. They are often more independent and better able to take care of themselves." Some directors share this opinion and praise the mutual enrichment a variety of backgrounds provides. Others disagree. They feel that their more homogeneous classes allow them to spend more time on teaching and less time on negotiation and intervening.

If you are looking for a school with diversity at the primary and elementary levels, contact **Early Steps**,** an organization that acts as the liaison for independent schools seeking students with a variety of backgrounds. It is the clearinghouse for information about programs, admissions procedures, and financial aid; it will assist families to negotiate the admissions process.

Where can you get information to help make your decision about the right preschool for your child?

Neighbors are a terrific source of candid information, so call everyone you know with children in preschool. Finding a nursery school is a memorable experience for parents and most are happy to talk about it, while others' egos are deflated and they feel as if they have just been denied membership to the "club" of their dreams.

* See ACS, p. 389, *infra*.
** See p. 393, *infra*.

Also, look into **Center for Children's Initiatives.**° This is the leading private childcare advisory and advocacy organization. It is non-profit and provides a great array of services. Telephone counselors give advice and information on over 2,000 licensed infant-toddler programs in the city, on nursery schools, all-day centers, after-school programs, kindergartens, and camps.

For a small fee, you can get a listing of all the licensed programs, and a counseling session will be arranged for you once you have several candidates in mind.

A professional advisor can also be retained.°° Fees range from roughly $200 to $3,000, but still there are no guarantees.

Understanding the Program

Technology has clearly become of greater importance than the learning of handicraft activities at many nurseries. However, a school like the Rudolf Steiner School continues to value the organic and natural, and handicraft activities; there is little if any plastic in the entire school, and none in the nursery school.

What is "dramatic play"?

Dramatic play is simply make believe, or pretending. In most schools this consists of imaginative role-playing in the housekeeping corner, often including dress-up.

What are creative movement, music and movement, rhythms?

Anything from dancing around to a guitar or piano accompaniment, to extremely imaginative choreographic inventions that evolve in a rhythms program, answers to these descriptions.

What is large motor activity?

Active physical play on slides, see-saws, climbing equipment, swings, and tricycles, and construction with large building blocks. Today, most nursery schools have yoga as an integral part of the progam.

° See p. 389, *infra*.

°° See Advisory, Testers, and Other Resources p. 399, *infra*.

What are "manipulatives"?

Small play objects: beads, Legos, and the like.

The best way to get to know a school is to sit in the classroom and observe. Unfortunately, many schools do not allow this. It is not practical for them, and also many parents cannot commit the time this would entail. If an open house is coming up, go. Most schools arrange such visits.

In most instances, the director strongly sets the tone of the school, so the director's willingness to respond to your concerns is a significant clue as to what the school is or isn't. If you feel comfortable at a school, chances are so will your child. So, follow your instincts and your child will more than likely have a healthy and productive nursery school experience, and you will, too.

GLOSSARY OF ACRONYMS

ACEI   Association for Childhood Education International
ACS   Agency for Child Services
AMI   Association Montessori Internationale
AMS   American Montessori Society
ATIS   Association of Teachers in Independent Schools
BJE   Board of Jewish Education
ERB   Education Records Bureau (also may refer to the test administered by the organization to pre-kindergarteners)
ISAAGNY   Independent Schools Administration Association of Greater New York
NAES   National Association of Episcopal Schools
NAEYC   National Association for the Education of Young Children
NAIS   National Association of Independent Schools
NEST   New Explorations for Science, Technology + Math
NYSAIS   New York State Association of Independent Schools
SEIT   Special Education Intervention Teacher

EAST SIDE

All Souls School

Ages: 2.6–6 yrs

Nonsectarian Nursery School

1157 Lexington Avenue	Established 1965
(between 79th and	Dr. Marjorie Goldsmith,
80th Streets)	Director
Zip: 10075	Renee Mease,
Tel: 861-5232	Director of Admissions
Fax: 737-5271	Enrollment: 165

School year. September through early June.

Age	Hours	Days	Tuition
2s°	9:00–11:30	Tues and Thurs	$9,475
2s	9:00–11:45	Mon Wed Fri	$11,430
old 2s/young 3s	1:00–3:45	Mon–Thurs	$13,600
3s	9:00–11:45 or	Mon–Fri	$16,170
3s	1:00–3:45	Mon–Fri	
4s	9:00–12:00 or	Mon–Fri	$16,170
4s	1:00–4:00	Mon–Fri	
5s	9:00–3:00	Mon–Fri (until 12:00)	$21,530

°Must be 2.6 by September. Extended hours for 4s: The cost is $1,350 for one after-noon and $2,700 for two afternoons per year. Scholarships are available.

Program. Traditional/Developmental. The educational approach of the school is based on two principles: Children learn best when they are developmentally ready for new experiences and when these new experiences build upon earlier ones. Learning depends on the child's interaction with the social and physical environment. Long-range group projects and opportunities for individual work flow from children's interests and their readiness.

Activities include language arts (dictating stories, storytime, reading-readiness, and writing), block building (to discover math and aesthetic concepts), art, cooking, woodworking, sand and water play, math-readiness (measuring, quantifying, categorizing), science experi-ences, dramatic play, music and movement, social studies, and active play. Children do not use workbooks, worksheets, or computers.

Class projects develop from the interests of the children. Teachers and children collaborate on ideas that grow into trips, talks by guest experts, and other special events.

All Souls is unusual in the amount of time it devotes to studying each child. Children are observed closely by all members of the staff in an attempt to see the world through each child's eyes, to learn who the child is, as opposed to evaluating that individual according to achievement norms (although this is done too, to meet ongoing school requirements). The staff's observations are discussed in staff meetings devoted to the children, and then a curriculum is developed.

ERB tests are given on the premises.

Scholarships are available.

Admissions. The application fee is $50. Inquire the first week after Labor Day. An open house is usually held in October. A lottery is being used to limit the number of applications. Completed applications are processed in the order received.

Once the application is filed, the admissions director schedules a visit for the parents and, for another time, an afternoon play session for the applicant, at which four or five children of about the same age are brought together for about forty-five minutes with parents and faculty present.

Notifications are sent by early March. Preference is given to siblings.

Class size and staff. 2s have three teachers for each class of ten. 3s and older have fifteen or sixteen in each class, with three faculty. Most of the faculty, senior and junior, hold advanced degrees in early childhood education. Teachers are assisted by student teachers and a creative movement teacher. The school has a teacher's enrichment fund to support courses taken by teachers to increase their professional expertise. Teachers can obtain interest-free loans. The school has a faculty that is unusual in its seniority and professional qualifications. The school sponsors staff attendance at important conferences, seminars, professional workshops, and conventions, as well as further courses.

Facilities. The entry is through a garden. The classrooms are on the third, fourth, and fifth floors; the school's reception office, director's office, and a 2,500-book lending library are on the fifth floor. Since the elevator is tiny, many parents prefer to take the stairs. There are six well-equipped, modern classrooms, two on each floor, and a large multi-purpose basement room for movement and music. A roof playground houses a play structure, climbing and riding equipment, and large building blocks.

Summer program.   An optional three-week summer program in June, from 9:00–12:00. Activities are similar to the regular curriculum with an expanded outdoor program.

Separation.   Children are brought into the program in small groups for short class sessions. Separation may take a month for younger children. A home visit is made to each new child beforehand.

Parent involvement.   Class-parent meetings and parent/teacher conferences are held periodically. Class-parent newsletters provide additional information. The school's Board of Trustees includes parents of children in the school. An active Parents Association sponsors many events, such as a pancake breakfast, a cocktail party, and educational speakers. Parents also serve as classroom substitutes, librarians, and trip escorts. The Annual Benefit, held in the community hall of the Unitarian Church of All Souls, is the school's major fund-raising event, along with the book/bake fair. Funds raised go to the school's Scholarship Fund, Teacher's Enrichment Fund, and the Director's Fund for Children's Special Needs. Parents meet regularly with the director to discuss issues of early childhood education, child development, and parenting.

Financial.   Significant financial aid is awarded annually. There is a large endowment that helps keep tuition somewhat lower than at comparable schools.

Transportation.   Parents or caregivers bring their children to the classroom.

Graduates.   Have gone to Allen-Stevenson, Bank Street, Brearley, Browning, Buckley, Caedmon, Chapin, Collegiate, Columbia Grammar, Convent of the Sacred Heart, Dalton, Ethical Culture, Fieldston, Friends Seminary, Hewitt, Horace Mann, Hunter, Marymount, Nightingale-Bamford, Riverdale Country, St. Bernard's, St. David's, Lab School, Spence, Town, Trevor Day, Trinity, PS 6, PS 158, PS 290, and UNIS.

Chartered.   By the Board of Regents of the State University of New York.

Member.   ERB, ISAAGNY, NAEYC.

The Brick Church School

Ages: 3–6 yrs

Nonsectarian

62 East 92nd Street (between
  Madison and Park Avenues)
Zip: 10128
Tel: 289-5683
Website: www.brickchurchschool.org
E-mail: lspinelli@brickchurch.org

Established 1940
Lydia Spinelli, Ed.D.,
  Director
Enrollment: 162

School year.   September through May. An optional summer camp
program runs the first three weeks in June.

Ages	Hours	Days	Tuition
3s	9:00–12:00	Mon–Fri	$17,200
3s	1:00–4:00	Mon–Thurs,	$16,800
	1:00–3:30	Fri	
4s–5s	9:00–12:00	Mon-Fri	$17,200
4s–5s	9:00–2:30	Mon–Thurs,	$21,700
		Fri to 12:00	
K/5/6s	9:00–2:30	Mon–Thurs,	$21,700
		Fri to 12:00	

Children bring their lunches for the extended-day program, which is nonacademic.
Morning drop-off and extended day available for a fee.

Program.   Traditional. Lydia Spinelli has been director at Brick
Church School for close to thirty years. She runs the school with a
combination of expertise in early childhood, humor, grace, and
good manners. Classrooms are well organized. Children choose
from a variety of age appropriate early childhood materials, and
take part in art, music, and cooking, as well as pre-academic programs, which include science, math, social studies, language arts
and literacy. There is a posted daily schedule of activities. The children have rooftime, activity time, etc. There is some scheduling
flexibility except for the use of communal spaces. Although orderly
and traditional, students can move freely from one activity area to
the next. The school recognizes that play is the work of the child.
Project work based on areas of children's interest fosters basic skills.
All children attend a weekly chapel service.

ERBs are administered on the premises.

Admissions. The application fee is $50. Inquiries begin right after Labor Day and families may request applications and apply online. The application deadline is October 1st. Ask about tour schedules. Group interviews are scheduled by the admissions director. The applicants are observed in a classroom. Parents sit along the side and are asked to fill out a questionnaire, mainly (according to the school) so that the youngsters will see they are somewhat on their own and feel free to focus on their play.

There are very few openings for older children. Preference is given to children of Brick Church members who have joined the church at least two years prior to the application deadline, and to siblings. The school is committed to giving financial aid to at least 10 percent of its students. Children of church members account for about fifty percent of the enrollment. Notifications are sent according to ISAAGNY guidelines. The school maintains a waiting list.

Class size. There are five classes of 3-year-olds; three in the morning and two in the afternoon. Each has ten to fifteen children with two or three teachers per class. The 4s and 5s classes have eighteen to twenty children and three teachers. There are also art, movement, and music teachers.

Facilities. This Carnegie Hill gem of a preschool recently renovated its building and church. The back wall of the large lobby is glass and faces the church's pleasant, walled garden which is where the children play on climbing structures, with wagons, and with other outdoor play items. A beautiful, spacious, light-filled art studio is used by each class at least once a week. Corridors and anterooms have cubby and storage space.

The classrooms are bright, clean, well organized, and well-equipped. There is a large, rubber-padded rooftop play area, as well as a carpeted music room and a chapel where the entire school gathers weekly for a brief chapel service. The downstairs area serves as a rainy-day play space. The children also use the church kitchen and gym.

Separation. After teachers visit the homes of new students, school begins with a four-day orientation period during which half of each class meets for a short time. Parents stay with their children or wait in the garden room, depending on the child's ability to separate.

Parent involvement. Parents can visit classes by appointment. Conferences are held with teachers semi-annually. Seminars are conducted on various aspects of parenting. There is a mix of working and nonworking parents who volunteer to various degrees, from occasional service to running the school library, Fall Fair, and other major fund-raising events. Parents serve on the Day School Committee and the director meets with class representatives approximately once a month.

Financial.   A deposit is required on signing the contract. The remainder of the tuition is payable in two installments due June 1 and October 1. An alternative payment schedule may be arranged upon request. About 13 percent of the students receive financial assistance, and the school encourages scholarship applicants.

Transportation.   Most of the youngsters come from the immediate neighborhood and are brought by parents or caregivers.

Graduates.   Have gone to Allen-Stevenson, Brearley, Browning, Buckley, Collegiate, Convent of the Sacred Heart, Chapin, Hewitt, Marymount, Nightingale-Bamford, Spence, St. Bernard's, and St. David's as well as to such co-ed schools as Birch Wathen-Lenox, Cathedral, Dalton, Manhattan Country, Riverdale, Town, Trevor Day, Trinity, and to public schools.

Affiliations.   Brick Presbyterian Church.

Member.   ERB, ISAAGNY, NAIS, NYSAIS, Early Steps.

The Caedmon School
Ages: 2.8–5th Grade

Modified Montessori Nursery and Elementary School

416 East 80th Street (between
First and York Avenues)
Zip: 10075
Tel: 879-2296
Fax: 879-0627
Website: www.caedmonschool.org
E-mail: admissions@caedmonschool.org

Established 1962
Honor Taft,
Head of School
Erica L. Papir,
Admissions Director
Nursery enrollment: 110
Total enrollment: 275

28

School year. Mid-September through mid-June. Summer camp and vacation programs are available.

Ages	Hours	Days	Tuition
2.8/3s/4s	8:30–11:30/3:30°	Mon–Fri	$15,851–$27,315
2.8–4s, (*Discovery Program*)	11:30–3:30	Mon–Fri	$11,224
Kindergarten–5th grade	8:30–3:30	Mon–Fri	$31,883

Children must be 2.8 by September 1st to begin and must be 5 years old by September 1st for kindergarten.
°Extended day options are available for an additional fee.

Program. Modified Montessori. The Caedmon School is a small, nursery through fifth grade school with a strong sense of community and an actively involved group of families. Students have the unique opportunity to learn in a nurturing and academically challenging environment among a richly diverse group of peers. They graduate after completing the fifth grade, before entering adolescence, allowing the school to dedicate all of its attention and resources solely to these years of development. All grades are single ages except for the 3s/4s and first and second grade.

The Beginners' Program, for children 2.8 to 3.0 years old, is specifically designed with developmentally appropriate tasks aimed to foster a sense of competence and confidence and social and emotional development. There is a predictable daily routine, a clear, accessible arrangement of materials, and special activities, all geared to make the experience a successful one. Social interaction within the deliberately small class with up to fourteen students and two teachers is emphasized.

The Early Program for 3- and 4-year-olds, combines ages and Montessori philosophy and materials with art, open-ended activities, outdoor play, music and movement classes. In the Early Program, the curriculum emphasizes social and emotional development, as well as cognitive and sensory development, all geared to a child's individual pace. Caedmon utilizes and provides materials for fantasy play, and there is a strong emphasis on group work and relaxed socialization among children. Classrooms are carefully organized and arranged to create a Montessori environment. The program includes math, language arts, and geography along with art, science, and library classes for the four-year-olds once a week. Academics are taught in the afternoon and prepare

29

children for the school's Elementary Program, kindergarten through fifth grade.

The Caedmon music school is available to students of all ages and abilities. Music lessons are offered in piano, violin, voice, guitar, cello, flute, recorder, trumpet, and rock and roll instruments. There are also music technology classes, all open to children from other schools.

Twenty-five percent of the students are from international families, representing twenty-two countries. Religious holidays are celebrated from a historical perspective and Catholic parents may request that their children receive religious instruction beginning in Kindergarten.

Admissions.   The application fee is $50. The application deadline is November 30th. There are three required appointments: a morning or evening tour, a parent interview, and a child play group. In accordance with ISAAGNY policy, notification letters are mailed in early March for Beginners and the Early Program; and in mid-February for kindergarten and above. Early notification is available for siblings.

Tests.   Applicants for the elementary program must take the ERB.

Class size.   The Beginners class has fourteen children (2.8–3 years old) with two teachers. The Early Program classes (3–4 years), have twenty-four children with three teachers. The Elementary Program classes average twenty-two children and also have two to three teachers as well as specialists for all grades.

Staff.   Caedmon has a highly trained, dedicated, professional staff of teachers. Early Program head teachers are experienced Montessori-trained educators and the Elementary teachers have high level credentials. Teachers meet weekly, as a group and individually, with the Division Heads and faculty to discuss each child's progress, the curriculum, and to share ideas. Experts, a school psychologist, and early intervention are available when needed.

Facilities.   Caedmon occupies a cheerful, bright, and spacious building with four floors housing classrooms, an art studio, science lab, gym, outdoor play space, and patio, lunchroom, library, computer lab, and music room. The science lab was recently renovated and has all brand new, state-of-the-art equipment. The gymnasium was also renovated to include new gymnastics equipment and a rock-climbing wall (for Elementary Program students only). Classrooms are beautiful, bright, and well equipped with Montessori and traditional equipment, laptop Macs and SMART Boards in kindergarten. The 3s and 4s use the large, spacious lunchroom for movement classes, often conducted by a professional dancer. They also visit the school's art room, library, and science lab each week and use the fully equipped music room. Elementary children use the school's gym three days a week, as well as the art, library, computer room, science, and music rooms.

Separation.   Separation is explained at a parents' orientation meeting before school begins. It is gentle and nurturing. In September, new children begin school in small groups of four to six, and work up to the full program within two weeks. Most children settle in easily within that time period. Children's needs to take longer are respected. New parents have the opportunity to meet other parents and teachers to learn more about the school.

Parent involvement.   The Caedmon Family Association (CFA) acts as a formal liaison between the parents and staff. It's warm and welcoming. It organizes fund-raising events and sponsors social functions. Formal conferences are held three times each school year. The school also gives several workshops throughout the school year to demonstrate the use of educational materials and discuss various aspects of the curriculum. Parents may be invited to read a favorite book, share a holiday treat, or tell a story about their family. There is excellent communication between the school and parents.

Financial.   A non-refundable deposit of $5,000 is required with the enrollment contract.

Transportation.   Private bus service can be arranged for children 4 and older with a company recommended by the school. Each day an administrator greets the children upon arrival.

Graduates.   Have gone to a wide variety of schools including Allen-Stevenson, Birch Wathen-Lenox, Brearley, Brooklyn Heights Montessori, Browning, Calhoun, Chapin, Collegiate, Cathedral, Columbia Grammar, Convent of the Sacred Heart, Dalton, Dwight, Ethical Culture, Friends Seminary, Fieldston, Hewitt, Horace Mann, Hunter Elementary, Manhattan Country School, Marymount, The Master's School, Nightingale-Bamford, Poly Prep, Professional

Children's School, Riverdale Country, Rudolph Steiner, Sacred Heart, Spence, Trevor Day, Trinity, York, and gifted and talented public school programs.

Chartered. By the Board of Regents of the State University of New York.

Member. AMS, ERB, the Guild of Independent Schools, NYSAIS, NAIS, ISAAGNY, Early Steps.

Central Synagogue
May Family Nursery School
Ages: 2.5–5 yrs

The Parenting Center
Ages: 5–30 months

Jewish, Reform

123 East 55th Street (between
Park and Lexington Avenues)
Zip: 10022
Tel: 838-5122 ext. 233
Website: www.centralsynagogue.org

Established 1965
Susan Alpert,
Director
Ann Obsatz,
Associate Director
Enrollment: 175

School year. September through first week in June. Separate June program.

Ages	Hours	Days	Tuition
2.6	9:30–12:00	3 days	$11,060/$12,240
3s	9:15–12:15	Mon–Fri	$19,350
4s	9:15–2:15	Mon–Fri (Fri till 12:15)	$20,640

Sibling and congregant families enrolled are eligible for priority enrollment. Synagogue membership is billed separately.

Program. Developmental. Children's intellectual and emotional growth, competence, and work habits are addressed in a warm and healthy learning environment. The program welcomes children from diverse backgrounds, and its objective is to encourage each to reach optimal development as an individual as well as a participant in group life. The staff give the children hands-on, open-ended, explorative materials and activities such as art, water and sand play, music, literature, expressive writing, science, cooking, dramatic play, and discussion. Children have music and movement once a week as well as a library class. For older children there are class trips to Donnell Library, The Jewish Museum, an apple orchard to pick apples, a picnic in Central Park's Conservatory Garden, etc.

Shabbat is celebrated every Friday.

ERBs are given on the premises, and the school works closely to counsel parents in selecting an ongoing school. Early in the fall a meeting for parents of 4s/5s is held to discuss admissions procedures to public and private ongoing schools.

Admissions. The application fee is $40. Inquiries are from the end of August through the middle of September. Call for an application and to sign up for the parent tours, held throughout the fall. Children are seen in January for a half hour of play and snack. Notifications are sent in accordance with ISAAGNY guidelines.

Class size. Each class has a head, associate, and an assistant teacher.

Staff. The staff is notable for its experience and its low rate of turnover.

Facilities. The school occupies the second and third floors of the Synagogue's expansive, adjacent Community House, built in 1966. There are cheerful, light, and well-equipped rooms on each floor, also offices, a well-stocked library of children's and professional literature, and kitchenettes. The rooftop playdeck is equipped with an extremely large climbing and exploration structure and slide. The floor is safety-surfaced. It has a large toy-filled sandbox and is well equipped with tricycles, wagons, building blocks, planks, and other riding toys housed in a charming barn structure. Children bring their lunches and the school provides snacks.

Separation. Teachers pay home visits to the children shortly before school begins. Separation is gradual. The youngest children are introduced to one another and to the school in groups of as few as three youngsters. Size and length of stay increase until, after a month, all the children come together for the full session. Parents remain in the classroom or nearby as long as needed.

Parent involvement. Parents are welcome in the classroom for various activities, including art or music projects, storytelling, and cooking. They also join the classes on field trips, run the major benefit/fundraiser, and join holiday observances, including weekly Shabbat, outdoor Sukkah, and Hannukah and Purim services. Parents are occasionally asked to attend school events during the daytime. One day a week a consultant from the Jewish Board of Family and Children's Services is available. There are also two additional consultants, an occupational therapist and a speech and language specialist. Parent/teacher conferences are held twice yearly.

Financial. Some financial aid is available.

Transportation. Private bus transportation can be arranged for children age 3 years and older.

Graduates. Go on to both public and private schools.

Affiliations. Jewish Board of Family and Children's Services, ECE-RJ, NATE.

Member. ERB, ISAAGNY, Parents League of New York.

Special Programs:

The Parenting Center. The Parenting Center offers support and guidance to enrich parents' relationships with their very young children during the critical early years. Once a week, professional facilitators meet with mothers of same-age children (0–12 months, 12–18 months, 19–30 months) to discuss child development, parenting skills, women's issues, etc. The children play in a cheerful adjacent space under teachers' supervision. (Children unwilling to separate may stay with their mothers.) The session ends with a snack, music, and a story. PC Sunday is offered twice during the year for the parent who does not attend regularly. Jewish holidays are celebrated. A similar weekly program is offered for caregivers.

Children's All Day School and Children's All Day Pre-Nursery

Ages: 6 mos–5 yrs

Nonsectarian

109 East 60th Street (between
Park and Lexington Avenues)
Zip: 10022
Tel: 752-4566
Fax: 752-4567
Website: www.childrensallday.org
E-mail: cadskids@aol.com
Enrollment: 95

Established 1975
Roni Hewitt,
Director
Karen Lee,
Administrative Assistant
Karen Vernoski,
Educational Consultant

School year. Year round.

Ages	Hours	Days	Tuition
Infants (6–15 mos)	8:00–6:00	Mon–Fri	$28,900
Toddlers (1–2)	8:00–6:00	Mon–Fri	$27,800
2s	8:00–6:00	Mon–Fri	$26,600
3s and 4s	8:00–6:00	Mon–Fri	$25,500
Half-day*	8:30–12:30	Mon–Fri	$18,500

*Half-day programs are only available for children over two.

Program. Developmental Interaction. Young children are provided safe, nurturing, and developmentally appropriate environments where learning takes place through play, hands-on, and academic experiences.

The developmental interaction philosophy is the main focus of the school's approach. The youngest children are afforded an individualized approach to learning through play. In the 3s and 4s, more emphasis is placed on reading and math readiness activities so that children will be able to handle an academic kindergarten. Social skills and emotional well-being are important aspects of the program. Movement specialists work with all groups each week.

Admissions. The application fee is $40. The school has a fall admissions process but will enroll children throughout the year if there is a place available. An application form and fee must be sent before the school will schedule a tour. Parents are met in small groups and children are observed in play groups of four to six. Admissions preference is given to siblings and legacies. The ERB test is given on the premises.

Class size.   There is one Infant Group of 9 children (ages six to fourteen months) with three full-time caregivers, and two Toddler groups of 8 children, each with two full-time and one part-time teachers and one part-time floater. There are two 2s classes of 12 children with three full-time teachers; two 3s classes of 15 children, each with two full-time and one part-time teacher; and one 4s or Pre-K class of 18 to 20, with three full-time and a part-time teacher.

Staff.   Seven teachers currently have masters degrees in early childhood education. There is a music teacher on staff and an outside movement specialist for all classes, from toddlers on. The educational consultant works with all teachers on curriculum and child development concerns.

Facilities.   The school occupies most of two contiguous townhouses. The school is open from 8:00–6:00, and children arrive between 8:00 and 9:30 and leave between 4:30 and 6:00. Parents and children climb stairs to the various rooms, which are colorful and bright. All eight classrooms have either lofts or climbing platforms. Rooms and hallways are decorated with children's art. On the first floor is the director's office and a large, handsome, and formally furnished parlor. The school has one infant class, two toddler classes, two 2s, two 3s, and one 4s–5s class.

A tree-shaded backyard contains a tree, climbing and sliding structure, outdoor building blocks, tricycles, wagons, and other toys. The school uses a closed-circuit television camera for security purposes.

Children bring lunch from home. Healthy snacks are provided by the school in the morning and afternoon.

Summer sessions (July and August) are part of the yearly contract and offer sprinklers, water play, bi-weekly shows, and weekly picnics.

Separation.   Parents of children under age 4 are required to participate in a seven day orientation process to assist with separation. Young children are gradually introduced into the program, in small groups, for progressively increased time periods. For the first three days parents remain in the classroom. Generally, by the end of seven school days, children are ready to be on their own but if necessary, parents are asked to stay longer. For older children the process is modified.

Parent involvement.   Parents may visit without an appointment. Most parents participate in fund-raising events and field trips. Conferences are arranged twice a year or at the parents' or teachers' request.

The student body is diverse and international, coming from NYC and surrounding areas.

Financial.   Upon signing a contract (which runs from September through August), a deposit of ten percent of the total annual tuition is required. The year's tuition is paid in ten installments. About ten percent of the students receive some financial aid, and sibling discounts are offered.

Transportation: All students are brought and picked up by parents or caregivers.

Graduates.   Have gone on to such schools as Birch Wathen-Lenox, Brearley, Browning, Buckley, Chapin, Columbia Grammar, Dalton, Ethical Culture, Hunter Elementary, Lycée Français, Manhattan Country, Trinity, and UNIS.

Chartered.   By the Board of Regents of the State University of New York.

Member.   ERB, ISAAGNY, NAIS, National Association for the Education of Young Children.

Christ Church Day School
Ages: 2.3–6 yrs

Nonsectarian Nursery School

520 Park Avenue
   (at 60th Street)
Zip: 10021
Tel: 838-3039
Fax: 593-3744
Website: www.christchurchnyc.org
E-mail: pmarble@christchurchnyc.org

Established 1949
M. Margaret Marble,
Director
Luanne Vrattos,
Administrative Assistant
Enrollment: Approximately 100

School year: September to end of May. June camp available to currently enrolled students.

Ages	Hours	Days	Tuition
2s	9:00–11:15	Tues Thurs or	$10,875
		Mon Wed Fri	$13,145
3s	9:00–11:45	Mon–Fri	$18,420
4s	9:00–11:50	Mon–Fri	$18,420
5s	9:00–2:30	Tues–Thurs,	$24,725
		Mon and Fri until 12:00	

Extended day option available Tues and Thurs for 3s and Tues, Wed, and Thurs for 4s until 2:30 at an additional cost of $3,700 and $4,510, respectively.

Program. Developmental. Founded in 1949 by the Board of Trustees of Christ Church United Methodist as a day nursery for parishioners as well as neighborhood families, but without religious instruction.

M. Margaret Marble, known as "Peggy," has been with the school as director for over thirty years. Ms. Marble's expertise in early childhood development, as well as her strong leadership, is the reason why the Day School has become one of the prominent nursery schools in the city.

The Day School emphasizes a child centered program. The school sees learning as a process in which children gather information and concepts through direct discovery and exploration and then externalize them through creative activities. The children are expected to have a good time, with a wide range of materials and activities, including block building, art, music and movement, woodworking, and dramatic play.

ERBs are given on the premises. The school has set aside a quiet room for ERB testing. At the beginning of the year, teachers introduce the tester. The children visit and play in the testing room with the teacher before any of them are tested. A number of meetings are arranged for parents to discuss the ongoing schools' application process.

Admissions. The application fee is $60. Inquiries are received by e-mail from the first Monday in October for the duration of that week. Apply promptly. The school automatically accepts siblings, who occasionally take most of the openings. Reserve a place in a group tour, given during January, when you call for an application form. The school notifies parents by mail that it has received their application and requests that they call to make an appointment in January or early February for the child's interview. Children are seen individually with their parents for half an hour to forty-five minutes. Parents who apply after the application cutoff pay no application fee unless the school is able to schedule an interview. Notifications are sent by early March.

Class size. There are two classes of 2s, with ten to twelve children and one of twelve to fourteen children. The two 3s classes have fifteen children each, and there is one class each of eighteen to twenty 4s or 4s/5s.

Staff. The larger classes have three staff members: two co-teachers with an assistant, including at least one teacher with a masters in early childhood education. The faculty are reputed to be among the highest paid in any New York City nursery school. The school has a Teachers Fund, the interest from which is used for yearly bonuses for all teachers. In addition, ongoing workshops within the school provide continuing professional development, and further training is paid for by the school. A professional artist works with the four- and five-year-olds in the extended day program. There is also a music and movement specialist for the children as well as a beautiful library staffed by a librarian.

Facilities. Visitors enter through the church's small courtyard on Park Avenue, or through the main entrance to the church. Once inside, there is a manned elevator to the sixth floor, where you are buzzed into the school through a glass door. The stairs are locked above the second floor, although parents can use the stairwells. The school has five spacious classrooms and a large, well-equipped state of the art playroof with a colorful modular play system. An indoor playspace is used for movement and music classes.

Separation. A separation workshop is given by the director before the term begins to explain how parents can help their child. Parents of 3s are encouraged to step out of the room on the second day, if the child is comfortable with this. The 2s have a longer separation period. However, because each child's needs are different, separation is handled individually.

Parent involvement. The parent body is cohesive, and very involved in the school. In addition to arranging social and fund-raising events, parents are involved in classroom activities. There are frequent workshops on parenting issues such as children's fears, sibling rivalry, discipline, and ongoing school selection given by outside experts. Conferences are arranged twice yearly and as needed.

Financial. Financial aid is available.

Transportation. No bus service.

Graduates. Parents tend to prefer single-sex schools, a fair number go on to schools such as Allen-Stevenson, Brearley, Chapin, Collegiate, Nightingale, and Spence as well as to Columbia Grammar, Dalton, and Trinity.

Affiliations. Christ United Methodist Church, but school is nonsectarian.

Member. ERB, ISAAGNY, NAEYC.

Convent of the Sacred Heart

Ages: 3–18 yrs

Girls Catholic Nursery and Comprehensive School

1 East 91st Street
(at 5th Avenue)
Zip: 10128
Tel: 722-4745
Fax: 996-1784
Website: www.cshnyc.org
E-mail: imullin@cshnyc.org
Pre-K enrollment: 15
Total enrollment: 695

Established 1881
Patricia Hult,
Head of Lower School
Imogene Mullin,
Associate Director of Admissions
and Financial Aid
Nursery enrollment: 33
JK enrollment: 18
Kindergarten enrollment: 54

School year. September through June. No summer program.

Ages	Hours	Days	Tuition
3s	8:15–12:15	Mon–Fri	$19,290
4s	8:15–2:00		$25,390
5s	8:15–3:00	Mon–Fri	$36,760
Fees for lunch for grades 1–4			$37,395

Program. Traditional. At 8:15, the young children pass through the school's enclosed, cobblestoned courtyard into a cavernous hall fragrant with flowers. Each joins the line for Morning Greeting and takes her turn, curtsying to and taking the hand of the Lower School Head before going on to class.

The children begin to wear uniforms (gray jumpers) in Pre-K. In kindergarten, work becomes distinctly academic, although there is time for free play. There is an emphasis on social skills; instilling confidence and a strong sense of self esteem is the focus of the lower school's program. Each student is encouraged to recognize the spiritual dimensions of their personality.

The oldest girls' school in the city, Sacred Heart has deep ties with an international network of 118 schools (22 in the United States) under the direction of the Society of the Sacred Heart, founded in France in 1800 and now headquartered in Rome. The schools are centrally evaluated every five years for their intellectual rigor, sense of community, social awareness, and ethical sense. The academic program is designed to foster competency and creativity. Children develop effective problem-solving skills; logical ways of thinking are taught and encouraged. There are exchange programs with European sister schools.

There is a daily community prayer, and children from second grade on attend weekly mass.

Admissions.   The application fee is $65.
Inquire from April on. After the school has received the completed application and fee, parents are contacted to arrange an interview and tour. Plan to spend about one to one and a half hours for this visit; your daughter's interview will be in a group setting and last about half an hour and will consist of free play, teacher-directed activities, and a story. The school's multiracial, multicultural student body consists of girls from the New York area as well as many foreign countries. While religion plays little part in the preschool, it enters the curriculum in later grades.

The preschool admits older 3s for a two-year program. The school maintains a waiting list, but will not admit a child who has already accepted a place at another ISAAGNY school.

The preschool was founded to accommodate families already involved with Sacred Heart. Preference is given to qualified siblings and children of alumnae.

Notifications are sent by early March. ERB tests are required for kindergarten applicants. Children who enter the school through the nursery program go automatically into kindergarten and therefore need not prepare for the ERB. ERBs are not required for Pre-K.

Class size.   There are two preschool groups, one for 3s and one for 4s, of between fifteen and seventeen children, with two teachers each. There are fifty-four children in the kindergarten in three sections with two teachers each.

Facilities.   These are easily among the most elegant school buildings in the city—two interconnecting mansions, the James Burden House (circa 1900) and the magnificent Otto Kahn mansion (completed in 1918 in the Italian Renaissance style), both landmark buildings. The Burden House was built for a granddaughter of Cornelius Vanderbilt and was designed by Warren & Wetmore, the architects who designed Grand Central Terminal and the old Biltmore Hotel. Its marble staircase swirls up several flights to a cupola executed by the French artist Hector d'Espouy. On the third floor is a ballroom with mirrored panels and doors, rose and white marble walls, and an ornately decorated ceiling. There is a large music room. Older children lunch in a banquet hall with immense, deeply inset, arched windows and green marble walls accented with gold.

The school completed an extensive construction and renovation project in 2004. It has thirty-six classrooms, a large chapel, two libraries with automated card catalogues and over 25,000 volumes, five science laboratories, five computer centers, an independent computer network, a theater, five art and music studios, two gymnasiums, a ballroom, and a banquet hall, as well as a dining hall. There are two handsome, cheerful prekindergarten classrooms. These are arranged into distinct activity areas and filled with well-ordered materials, both task-centered and open-ended. There are two rooftop play areas; one extends the length of the building fronting 5th Avenue and has a spectacular view of Central Park and the reservoir. Preschoolers use the lower school library, the ballroom for dancing lessons, the rooftop play spaces, and the gyms.

Separation.   Children are brought into the school in small groups for three days to acclimate them. Parents remain on the premises until the child is comfortable. A parents' office is computerized and also has telephones. It is staffed five days a week.

Parent involvement.   There is an active parents association. Conferences are scheduled twice a year and can be called for by parents or teachers whenever a need arises.

Financial.   Limited financial aid is available for students of special ability. The endowment is approximately $25 million.

Transportation.   Children come from all over the metropolitan New York City area. Private bus transportation can be arranged.

Graduates.   Approximately half those enrolled eventually graduate from the upper school. Those who leave usually do so because their families leave the New York area.

Affiliations.   The school is informally affiliated with the Archdiocese of New York. It is chartered by the Board of Regents of the State University of New York.

Member.   The Network of Sacred Heart Schools, National Coalition of Girls' Schools, ERB, ISAAGNY, NAIS, NYSAIS, the European Council of International Schools, and the International Schools Association.

The Creative Playschool
Ages: 2.0–4.0 yrs

A Jewish Preschool

Fifth Avenue Synagogue
5 East 62nd Street
Zip: 10065
Tel: 750-8793

Paulette Stein Meyer,
Director
Rochelle Hirsch,
Chairperson
Enrollment: 48

School year.   Third week in Sept.–June.

Age	Hours	Days	Tuition
2.0–2.3	9:15–12:15	Tues, Thurs	$10,000
2.3–2.7	9:15–12:15	Mon, Wed, Fri	$13,200
2.6–3.0	9:00–1:00	Mon–Fri	$18,000
2.11–4.0	9:00–1:30	Mon–Fri	$18,500

°Children need not be toilet-trained.

Program.   Eclectic, centered on experiential learning. Classroom atmosphere is warm, respectful, and unpressured. If they show an interest, 3/4s are encouraged to write their names, but this is not required. If a child does not want to join an activity, that choice is respected. Curriculum centers around the seasons, Jewish holidays and secular holidays, the development of self, and the recognition that each child is unique. As part of scientific study, children go on nature walks, picking a tree in autumn and making notes throughout the year.

Admission.   Inquiries should be made in autumn of the year preceding attendance. Applications are generally made by December with notification by March. After the application form is submitted with a $150 fee, the director will contact parents to arrange a meeting.

Class size.   Two classes of 2s with 12–13 children and 3 adults. Two classes of 3s/4s with 12 children and three adults.

Facilities.   Very clean and new. An elevator to the fifth floor opens into the entryway of the very large, high ceilinged 2s/3s class. Windows fill the top third of one long wall. The 3s/4s rooms are smaller but equally bright with the same high windows. A large windowed room serves as a gym where children play daily. Beautiful rooftop playground was added in Spring 2011.

Separation.   "Slow and easy," says the director. The first day is divided into two sessions with half the class attending each. Parents or caregivers are required to stay for the first day and thereafter, based on cues from their children and the teachers, take their leave usually within a few weeks.

Parent involvement.   An orientation meeting for parents is held one evening before the start of school. Parents are always welcome to visit, but must call first; they often come in for cooking and baking, to celebrate Shabbat or accompany groups on trips. A parent committee has been formed; it coordinates fund-raising activities like raffles, breakfasts, book fairs, and lectures. Close home/school communications are encouraged. Parents may call to arrange conferences.

Financial.   Upon a child's acceptance into the program, a nonrefundable deposit of $3,000 must be paid, credited towards tuition.

Fifty percent of tuition is due by July 1, the remaining half by September 1.

Graduates. Go to Ramaz School, Park East Day School, Horace Mann, the Abraham Joseph Heschel School, and Park Avenue Synagogue.

Affiliation. Fifth Avenue Synagogue.

The Elizabeth Seton Pre-School

Ages: 2 mos–6 yrs

An All Day Montessori Developmental Educational Program

1675 Third Avenue   Established 1972, 1980
(at East 93rd Street)   Mrs. Betzaida Stroz,
Zip: 10128   Infant Program Preschool Director
Tel: 369-9626   Susan Pomilla,
Fax: 369-1337   Assistant Director
Day Care Enrollment: 40 (2 mos.–36 mos.)
Preschool Enrollment: 35 (2.9–6 yrs.)

School year. All Year.

Age	Hours	Days	Tuition
2 mos–6 yrs	8:00–6:00	Mon–Fri	$460–485 weekly

Program. Montessori based. Seton serves as a model of Montessori day care programming. Observers from all over the country visit frequently. Children are introduced with remarkable gentleness to its modified Montessori curriculum, which includes many activities and materials found in more traditional programs: dramatic play, open-ended materials such as blocks, sand, and water, as well as many ordinary toys. There is a strong emphasis on the nurturing and personalized care of children as well as on their social and emotional growth.

In the preschool, children are given free choice in the various curriculum areas and are encouraged to work individually or in small groups. A teacher in each activities center pays close attention to the children's progress in a curriculum area, and encourages

45

development through small group and one-on-one work. Skills and materials are introduced in small groups or as one-on-one.

Admissions. The application fee is $40. Inquiries can be made at any time; filing an application form places your child on a waiting list. You may then make an appointment to visit the preschool or the infant/toddler program. Applicants are accepted on a first-come basis. In the infant/toddler program, a small number of families are eligible for sliding scale fees through a limited purchase of service plan with the Agency for Children's Services.

Class size. The four small groups in the infant/toddler center meet in separate rooms. There are seven infants, 2 to 10 months; nine toddlers, 10 to 18 months, and two classes of twelve children, each 18 to 36 months. Each group has a staff of three adults. Foster grandmothers and student interns assist staff.

Children in the preschool (which is really an extension of the infant/toddler program) function in flexible, constantly changing small mixed-age groups. Students on field placement assist the five regular staff members. There is also a music teacher.

Facilities. The school is located near two parks that are safe and homelike.

Separation. A phasing-in plan is worked out for each family based on its needs and the child's.

Parent involvement. On a daily basis parent involvement is informal. The staff works in partnership with parents. Throughout the year, small group and large group meetings are held. The school's PA supports the program through small fund-raisers and planning social events.

Financial. Tuition for the preschool and the day care center is payable monthly.

Affiliations. Sponsorship by The New York Foundling Hospital/Center for Parent and Child Development.

Member. Affiliated with AMS, ERB, ISAAGNY, Administration of Children's Services (ACS).

Epiphany Community Nursery School
Ages: 2–5 yrs

Nonsectarian

510 East 74th Street
  (off York Avenue)
Zip: 10021
Tel: 737-2977
Fax: 737-2993
Website: www.ecns.org
E-mail: w.levey@ecns.org

Established 1975
Wendy Levey,
Director
Enrollment: 150

School year.   Mid-September through the end of May.

Age	Hours	Days	Tuition
young 2s	9:00–12:00	Tues and Thurs	$13,500
older 2s	9:00–12:00	Mon Wed Fri	$16,000
3s	9:00–12:00 Tuesday to 2:30	Mon–Fri	$22,500
4s/5s	9:00–2:30	Mon Wed Thurs and Tues Thurs until 12:00	$25,750

Extended hours.   Children 3 through 6 may be dropped off at 8:30 for an additional daily charge of $5.

Program.   Traditional. The school has a strong program using a core curriculum for social, emotional, cognitive, language, and motor development. Weekly study units explore themes through experiment, cooking, painting, music, and other pursuits. The school celebrates holidays through food and music. For example, in celebration of the Chinese New Year there's a parade, the children make lanterns and prepare a typical Chinese dish. Current events and history are discussed with older children. Community service is a monthly activity.

The ERB tests used to evaluate kindergarten candidates are given on the school's premises.

Admissions.   The application fee is $150.
Inquire online from the day after Labor Day. There are openings for 20 to 24 young 2s, 24 to 28 older 2s, and openings vary for 3s, 4s, and 5s.

Group tours are scheduled during October and November. The application and fee may be submitted after the tour. Call right after your tour to arrange a forty-five minute interview with the director, during part of which the child will be observed at play with parents present. Interviews for 2s, 3s, and 4s applicants are conducted after Thanksgiving until the end of February with both parents and the child.

Acceptance notifications are sent in March in accordance with ISAAGNY guidelines.

Class size: There are four classes of 12 to 14 2s with 3 teachers; 16 3s with 3 teachers; and 20–24 4/5s with 3 teachers.

Staff. All head teachers have masters degrees in early childhood education. Parent/teacher conferences are held twice a year. The school pays for teachers to attend workshops, lectures, and weekend classes.

Facilities. The school located on East 74th Street under a bright red canopy is a large, air-conditioned, newly painted four-story facility. There is a playground on the roof. The facility has ten classrooms. There is a full kitchen, conference room, and library. Children bring their own lunch; parents provide the school's snacks. No nuts are allowed.

Summer program. From June through August there is a summer day camp for 2–5.5s on the premises. Schedules are flexible; an additional fee is required.

Separation. All children are visited at home by their teachers before school begins. They are eased in slowly, especially the 2s, who are introduced to the school environment in fifteen-minute sessions with half of their eventual classmates. The length of each introductory visit is increased and the class members are brought together, so that by the first week in November they are on the full morning schedule.

Parents stay in the classroom the first day, and can stay outside of the classroom thereafter, unless a child seriously objects. They are encouraged to stay in the school in a room other than the classroom, until their child is comfortable with complete separation. For 3s and 4s the process is faster.

Parent involvement. Parents are encouraged to take part in classroom activities and field trips, to share their expertise with students and faculty, and to help in fund-raising and development drives, community service projects, with admissions tours, and with the school's newsletter.

Several meetings are held each year on curriculum, ongoing schools, and other topics of interest. These are usually held during the day, often at breakfast.

Parents' visits are by appointment. They confer with their child's teacher twice a year for formal developmental progress reports.

Financial. A $3,000 deposit is due upon signing the contract. Half the balance remaining is due May 1st, the last installment by August 1st. There are no refunds. Some scholarship aid is available.

Transportation. No private bus service.

Graduates. Have gone on to schools such as Allen-Stevenson, Birch Wathen-Lenox, Brearley, Browning, Buckley, Chapin, Collegiate, Convent of the Sacred Heart, Dalton, Ethical Culture, Friends Seminary, Hewitt, Horace Mann, Marymount, Riverdale, St. Bernard's, St. Davids, Spence, Town, Trevor Day, Trinity, UNIS, and PS 158, among others.

Chartered. By the Board of Regents of the State University of New York.

Member. ERB, ISAAGNY, Parents League, ATIS, NAEYC.

The Episcopal School

Ages: 2.6–5+ yrs

Non-sectarian Early Childhood School

35 East 69th Street (between Park and Madison Avenues)
Zip: 10021
Tel: 879-9764
Fax: 288-7505
E-mail: office@episcopalschool.org

Established 1961
Judith Blanton, Director
Jane Arnold, Director of Admissions
Enrollment: 220 boys and girls;

School year.   September through mid-June

Ages	Hours	Days	Tuition
2s	9:15–11:15 or 1:15–3:15	Mon–Fri	$15,800
3s, 4s,5s	8:30–11:30 or 12:30–3:30	Mon–Fri	$17,400

Program.   Traditional. Instruction is individualized to meet each child's needs. The program provides experiences in reading- and math-readiness, science, cooking, music, art, and literature. Creative movement and storytelling are also offered. The atmosphere of the school is formal. Both upon arrival and departure from school children are greeted with a formal handshake for each child. Children are accompanied to the classroom by a parent or caregiver. Weekly chapel services are held.

ERBs are given on the premises, and the admissions directors of some of the ongoing schools visit to observe the children they are considering for admission.

Admissions.   The application fee is $60. Inquiries from the Wednesday after Labor Day on. Openings are limited. Call for an application form and return it promptly. Upon receipt, the school contacts the parent and arranges a parent tour and interview, given in October and November. The child will visit later in the winter for a play session at which parents are present. Notifications are sent by early March.

Facilities.   The school occupies a well-appointed, seven-story townhouse with a rooftop playdeck. In addition to spacious, sunny classrooms, there are an indoor all-purpose room, a library, and a small backyard play area.

Summer program.   For three weeks in June, 9:00 to 1:00.

Separation.   New children are visited at home by their teachers before school begins. Twos and threes are introduced to the program in small groups and shortened sessions.

Parent involvement.   The parent body is cohesive. Parents are heavily involved in school activities.

Financial. A non-refundable deposit of $3,000 is due by mid-March with the signing of the contract. Financial aid is readily available. A form should be requested when applying.

Chartered. By the Board of Regents of the State University of New York.

Graduates. Tend to choose single-sex ongoing schools as well as various co-ed schools.

Member. ERB, ISAAGNY, ISM, NAES, NAEYC, NYSAIS, NAIS.

The Family Schools
Ages: 1.6–12 yrs

Nursery and Elementary School

Dag Hammarskjold Plaza
323 East 47th Street
  (between 1st and 2nd
  Avenues)
Zip: 10017
Tel: 688-5950
Fax: 980-2475
E-mail: famschool@aol.com

Established 1975
Lesley Nan Haberman,
Founder and Headmistress
Total enrollment: approximately 160
Preschool enrollment: approximately 130

See also Family School West under West Side listings.

School year. September through June.

Age	Hours	Days	Tuition
1.6–3s	8:15–3:00	Mon–Fri	$19,000
1.6–3s	8:15–11:15	Mon–Fri, 2 or 3 days	$11,300– $17,500
	12:30–3:30	Mon–Fri	
3s°–6s	8:15–11:15	Mon–Fri, 2, 3 days half or full	$11,600– $19,500

°Must be toilet-trained.
Extended day programs are available until 6:00 P.M. for an additional fee.

51

Program.   Montessori. Toddlers spend time in both cognitive and gross motor rooms each day. The cognitive room offers children a variety of areas to choose from including language, math, sensorial, practical life, and cultural arts. Toddlers start the day with circle time, where they learn to focus and use language for increasing periods of time. Music, art, storytelling, and foreign languages as well as social interaction are central to the toddler program. Toddlers have their own enclosed outdoor play area.

The pre-primary program for three-, four- and five-year-olds, also includes language, math, activities of sensorial, practical life, science, and geography. Children begin their day with a group meeting in a circle, then break up into smaller groups for independent and collaborative work during which they are exposed to academic materials. They have recess outdoors before lunch. Specials include music, art, foreign languages, physical education, martial arts, drumming, and yoga; violin and chess for older and preprimary students.

ERBs are offered on the premises; applicants 5-years-old and older must take the ERB. The headmistress works closely with parents during the ongoing school process.

Admissions.   The application fee is $50. Inquiries are always welcome. Applications are followed up with a call to schedule an appointment for parents to visit and observe a classroom. Families are encouraged to visit the school as many times as they desire. Children join their parents during the first visit; the headmistress is available to meet with applicants and their families.

Class size.   Including both part- and full-time students, there are approximately sixty children in the toddler program, with no more than twelve to a class, each with three teachers; 3s through 6s, have three groups of seventeen to twenty-one children, with two collaborative teachers and specialists.

Facilities.   There are seven classrooms, a gym, an art room, a library, and an outdoor play area. Dag Hammarskjold Plaza, of which the headmistress is a vice president, is a commonly used play area.

Summer program.   Mid-June through August; $5,000 for the full 11-week program, or $100 a day for any combination of days. Camp includes instructional swimming, art, music, field trips, special on-site events, and academic maintenance.

After-school program.   All children may take part in creative and recreational activities on a full-time basis or at a per diem cost.

Separation.   The school's summer program is a good time to introduce new students to the school. In September children have several days of transition with their parents.

Parent involvement.   Parents are encouraged to share their cultural backgrounds and traditions in the classrooms. Two parent workshops are offered each year; parents receive two detailed narratives each year, attend mandatory parent/teacher conferences, and optional observations. There are many in-class celebratory events to which parents are invited. Class parents are well-informed and accessible.

Financial.   A $1,500 non-refundable deposit is required on contract signing. The remainder of the year's tuition is payable July 1st and December 1st. Payment plans are available.

Transportation.   About a quarter of the children come from the immediate neighborhood: 1st to 5th Avenues, between 37th and 57th Streets. The remainder come from other parts of Manhattan or other boroughs.

Graduates.   Have attended Allen-Stevenson, Brearley, Browning, Chapin, Collegiate, Columbia Grammar, Convent of the Sacred Heart, Dalton, Hewitt, Horace Mann, Nightingale-Bamford, Riverdale, Spence, Town, Trinity, Trevor Day, and UNIS, as well as Hunter, and Gifted and Talented programs in the public schools.

Chartered.   By the Board of Regents of the State University of New York.

Member.   AMS, ERB, ISAAGNY, Parents League.

Garden House School of New York
Ages: 2.6–6 yrs

Nonsectarian Preschool

37 East 63rd Street
Zip: 10065
40 Sutton Place (at 59th Street)
Zip: 10022
Tel: 421-3282
Website: www.gardenhouseschool.org
E-mail: info@gardenhouseschool.org

Natalie Williams,
Co-Director
Mary Cantwell,
Co-Director
Enrollment: 220

Ages	Hours	Days	Tuition
2s	8:45–11:15 12:30–3:00	Mon–Fri	$17,000
3s–6s	8:45–11:45 12:30–3:25	Mon–Fri	$25,000

Program. Traditional/academic. Programs are designed to meet the social, physical, emotional, and intellectual growth of each child. The day is structured with an enriched curriculum that includes art, singing, gym, cooking, early science, and math-readiness. There are daily class discussions as well as storytime, dramatic play, and use of small motor manipulatives. The juniors (3s/4s) and seniors (4s/5s) are introduced to French, ballet/movement, computer, as well as an early reading and writing program. The 4s and 5s take field trips throughout the year.

Typical units of study are introduced through projects, readings, trips, and discussions. They include farm animals, friendship, and personal stories.

The core of the program is traditional values combined with academic learning. The school maintains a structured, but playful, nursery environment which is beautiful, comfortable, and orderly. There are always fresh flowers in the school's entryway, and the children wear uniforms designed uniquely for Garden House School.

ERBs are given on the premises. The examiner is introduced to the children before testing begins. Directors from ongoing schools visit to observe children they are considering for admission.

Admissions. The application fee is $100. Requests for applications begin the Tuesday after Labor Day. Upon application, visits and interviews for the parents and child are scheduled from October through mid-December. Parents are given a group tour and an informal interview. The child is invited to a brief playdate. Families are notified in March.

Staff. Each class has a head teacher with a masters degree and an assistant teacher. A ballet/movement teacher, a music teacher, and a French teacher work with the children throughout the school.

Facilities. The 63rd Street facility is a newly built beautifully crisp space that occupies three floors of three combined townhouses.

The Sutton Place facility is the flagship for Garden House School of New York. It occupies the entire ground floor of a condominium building.

Summer program. A two-week program is available in June. Daily activities include arts and crafts, gardening, dramatic play, music, and outdoor water play.

Separation. Toddlers are gently introduced to school for shortened sessions and in smaller groups over a two- to three-week period. A parent or caregiver stays in the classroom for the first few days and then remains nearby until the child is comfortable.

Parent involvement. Parents participate in field trips. All parents are members of the Parent/Teacher Association. A class representative(s) from each class organizes social events. Parent/teacher conferences are arranged in November and May.

Financial A non-refundable deposit is required to secure a place. The remaining tuition is paid in three additional installments due in April, September, and November.

Graduates. Have gone to all "the leading ongoing independent and public schools."

Affiliations. Garden House School of London.

Chartered. By the Board of Regents of the State University of New York.

Member. ERB, ISAAGNY.

Horace Mann School Nursery Division

Ages: 3–5 yrs

Nonsectarian Nursery School

55 East 90th Street (between
Madison and Park Avenues)
Zip: 10128
Tel: 369-4600
Website: www.horacemann.org
E-mail: admissions@horacemann.org
Enrollment: 150

Established 1954
Dr. Thomas M. Kelly,
Head of School
Mrs. Marsha Levy,
Head of the Nursery Division
Ms. Meredith Berman,
Associate Director of Nursery
and Kindergarten Admissions
Mr. Jason H. Caldwell, '97,
Director of Admissions

School year. September to June.

Ages	Hours	Days	Tuition
3s	9:00–3:00	Mon–Fri	$37,275
3s	12:15–3:00	Mon–Fri	$26,750
4s	9:00–3:00	Mon–Fri	$37,275
5s	9:00–3:00	Mon–Fri	$37,275

Program. Developmental/Traditional. Active learning is the opera-
tive principle here with a strong focus on social and emotional,
as well as intellectual, development in an academically appropriate environment. Activities include block building, cooking,
free or structured dramatic play, including puppetry and putting
on plays; art, woodworking, music, including singing, improvisa-
tion, instruments, and movement to music; daily storytime,
reading- and math-readiness, and science, computer readiness,
physical education, and chess. Phonics, sight words, and writing
are introduced.

The school was founded in 1954 as the New York School for
Nursery Years by the staff of the former Harriet Johnson Nursery
School. In 1968, as a service to alumni, it merged with the Horace
Mann School in Riverdale and then the Horace Mann-Barnard
Elementary School, providing an academically appropriate preschool program of the ongoing school. There are approximately
1,780 children in the entire school, ages 3 through 18. Many children admitted to the nursery division go all the way through twelfth
grade at Horace Mann.

Admissions.   The application fee is $60. Inquire from May 1st on; apply promptly. The school requires two interview appointments for nursery 3s and 4s: one for the parents, and one for the child. For kindergarten, one appointment is required for parents and child. The children are observed in play groups of five or six (with parents sitting on the side for threes), for about forty-five minutes, ending with juice and cookies. Notifications are sent by early March. Preference is given to siblings and legacies.

Test.   Kindergarten applicants must take the ERB.

Class size.   There are nine classes for the various age groups, including kindergarten. Each class has a head teacher and an assistant teacher or two head teachers. Often there is a third adult present. Threes classes have up to sixteen children, 4s have eighteen to twenty, and kindergartners have fifteen to twenty.

Staff.   A psychology consultant is available to parents and teachers on a regular basis.

Facilities.   The school is located in a completely renovated coach house between Park and Madison Avenues. Each group has a colorful, comfortable, and well-ordered classroom. Two rooftop playgrounds are equipped with a sandbox, large blocks, and climbing apparatus, and there is a large yard. Fours and 5s go to Central Park or to a neighborhood gym. A hot lunch is provided for full-day groups. The 5s take a school bus to Riverdale to use the gym facilities and become acquainted with the lower division.

Parent involvement.   There is an active parent association. Conferences are scheduled twice yearly, and other conferences are encouraged as needed. Parent volunteers run the school library.

Separation.   The teacher visits the child at home at the start of the school year, and each child is helped to make a comfortable transition from home to school.

Financial.   A nonrefundable deposit of $7,125 is payable upon contract signing.

Financial aid is available. A form may be requested from the Nursery Division and filed with the admissions office of the Horace Mann School at 231 West 246th Street, Riverdale, NY 10471.

Transportation. Children from all parts of Manhattan attend. Private bus transportation can be arranged.

Member. ERB, ISAAGNY, NYSAIS.

House of Little People
Ages: 3 mos–5 yrs

Nonsectarian

122 East 91st Street

Zip: 10128

Tel: 369-2740

Fax: 369-3298

E-mail: hlp90@verizon.net

Website: thehouseoflittlepeople.com

Established 1976

Barbara Robinson, RN,
Founder, Executive Director

Enrollment: approximately 35

Second location:

House of Little People, Too

Ages: 3 mos–2.9 years

129 East 90th Street

Zip: 10128

Tel: 860-8118

Established: 1999

Debra Tuohy, M.S.Ed.,
Managing Director

Enrollment: 45

Third location:

Your Kids "R" Our Kids (see entry page 345)

Age	Hours	Days	Tuition (monthly)
All	7:30–6:00	5 days, M–F	$1,725

The school offers a year-round program.

Program. The program is designed to provide a warm, nurturing, and family-like atmosphere. The environment demonstrates sensitivity to the different needs of infant, toddler, and preschool children, affording comprehensive learning experiences, socialization skills, and growth enhancement. The comprehensive program is recognized by the New York City Department of Health as an innovator within the field of infant/toddler and preschool care.

Admission.   Open enrollment: children are enrolled as space becomes available. Interested parents may call to arrange enrollment and/or tour. Tuition is payable monthly. There is no financial aid.

Class Size.   Class size is age appropriate as indicated below:
Infants = 1 adult to 3 infants
Toddlers = 1 adult to 5 toddlers
Preschool, 4–5 years = 1 adult to 6 preschoolers

Facilities.   The school is located in the first two floors of a brownstone with a garden play yard area. Two neighborhood parks are within safe walking distance offering substantial physical activity opportunities. There's also an onsite playground for all ages.

Parent Involvement.   Parent meetings are held throughout the year. Children's progress conferences are conducted twice a year. Special issues and/or concerns are managed on a daily basis with parent input. Parents participate in all field trips and special in-house activities.

Graduates.   House of Little People graduates have been accepted at many private schools including Chapin, Dalton, Nightingale-Bamford, St. Ignatius, Spence, PS 6, 87, 151, Hunter Elementary, and gifted and talented public school programs.

House of Little People, Too
Ages: 3 mos–2 yrs, 6 mos

Established 1999
Debra Tuohy, M.S.Ed,
Managing Director

Program.   Infant Toddler Learning Program, specializing in quality care for very young children. The environment is nurturing and stimulating. Activities are sensory related, giving each child the opportunity to develop at his/her own pace.

Admission.   Registration is open all year. It is recommended that parents apply as early as possible, as spaces fill up rapidly. Call to arrange an onsite tour. A one-time registration fee and one-month advance payment are required at the time of enrollment. Tuition is paid monthly.

Class Size.   There are three age groups: infants, young toddlers, and older toddlers, staffed at a ratio of 1 adult : 4 infants; 1 adult : 5 toddlers.

Staff.   Staff members all have early childhood education backgrounds. The music teacher plans creative music and movement activities weekly. Directors hold masters degrees in education and Infant/Toddler Development from Bank Street College.

Facilities.   A safe, clean, cozy, and stimulating environment on Manhattan's East Side. Located on the ground floor of a brownstone, the center has central air-conditioning and heat. Children's bathrooms have age-appropriate fixtures, which encourage toilet training. A private backyard contains climbing equipment designed for infants and toddlers. During the summer months, outdoor water play and sanitized creative sand related activities are available.

Parent Involvement.   Parents may request individualized conferences regarding progress and development at any time. Parents are encouraged to participate in holiday celebrations and special occasions as well as field trips.

Graduates.   Have gone on to attend some of Manhattan's most selective schools, including Dalton, Nightingale-Banford, St. Ignatius, Spence, PS 6, 87, 151, Hunter, and other gifted and talented programs.

The International Preschools

Ages: 1.6 yrs–6 yrs

Nonsectarian

330 East 45th Street (between
1st and 2nd Avenues)
Zip: 10017
Tel: 371-8604
Website: www.ipsnyc.org
E-mail: 45street@ipsnyc.org
(for all locations)
E-mail for admissions:
admissions@ipsnyc.org
28 East 35th Street (between
Park and Madison Avenues)
351 East 74th Street (between 1st and 2nd Avenues)
120 West 76th Street (between Amsterdam
and Columbus)

Established 1963
Donna Cohen,
Director
Kevin Abernathy,
Admissions Director
Total enrollment approx. 600
Enrollment: 200
(for 300 East 45th Street)

Enrollment: 124
Enrollment: 164
Enrollment: 164

School year. Mid-September through early June.

Age	Hours	Days	Tuition
1.6–2 years (Crèche program)	8:30–10:30 or 11:00–1:00	2 days	$8,550
2.4–3.3 (Toddler program)	9:00–11:30 or 1:15–3:45	2, 3 days	$9,000–$12,500
3s	9:00–12:00 or 1:00–4:00	3 days	$12,500
3s/4s	9:00–12:00 or 1:00–4:00	Mon–Fri	$15,250–$15,650
4s/5s; Kindergarten	9:00–3:00	Mon–Fri	$21,730

Different schedules are available at each location; the most common are listed above. A young toddler program, "The Crèche," for children under 2, is only available at the 45th Street location. There are additional charges of from $85 to $110 per year; $150 for kindergarten, for books and computer fees.

Program. Developmental/Interactive. The academic approach is learning through play that encourages children to be creative and independent thinkers. Through structured play students learn math concepts, pre-reading skills, and writing. Fine and visual motor development is encouraged through puzzles, pegs, small manipulatives, and the school's writing center. Social emotional growth takes place as children learn to share, take turns, and engage in dramatic play, block building, and circle time activities. Specialty teachers work with children in music, science, movement, and library. Pre-kindergarten and kindergarten children have the opportunity to use iPads.

The celebration of varied national customs, cultures, languages and cuisine, and dress are part of the curriculum, as well as stories, songs, and games from around the world.

Admissions. There is a $75 application fee. The school's admissions process begins the fall prior to the year in which the child will be enrolled. Applications are available either by phone, mail, or online. After a completed application is received, parents are invited to an admissions information meeting. An admissions representative will call parents to schedule a visit to the location of their choice with their child. Notifications are sent out by early March but IPS accepts applications from families being transferred to New York throughout the year.

Class size. Young toddlers (crèche and young 2s), are limited to ten children per group. Older 2s and young 3s have ten to twelve children with three teachers. Older 3s have up to fifteen per class; 4s and 5s classes each have between fifteen and twenty children with two or three teachers.

Staff. One teacher in each class is "international." Each class has a licensed early childhood teacher and one or two qualified assistant teachers. There's a librarian, and there are specialists in science, music, technology, and creative movement, and an education director who works closely with teachers for all children. A development specialist works with children who have special needs.

Facilities. Parents have called the school warm and boisterous. Those with children in the most "international" of the preschools feel the varied cultural exposure is invaluable. The school's major center is located on East 45th Street with a modern preschool facility funded with the help of the United Nations Development Corporation's Board of Directors.

Each location has its own character and personality. Outdoor and indoor active play areas provide plenty of space for exercise.

Summer program.   There is a creative and recreational program from early June through the end of July. The program is open to children 2 to 5 years old. Preference is given to children currently enrolled.

Separation.   Special care is taken with children of all ages, since many of them face major adjustments in coming to a new country. The crêche and toddler programs offer a gradual separation process that includes parents and caregivers who stay until the child is comfortable. According to the director, "We don't hurry parents out of the classroom."

Parent involvement.   The Parents Association is active; it organizes social and fund-raising events. Educational meetings are held on a variety of subjects and there are social activities and events. Parent/teacher conferences are held each semester. Parents join on field trips and classroom celebrations.

Financial.   Financial aid is available based on need. There are payment options available.

Transportation.   Parent or caregiver brings the child directly to the classroom.

Graduates.   Have attended most private schools in Manhattan including, Allen-Stevenson, Brearley, Buckley, Chapin, Collegiate, Convent of the Sacred Heart, Dalton, Ethical Culture, Friends Seminary, Grace Church, Hunter Elementary, Lycée Francais, Nightingale-Bamford, St. Bernard's, St. David's, Spence, Town, Trinity, UNIS, other independent schools, and various public gifted and talented programs, and parochial schools.

Member.   ERB, ISAAGNY, NAEYC, Parents League, chartered by the Board of Regents of the State University of New York.

The Stanley H. Kaplan Nursery School
of Sutton Place Synagogue
Ages: 2–5 yrs

Jewish Nursery School

225 East 51st Street
(Between 2nd & 3rd Avenues)
Zip: 10022
Tel: 826-6204
Fax: 893-8116
E-mail: akmorgano@aol.com

Established 2001
Amy K. Morgano,
Director

School year: September through May; June camp for in-house students.

Ages	Hours	Days	Tuition
2s°	9–11:30	Tues Thurs or	$9,900
		Mon Wed Fri	$11,900
3s°°	9–12	Mon-Fri	$14,000
4s	9–1:30	Mon–Thurs	$18,500
5's	9:00–2:15	(Fri until 12)	$20,200

°Children entering the 2s class must be 2 by September 1st.
°°Extended day option is available at an additional cost.

Program. Developmental. The Kaplan Nursery School just completed its tenth year of operation. Amy Morgano is the school's founding director. This preschool aims to "foster a deep sense of community, where a young child's social and emotional growth and intellectual development can flourish." The program offers both structured and open-ended play. Children are encouraged to ask questions and interact with a variety of stimulating materials. The Jewish holidays are integrated into the school's curriculum and on Fridays the children take part in a Shabbat snack.

Admissions. The application fee is $50. Inquiries are from September on. Preference is given to long-term synagogue members and siblings. Group tours are given. Families come for individual visits in December through February. Notifications are sent in accordance with ISAAGNY guidelines.

Class size. There are ten to twelve children in the 2s classes with two teachers; ten to fifteen children in the two 3s classes, and ten to sixteen children in the Pre-K classes.

Staff. All head teachers have a graduate degree in Early Childhood Education and all assistant teachers have an undergraduate degree in Early Childhood Education or a related field.

Facilities. Classrooms are housed in a six-story building that includes a large outdoor play area and a children's garden.

Parent Involvement. Parents are welcomed in the classrooms to read books or cook. The Parents Association is an integral part of the school's community; parents can volunteer to work on a variety of fund-raising and community building events.

Transportation. None

Graduates. KNS graduates attend Allen-Stevenson, Brearley, Browning, Collegiate, Ethical Culture, Hewitt, Spence, Chapin, Horace Mann, Nightingale-Bamford, Trevor Day, Lower Lab, Hunter, and other private and public schools such as The Anderson Program, Lower Lab, NEST, and other neighborhood schools and gifted and talented programs.

Affiliations. Sutton Place Synagogue.

Member. ISAAGNY, ERB.

La Scuola d'Italia "G. Marconi"
Ages: 3yrs–12th grade

Bilingual Italian Preschool and Comprehensive School

12 East 96th Street

Zip: 10128

Tel: 369-3290

Fax: 369-1164

Website: www.lascuoladitalia.org

E-mail: secretary@lascuoladitalia.org

Established 1977

Pia Pedicini,

Deputy Headmistress and

Director of Admissions

Preschool enrollment: 35

Total enrollment 230

Ages	Hours	Days	Tuition
3–5°	8:30–2:50	Mon–Fri	$20,000 plus $1,600 in fees, (3s–12th grade)

°The birthday cut-off for kindergarten is 5 years of age by December 31st.

Program. The school was founded by the Italian Ministry of Foreign Affairs to meet the academic needs of Italians living in the New York City area. The curriculum seeks to foster self-esteem, trust, and autonomy by building physical and linguistic abilities and introducing children to the first elements of literacy. Preschoolers are introduced to Italian through a variety of activities in language, drama, art, music, science, and psychomotor projects. There is total immersion in foreign languages from preschool on, and an in-depth study and appreciation of American, European, and Italian civilizations and cultures.

Admissions.   The application fee is $100. There is no deadline for submitting applications but parents should be prepared to apply as early as September for the following school year. After the application is completed, the family is invited for an interview. The child stays in the classroom, where the head teacher evaluates social skills and capacity to relate to peers. Notifications are sent in accordance with ISAAGNY guidelines.

Class size. There are about 8 to 15 children per class.

Staff. Two head teachers, one who instructs in Italian, one in English, alternate during the school day. Larger classes have bilingual assistants who remain in class at all times.

Facilities. Entering the school's limestone, five-story mansion through a bright-red door, one crosses the hall and takes a central staircase down to the high-ceilinged rooms of the preschool area. The main room, walls hung with murals painted by the children, has two windows onto the yard. Another long, bright room with easels, kitchen facilities, and long tables on which children were shaping playdough and painting, has windows and a door opening onto a ground-level wooden deck with riding toys, seesaws, and a balance beam. A child-size bathroom adjoins.

Separation.   For the first week, children attend a half class, on an abbreviated schedule, and parents stay as needed.

Parent involvement.   A curriculum meeting opens the school year, and three parent/teacher conferences are held during the year. An annual open house offers prospective parents the opportunity to become acquainted with the bilingual curricula and educational activities. The Parents Association is very active in organizing annual fund-raising events.

Financial.   A $1,700 plus 20 percent tuition deposit is required upon acceptance. Tuition is paid in three installments. No financial aid is available at the preschool level.

Graduates.   Most children stay on at La Scuola through 12th grade. At the end of their senior year, the students are required to take the Italian Ministry of Education State Exam, the *Maturita*, equivalent to the International Baccalaureate degree honored by all universities in Europe and the United States.

Affiliations.   Chartered by the Board of Regents of the State University of New York, the Ministry of Education of Italy, and a member of the New York City Association of Independent Schools (NYSAIS).

Le Petit Paradis Preschool
Ages 2.8–5

Preschool

1656 Third Avenue Ground Floor
(between 92nd & 93rd Street)
Zip: 10128
Tel: (212) 410-0180
Website: www.lepetitparadispreschool.com

Established in 2008
Christina Houri,
Director
Total Enrollment 40

Shool year.   Early September through mid-June.

Hours for all ages.   Mon–Fri 8:30 A.M. to 3:30 P.M. Full day program 8:30 A.M. to 11:30 A.M. or 12:30 to 3:30 P.M. half day program

Tuition. $24,975 full day; $19,995 half day

Staff.   Christina Houri is the Founder, President, and Director. There is one French teacher and one English teacher certified by the Board of Education for Early Childhood education in each classroom co-teaching both languages.

Facilities.   The school has 2 classrooms and 2 children's restrooms. Children go to the public playground which is 2 blocks away accompanied by their teachers.

Summer camp.   A four-week summer camp in July is available for an additional fee.

Separation.   Parents stay with their children for 4 days during the first week of school after Labor Day. The hours are increased each day during that week. After that, parents are not permitted to stay.

Financial.   A 25 percent of the tuition total non-refundable deposit is required on signing the contract in order to reserve a spot for your child. Also a non-refundable deposit is required on signing the contract in order to reserve a spot for your child. Also a non-refundable $200 application free is required upon submitting the application.

Graduates.   Most graduates go on to the Lyée Français de New York.

Affiliations.   The Parents League (in process).

Program.   Bilingual French/English Progressive mixing Montessori and Bank Street philosophies in an international environment. Children from various cultural backgrounds work in a relaxed, positive atmosphere. Children learn about ecology, and French as a second language.

Admissions.   Open Houses are scheduled in mid-September and mid-October. Applications should be submitted during that time. Children are interviewed and response letters are mailed out promptly.

Class Size.   There are 15 children in each classroom with 2 teachers. The student teacher ratio is 1 to 7.

Parent involvement. Parents are encouraged to participate during field trips and during children's presentations. Parents are expected to attend parent/teacher conferences, class meetings held once a month, the holiday potluck party, and the end of school year picnic in Central Park.

Lycée Français de New York

Ages: 4–18 yrs

Bilingual French Nursery and Comprehensive School

505 East 75th Street
(York Avenue)
Zip: 10021
Tel: 369-1400
Website: www.lfny.org
E-mail: mail@lfny.org
Total enrollment: 1346

Mr. Yves Theze,
Head
Vannina Boussouy,
Primary School Director
Martine LaLa,
Director of Admissions
Preschool enrollment: 180

School year. Mid-September through mid-June. There is also a summer program, from mid-June to mid-July.

Ages	Hours	Days	Tuition
4s	8:30–2:30	Mon–Fri	$24,650
5s	8:30–2:30	Mon–Fri	$24,650

°Children must be toilet-trained upon entrance, but extra clothes are kept on hand in case of accidents.

Extended hours. Afterschool activities are available until 6:00 P.M.

Program. Traditional. The early childhood program offers a complementary bilingual English and French educational curriculum for 4s and 5s. Children starting kindergarten must be proficient in French. An American certified teacher and a French-educated and certified teacher share the classroom at all times, encouraging the students to develop their personality, talents, and skills while acquiring a new language. This is accomplished by means of interrelated individual and small-group activities planned by the co-teachers around a class project, with common pedagogical objectives covering all facets of the curriculum, including art, music, and movement. There are clear academic expectations for each age. At the same time, a calm, nurturing, and accepting atmosphere prevails.

The children participate in a music and movement class, two to three times a week. Physical education classes are held in the gym. The children keep song and poetry books. The 4s and 5s are prepared for cursive writing. School trips are planned regularly and include a variety of local attractions. The student body represents over 50 countries.

The Lycée confers a New York State high school diploma and prepares its students to pass the baccalaureate at the end of "Terminale." The dual French and English curriculum allows students to attend leading American as well as foreign colleges and universities. The Lycée is neither owned nor operated by the French government. It is accredited by the French Ministry of National Education and chartered by the Board of Regents of the State of New York.

Admissions. The application fee is $200. Inquiries are from mid-September on. Preschool applicants are given individual evaluations in a small-group setting conducted by a faculty member. A tour follows the evaluation. Admissions are rolling. Notifications are sent in February or March, and are ongoing for international transfers, depending on availability.

Class size. From 15 to 22. Each classroom is shared by two co-teachers.

Staff. All American teachers are certified by New York State and hold a masters degree. All native French teachers are certified by the French Ministry of Education.

Facilities. The new building, situated on 75th street at York Avenue, offers a spectacular space with large gymnasiums, gross motor climbing structures, a roof play area cushioned with a rubber surface for the youngest, computer and science labs, art and music studios, and a spectacular 350-seat auditorium which opened in May 2005. With this opening, the Lycée has a cultural center which provides a unique venue in which students can express their artistic creativity or to listen to leading speakers addressing a variety of international topics.

Dress code. Beginning at age 4, boys wear a navy-blue blazer, classic-cut gray pants, a white shirt and tie, or a white turtleneck and blue pullover. Girls wear a navy-blue blazer; a gray skirt, jumper, or slacks; a white blouse or turtleneck and navy-blue cardigan. A chambray smock is worn over the "uniform."

Parent involvement. Parents are encouraged to participate in their child's education and in all major social, cultural, educational, and fund-raising events. These activities include pedagogical meetings and conferences, regularly scheduled school trips, concerts, United Nations week, the spring fair, and other special projects. Progress reports are issued two to three times a year. Parent/teacher conferences are scheduled in the spring.

Financial. 30 percent of the student body receives some form of aid.

Transportation. Arrangements for private transportation are made by parents. Children 5 and older may use Department of Education buses.

Graduates. Most students continue at the Lycée through 12th grade.

Chartered. Chartered by the Board of Regents of the State University of New York and the French Ministry of Education.

Member. Association of French Schools in America, NYSAIS, Parents League.

Lyceum Kennedy French International School
Ages: 3–18 yrs/High School

French American School

225 East 43rd Street
Zip: 10017
Tel: 681-1877
Fax: 681-1922
Website: www.lyceumkennedy.org
E-mail: LKManhattan@lyceumkennedy.org

Established 1964
Dr. Laurent Bonardi,
Head of School
Christine Grunfelder,
Preschool Director
Preschool enrollment: 60
Total enrollment: approximately 200

School year. September through mid-June.

Ages	Hours°	Days	Tuition
3s/4s/5s	8:30–3:30	Mon–Fri	$19,620

°Extended hours of daycare as well as extracurricular activities, from 3:40 to 5:40, are available at a reasonable fee.

Program. The preschool or Marternelle program is divided into three levels, the Petite section (nursery 3s), the Moyenne section (prekindergarten 4s), and Grande section (kindergarten 5s). French is the primary language in the preschool. Pre-reading, writing, speaking, and math are taught in English. The goal of the preschool program is to foster pre-academic, social, and emotional skills in both French and English. The schedule allows for play, indoors and outdoors, as well as individual and group activities. In kindergarten, there is a greater emphasis on phonics, reading readiness, and beginning math concepts. Each day has a structured time for academics and other activities.

Admissions. The application fee is $200. Children must be 3 years old by December 31st and completely toilet-trained by the start of school. Children participate in either a half-day or full-day visit at the school called Discovery Day where children are evaluated on their developmental readiness.

Class size. Fifteen to twenty children.

Financial. A deposit of $1,000 is required upon admission. The first tuition payment is payable on June 1st. Children of French citizens may receive a scholarship from the French government.

Transportation. Children receive free public bus or subway passes starting in first grade.

Affiliations. The school is managed by a French head of school and is accredited by the French Ministry of Education as well as by the Board of Regents of the State University of New York and the New York State Education Department; registered with the Independent School Association.

The Madison Avenue Presbyterian Day School
Ages: 2.9–5.11 yrs.

Nonsectarian Nursery School

921 Madison Avenue
(between 73rd and
74th Streets)
Zip: 10021
Tel: 288-9638
Fax: 717-4152
Website: www.mapc.com
E-mail: mapds@mapc.com

Patricia Pell,
Director
Michael Zimmerman,
Admissions Coordinator
Enrollment: 110

School year. Mid-September through May. June program.

Ages	Hours	Days	Tuition
All°	8:30–12:45	Mon–Thurs (Fri until 12:00)	$17,900
	8:30–2:45°°	Mon–Thurs	$5,000°°°
2.10–3.4	11:30–3:00	Mon–Thurs	$13,680

°Must be 3 by December 31.
°°optional extended day.
°°°in addition to tuition listed above.

Program. Developmental/interactive. The school's goal is to provide, and encourage children to engage in, activities that will allow them to acquire skills, learn new concepts, and discover by themselves the information that they need. Using a Bank Street/Constructivist approach influenced by Reggio Emilia philosophy, the school recognizes that play is the work of children. Tactile materials such as sand, water, clay, paint, and blocks are emphasized. Explorations with pre-academic materials encourage children to think, plan, recreate, and thereby to make sense of the world. The programs are rich in language-usage experiences as well as reading and math readiness so as to encourage in each child a love of learning, curiosity, creativity, self-confidence, and independence.

Each class visits the school library weekly. Chapels and assemblies are held for Christmas, Hanukkah, Passover, and Easter as well as other significant cultural holidays celebrated by families in the school.

The school is an integral part of the church and serves not only the member families but also the community beyond.

Admissions. The application fee is $75. Inquiries begin in September, and parents may tour the school prior to applying for admission. Children are seen later in groups of six.

Church members and siblings may request an early decision on admissions.

Class size. There are seven classrooms; group size depends on the ages of the children as well as the size of the classroom. There are twelve to fifteen 2s and 3s, fifteen to sixteen each of 3s and 4s, and eighteen to twenty-one 4s and 5s.

Staff. There is a Lead Teacher and two associates or assistants in each class. Specialists teach music, movement, and art.

Facilities. The eighth, ninth, and fourth floors of the church house contain the school's seven classrooms with self-contained bathrooms, as well as staff offices, along a cubby-filled corridor. All of the rooms enjoy plenty of natural light. The two largest rooms overlook Madison Avenue and are windowed on three sides.

Classroom materials include a wide variety of manipulative items, including blocks, games, and puzzles. Children's artwork is displayed on classroom walls and the school hallways. Portable ovens and hot plates are available for cooking in the classrooms.

On the eighth floor there are two classrooms, a full kitchen used by all classes, a children's lending library, and a multipurpose room used for music and movement, as well as for assemblies. The eleventh floor play roof is extremely large, enclosed, and well equipped for play.

Parent involvement. The school's parent committee plans social and fund-raising events. There is a library committee and parent volunteers are responsible for the lending library and weekly storytime.

Financial. An initial payment of 25 percent of the annual tuition is due with the contract. Tuition aid is supported through fund-raising and an endowment fund.

Transportation. Most parents bring their children to school. Private bus service is not available.

Affiliations.   The Madison Avenue Presbyterian Church.

Member.   ERB, ISAAGNY, NAIS, NYSAIS, Early Steps, ACEI, ATIS.

Marymount School of New York
Ages: 3–18 yrs

Catholic Nursery and Comprehensive Girls' School
Nursery Program includes boys 3–4 yrs

1026 5th Avenue (between
East 83rd and 84th Streets)
Zip: 10028
Tel: 744-4486
Fax: 744-0163
Website: www.marymountnyc.org
Nursery enrollment: 24
Uniforms are required of all students.

Established 1926
Concepcion Alvar,
Headmistress
Katie Bergin,
Head of Lower School
Lillian Issa,
Admissions Director and
Deputy Head

School year.   First week in September through second week in June.

Ages	Hours	Days	Tuition
3s	8:20–11:30/12:30–3:30	Mon–Fri	$21,835
4s	8:20–11:45	Mon–Fri	$21,835
5s	8:20–3:00	Mon–Fri	$37,275

°The birthday cut-off is August 31st.
°°Extended day options are available.

Program.   Traditional. It is one of an international network of Marymount schools founded by the religious order of the Sacred Heart of Mary. Chapel services, lessons and carols, vespers, and other Catholic rituals, are part of the curriculum. Nursery children follow a balanced program of work, rest, and play, which prepares them for later learning. Nursery students are the youngest users of the lower school science lab. They are exposed to language arts, mathematics, science, social studies, and religion. Music, art, and physical education are also part of the curriculum.

Reading instruction for kindergartners is approached with structured phonics lessons, whole language and literature-based instruction. Mathematics instruction employs materials such as unifix cubes, cuisenaire rods, weights, and graphs. Language arts and math are taught in small groups of 3 to 5 children.

Admissions. The application fee is $70. Inquiries are accepted throughout the year. Sixty percent of the students are Catholic, but the school welcomes students of other faiths.

Parents should call in September for an admissions packet. After a completed application is received, parents are called to schedule a parent interview, a child interview, and a tour. Notifications follow ISAAGNY guidelines.

Facilities. The school is housed in three adjoining landmark Beaux Arts mansions, constructed near the turn of the century—the Vanderbilt Burden Mansion, the Herbert Pratt, and the Dunlevy Milbank. These form part of the Metropolitan Museum historic district known as "Museum Mile." A middle school building is located on East 82nd Street just off Fifth Avenue and the school occupies an additional 42,000 square feet at East 97th Street. The buildings contain classrooms, a chapel, an auditorium, two gymnasiums, five science laboratories, three computer centers and a language lab, three libraries, four art studios, a commons and a courtyard play area.

After-School Program. Starting in kindergarten, a variety of optional activities are available, Monday–Thursday until 6:00; Friday until 2:00.

Summer program. Three 5-week co-ed sessions; varied programs are open to children from ages 3.5 years old to 13. Cost: $2,900–3,150.

Financial. A non-refundable deposit of $5,000 is required upon enrollment. It is credited toward the second term tuition. Two-thirds of the annual tuition is due by May 2nd, and one-third by November 1st.

Graduates. Girls attending nursery usually continue at Marymount; boys attend a variety of independent schools including Allen-Stevenson, Browning, Buckley, Collegiate, Dalton, St. Bernard's, Saint David's, and Trinity.

Chartered. By the Board of Regents of the State University of New

York and accredited by NYSAIS and the Middle States Association of Colleges and Schools.

Member. ERB, Guild of Independent Schools, IES, ISAAGNY, NAIS, the National Catholic Educational Association, NCGS (National Coalition of Girls' Schools), RSHM Schools (Religious of the Sacred Heart of Mary).

Merricat's Castle School
Ages: 2–5 yrs

Nonsectarian Nursery School

316 East 88th Street (between 1st and 2nd Avenues)
Zip: 10128
Tel: 534-3656
Fax: 534-4141
Enrollment: 120

Established 1974
Linda Wosczyk and Mimi Broner, Co-Directors
Gretchen Buchenholz, Executive Director
Association to Benefit Children

Ages	Hours	Days	Tuition
2s/3s	9:10-11:40 or	Tues/Thurs	$6,500
	12:40-3:10	Mon/Wed/Fri	$9,000
3s/4s*	9:15-11:45 or	Tues/Thurs	$6,300
	12:45-3:15	Mon/Wed/Fri	$8,700
		4 days	$11,600
		Mon-Fri	$14,500
4s/5s*	9:05-3:05	Mon/Wed/Fri	$16,200
		4 days	$20,800
		Mon-Fri	$24,000

*Combined full- and half-day weeks available, tuition is adjusted to reflect the program selected.

Program. Developmental. Merricat's Castle offers a preschool program where children come together in a supportive and nurturing environment. Children are encouraged to participate in both structured pre-academic work and open-ended activity such as dramatic play, cooking, music, reading, arts and crafts, social studies, science, block building, physical activities, and outdoor play. The school serves as a model for preschool integration, blending some children with special needs into three classrooms. Merricats has a richly diverse group of children from many New York City neighborhoods. The directors see Merricat's as a family, for other families to join.

Admissions. The application fee is $35. Applications are available after Labor Day. There are about forty openings per year. After receiving the application, the school will call to schedule a tour for parents without the child. The child will be invited at a later date to participate in a short play group.

Class size. The school accommodates fifty-five children at a time, in three groups with four staff members each plus volunteers. There are twelve 2/3s, seventeen 3/4s, and twenty-two 4/5s.

Staff. In addition to the full-time teaching staff, teaching interns from Hunter, BMCC, CUNY, La Guardia, Bank Street, Marymount, NYU, and Columbia Teachers College are present in the classrooms.

Facilities. On the second floor of St. Christopher's House, a four-story building constructed in 1887 and part of the complex belonging to the Church of the Holy Trinity (inspired by England's Litchfield Cathedral). The school has three large classrooms, divided into activity centers. In addition, there is an office, kitchen, conference room, and parents' lounge. There are two outdoor play areas with climbing structures.

Separation. Parents are asked to remain nearby during the first two weeks of school. Coffee and treats are served in the parents' lounge, where new parents have the opportunity to meet each other and returning parents.

Parent involvement. The active parents' association comprises a number of committees, with opportunities for involvement for all parents. Parent/teacher conferences are scheduled annually at mid-year and as needed.

Financial. A 20 percent deposit is required upon signing of contract. A monthly payment plan is available for families upon request. The school, committed to racial and economic diversity, makes every effort to provide financial assistance.

Graduates. Have gone on to Allen-Stevenson, Birch Wathen-Lenox, Brearley, Browning, Cathedral, Caedmon, Chapin, Collegiate, Columbia Grammar, Convent of the Sacred Heart, Dalton, Ethical Culture, Manhattan Country, Marymount, Riverdale Country, St. Bernard's, St. David's, St. Ignatius, Spence, Town, Trevor Day, and many other private schools as well as Hunter Elementary and a variety of public school programs.

Member. ERB, ISAAGNY.

Special programs. Merricat's is one of the programs of the Association to Benefit Children, a service-based advocacy organization. ABC serves hundreds of children each year from families struggling with poverty, homelessness, serious illness, and disability, through programs at several sites in Manhattan.

The Montessori School
of New York International

Ages 2–14 yrs
(Nursery–8th grade)

Nonsectarian Montessori Nursery and Elementary School

347 East 55th Street
(between 1st and
and 2nd Avenues)*
Zip: 10022
Tel: 223-4630
Fax: 644-7057
Website: www.montessorischoolny.com
Total Enrollment: 100

Established 1969
Mrs. Hannah Sinha,
Director
Ms. Donna Thomas,
Admissions Director

Nursery Enrollment: 50

*Other locations include: 105 Eighth Avenue (Park Slope), Brooklyn 11215 Tel (718) 857-3341, 55 Junction Boulevard, (Elmhurst), Queens 11373 Tel (718) 857-3474

School year. September through June. Summer camp and academic programs are available for children ages 4–14.

Age	Hours	Days	Tuition
2–14	9:00–5:45°	Mon–Fri	$10,000–$15,000

°Schedule depends on age group; after school program until 6:00 P.M..

Program. Montessori. The school's early childhood curriculum includes classes in practical life, language and speech, writing, reading, phonics, grammar, math, French, music and movement, science, art, social studies, and free play. Children choose activities in which they are interested and for which they are ready. Older children use workbooks. Conversational French and Spanish are begun in the early years. Admissions preference is given to siblings and international students.

Admissions. The application fee is $25. The admissions deadline is March 1st, though it may be earlier if applications are numerous. Admission is based on group orientations followed by an interview with the child, at which time parents may observe a class. If they wish, parents may visit the school first, without their children, after they have applied.

Class size. The primary class contains children age 2 to 5 years. The children meet together in one large room with four teachers. The room is divided into two areas, one for older and one for younger children, with mixed age groups.

Staff. Staff have postgraduate Montessori diplomas from the Association Montessori Internationale.

Facilities. The school occupies a specially designed townhouse and has branches in Brooklyn and Queens.

Separation. Children are phased in during the first two weeks of school according to their comfort and ability to separate.

Financial. A non-refundable deposit is required on enrollment. Approximately half the tuition is due by spring/summer, another third in fall, and the remainder in December and January.

Chartered. By the Board of Regents of the State University of New York.

Member. Staff members belong to a variety of educational societies including AMI and AMS.

92nd Street YM-YWHA Nursery School
Ages: 2.6–5 yrs

Jewish Nursery School

1395 Lexington Avenue
(at 92nd Street)
Zip: 10128
Tel: 415-5532
Website: www.92y.org

Established 1938
Ellen Birnbaum,
Director
Shereen Rutman,
Associate Director
Enrollment: 175

School year. Third week in September through the first week of June.

Age	Hours	Days	Tuition
2.6–2.8	9:00–11:30	Tues Thurs.	$13,500
2.4–2.11	9:00–11:45	Mon Wed Fri	$16,000
3s	9:00–12:00	Mon–Fri	$22,150
4/5s	9:00–2:00 (Fri until 12:30)	Mon–Fri°	$27,150

Extended hours. Parents may drop children off early (at 8:30).

Program. Developmental/Traditional. The 'Y' was founded in 1938 with three classes and has grown to ten classes. Ellen Birnbaum has been at the Y since 1981 as Associate Director, Camp Director, and teacher prior to her new appointment in 2011 as Director. The school's warm, creative atmosphere fosters young children's imagination, curiosity, and intellect. The children's social, emotional, physical, and intellectual growth is facilitated through a curriculum attuned to the children's unique pattern of development. The school feels children learn best in a clearly structured program which emphasizes creative expression through hands-on experiences, provides opportunities for play, and encourages respect for others. Favorite projects include an archeology "dig" and a sculpture unit and gallery opening. Tzedakah (community service) is performed through Passover Food Drives for the elderly and toy

81

collections for needy children. The school's goal is to help children establish a secure sense of self-esteem in order to fulfill their potential. Shabbat and the Jewish holidays are celebrated.

Admissions. The application fee is $75. Inquiries are from the day after Labor Day. Most children enter as 2s or 3s but the school accepts older children as well. Application forms are not mailed. Call early to arrange a parents-only visit between mid-October and the end of November. Children are observed in playgroups of six to eight, with one parent present, for thirty minutes.

The school welcomes children of all faiths.

Class size. The 2s classes have about ten children, with three teachers. The older classes have fifteen to twenty-one children, with three teachers each.

Staff. There are specialists for movement, science, music, gymnastics, learning specialist, and a psychologist visits once a week. The director meets with all members of the staff once a week. There is a teacher enrichment fund that is used for enhancing teacher salaries, funding teacher education and for special projects.

Facilities. Parents enter the large marble lobby of the Y's "old building" and take the elevator to the sixth floor. There are extremely large, inviting, and well-furnished classrooms, offices, a music/assembly room with a skylight, a quiet-time room (where ERBs are given), and three rooftop play areas (one with a retractable roof), with innovative climbing structures that run nearly the full length of the building. Children are escorted to after school programs at the Y such as pottery, gymnastics, sports, and dance.

Summer programs. Summer day camp is housed in the nursery school.

Separation. Teachers visit children starting school for the first time at home before school starts. Twos begin with brief, small-group classes; the full session begins after about six weeks. A parent or caregiver needs to be available during phase-in. The schedule is staggered for the beginning weeks of school.

Parent involvement.   The parents association takes an active role in fund-raising. The Nursery School Benefit usually held in March is legendary; about 400 people attend including the parent body. Parents participate in classes frequently, there are class parents, a Book Fair, newsletters, and monthly parent meetings with the Director. Conferences are arranged twice yearly.

Financial.   Approximately 5 percent of children receive financial aid.

Graduates.   Graduates attend approximately 25 different private and public schools including Allen-Stevenson, Brearley, Chapin, Collegiate, Columbia Grammar, Dalton, Ethical Culture, Heschel, Hewitt, Horace Mann, Nightingale-Bamford, Ramaz, Riverdale, Spence, Trevor Day, Town, Trinity, PS 6, and PS 290.

Affiliations.   YMHA, UJA/Federation.

Member.   ATIS, ERB, ISAAGNY, NAEYC.

Park Avenue Christian Church Day School

Ages: 2.7–5 yrs

Nonsectarian

1010 Park Avenue (between   Established 1963
    84th and 85th Streets)   Betsy Newell,
Zip: 10028   Director
Tel: 288-3247
Enrollment: 180

School year.   September through June.

Age	Hours	Days	Tuition
2s	9:15–11:30/1–3:15	2 or 3	$11,300–$13,390
3s	9:00–11:45/1–3:45	Mon–Fri	$18,300
4s	8:50–12:00	Mon–Fri	$18,800
4s	optional three afternoons until 2:30		$2,500
5s	8:50–2:30 (Fri until 12)	Mon–Thurs	$22,400

Program. Developmental. Emphasizes blocks, dramatic play, learning from hands-on experience rather than traditional academic skills. Children's social skills and interaction are of the foremost importance. There are no worksheets. In art, teachers do not show a model for replication. Representational drawing and abstract work are equally valued.

Threes study the family, talk about themselves as babies, and make family books to take home. Walls display each child's artwork. Fours begin to explore the neighborhood with trips, e.g., to the shoe store. There is no formal math for 4s, but measurement is introduced. 5s use a modified version of the Writing Process. 5s also have scheduled work time for math, writing (inventive spelling is used), and reading, but reading is not expected of the children.

Children in all groups were observed to listen attentively while teachers read aloud, and readily joined in discussion. Teachers take dictation of the children's own stories.

ERBs are given on the premises and directors from ongoing schools visit the classrooms.

Admissions. The application fee is $75. Inquiries begin after Labor Day. The school accepts thirty-two toddlers and sixty-five 3s. A few places are sometimes available for 4s and 5s. It is best to call anytime the week after Labor Day for an application. When parents have submitted an application, they will be contacted by the school to schedule a parent tour and a child interview. Small group visits begin in October and continue through January. Children visit with the director for half-an-hour in groups of four. One parent per child stays through the interview.

Applicants for the 4s and K are usually seen in January and February and visit one at a time in a classroom setting. Applicants for 3s are seen mainly in November and December. Toddler interviews are January through February. The school follows ISAAGNY notification dates.

Admissions priority is given to siblings of current and past students and to children of church members.

Class size. The morning toddler classes have ten children each, the afternoon has 12. Two of the 3s classes have ten children, the youngest 3s, and there are five 3s classes with fifteen children grouped loosely according to age. The three 4s classes have eighteen to twenty-one. The 5s class has up to 23 children.

Each class has a head teacher with a masters degree and a flexible assistant. There are two music teachers, one for the morning and another for the afternoon classes.

Facilities.   Children and mothers climb a short flight of stairs once they enter the building. Children escorted by a parent use the elevator to reach the four floors of spacious, bright classrooms with white brick walls and large windows. There is a separate kitchen on each floor. Each class spends 30 minutes daily in free play in the big cheerful rooftop playground with extensive equipment, and an equally large basement used for cold or rainy-weather play.

Separation.   Varies with the child's age. Teachers make home visits to all toddlers and 3s before school begins in September. The school requires parents to stay in the room for a minimum of six days with toddlers; three days in the room with 3s and on site for the fourth day; on site for one day with the 4s, or as needed.

Parent involvement.   The connection between home and school is highly valued and nurtured. An active parents' association organizes the fund-raising for scholarship, teacher tuition reimbursement, and other program enrichments around the building. Scheduled parent visits—to share a special skill, introduce a new baby or tell a story—form a crucial part of the curriculum in the 3s and 4s. Parents may also visit to observe by appointment. Conferences are held twice a year.

Financial.   A deposit is due with the signed contract. Diversity in racial and economic backgrounds is encouraged. A generous scholarship program exists, ranging from almost full scholarships to 50 percent aid.

Transportation.   Bus transportation cannot be arranged.

Graduates.   Go to the full range of ongoing independent schools, including Allen-Stevenson, Brearley, Browning, Buckley, Chapin, Collegiate, Dalton, Hewitt, Nightingale, Sacred Heart, Spence, St. Bernard's, St. David's, Town, and Trinity. Some parents choose parochial or public schools, including PS 6, 158, 290, and Hunter.

Affiliations.   The church founded the school in 1963. Nonsectarian. Children do not attend chapel.

Member.   ERB, ISAAGNY.

Park Avenue Methodist Day School

Ages: 3–6 yrs

Nonsectarian

106 East 86th Street
  (between Park and
  Lexington Avenues)
Zip: 10028
Tel: 289-6997
Fax: 534-0410
Website: www.pamdayschool.org
E-mail: information@pamdayschool.org

Established 1953
Pamela J. Melasky,
Director
Enrollment: 72

School year.   Mid-September through May.

Summer Camp: June and July

Age	Hours	Days	Tuition
3–6°	9:00–12:00 or 1:00–4:00	Mon–Fri	$16,200

°Extended day program M/T/W, $4,200; parenting program T/Th.

Program.   The philosophy of the school is play based. There are no workbooks. Teachers talk a lot with the children and encourage them to talk to one another and value the social and emotional development of each child.

Activities include sand and water play, housekeeping, dress up, play-dough, painting and other art materials, block building, play with small objects, musical instruments, toys, and books. Group activities include music and storytime.

Admissions.   The application fee is $75. Applications are available from Labor Day on and can be downloaded from the school's website or call. Parents tour in small groups. After filing an application, parents make an appointment to come in with their child for a visit in a play group setting with four to five other families for half an hour. Notifications are sent in March.

Class size.   There are two groups of younger children, one in the morning and one in the afternoon, each with sixteen children and three teachers. There are two groups of older children, one in the morning and one in the afternoon. Each group has sixteen children who stay half day, and an additional 8 children stay for an extended day.

Facilities.   The school uses the fourth floor of Park Avenue Methodist Church. Parents or caregivers bring the children up in the elevator. Everything is well maintained. The school has an extremely large room divided in half by cubbies. One side accommodates the younger children, the other, slightly larger area is occupied by the older children. There is plenty of room for both, but they are not in the room at the same time. At the far end is a large area rug which houses the blocks, musical instruments, CDs, and dress-up clothes. Shelves and cupboards line the walls, and there are lots of small tables and chairs. There is also a science area and art materials, small play objects, puzzles, games, and toys. There are large windows all around. The room is organized, yet messy, and the children's art and projects are everywhere. Down the corridor are staff offices, a small kitchen, and a small, inviting library is nestled at the end of the hall. Up two short flights of stairs is the rooftop playground, quite large, with lots of climbing equipment, two slides, wagons, blocks, crates, and chairs. For rainy-day play, the children use the basement play area.

Summer program.   The eight-week summer program, June through July, is open to children currently enrolled in the school; a 3-week camp in July for incoming 3-year-olds.

Separation.   Gradual. School begins with small groups coming for short sessions. It takes one to three weeks to get the whole group together for the whole session.

Parent involvement.   There is no formal parents association, though parents do involve themselves in various school activities including administration of the school library. They host the holiday party, as well as Spring Carnival. Parents also participate by cooking and helping with music and art or science activities among others.

Graduates.   Go to the full range of public and private schools. ERBs are given on the premises.

Member.   ERB, ISAAGNY.

Park Avenue Synagogue
Early Childhood Center

Ages: 2.6–5 yrs

Jewish Nursery School

50 East 87th Street (corner
  Madison Avenue
  and 87th Street)
Zip: 10128
Tel: 369-2600
Fax: 410-7879
Website: www.pasyn.org
E-mail: ecc@pasyn.org

Established 1965
Carol Hendin,
Director
Enrollment: 125

School year. Mid-September through first week in June.

Ages	Hours	Days	Tuition
2.6	9:00–11:30	Tues Thurs	$12,500
2.9	9:00–11:30	Mon Wed Fri	$14,500
Middle 3s	9:00-12:00	Mon-Fri	$19,500
Young 3s	1:00-3:30	Mon–Thurs (Fri till 12:00)	$15,650
Older 3s/ Young 4s	9:00-1:00	Mon–Thurs (Fri till 12:00)	$21,600
4s/5s	9:00-2:00	Mon–Thurs (Fri till 12:00)	$23,600

Children should be toilet-trained for the 3s program.

Program. Developmental. The school strives for a balance between flexibility and structure and between self-initiated and guided work and play. There is block building, dramatic play, music, art, language arts, math, science, and trips. There is no specific reading program, but teachers respond to their children's readiness in an individual way.

The children celebrate major Jewish holidays and close each week with a Shabbat celebration. Blessings are said in Hebrew and English.

ERB testing is done on the premises. The director sees each parent individually to talk about ongoing school options. A mid-Spring meeting is held to discuss the admissions process.

Admissions. The application fee is $40. Inquiries begin in early September. Most children enter as 2s or 3s.

Once an application has been submitted, parents call to schedule a date for a group tour. Children are seen in groups of about seven beginning in late December or January. There is no separate interview for parents. Special consideration is given to siblings and active long-term synagogue members. Notifications are sent in March.

Class size.   There are two 2s classes of eleven to thirteen children each, three 3s classes of fifteen to seventeen, and three 4s classes of eighteen to twenty children each.

Staff.   Three teachers for each class. There are also a part-time music and movement teacher and several consultants available one day a week.

Facilities.   On the fifth and sixth floors, there is a small, cheerful lobby surrounded by benches. Hallways on either side lead to the classrooms and an interior space used for indoor play on rainy days. The classrooms are large and beautifully equipped with a bathroom in each one. A full kitchen opens off the interior playroom and is used for cooking by all but the toddlers. A comprehensive children's library is available to families and classrooms. There is also a large rooftop play space.

Children bring their own dairy or vegetarian lunches.

Separation.   All children who are new to the school are visited at home before school begins. Returning students make classroom visits prior to the beginning of school. Parents and caregivers are encouraged to be available for the first few weeks of school, sometimes longer. Parents will spend some time in the classroom. The children begin classes in small groups for gradually increasing hours. The whole process takes less than a month. An effort is made to allow the children to come to trust the adults involved.

Parent involvement.   Family orientation meetings are held in the fall and spring. There is an active Parents Association and parents are closely involved through holiday celebrations. Parent/Teacher conferences are held twice yearly. Additional conferences may be requested.

Financial.   Once children are enrolled in the school, families are required to become members of the synagogue. Financial aid is available.

Graduates. Go on to a variety of public and private schools.

Affiliations. Park Avenue Synagogue, a Conservative congregation.

Member. ERB, ISAAGNY.

Philosophy Day School
Ages: 2.11–9

12 East 79th Street (between Madison and 5th Avenue)
Zip: 10021
Tel: 744-7300
Fax: 744-6088
Website: www.philosophyday.org
E-mail: info@philosophyday.org

Nursery program
(Formerly The Ark Nursery School)
Established 1975, the Day School (formerly Abraham Lincoln School) Established 1994
William Fox, Headmaster
Kathy Kigel, Director Preschool Program
Enrollment: 110

School year. Early September–early June; extended day program for nursery and pre-K until 3 P.M. for an additional fee.

Ages	Hours	Days	Tuition
2.11–4.11	8:30–12:45	Mon–Fri	$16,500
5–9	8:10–3:20	Mon–Fri	$25,000

Program. The mission of the Philosophy Day School is to provide a rigorous classical education incorporating knowledge and approaches to life from Eastern and Western civilizations.

The school's focus is on educating the "whole child": intellect, body, and spirit. The school values academics, arts, and athletics and is integrated with teachers who encourage students to make connections not only between subject areas but also between subjects and themselves and their fellow students.

In a structured, unpressured environment, the physical surroundings are intended to enhance the sense of intimacy, beauty, and light. There is a dress code, and a formal system of address between students and teachers.

Teachers model personal values, good manners, and social

skills to develop a sense of self, a respect for others, a commitment to community, and a belief in a Divine Spirit. Students take responsibility for areas of the classroom and parts of the daily schedule in an atmosphere that values each individual's thinking and efforts so that students do not shy away from taking risks or doing their best.

Admissions. The application fee is $55. Parents should call or e-mail inquiries on or after Labor Day. Parents are encouraged to attend an open house (held every Wednesday, September through December) before applying. After applying, parents are given a 45-minute personal tour with the preschool director, or with the headmaster if applying for K–5th grade. Play-groups of one hour with 3–4 children are held during the winter. Parents or babysitters stay in the room.

Class size. There are 15 3s and 18 4s.

Staff. Head teachers have their masters and certification, or are in graduate school. Assistant teachers have BA degrees.

Facilities. The school is located in a beautiful townhouse with large rooms near both Central Park and the Metropolitan Museum of Art.

Separation. Gradual separation for 3 year olds: At first they stay for 1½ hours for two days, parents welcome to remain; 2 hours for the next week; 3 hours for the third week; and have a full program by the 4th week. Parents can remain as long as necessary.

Parent involvement. The school has an active Parents Association.

Financial. Tuition assistance is available from K–5th grade.

Member. NAIS, NYSAIS, ISAAGNY.

Rabbi Arthur Schneier Park East Day School

Ages: 2–13 yrs

Jewish Nursery and Elementary School

164 East 68th Street	Established 1976
(between Lexington and	Mrs. Barbara T. Etra,
Third Avenues)	Principal
Zip: 10021	Mrs. Debbie Rochlin
Tel: 737-6900	Director of Admissions
Fax: 570-6348	Total Enrollment: 350
Website: www.parkeastdayschool.org	Nursery/K Enrollment: 250
E-mail: debbie@parkeastdayschool.org	

School year.　Early September through mid-June. Summer program available for registered students only.

Ages	Hours	Days	Tuition
2s	9:00–12:00	3 days	$13,600
3s	9:00–12:00	5 days	$17,280
3s	9:00–2:00	Mon–Fri	$19,160
4s	9:00–2:00	Mon–Fri	$20,600

A tuition reduction is available for families with more than one child enrolled. Members of Park East Synagogue receive a tuition reduction of $500 for one child.

Program.　Developmental. The Park East Day School was founded by Rabbi Arthur Schneier as a nursery school and merged with East Side Hebrew Institute in 1979, when an elementary division was added. The school is sponsored by a traditional orthodox Jewish synagogue; all the Jewish holidays and Shabbat are observed. Classes for children in the toddler and nursery programs are experiential; they learn through play and hands-on activities. Formal reading instruction begins in the 4s class, computers are used beginning with the 4s, and 5-year-olds have chess instruction. In kindergarten, children also begin to learn about The Writing Process.* For those who choose to continue at Park East, the elementary school offers an award-winning program in math, and also has strong programs in science, art, and computers.

---

* Sometimes called Writers' Workshop, this is a four-step program in which students learn to clarify their thoughts by drafting ("brain drain"), revising ("sloppy copy"), editing ("neat sheet") and, finally, publishing ("final fame"). Formal grammar and spelling are taught in this context.

Admissions. The application fee is $50. Inquiries are from mid-September on. The school has a three-to-one applications to acceptances ratio. Call no earlier than mid-September. After an application form has been submitted, the school will arrange a conference with the parents. A play session will be arranged for the child in late January or the beginning of February. Notifications are sent in March.

Class size. "A Taste of School" for sixteen-month to twenty-four month-olds meets twice each week in two groups for ninety minutes, with a parent or caregiver. For 2s there are two classes, there are three classes of 3s, three classes for 4s and two classes for 5s.

Staff. Each class has two staff members. There are specialists for music and movement, computers, and other activities.

Facilities. The school is located in ten large, modern classrooms on the third, fourth, and fifth floors of the Minskoff Cultural Center. There is a large outdoor play terrace and a large gym, as well as other facilities of the ongoing school. A Kosher lunch is served.

Separation. The children are introduced with short schedules and in small groups over two weeks. Parents usually stay in the hall.

Parent involvement. The parents council is extremely active and arranges many programs for parents and children. The school psychologist is available for consultations. A social worker is also available and holds parent workshops.

Financial. A deposit of $1,000 is required on signing the contract. Parents must pay by four quarterly checks postdated June 30 to March 30 enclosed with the contract.

Transportation. Private bus service can be arranged.

Graduates. Many continue on to the upper school.

Affiliations. Park East Synagogue. Chartered by the Board of Regents of the State University of New York; BJE.

Member. ERB, ISAAGNY.

Ramaz School

Ages: 3–18 yrs

Orthodox Yeshiva (bilingual Hebrew School)

Early Childhood and Lower school:
125 East 85th Street
Zip: 10028
Tel: 774-5610
Tel: Early Childhood Center:
744-8005 or 744-8025
Fax: 774-8039
Website: www.ramaz.org
E-mail: admissions@ramaz.org

Established 1937
Rabbi Haskel Lookstein,
Principal
Rabbi Alan Berkowitz,
Headmaster, Lower school
Ms. Judith Fagin,
Head of School
Ms. Lori Ash,
Director, Early Childhood Center
Ms. Shira Baruch,
Assistant Director of Admissions
Ms. Laurie Bilger,
Director of Admissions
Total enrollment: 1085
Early Childhood Center: 176

Ages	Hours	Days	Tuition
3s	9:00–2:00	Mon–Fri	$20,150
4s	9:00–3:00	Mon–Fri	$20,800
5s	8:20–3:15	Mon–Fri	$22,200

Program. Academic. Ramaz offers a rigorous curriculum of general and Judaic studies as well as a program in the Torah and mitzvot, Zionism, the State of Israel, and the religious and cultural traditions of Judaism. It gives equal emphasis to American democracy and Western culture.

The Early Childhood Center's curriculum includes cooking, math, verbal and social skills, science, music, art, dance, social studies, field trips, and physical activity. Jewish and national holidays are celebrated and Jewish history, laws, customs, prayers, and blessings are explored. The program also stresses social and emotional growth.

Children who may require extra support in developing readiness skills may participate in the school's Early Intervention program.

Admissions. The application and testing fee is $150. Parents should call for an appointment as early as possible.

Class size. There are two classes of eighteen 3-year-olds, two classes of eighteen 4s, and three kindergarten or 5s classes of 22 children each.

Facilities The Early Childhood Center is located in the lower school, and has two outdoor play areas, one with a custom-designed play sculpture the other with a full-sized playground. There is also access to a fully equipped gym, library, a media center, science lab, and music and art centers.

Financial. A variety of additional fees for 3s through 5s.

Transportation. Private bus service can be arranged.

Affiliations. Congregation Kehilath Jeshurun.

Member. NYSAIS, Middle States Accredited.

Renanim Preschool and Nursery
18 mos–5 yrs

Jewish

336 East 61st Street (between
First and Second Avenues)
Zip: 10021
Tel: 750-2266

Established: 1977
Rachel Goren,
Director

School year. September through June, plus summer camp.

Ages	Hours	Days	Tuition
All	8:30–12:00	Mon–Fri	$13,825
	8:30–3:30	Mon–Fri	$20,000
	8:30–6:00	Mon–Fri	$21,000

Flexible schedules are available and tuition is prorated.

Extended stay. $12.00 per hour, by prior arrangement.

Program. Developmental. "Renanim" means happiness in Hebrew.

The school, founded in Israel, offers an English-Hebrew education, although no prior knowledge of Hebrew is required or necessary. The program seeks to develop the whole child—i.e., the social, emotional, physical, and cognitive aspects—through meaningful, concrete experiences. There is a strong focus on the arts, including drama, arts and crafts, music and dance. In addition, the school offers an emergent literacy curriculum, computer, math and science, cooking, and fun-filled educational trips. The goals are to build self-esteem, to develop a positive attitude toward school, to learn respect for oneself and others, to develop math and reading readiness skills among the older children, and to encourage curiosity and foster independence.

Admissions. The application fee is $85. Inquiries are welcomed from Labor Day on. The school offers two open houses, one in November, one in December. Parents are encouraged to call to schedule a tour with their child throughout the year.

Class size. All classes have two head teachers, one who speaks Hebrew, one who speaks English, as well as an assistant teacher or aide. There are twelve children in the 20 mos–2.6 yrs group, fourteen in the 2.6–3.6 group, and sixteen in the 3.6–5 group.

Staff. All head teachers have a masters degree in early childhood education. A music, a yoga, and a ballet teacher work with the children on a weekly basis.

Facilities. Open, spacious classrooms with custom-made and brightly painted furniture provide a unique and cheerful environment for indoor play and learning. Every classroom has its own bathroom, which allows the teacher to help children become successfully toilet-trained. A special diaper-changing area is also available. A large, safe outdoor playground is connected to the school and is used exclusively by Renanim children. In addition to balls, hoops, and sand play, it is fully equipped with a carousel, climbing apparatus, two slides, and bicycles.

Separation. For the first week, the parent is asked to be available, either in the classroom or outside in the lounge, as needed. The school wants both the parent and the child to be comfortable.

Parent involvement. Parents are encouraged to visit the classroom. There are three parent/teacher conferences each year and two Sunday afternoon arts-and-crafts workshops for parents and children. Parents are invited to accompany the class on field trips and also to celebrate holidays and their children's birthdays with special programs. A monthly calendar and weekly letters inform parents of activities the children will be involved in during the coming week.

Summer program. A separate summer program is available during July and August. The children play outdoors, garden, swim, and exercise; indoor activities include cooking, arts and crafts, music, musical instruments, movement and dance, movies, and visits to museums.

Financial. A non-refundable registration fee of $85 and a non-refundable deposit (applied toward tuition) of $500 is due upon registration. The remainder of tuition is due in equal installments upon arrangement with the school administration.

Graduates. Have gone on to private schools such as Abraham Joseph Heschel, Rabbi Arthur Schneier Park East Day School, and Solomon Schecter, as well as a variety of public schools, including Hunter.

Affiliations. BJE.

Member. ERB.

Resurrection Episcopal Day School (REDS)
Ages: 2.9–6 yrs

Episcopal Nursery School

119 East 74th Street
(between Park and
Lexington Avenues)
Zip: 10021
Tel: 535-9666, Admissions, ext 11
Fax: 535-3191
Website: www.redsny.org
E-mail: admissions@redsny.org

Established 1990
Laurie Boone Hogan,
Director
Rhea Shome,
Assistant to Director and
Director of Admissions
Enrollment: 84

School year: Second week in September until early June. Two-week summer program for current students only.

Ages	Hours	Days	Tuition
2.9–6°	8:45–11:45	Mon–Fri	$18,520
3.6–5	8:45–2:45 (Fri until 11:45)	Mon–Fri	$23,800

Full-day children bring their own lunches. A snack is laid out for half-day children who help themselves to it.

° There is an afternoon enrichment program (AEP) for younger children from 1–2:45 P.M. in art, music, and community projects.

Extended hours.   For children 3.6–4.6, the Afternoon Enrichment Program operates from 12:00 to 2:45. On any particular day there may be three or four activities for children to choose from.

Program.   Classic Montessori curriculum, member of the Association Montessori Internationale. REDS, the school's nickname, is an Episcopal Montessori school founded by the Church of Resurrection Ultimate, and is governed by a board of trustees. Children are given the freedom to learn at an individual pace and are allowed to gain in self-confidence, initiative, and independence as they master each level of material. There is a three-year age span in the classroom, which allows the individual to socialize with both older and younger children, and an opportunity to experience help joyfully given and received.

Admissions.   The application fee is $75. Inquiries start in the fall prior to the application year. Parents attend an open house with a school tour, complete an application, along with an essay. Parents are invited to observe a classroom, and have an interview. A child visit follows. Parents are notified in early March.

Class size.   The ratio is 8 to 1.

Staff.   Two staff members per class: one AMI°-trained teacher and one credentialed assistant. There are two full-time assistant teachers (floaters) and four specialists, one to four days a week.

°Association Montessori Internationale

Facilities.   The school's four sunny, attractive, and well-organized rooms on the second and third floors of the parish house of the Church of the Resurrection. The rooms are filled with colorful and beautifully displayed Montessori materials. There are child-sized bathrooms. The whole environment is designed for children.

Separation.   Before school starts, a parent accompanies the child for a visit, an opportunity to meet the teachers, become familiar with the classroom. Once school starts, new children are "phased in" a few at a time. Some new children are more comfortable with shortened sessions. For the first week of school, all new parents are encouraged to remain at the school.

Parent involvement.   All REDS parents are automatically members of the Parents Association. Parents volunteer as classroom parents, admissions guides, field trip chaperones, party organizers, librarians, and more.

Financial.   A $1,000 deposit is required on signing the contract. The balance of tuition is paid in two equal installments. Limited financial aid is available.

Transportation.   Most children come from the immediate neighborhood and are brought by parents or caregivers.

Graduates.   Have attended leading ongoing independent and public schools.

Member.   AMI, ISAAGNY, North American Montessori Association, NAEC.

The Rhinelander Nursery School
Ages: 2.6–5.0

350 East 88th Street
   (between First and Second Avenues)
Zip: 10128
Tel: 876-0500
Fax: 876-9718
Website: www.rhinelandercenter.org
E-mail: dianef@rhinelandercenter.org

Established in 1993
Diane E. Farley,
Nursery Director
Lauren M. Stelzer,
Assistant Director
Enrollment: 75

School year. Second week in September through the last week in May.

Summer program. Optional summer program June through August.

Ages	Hours	Days	Tuition
2s	12:45-3:15	Mon, Tues, Thurs	$7,850
3s	8:45–11:45	Mon–Fri	$12,600
3s	12:30–3:00	Mon, Tues, Wed, Thurs	$9,450
4s/Pre-K	8:45–12:45	Mon-Fri	$14,950
4s/Pre-K	1:00–3:30	Mon,Tues,Wed, Thurs	$9,450

Program. Developmental. The program focuses mostly on the development of social skills, self-esteem, and individuality, through relationships with the other children and with teachers. Children learn through hands-on play that is tailored to meet their individual abilities and interests. The core of the program consists of support and enhancement of each child's ideas, feelings, and thoughts. Age appropriate activities with a multi-sensory approach are incorporated into group and individual instruction times in the school's learning centers. Onsite outdoor playgrounds provide a place for the children to exercise and play. Specials include library, music, yoga, and Spanish.

Admissions. The application fee is $50. Applications are accepted the day after Labor Day for the following year. After applying, parents are invited to join a small group tour of the school. Children are invited to return for a playgroup along with their parents or caregiver later in the year. Parents are notified in early March.

Class size. There are fifteen children in each 3s class and sixteen children in each 4s class. The 2s classroom has thirteen children. All classes have three teachers, one head teacher and two assistants.

Staff.   Head teachers are certified teachers with education degrees.

Facilities.   The school is located in a brownstone. There are two sunny classrooms with areas for block building, art, science, reading, dramatic play, puzzles, and manipulatives. The children play outdoors on two rooftop decks.

Separation.   Separation is a two-step process: For the first three weeks the school day is shorter and classes are smaller. Parents or caregivers bring their children into the classroom and either stay in the classroom or in an adjacent family room that has a one-way mirror. Parents or caregivers are expected to stay at school until their child is comfortable. If the process takes longer than three weeks, the school is flexible and gently guides parents through the separation process individually.

Parent involvement.   Parents play an important role and choose to be involved in many ways. There is a parent association, conferences, newsletters, and trips. Parents are welcome in the school at any time.

Financial.   A nonrefundable deposit of $2,000 is required upon signing the contract. The balance of tuition is to be paid in one or two payments. There are flexible payment plans and financial aid is available.

Transportation.   Most students come from the Upper East Side and walk to school.

Graduates.   Have attended leading ongoing private and public schools.

Affiliations.   Children's Aid Society.

Member.   ISAAGNY, Parents League, ERB.

The Rockefeller University Child and Family Center

Ages: 3 mos–5 yrs

Nonsectarian Nursery School

1230 York Avenue	Established 1966
(at 66th Street)	Karen J. Booth,
Zip: 10065	Director
Tel: 327-7072	Enrollment: 110

Ages	Hours	Days	Tuition*
3 mos–3 yrs	8:30–6:00	Mon–Fri	
3s–5s	8:30–2:30 or 8:30–6:00	Mon–Fri	

*The Child and Family Center accepts only children whose parents are affiliated with Rockefeller University. These affiliated families pay tuition on a sliding scale depending on the amount of hours their children attend.

Program and Admissions. There is no application fee. Applications are accepted throughout the year. Parents may visit the school during January and February. The director does not meet the children until after they are admitted.

Class size. There are two infant groups, four toddler groups, one 2/3s group, two 3s groups, and one 4s/5s group, ranging in size from eight to eighteen children, depending on the age.

Staff. The director, thirty-six full-time teachers, and ten part-time teachers, and music, creative movement, and art teachers.

Facilities. The school occupies the ground floor of the Graduate Students Residence and Sophie Fricke Hall on the Rockefeller University campus. Its classrooms look out on the beautifully landscaped fifteen-acre campus. There are three outdoor playgrounds. A large children's garden, planted, tended to, and harvested by the children.

Summer program. The summer program is for students already enrolled and runs five days a week from July through August.

Separation. Children attend for short periods in small groups during the first week. Parents are expected to stay until their child is comfortable.

Parent involvement. Parent involvement in the school's activities is encouraged. An active Parent Association organizes fund-raising events as well as activities and events for families.

Financial. There is a non-refundable registration fee of $400 applicable to tuition.

Transportation. No private bus service is available.

Graduates. Have gone on to such schools as Brearley, Caedmon, Collegiate, Dalton, Ethical Culture, Marymount, Nightingale-Bamford, Spence, Trinity, Hunter, as well as neighborhood public schools.

Affiliations. Rockefeller University.

Member. ERB, ISAAGNY, NCCCC.

Roosevelt Island Day Nursery
Ages: 2.6–5 yrs

Nonsectarian

4 River Road
Zip: Roosevelt Island 10044
Tel: 593-0750
Fax: 593-1342
Website: www.ridn.org
E-mail: preschool@ridn.org

Established 1977
Diana Carr
and Mandi Ridler,
Directors
Enrollment: 50

School year. Early September through mid-June. Working parents may drop off children at 8:00.

Age	Hours	Days	Tuition
2.6/3s	9:00–12:00	Mon–Fri	$12,000
3s	9:00–3:00	Mon–Fri	$14,575
4s	9:00–3:00	Mon–Fri	$15,500

Program.   Eclectic. The school describes itself as an open-classroom, child-centered school. The curriculum stresses the development of concepts and skills that are needed for the formal learning of reading, writing; math, science, and social studies. Block building, dramatic play, art, music, and physical development are an integral part of the curriculum.

Admissions.   The application fee is $25. Registration begins in March. Most children enter as 3s, although there are usually some openings for 4s as well. Children are admitted on a first-come basis. Parents visit the school with their children.

Class size.   Classes for 2.6s/3s, have 15 children, and for 4s, up to 20 children. There are 2–3 teachers in each classroom.

Facilities.   The rooms are spacious, bright, and well equipped, with views of the river. All classrooms are divided into activities areas for block-building, art, science, cooking, dramatic play, puzzles, and games.

Summer program.   There is an eight-week summer program similar to the school-year program with emphasis on water and other outdoor activities.

Parent involvement.   Parents may visit any time and are involved on the board of directors, with fund-raising, and with classroom activities such as cooking, art projects, field trips, and parties.

Financial.   A tuition deposit is required on registration. Payments of the balance are made quarterly or monthly. There is a $10 book-keeping charge for monthly payments. Financial aid is available from the school's scholarship fund.

Graduates.   Have gone on to local public schools and private schools such as Brearley, Browning, Caedmon, Collegiate, Dalton, Dwight, Ethical Culture, Friends Seminary, Manhattan Country, Spence, Town, Trevor Day, and UNIS.

Member.   ERB, ISAAGNY

The Rudolf Steiner School

Ages: 2–18 yrs

Nonsectarian Nursery and Ongoing School

Lower School:	Established 1928
15 East 79th Street (between Fifth	Josh Eisen,
and Madison Avenues)	School Administrator
Zip: 10021	Irene Mantel,
Tel: 327-1457	Director of Admissions
Fax: 744-4497	Early Childhood Enrollment: 70
Upper School: 15 East 78th Street	Total Enrollment: 350
Tel: 879-1101	
Website: www.steiner.edu	

School year.   September to early June.

Ages	Hours	Days	Tuition
2s	90 minutes	Tues or Thurs	$1,050
3s	8:30–12:00	Mon–Fri	$22,600
4s/5s	8:30–12:00	Mon–Fri	$23,570
4s/5s	8:30–2:45	Mixed Week	$28,300
4s/5s	8:30–2:45	Mon–Fri	$32,100

The 2s attend ten parent/child sessions. For all other programs, children must be age-appropriate by June 30th.

Program.   Developmental. The Waldorf method, established by Rudolf Steiner, is based on the belief that children pass through three basic stages of development, and the curriculum is designed to engage the abilities of the growing child at each of these stages. In preschool this is accomplished through creative guided play and activities that foster imagination. Movement and eurythmy, a form of music and movement, and counting games, which build a foundation for later learning. The preschool uses only natural materials including chestnuts, sand and water, shells and stones, pinecones, and other objects found and gathered from nature. Regular guided activities include paint with watercolors, baking, cooking, sewing, and woodworking. You will never find a LEGO here.

Rudolf Steiner (1861–1925), an Austrian scientist, artist, educator, and founder of anthroposophy, began the first Waldorf school in Stuttgart in 1919. Integrating intellectual and artistic development, Steiner sought to sustain and deepen the child's capacity for life and creative thought. Driven underground during the Hitler years, Steiner's ideas survived and now inspire some 1,000 schools in more than 83 countries. There are approximately 300 Waldorf schools in North America.

Admissions. The application fee is $55 Inquiries begin after Labor Day. The application deadline is November 1st. Tours and open houses are offered in the fall and require a reservation. Applicants' parents meet with the admissions director, while children are interviewed in small groups.

For the 2s Plus Program, children must be 2 by June 30th. There are 23 spaces available for 3-year-olds. Places for 4 and 5 year olds are limited and depend on attrition. The 2s program offers 24 places but does not provide automatic acceptance into the 3-year-old nursery program. Five years of age is a typical entry point. Preference is given to siblings and legacy applicants.

Notifications are sent in February and March. Children may be put on a waitlist pending openings that can sometimes occur in late spring or summer.

Class size. There are two classes of 3-year-olds, one group of fifteen older 3s, and a second group with nine young 3s, each with two teachers. There are also two mixed-age (4s/5s/6s) kindergartens, one with twenty-four students and the other with twenty-one students, each of which has a head teacher with two assistants. The parent/child program has two groups of twelve children with three teachers.

Staff. The head teachers hold several levels of university credentials, some have masters degrees in Early Childhood Education as well as training in Waldorf education, others range from bachelor's to PhDs. An elected committee composed of faculty and staff governs the school. This committee must approve all decisions affecting the school and the students.

Facilities. The lower school building houses the nursery; kindergarten and first through sixth grades and is located in a limestone mansion by McKim, Mead & White fronting East 79th Street. Its entrance hall is white marble. On the first floor are two nursery rooms, and one mixed-age kindergarten; a second kindergarten is on the second floor. The rooms are filled with materials chosen to stimulate the children's imagination such as building blocks, soft dolls and puppets, and colorful cloths. Each classroom is equipped with a kitchen area for baking, cooking, and preparation of a daily snack. An organic lunch is served to full-day students. Central Park is the school's play yard. Everyday the children walk the half block from the school and cross Fifth Avenue holding on to a long rope with loops. They carry buckets for gathering acorns or leaves, jump ropes, balls, and in the spring their snack and a large blanket for picnics.

Separation.   Separation is gradual and varies with the needs of each child. Threes come together in small groups for a phasing-in period. After a few weeks they are in their regular group for a full morning. Most children learn to separate within two to three weeks.

Parent involvement.   Ongoing parent education is offered. Formal parent/teacher conferences are held twice a year, and informal exchanges are frequent. Either the parent or the teacher may request a meeting at any time. There is also an active parents association, which has a role in community building activities such as the annual Fall Fair, where beautiful crafts are sold, a major showcase for Waldorf education.

Financial.   Tuition includes all fees. A non-refundable tuition deposit of 15 percent is required on signing the contract. Sixty-five percent of the tuition is due July 1st, the remainder on December 1st. Parents can subscribe to a commercial tuition payment plan. Financial aid is not available at the nursery and rarely at the kindergarten level.

Transportation.   About half the school's students come from the immediate neighborhood, the remainder from the Upper West Side, downtown, Brooklyn, Queens, the Bronx, and New Jersey. Most children are brought to school by their parents or caregivers.

Graduates.   Many children continue through high school.

Member.   ERB, ISAAGNY, NAIS, NYSAIS, Early Steps, Waldorf Schools Association, AWSNA, AISAP.

St. Bartholomew Community Preschool
Ages: 2.6–5 yrs
Non-denominational

325 Park Avenue
  (at 50th Street)
Zip: 10022
Tel: 378-0223/0238
Website: www.stbarts.org

Established 1973
Allison O'Melia,
Director
Mary Ponce,
Admissions Director
Enrollment: 60

School year. September through May.

Ages	Hours	Days	Tuition
2s/young 3s	9:00–11:45	2, 3 or 5 days	$10,400–$17,300
3s/4s	9:00–12:00	Mon–Fri	$17,300
4s/5s	9:00–3:00	Mon–Fri	$22,500

Children in the 3s program must be toilet-trained. Early morning drop-off is available from 8:30–9:00 A.M. at a minimal fee.

Program. Eclectic. The preschool cultivates an environment in which children are encouraged to learn about themselves, and the community around them. Teaching is tapered according to the child's need, development, and readiness. The program is structured but not rigid and includes weekly music and movement, yoga, swimming, library, chapel, and cooking. One of the main goals of the school is to foster a sense of enjoyment and help children feel confident about going to school and learning. ERB testing is offered on-site.

French, tennis, and cooking are offered as afterschool activities.

Admissions. The application fee is $75. Applications can be downloaded from the school's website and mailed to the preschool after September 1st. The first 150 applicants are contacted to schedule a tour and family meeting. Notifications are sent in accordance with ISAAGNY guidelines.

Class size. There are two 2s groups of ten to twelve, one group of fifteen to seventeen 3s, and one group of eighteen or nineteen 4/5s. Each class has two staff members. Specialists teach dance and movement, swimming, and science.

Facilities.   Children enter the building through the school entrance on 50th Street between Lexington and Park Avenues. They take the elevator with their parents to large, sunny, cheerful classrooms on the fourth and fifth floors of the church's community house. The children make use of a large multi-purpose room for music, dancing, and other activities; a children's 2,500-volume circulating library; a swimming pool (with a special tot "dock") and full-size gymnasium; and a new 1,900-square-foot fully equipped rooftop playground with a garden and climbing equipment. Many of the school's resources (the library, video equipment, gym equipment, the charming cubby mural) were donated by generous parents of past and present students.

There are newly renovated child-size bathrooms, and a heated pool in the basement of the community house.

Summer program.   The June program—three weeks of "Adventurous Summer" camp—is open to the community.

Separation.   Handled gradually and individually. The 2s begin with small groups and short sessions. Parents remain in the classroom until children are comfortable with their leaving.

Parent involvement.   The school strongly encourages parent participation in their children's lives at school. There are monthly parent/child luncheons that parents gladly attend, a newsletter staffed by parents, library activities, and numerous committee, fund-raising, and social events (Family Play Days, Thanksgiving/Passover exchange program with Central Synagogue, Parents Night, farewell picnic) that bring the community of families together. As one parent said, "Finding a school that allows parents to be this involved makes us feel like we are a part of, and not just an observer of, our children's school experience."

Financial.   A deposit is required on signing the contract. Limited scholarship aid is available.

Graduates.   Go on to such schools as Allen-Stevenson, Brearley, Browning, Buckley, Chapin, Collegiate, Dalton, Friends, Hewitt, St. Bernard's, Spence, Trinity, as well as public schools.

Affiliations.   St. Bartholomew's Episcopal Church.

Member.   Day Care Council of New York, Child Care Inc., Ecumenical Child Care Network, ERB, ISAAGNY, National Association of Episcopal Schools.

St. Ignatius Loyola Day Nursery
Ages: 2–5 years
Catholic

240 East 84th Street   Established 1915
Zip: 10028   Theodora L. Crist,
Tel: 734-6427 (Office);   Director
Ext 25 (Admissions)   Luz M. Mezza Robledo,
Fax: 734-6972   Assistant Director
Website: www.saintignatiusloyola.org   Rosario Murray,
                                                    Admissions Director
                                                       Enrollment: 130

School year.   September through June.

Ages	Hours	Days	Tuition
2–5	8:00–5:30	Mon–Fri	$20,000
2s and 3s	9:00–12:00	3, or 5 days	$15,200–$16,200
3s and 4s	1:30–4:30	3, or 5 days	$15,200–$16,200

Program.   The Day Nursery offers a challenging child-centered preschool program that stresses social, emotional, and cognitive growth. Creative play with manipulatives (blocks), as well as a variety of other materials is stressed. Teachers support learning and act as nurturing guides in a variety of ways. There's age-appropriate instruction in math, language arts, music, movement, art, science, and social studies. Twice a week, each class receives Spanish language instruction; once a week there's a yoga class with an expert in early childhood yoga. Themes are central to the program: units include *Aesop's Fables* to life in the North Pole to recycling.

The lunch menu (from a full-service kitchen with a full-time cook), reads like those of many Madison Avenue restaurants offering raisin bread, frittatas, pasta primavera, puddings, and parfaits. ERBs are given onsite.

Admissions. The application fee is $75. Inquiries and requests for applications from September on. Once a completed application is received the admissions office will call to schedule a meeting and a tour. Preference is given to children of members of the parish of the Church of St. Ignatius Loyola and siblings.

Class size. There are two classes of 2s, four classes of 3s, two classes of 4s, and one junior kindergarten of 4s and 5s. Each class has a head teacher and an assistant teacher.

Staff. There's a strong feeling of connection and continuity. Faculty members teach at the school on average of fifteen years. There are professional development opportunities both in-school and off-site as well as funds for higher education. A consulting psychologist is available to meet with parents and teachers on a weekly basis. A Spanish teacher meets with children twice a week integrating art, music, and movement into the foreign language program. A yoga instructor introduces the fundamentals of yoga weekly.

Facilities. The Day Nursery occupies an historic five-story building on the Upper East Side. Each floor contains two generously proportioned, sunny classrooms, divided into separate areas for instruction, play and reading, eating, and napping. The rooftop playground includes 2,000 square feet of open play space, equipped with tricycles, slides, climbing equipment, and plenty of room for running and playing.

Parent involvement. Parent/teacher conferences are held twice a year, more frequently if requested. Each class has parent representatives who fund-raise, arrange special classroom activities, and volunteer for field trips.

Separation. A gradual process that begins with abbreviated sessions and small groups.

Financial. There is an enrollment fee of $2,300 due upon signing the contract. Tuition payments are made in three installments: April, September, and January. A building maintenance fee of $1,000 is due in April. Financial aid is available for the full-day program.

Transportation. The school does not provide bus service. The closest public transportation includes the numbers 4, 5, and 6 Lexington Avenue trains and the 86th Street, Madison, Fifth, Second, and Third Avenue bus routes.

Graduates. Have been accepted to Allen-Stevenson, Bank Street, Birch Wathen/Lenox, Brearley, Browning, Buckley, Caedmon, Chapin, Collegiate, Convent of the Sacred Heart, Dalton, Ethical Culture, Horace Mann, La Scuola, Lycée, Marymount, Spence, St. Bernard's St. David's, St. Ignatius Loyola, St. Joseph's Yorkville, St. Stephen's of Hungary, P.S. 6, 158, 290, The Anderson Program, Hunter, and Lower Lab.

Affiliations. The Church of St. Ignatius Loyola, Parents League, ACEI, ASCD.

St. Thomas More Play Group

Ages: 2–5 yrs

Nonsectarian Nursery School

65 East 89th Street
 (between Madison
 and Park Avenues)
Zip: 10128
Tel: 534-3977
Fax: 427-9015

Established 1972
Nancy Godreau,
Director
Deirdre Groescup,
Admissions Director
Enrollment: 120

School year. September through May.

Ages	Hours	Days	Tuition
2s	1:15–3:15	T/W/Th	$14,870
3s	12:45–3:00	M/T/Th	$17,150
	8:45–12:00	Mon–Fri	$20,350
4s/5s	8:45–1:00	Mon–Fri	$21,670

Program. Traditional/Developmental. The Play Group provides a nurturing and supervised environment where separation is sensitively handled. Daily schedules and movement of the groups between rooms and interest areas is structured yet flexible enough to allow for spontaneity. Developmentally age-appropriate activities include arts, science, movement, and music. Children make weekly visits to the school's library where even the youngest children are encouraged to explore and borrow books of their choosing.

Admissions. The application fee is $50. Inquiries are in September. Parents call the day after Labor Day to arrange for a visit to the school between October and December. Applications are given after the school tour. No interview is required of the child. Parents are notified of decisions in late-February and must respond by early March.

Class size. There are two 2s classes with ten to twelve children and two 3s classes with fifteen children. The 4s class and the two 4s/5s classes each have fifteen to eighteen children. Each class has three teachers.

Facilities. When children enter the school they are met by their teachers and escorted downstairs where they each have a cubby. The classrooms and special activity areas are well lit and well equipped, and there are two padded outdoor play area. The children have music or creative movement each day in a large music room with a piano. In addition, there is a science program and special arts program for all 4s.

Summer program. Two weeks in June, for enrolled students only.

Separation. Teachers make home visits from prior to the beginning of the school year. The 2s and 3s begin school in small groups, which meet for shortened sessions during a three-week orientation period.

Parent involvement. There is an active parents association, which meets monthly and serves as liaison between parents and school. The parent body is homogenous; families are likely to reside in the immediate Upper East Side neighborhood.

Transportation. No private bus service is available. Most children walk to school with a parent or caregiver.

Temple Emanu-El Nursery School and Kindergarten

Ages: 2.7–6 yrs

Jewish Nursery School

One East 65th Street
(between 5th and
Madison Avenues)
Zip: 10021
Tel: 744-1400
Enrollment: 135
Website: www.emanuelnyc.org
E-mail: info@emanuelnyc.org

Established 1950
Mrs. Ellen Davis,
Director
Mrs. Suzanne Fischer,
Registrar

School year. September through beginning of June. Seven-week summer program available to children in and outside of the school community.

Ages	Hours	Days	Tuition
2.7–2.9	9:00–12:00	2 days per week	$10,165
2.10–3.1	9:00–12:00	3 days per week	$12,035
3.0–3.5	9:00–12:00	Mon–Fri	$17,190
3.5–4 yrs	9:00–2:00	5 mornings + 3 afternoons	$19,900
4–5.3 yrs	9:00–2:00	5 mornings + 4 afternoons	$20,900

Children of temple members and siblings may be 2.5 on entering. Toilet training is not necessary for 2s or 3s.

Program. Traditional. The curriculum includes a full readiness program. In a typical day, children have an hour of free-choice time, which includes group time, music, gym, nature, science, a cooking or art project, or library time. The older children dictate and illustrate stories, which are collected and saved for their parents. The last part of the morning is spent on one of the school's two outdoor playgrounds. The children also take many field trips. The classes contain a balanced number of boys and girls.

The director stresses that the children are not schooled for the ERB other than by being helped to learn to sit, focus, and complete a task. She strongly disapproves of tutoring and considers it self-defeating for children to be placed in schools that are inappropriate for them. The ERB test is given on the premises.

Major Jewish holidays are celebrated and others are discussed when appropriate. The children's snack on Fridays is challah.

Admissions. The application fee is $75. Inquiries are from Labor Day on. Parents begin calling after Labor Day to reserve a place in a group tour. These commence in October. Parents are notified by letter of their tour date. Applications must be received before a tour is scheduled. The school invites children for play sessions with members of the staff in January and early February. Five or six children come at a time, and the session lasts thirty minutes. Only one parent accompanies the child. Preference is given to siblings and children of congregation members.

Class size. There are three 2s classes of thirteen students each. The two 3s classes have eighteen children, the 4s and 4/5s each have nineteen. Each class has at least three staff members, allowing teachers to split up the group for concentration in various areas, such as woodworking or cooking. There are floating teachers on staff. Movement, music, yoga, and nature specialists work with each group once a week. The nature specialist brings in a variety of plants and animals—from parrots to snakes—to enrich nature presentations. Each Friday a reading program takes place in the library. This program is run by parent volunteers.

Facilities. In addition to six spacious, beautifully equipped and maintained classrooms on the third floor of the temple's Community House, there are two large outdoor playgrounds (equipped with playhouses, large construction blocks, slides, tricycles, wagons, and intricate climbing structures), a large carpeted playroom, a library, a conference room, offices, and a room for cooking and woodworking. The classrooms have adjoining toddler-sized toilets, sinks for water play, and mirrored-window observation booths for parents. Many of the rooms have pianos. Classrooms are divided into well-equipped activities centers, including a block corner. Creative artwork as well as project art adorn walls and bulletin boards. Sand tables are filled with kosher salt or cornmeal. The children gather together for a school sing-along once a month.

Summer program. A seven-week summer program is available Monday through Thursday at 9 A.M. to 1 P.M., at an additional cost of $3,960. It is held in the school's facility and is open to the community.

Separation.   Handled gradually and individually. Parents of new children meet with the director in the spring before their children begin school. Children and parents visit the classroom before school begins. In addition, there is a tea and a breakfast in the classroom for new parents to meet one another before school begins.

Parent involvement.   Parent involvement is welcomed. There are two formal conferences each year and others as needed. Teachers are always available by phone. Parents are encouraged to join the class for lunch, to read a story or to arrange an art project. They are also involved in the book fair, family day, library, and they help arrange events such as the Seder.

Financial.   Some scholarship aid is available.

Transportation.   Parents bring their children to the school floor where they are greeted by their teachers. No bus service is provided by the school. The children come from the East and West Sides down to Tribeca and uptown as far as 105th Street.

Graduates.   Have gone to Abraham Joshua Heschel, Allen-Stevenson, Birch Wathen-Lenox, Brearley, Browning, Buckley, Chapin, Collegiate, Columbia Grammar, Dalton, Ethical Culture, Friends Seminary, Hewitt, Horace Mann, Nightingale-Bamford, Riverdale, St. Bernard's, Spence, Town, and Trinity.

Affiliations.   Temple Emanu-El.

Member.   ERB, ISAAGNY.

Temple Israel Early Childhood Learning Center

Ages: 2.4–5 yrs

Jewish Nursery School, Reformed

112 East 75th Street
(between Lexington and
Park Avenues)
Zip: 10021
Tel: 249-5001
Website: www.templeisraelnyc.org

Established 1966
Nancy-Ellen Micco,
Director
Lindsay Bennett,
Assistant Director
Enrollment: 95

School year. September through early June. Camp Chaverim held in June and July.

Ages	Hours	Days	Tuition
2s	9:00–11:30	2, 3 days a week	$10,815–$12,675
3s	9:00–11:45	Mon–Fri	$17,325
3s	12:30–2:45	Mon–Thurs	$13,125
4s	9:00–2:15	Mon–Fri (Fri to 12)	$20,900
5s	9:00–2:45	Mon–Fri (Fri until 12)	$21,800

Extended days available for 3s (11:45–2:00) for an additional fee of approximately $3,000, Tuesday and Thursday afternoons.

Program. Developmental. The Early Childhood Learning Center provides a warm, nurturing, structured, and stimulating environment emphasizing individual and small group activities. Teachers understand the individual needs of young children. Experiences are provided in the arts, math, reading readiness, handwriting without tears, music, literature, science, block building, and science. Each child is encouraged to develop his or her own strengths. The goal is to have all the children leave school feeling confident, independent, and secure in themselves and their abilities.

Learning through play on an age-appropriate level is stressed. Projects related to the individual curiosity and interests of the child are incorporated into the curriculum. There are always specific projects available, as well as a range of other activities. Each group is offered a cooking curriculum which incorporates aspects of math and science.

117

There is a strong Jewish component to the curriculum. Children are introduced to Jewish traditions and holiday celebrations, through art, music, and food. Shabbat is celebrated on Fridays in every classroom; families participate.

ERBs are given on the premises, in both spring and fall.

Admissions. The application fee is $65. Requests for applications begin on the first Monday in October, unless this conflicts with the High Holy Days. Dates to call may be found on the summer voice mail message. Parents should call for an application form and return it with the fee. The school will call to arrange a parent group tour. Individual family interviews begin in early December. Preference is given to siblings and children of long-term temple members.

Class size. There are two 2s classes, two morning classes for 3s, one afternoon 3s class, one class for 4s, and a class of older 4/5s. There are three teachers for each group.

Facilities. Located on the fourth floor of Temple Israel, the school's walls are fire brick, painted white and accented with primary-color-painted doorways. Each of the five classrooms has a wall of windows, its own bathroom, and direct access to the play terraces. The rooms are well equipped and divided into activity areas for art, block building, storytime, dramatic play, science, puzzles, manipulatives and special projects. The school has a new library and a music and movement room. In warmer weather children can take classroom activities out onto the terrace; in rainy weather they use the temple's auditorium for active play.

Separation. All children visit their classrooms before school begins. There is a separation workshop, prior to the first day of school, for all incoming parents. Separation for the 2s is gentle and gradual.

Parent involvement. The parents association sponsors social events, parenting seminars, and special programs for children and is solely responsible for all fund-raising events. Parents are welcome to visit any time to observe. The staff makes a point of being accessible. Formal conferences are held twice yearly, in November and April.

Transportation. This is primarily a neighborhood school. Parents or caregivers bring their children to the classrooms.

Graduates. The majority of students go on to independent schools such as Abraham Joshua Heschel, Allen-Stevenson, Bank Street, Beit Rabban, Birch Wathen/Lenox, Brearley, Browning, Collegiate, Calhoun, Cathedral, Chapin, Columbia Grammar, Dalton, Dwight, Ethical Culture/Fieldston, Friends Seminary, Hewitt, Horace Mann, Manhattan Country, Nightingale/Bamford, Rabbi Arthur Schneier Park East, Ramaz, Riverdale, Rudolf Steiner, Rodelph Sholom, Solomon Schecter, Spence, Speyer Legacy School, St. Bernard's, St. David's, Town, Trevor Day, Trinity, UNIS, The Anderson Program at PS 9, Hunter, Lower Lab, and PS 166.

Affiliations. Temple of Israel. Chartered by the Board of Regents of the State University of New York.

Member. ERB, ISAAGNY, BJE.

Temple Shaaray Tefila Nursery
Ages: 2.5–5 yrs

Jewish Nursery School, Reformed

250 E. 79th Street

Zip: 10021

Tel: 535-2146

Fax: 288-3576

Website: www.shaaraytefilanyc.org

E-mail: nurseryschool@tstnyc.org

Established 1993

Sari Schneider, Director

Bonnie Blanco, Associate Director

Enrollment: 135

School year. September through June.

Ages	Hours	Days	Tuition
2.6	9:00–11:30	Tues Thurs	$11,500
		Mon Wed Fri	$12,865
2.9–3.9	9:00–11:30	Mon–Fri	$15,250
3	8:45–11:45	Mon–Fri	$16,410
3	12:45–3:15	Mon–Thurs	$12,970
3.6–4.6	8:45–1:00	Mon–Fri (Fri till 12:45)	$18,025
4	9:00–2:30	Mon–Fri (Fri till 12:45)	$19,665

There is a $2,000 discount for temple members.

Program.   The school incorporates the traditions and values of Judaism in a nurturing close-knit environment. The curriculum is designed to promote self-esteem and offers a program that includes block building, art projects, dramatic play, and the exploration of many different kinds of open-ended materials.

Children are introduced to Jewish traditions through weekly Shabbat and holiday celebrations, songs and games.

Admissions.   The application fee is $40. Parents fill out an application and call ahead for a tour appointment. During the tour, they meet the director. The school gives priority to temple members and siblings. Remaining spaces are filled via lottery. Notifications are sent out in March.

Class size.   Class size varies from 10 to 20, depending on age and class. There are three teachers per class.

Staff.   The head teachers are certified with masters degrees in early childhood education.

Facilities.   The school is located in the temple building on the third and fourth floors. There is a rooftop playground, and a playroom in the basement. The seven classrooms all have windows. There are rugs in the reading area. Children display their art on the walls. There is a library. The bathrooms have been adapted for children. Children bring their own lunches.

Separation.   Gradual phasing-in process. Parents and caregivers are asked to remain in the classroom until the school feels that the child is comfortable. Separation is considered an individualized process.

Parent involvement.   There is a strong Parents Association. Parents are very involved in fund-raising activities, organizing parent programs, working in the library, and publishing a bi-annual school newspaper. There are also monthly discussions on child development with the director.

Financial.   Partial financial aid is available. Payments are made four times a year. Parents sign a contract for the year. There is a non-refundable deposit of 30 percent of the tuition.

Transportation.   Transportation must be provided by parents.

Graduates.   Have gone on to independent and public schools, with about one-half of the children choosing private schools including Jewish and single-sex schools.

Affiliation.   Temple Shaaray Tefila.

Member.   BJE, ERB, ISAAGNY, NAEYC.

Town House International School
Ages: 2–6 yrs

Nonsectarian Nursery School and Kindergarten

1209 Park Avenue
  (at 94th Street)
Zip: 10128
Tel: 427-6930
Fax: 427-6931
Website: www.thisny.org

Established 1976
Ms. Nenita Dillera,
Director and Director of Admissions
Enrollment: 42

School year.   September through June.

Ages	Hours	Days	Tuition (monthly)
2–6	8:00–12:30	Mon–Fri	$898–$1,098
2–6	8:00–4:00	Mon–Fri	$1,098–$1,448
2–6	8:00–6:00	Mon–Fri	$1,298–$1,798

Two or three half or full-day sessions can be arranged. Children on these schedules can occasionally be accommodated for additional half or full days for which an additional payment is required.

Program.   Developmental. The school was started by former Head of School and present chairman of the board, Joseph Villamaria III, 25 years ago as an early childhood center. Emphasis is placed on nurturing individual talents in an intimate, yet challenging way to foster confident learning.

Admissions. The application fee is $50. Students are accepted throughout the year.

Facilities. The school is located in the headquarters of the Filipinas-Americas Science and Art Foundation (which founded and partially funds it) with an indoor and outdoor area for gross motor skills development and other activities. Children bring their own lunches; the school provides snacks.

Summer program. July and August.

Parent involvement. Conferences are as parents request them. A parent advisory committee works on two fundraisers each year. The funds help purchase more educational materials. There is a parent head in each of the four classes who assists teachers, go on field trips and fundraisers.

Financial. An initial payment of one month's tuition is due before school begins. There is a monthly payment plan. Financial aid is available.

Affiliations. Filipinas-Americas Science and Art Foundation, City University of New York. Chartered and accredited by the Board of Regents of the University of the State of New York, ISAAGNY, Parents League.

The Town School

Ages: 3–14 yrs

Nonsectarian Nursery and Elementary School

540 East 76th Street
(at the East River)
Zip: 10021
Tel: 288-4383
Fax: 988-5846
Website: www.thetownschool.org

Established 1913
Christopher Marblo,
Head of School
Jennifer Butler,
Admissions Director
Nursery enrollment: 80
Total enrollment: 395

School year. Second week in September through second week in June.

Ages	Hours	Days	Tuition
3s	8:15–12:00	Mon–Fri	$24,000
Pre–K	8:15–2:30	Mon–Fri	$31,800
K	8:15–2:30	Mon–Fri	$34,900

Program. Traditional. Each division of the school, nursery-kindergarten, lower, and upper, has its own director and an organization that reflects the developmental needs of its particular group.

In the nursery and kindergarten classrooms, which are alive with plants and animals, children are encouraged to make choices, ask questions, try new experiences, and find new friends. Learning is organized around simple themes, such as family, or the school itself, and is reinforced through books, songs, discussions, artwork, and trips. In the preschool, children are introduced to English, math, history, and science. In kindergarten, the children begin to learn a basic Spanish vocabulary.

Kindergarten applicants must take the ERB.

Admissions. The application fee is $65. Inquiries may be made at any time and the application is available online as well as by mail after Labor Day. Parents should reserve a place on a tour after Labor Day. Nursery threes candidates are seen in small groups (with parents) in January; Kindergarten applicants are also seen in small groups in October through January.

For applications completed by December 1, notifications are sent by February for kindergarten, March for nursery and PreK.

Class size. There is one class each of sixteen 3s and of eighteen pre-kindergartners. Each of these has two staff members. The two kindergartens each have twenty-two children with three staff members each.

Facilities. The four spacious and well-equipped classrooms in the nursery-kindergarten wing were recently refurbished in August 2001.

In addition to classrooms, the building complex includes a luxurious auditorium, a full-size gymnasium, a technology center, a two-tier library, studios for dance, music, and art, two science laboratories, a dining room, and three play roofs, one of them enormous and facing the river. Many classrooms have windows looking out onto the water. Children also use John Jay Park and Randall's Island sports complex.

Children below first grade do not wear uniforms.

After-school program.　Fees vary and are available for children 4 years of age and older.

Summer program.　SummerSault, is a day camp for three- through nine-year-olds, staffed both by Town School teachers and teachers from other independent schools.

Staff.　A full-time nurse is on staff as well as fourteen teachers in the nursery/kindergarten division. There are two reading specialists and one math specialist in the nursery and kindergarten division.

Separation.　The children are introduced in small groups with shortened sessions. The process is handled in a very individualized manner.

Parent involvement.　The parents association meets monthly, and its representatives liaise between parents and school. Annual dues are $100. The PA runs the Town School Store, the book fair, the uniform exchange, and special fund-raising events. Parent volunteers work in the library, on street patrol, share special talents or interests in the classroom, go on class trips, and join in other activities.

Conferences for the nursery-kindergarten division are arranged twice yearly, and written reports are sent at the end of the school year.

History.　Founded as the Hyde School in 1913, the school was purchased by four teachers in 1935 and renamed The Town School. It was the first in New York City to use a consultant psychologist and to require that teachers be trained in child development. Accorded non-profit status in 1952 and extended through eighth grade in 1956, it moved to its present location in 1962. In 1977 the school purchased and renovated an adjoining warehouse. The sale of its air rights in 1985 provided an endowment fund, and was used to raise teachers' salaries and improve facilities.

Financial.　A $6,000 reservation deposit is required on signing the contract. The tuition balance is payable on May 15th and December 1st. The school reserves the right to charge 1.5 percent per month on past-due invoices. A tuition refund plan is available. Parents are asked to support an annual fund-raiser.

The school has a budget of approximately $1.5 million for financial aid. Guidelines of the Princeton School Scholarship Service are followed in determining need; 17 percent of students receive assistance.

Transportation.   Private bus transportation is available. There's a free shuttle bus from the 77th Street and Lexington Avenue subway station.

Graduates.   Most graduates go to independent day schools, a few to boarding schools, and a few to selective public high schools. Among the schools graduates have attended in the last five years are: Trinity, Dalton, Horace Mann, Riverdale, Fieldston, Columbia Prep, Spence, Chapin, Brearley, and Nightingale.

Member.   ERB, Guild of Independent Schools, ISAAGNY, NAIS, NYSAIS, AISAP.

Trevor Day School
Ages: 3–18 yrs

Nonsectarian Comprehensive School

Early Childhood Division · Established 1930
11 East 89th Street · Pamela Clarke,
Zip: 10128 · Head of School
Tel: 426-3355 · Deborah Ashe,
Website: www.trevor.org Admissions Director (Nursery through Gr. 5)
Total Lower School enrollment: 391
Preschool enrollment: 117
Elementary enrollment: 274

School year.   September 7th through June 8th.

Ages	Hours	Days	Tuition
3s° mornings	8:30–12:00/1:00	Mon–Fri	$25,000
Pre-K/4s°	8:25–2:00/3:00	Mon–Fri	$30,000
Kindergarten/5s°	8:25 – 3:00	Mon–Fri	$35,250

°Must be 3 by September 1st, 4s must be 4 by September 1st, and 5s must be 5 by September 1st.

Extended hours. Afterschool programs are available Monday through Friday, for Pre-kindergarten–Grade 5 from 3:00–6:30 P.M. at an additional cost.

Program. Developmental. Emphasis is placed on providing a nurturing, appropriate environment, with careful attention to developmental and cognitive milestones. Activities in all classes include block building, cooking, art (painting, clay, rubbings, collage, sculpting, weaving, puppetry), dramatic play, sand and water play, games, puzzles, and stories. The pre-kindergarten and kindergarten curriculum includes formal reading and math instruction as well as social studies, science, and field trips. Specialists teach art, music, physical education, and Spanish.

Admissions. The application fee is $50; Applications are available online beginning August 1st.

A parent visit and interview are arranged following receipt of an application. Nursery and Pre-K applicants are observed by teachers with parents in the room. Kindergarten applicants are observed in groups without their parents. Notifications are sent according to ISAAGNY guidelines. Preference is given to children of alumni and to siblings.

Class size. There is one class of fourteen to sixteen nursery students; two classes of approximately sixteen 4s (pre-kindergarten), and four classes of approximately sixteen each for 5s (kindergarten).

Staff. All head teachers and many assistants have masters degrees in early childhood education. Professional development opportunities are available in various forms such as workshops and conferences. The school utilizes a variety of innovative techniques employing traditional manipulatives (blocks, etc.) as well as technology. Faculty meet weekly across the grades and disciplines.

Facilities. Trevor Day School occupies a former townhouse across from the Guggenheim Museum. Four floors house the nursery, prekindergarten, and kindergarten. There are two rooftop play areas. In addition, there are dedicated rooms for art, music, a gymnasium, kitchen, and library. Bright, cheery, and stimulating, the school was built for children.

Children enrolled pre-K and kindergarten bring their lunches.

Snacks include fresh fruits and crackers, which are provided by the school. The school is a peanut-controlled environment.

Summer program.   The summer program, Summer Day, which is open to the community, is a five-week program for 3s–6s, in late June to late July. For more information, call Shelley Miller, Director, at 426-3351; two, three, four and five week options are available.

Separation.   Nursery children and their parents visit individually with homeroom teachers on the first day of school. As the term progresses, the new children come together in small groups for a week for periods that gradually lengthen over about three weeks, building up to a full day's program. Gradually parents leave the classroom. Separation is very individual, and the teachers work out plans to suit the needs of each family.

Parent involvement.   All parents are members of the Parents Association. Parents also serve on the board of trustees, are involved in fund-raising and school committees, give admissions tours, read to children in the library on a regular basis, and assist with field trips. Evening workshops for parents are given two or three times a year, and family conferences are held twice a year.

Financial.   A non-refundable deposit of 15 percent of the tuition is due in February on signing the year's contract. Three payment plans are available. The school has a tuition refund plan for emergency withdrawals from school. About 20 percent of the full student body receives financial aid, which becomes available in kindergarten.

Transportation.   Children come from the East Side and West Side, as well as downtown, Roosevelt Island, New Jersey, Brooklyn, Queens, and the Bronx. Most are brought by parents or caregivers, but starting in kindergarten transportation is available by either private or Department of Education buses.

Graduates.   Most children go directly into the Trevor Day School Elementary School.

Chartered.   By the Board of Regents of the State University of New York.

Member.   ERB, ISAAGNY, NAIS, NYSAIS, Early Steps.

Vanderbilt YMCA

Ages: 6 mos–5 yrs

Nonsectarian Nursery School

224 East 47th Street
Zip: 10017
Tel: 912-2507
Fax: 752-0210
Website: www.ymcanyc.org
E-mail: aharvey@ymcanyc.org

Anita Harvey,
Early Childhood Director
Enrollment: 70

School year. Open year round, except the last week of August and the week between Christmas and New Years.

Ages*	Hours	Days	Tuition (monthly)
6 mos–5 yrs	8:30–6:00	Mon–Fri	$1,733
		Mon Wed Fri	$1,166
		Tues Thurs	$835
	8:30–12:30	Mon–Fri	$1,145
		Mon Wed Fri	$740
		Tues Thurs	$536
	2:00–6:00	Mon–Fri	$1,092
		Mon Wed Fri	$662
		Tues Thurs	$478

*Call for more information. Full-day children bring their own lunches. A snack is provided in the morning and afternoon. There is an annual membership fee of $105.

Program. Developmental. Children learn through hands-on play using the plentiful supply of blocks, weighing and measuring, and utilizing other forms of direct experimentation. Exploration of materials is open-ended. Children's self-esteem and feelings of success are encouraged. Children have a choice of activities provided within the structure created by teachers.

The Infant/Toddler class follows the same curriculum as the other aged classes, which includes nurturing active learning in all areas of development.

A music specialist visits all groups once a week and full-time children swim twice a week. Gym and play yard activities are scheduled daily. A science specialist and a movement specialist work with the 3s and 4s weekly; yoga is introduced.

Admissions. The application fee is $50. The school maintains an active and ongoing waiting list. Inquiries are year round and families should call to be placed on the school's extensive waiting list. A tour of the school is scheduled prior to enrollment. Parents do not sign a contract and there is no rigorous screening process for the children. The important requirement is that the school should be a good match for the child and family. A nonrefundable deposit of one month's tuition is required to hold a child's place. Tuition is payable monthly.

Class size. There are four classes. The Infant/Toddler and 2s classes have ten children and the 3s and 4s have fifteen children each.

Staff. There is one teacher in each class with three assistants in the toddler class, two assistants for the 2s and 3s, and one assistant in the 4s class.

Facilities. Large, clean classrooms have windows looking onto the inner court, water tables, art tables, tables for Legos and bristle blocks, adjoining bathrooms, and cots for rest time. Large areas are devoted to block play. The 3s/4s room has a listening loft with headsets and story cassettes. A long, narrow, sunny, outdoor yard, padded on three sides and screened on top, offers a climber, seesaw, wagons, tricycles, and outdoor blocks. In warm weather, water tables and sprinklers are made available outdoors.

Separation. Varies according to the individual child and is definitely not rushed.

Parent involvement. Parents help with fund-raising for scholarships. Monthly parent meetings and potlucks, to which parents bring food of their native countries, are held. Because of proximity to the U.N., families come from diverse ethnic backgrounds. Parents and teachers communicate on a daily basis.

Financial. Limited scholarships are available, based on need.

Graduates. Go on to Bank Street, Calhoun, City and Country, Dalton, Ethical Culture, Little Red School House, Rudolf Steiner, UNIS, Village Community, PS 6, PS 116, PS 178, PS 183, PS 59, Hunter Elementary, and other public school gifted and talented programs.

Wee Care Preschool

Ages: 6 wks–5 yrs

Nonsectarian Nursery School

451 East 83rd Street #BA (between
York and First Avenues)
Zip: 10028
Tel: 472-4481
Fax: 472-2622

Established 1994
Julie Josepli and
Serena Edmunds,
Co-Directors
Enrollment: 56

School year. September through June. Summer program July and August. (School is open year round.)

Ages	Hours	Days	Tuition (monthly)
Infants	8:00–6:00	3 days–5days	$1,050–$1,730*
Toddlers	8:00–6:00	3 days–5 days	$965–$1,485*
Nursery	9:00–3:30	3 days–5 days	$855–$1,215*
	8:00–6:00	3 days–5 days	$965–$1,465*
Preschool	9:00–3:30	3 days–5 days	$855–$1,215*
	8:00–6:00	3 days–5 days	$965–$1,465*

*Drop-in rates $88/day.

Program. Developmental. Children's learning is encouraged through interaction with their environment through play. Teachers plan activities that support emerging skills and recognize individual differences. The focus is on the development of the whole child: physically, emotionally, socially, creatively, and academically. The program aims to foster respect for others, the equipment and the materials. A wide variety of activities are provided within the daily routine and cooperative play is encouraged. Activities are drawn from the curriculum areas of art, math, science, cooking, music and movement, large muscle, social studies, practical life, dramatic play, language arts, and manipulative activities. Each child is encouraged to develop an active curiosity and an enthusiasm for learning which stimulates exploration and creativity.

Admissions. The application fee is $100. Prospective parents should call to schedule a tour. Siblings are given priority.

Class size.   The 2s' class has ten students and two teachers. The 3s' class has twelve students and two teachers. The pre-kindergarten has fourteen students and two teachers.

Staff.   Teachers are CPR certified.

Facilities.   The school has a play yard and the park is two blocks away.

Summer program.   The summer program features field trips, play in the sprinklers, picnics, and other activities.

Separation.   New children begin the program gradually, an hour or two a day to start with.

Parent involvement.   Parents are welcome anytime.

Financial.   Siblings are given a ten percent discount.

Graduates.   Go on to PS 290, PS 158, Hunter, Lower Lab and a variety of private schools.

The William Woodward Jr. Nursery School
Ages: 2.6–5 yrs

Nonsectarian

436 East 69th Street
Zip: 10021
Tel: 744-6611
Website: www.woodwardns.org
E-mail: wwjns@aol.com

Established 1961
Serena Fine English,
Director
Mary Fracchia,
Admissions Director
Enrollment: 90

School year.   Mid-September for 3s up, late September through May for 2s.

Ages	Hours	Days	Tuition
Younger 2s°	9:30–11:30	Tues Thurs	$7,530
Older 2s	9:30–11:30	Mon Wed Fri	$9,415
Young 3s	1:00–3:45	Mon–Fri	$10,415
3s	9:00–11:45 or 1:00–3:45	Mon–Fri	$11,550
4/5s	9:00–11:45 or 1:00–3:45	Mon–Fri	$12,900

°Toilet training is not essential for the 2s. Children must be 2 by March 31st.

Program.   Developmental/Traditional. The program includes a variety of experiences in block building, art, dramatic play, sand and water play, cooking, music, language arts, science, math, movement, and other activities aimed at developing social, emotional, physical, and cognitive skills.

Admissions.   The application fee is $50. Inquiries are from early September on. Parents should call for information and to arrange for a tour of the school, followed by a child's play visit. Admissions preference is given to families connected with New York-Presbyterian Hospital, New York Weill Cornell Center, Memorial Sloan-Kettering Cancer Center, and The Hospital for Special Surgery. This accounts for 65 to 70 percent of the available places. Community children are accepted as space is available.

Parents are notified in March. Families connected with affiliated hospitals are given the option of early notice.

Class size.   The school has two 2s classes of ten to twelve with three teachers each; three 3s classes of fourteen to fifteen each; and two 4/5s classes of fifteen. The staff is experienced in helping English and non-English speaking children communicate with each other. A music specialist works with the children. A consultant is available for children, families, and staff.

Facilities.   The school occupies four well-equipped classrooms; there is a one-way observation window. In addition, there is a library and a large multipurpose room for special events, movement, and rainy-day play; offices; and a large, landscaped outdoor playground equipped with sandbox, slides, climber, and wheeled toys. There is a full kitchen for cooking projects. Families provide snacks twice weekly.

132

Summer program.   There is a three-week morning June program for currently enrolled students ages 3 to 5 taught by Woodward staff.

Separation.   Children are introduced to school during two to three weeks of shortened, small-group sessions. Parents are expected to stay until children are comfortable.

Parent involvement.   The parent body is active and international. Evening meetings on parenting are held during the year by the school's parent facilitator. Parents serve on the board of directors and help with fund-raising and in the classroom. Conferences are held twice yearly, or as needed.

Financial.   A payment of $3,000 to $3,500 is required upon signing the contract. Tuition is payable in three annual installments. Children of families of affiliated hospitals pay tuition on a sliding scale.

Transportation.   Most children come from the East 50s through 80s and are brought by parents or caregivers.

Graduates.   Have gone on to leading independent and public schools such as Allen-Stevenson, Brearley, Browning, Buckley, Chapin, Collegiate, Dalton, Friends Seminary, Hewitt, Lycée Français, Marymount, Nightingdale-Bamford, Sacred Heart, Spence, St. David's, Town, Trevor Day, Trinity, PS 6, PS 9, PS 77, PS 158, PS 183, PS 290, and Hunter.

History.   The school was founded and is partially funded by grants from the Woodward Foundation.

Affiliations.   New York-Presbyterian Hospital, New York Weill Cornell Center, Memorial Sloan Kettering Cancer Center, Hospital for Special Surgery. Chartered by the Board of Regents of the State University of New York.

Member.   ERB, ISAAGNY, ATIS, NAEYC.

York Avenue Preschool
Ages: 2.3–5 yrs

Nonsectarian

1520 York Avenue (80th Street)

Zip: 10028

Tel: 734-0922

Fax: 861-8901

E-mail: admissions@yorkavenuepreschool.org

Website: www.yorkavenuepreschool.org

Established 1989

Dr. Michele Starr,

Director

Preschool Enrollment: 140

School year.   Mid-September through June.

Ages in September	Hours	Days	Tuition
2.3–2.6	8:50–11:45	Tues Thurs	$12,845
2.7–3.0	8:50–11:45	Mon Wed Fri	$15,985
3s	8:50–12:00	Mon–Fri	$22,465
4s	8:50–2:30	Mon–Thurs	$25,925

°Children in 3s program must be toilet-trained before school begins.

°°Children in the 4s stay for lunch. After school clubs program available for 3s and 4s.

°°°There is one extended day until 12:45 to the 2s.

Program.   Traditional/Developmental. The program is developmental, but the foundation is laid for the academic skills needed later on. Language, motor skills, and social and emotional development are taught in a sensitive and balanced way. The program includes art, music, yoga, movement, and "living science." French is taught to the 4s group.

ERBs are given at the school.

Admissions.   The application fee is $75. Applications are available online. After filing an application, parents call to schedule a tour. Following the tour parents schedule their child's playdate.

Class size.   The toddler group has twelve children. The 3s has about fifteen children. Pre-nursery 3s has eighteen children and nursery 4s has eighteen children. Each class has a head teacher and an assistant teacher.

Staff.   Dr. Michele Starr, the school's current principal is a licensed New York State School Administrator and holds a doctorate in early childhood education. All head teachers hold master's degree. Assistant teachers hold bachelor degrees.

Facilities.   The school has one spacious gym adapted for young children, a library, an art studio, and eight classrooms, each with its own kitchenette and toilets. There is a well-equipped playground.

Summer program.   June through mid-August; an additional fee is required.

Separation.   Before school starts there are meetings with parents. The separation process for the children is handled gently and on an individual basis. Toddlers begin with a schedule that consists of small group sessions and parents either remain in the classrooms, wait nearby, or join other parents for coffee.

Parent involvement.   Parents are expected to participate in their child's education, social activities, workshops, and scheduled conferences with teachers as well as take part in class trips and parent-run activities such as library and book club. The Parents Association sponsors activities that foster friendship and a strong sense of community.

Financial.   A non-refundable tuition deposit of $3,500 is required on signing the contract.

Graduates.   Recent graduates have gone onto both private and public schools, including competitive public school and gifted and talented programs.

Affiliations.   ERB, ISAAGNY, Parents League. Chartered by the Board of Regents of the State University of New York.

WEST SIDE

Abraham Joshua Heschel School
Ages: 3–18
Jewish

Nursery–Grade 12
West End Avenue
  (between 60–61st Street)
Zip: 10023
Tel: 246-7717
Website: www.heschel.org

Established 1983
Roanna Shorofsky,
  Director
Judy Wolf-Nevid,
Early Childhood Head
Nursery enrollment: 145
Total enrollment: 835

School Year. Early September through mid-June.

Ages	Hours	Days	Tuition
3s	9:00–12:00*	Mon–Fri	$23,850
4s	8:30–3:00**	Mon–Fri	$31,175
5s	8:30–3:15**	Mon–Fri	$31,400

*Optional afternoon hours available.
**Friday until 1:15.

Program. Eclectic/Progressive. The school describes itself as "a pluralistic independent Jewish school." Curriculum themes emerge from the Jewish and American holidays, nature, and Shabbat observance. The school believes that young children learn best by doing, and encourages experimentation and active involvement with their environment. The school aims to help children become independent, self-confident, and inquisitive learners.

Admissions. The application and testing fee is $45 for nursery and pre-K, $75 for K and above. Inquiries from September on. The admissions deadline is early December. Tours are given weekly from September through December. After the application is received, the Director of Admissions will call to schedule a half-hour play visit for the child and a meeting for parents with an administrator. The school expects that children who enroll in the nursery division will continue on at the school for the upper grades. ERB testing is required for kindergarten and above.

Class size.   There are two classes per grade in nursery and pre-K and three classes in K. Each class has two co-teachers (or three, depending on class size).

Facilities.   After many years of operating in various locations, the entire school is now located on West End Avenue. The facility is fully equipped with large classrooms, several libraries, science labs, chapel, art, and music studios, several gyms, a theater, cafeterias, and outdoor play areas.

Separation.   The school requires parents or caregivers to be available during separation. The children start with shortened sessions and work up to the full program over the course of two weeks. Parents or caregivers stay in the classroom or in the hall just outside as long as the child needs them.

Parent involvement.   Parents share personal and professional experience with classes, raise funds, escort school trips, plan and join in holiday celebrations and social events, serve on the board of directors, attend lectures on matters of general interest, and participate in the school's support group, which meets to discuss developmental parenting and curriculum topics.
Conferences are held twice yearly.

Financial.   A tuition deposit of $2,500 is required on signing the contract. Half of the balance is due July 1st; the remainder, December 1st. A monthly tuition plan is available. Each family makes the school an interest-free loan of $1,000 for the period of the child's enrollment. Financial aid is available.

Transportation.   Private bus service can be arranged. Department of Education buses are available for children 5 and older.

Graduates.   Few students go on to independent schools or select public schools and Jewish schools; the majority of students continue.

Chartered.   By the Board of Regents of the State University of New York.

Member.   ISAAGNY, NAIS, NYSAIS.

Basic Trust Infant/Toddler Center

Ages: 3 mos–5 yrs

Nonsectarian Day Care Center

225 West 99th Street
  (between Broadway
  and Amsterdam Avenues)
Zip: 10025
Tel: 222-6602
Fax: 665-6855
Website: www.basictrust.org
E-mail: basictrust@verizon.net

Established 1976
Mary Biggs,
Director
Enrollment: 39 per day

School Year. September through mid-August.

Ages	Hours	Days	Tuition*
3 mos–5 yrs	8:00–5:45	3 days	$19,930
		4 days	$24,430
		5 days	$28,080

*There are no make-up classes for absences. A non-refundable deposit of $1,000 is required.

Program. Progressive. The environment is warm and homelike, with many couches and chairs for snuggling. The children's day, structured around eating and sleeping, is filled with a wide variety of activities. The babies play with water, sing songs, read books, and are taken for walks. The Toddlers explore the neighborhood and nearby playgrounds. The Big Kids do all this plus baking, painting, block building, and eventually take on more sustained "project work." Social skills are a priority and relationships are fostered in many ways.

Admissions. The application fee is $75. Basic Trust has openings every September. Parents may make an appointment to look at the program after receiving a brochure. The school asks that both parents (of two-parent households) visit the program with their child. After visiting, parents are given an application. Applications must be completed by the end of January. Families will be notified by March 1st.

Class size. The infant group has between eight and nine children (3 months to 14 months) a day with three full-time caregivers. There are ten or eleven toddlers from 17 months to 2.6 years. The 3/4s group has eighteen children with four staff.

Staff. In addition to the director, twelve full-time teaching staff, a full-time chef, and seven part-time staff, Basic Trust often has interns from Bank Street, and BMCC. The staff have diverse backgrounds; some have master's degrees from Bank Street, some have BAs in early childhood education, others have no formal education but a wealth of experience and on-the-job training. When special needs children are enrolled, the school works closely with a variety of specialists.

Facilities. An exceptional, multi-level, well-lit, completely renovated space in the basement of St. Michael's Church thoughtfully designed for young children. Each age group has its own room but all areas are connected via a central, fully equipped kitchen. The bathrooms have child-size toilets; the kitchen has a low counter so children can bake and work on other projects; the couches are low and accessible to toddlers. The Baby Room is warm and cozy, with mobiles for the babies to gaze at, bells to ring, and many hanging plants. The Toddler Room has a pass-through window to the kitchen so children can watch and smell food being cooked. The Big Kids' Room has an upstairs level for working, eating, and reading, as well as a downstairs level for dress-up, blocks, toys, etc. There is also a large, carpeted gym area, and a large backyard with climbing equipment, and a room for bikes and balls.

Meals are cooked and served family-style, and snacks are provided. The school does not allow candy, gum, or nuts.

Separation. The separation process lasts a week, during which parents stay in the classroom attending to the needs of the child. Gradually the caretaking shifts from parent to teacher. Even if children will be attending part-time, the first week should be on a full-time schedule. The staff see separation as a developmental stage for both parents and children and therefore help both with the process.

Parent involvement. The staff feel their relationship with parents is central and are committed to sharing information with parents about child care as well as early childhood learning and development. Parents serve on the board of directors and are primarily responsible for the two to three major fund-raising events of the year. Parents are welcome to visit at any time.

Financial.   A nonrefundable $1,000 deposit is required on signing the full-year contract. Tuition is paid monthly on the first of the month from September to June. No financial aid is available.

Transportation.   No private bus service is available.

Graduates.   Go on to independent schools and select public schools such as Bank Street, Manhattan Country School, Manhattan New School, Trevor Day, Trinity, The School at Columbia, Hunter, Manhattan School for Children, PS 163, PS 87, PS 75.

Member.   ISAAGNY, Parents League.

The Brownstone School

Ages: 2–5 yrs

Nonsectarian

128 West 80th Street
  (between Amsterdam and
  Columbus Avenues)
Zip: 10024
Tel: 874-1341
E-mail: brownstoneschool@verizon.net
Website: www.brownstoneschool.com

Established 1963
Julia Harquail,
Director
Brooke Brodsky,
Assistant Director
Lorraine Lilley,
Director of Admissions
Enrollment: 100

School year.   September through mid-June.

Ages	Hours	Days	Tuition
2–5	9:00–12:30	2, 3, 4 or 5 days	$7,740–$15,500
	1:30–4:30	3, 4 or 5 days	$9,340–$14,500
	9:00–3:30	2, 3, 4 or 5 days	$9,900–$19,900
	8:00–5:45	2, 3, 4 or 5 days	$11,630–$23,100

Flexible schedules are available for 2, 3, 4, or 5 day attendance; fees vary according to schedule, not age. Children need not be toilet-trained; they must be 2 by September 1st of the year they enter.

Program.   Developmental. The approach is play-based, developmentally appropriate and child-centered, focusing on the social,

143

emotional, intellectual, and physical needs of each child. Traditional daily schedules offer a broad range of structured and unstructured activities, and provide children with the security of a routine. Working independently and in small groups, the children learn through play and hands-on exploration of selected materials. Dramatic play, children's literature, puppets, games, puzzles, blocks, various artistic mediums, music, creative movement, outdoor activities, water play, and manipulatives promote the development of pre-reading, pre-math, and scientific concepts. There are specialists in music, art, yoga and a play therapist. Social interactions with peers and teachers through such activities challenge children to learn appropriate ways to express their feelings and develop their interests.

Admissions.

Applications are available on the third Monday in September until an adequate pool of applications is received. Several classrooms have a lottery to get an application due to the large number of siblings. It is advisable to return applications promptly. After completing and submitting the application, parents should call to arrange a parent tour. Tours are scheduled for October through December, child visits for January through late February. Notifications are sent in accordance with ISAAGNY guidelines.

Class size.   Child-staff ratios are 3:1 for the 2s; 5:1 for all other classes. Most classes range from 9 to 18 children, "which averages out to 16 children with 3 teachers, except for the red room's 2s," says the school's Director.

Staff.   Each class is staffed with a qualified head teacher, and two assistant teachers. Music and creative movement classes are provided once a week, and a social worker is available as a consultant. Staff backgrounds are diverse but all have expertise in working with young children; in addition, all have been cleared by appropriate agencies.

Facilities.   The school occupies a roomy, five-story, renovated brownstone. The rooms are lofty, with handsome old fireplaces. The ground floor includes a well-equipped, child-friendly kitchen. Each classroom has a floor to itself except the first floor which also has offices. The rooms are divided into centers/activity areas. Standard early childhood equipment, such as water/sand tables, easels, and dramatic play and block areas are available. There are child-size bathrooms and sinks in each classroom as well as work areas for the teachers.

There is an outdoor play area, with slides and climbing frames with a poured rubber surface on the ground. The children use Central and Riverside Parks daily for outdoor and gross motor activities.

ERB testing is available onsite.

Summer program. From mid-June through end of July for Brownstone families only. Families may choose days and weeks in which their children will attend. Activities include arts and crafts, water play, outdoor recreation, various sports, and day trips throughout New York City.

Parent involvement. The school attracts families of diverse economic, cultural, and professional backgrounds. Although many live or work on the Upper West Side, some commute from the surrounding boroughs of the city. The strength of the school lies heavily on the participation of its parent body. Utilizing individual talents, skills, and professional affiliations, parents volunteer in and outside the classrooms. They become involved with the organization of social events, fund-raising, and are encouraged to become members of the board of trustees.

Financial. A nonrefundable reservation deposit of $2,500 is required. Parents sign a contract for the school year and tuition is payable in three installments. Details are explained in the contract. Financial aid is available.

Transportation. No private bus service is available.

Graduates. Go on to a wide range of school settings, both public and private schools such as Alexander Robertson, Allen-Stevenson, Bank Street, Browning, Buckley, Caedman, Calhoun, Collegiate, Columbia Grammar and Prep, Convent of the Sacred Heart, Dwight, Ethical Culture, Geneva School, Hewitt, The Ideal School, Mandell, Manhattan Country, Marymount, Nightingale, Riverdale, Rudolf Steiner, The School at Columbia, Saint Bernard's, Saint Hilda's & Saint Hugh's, Loyola, Saint David's, Spence, Town, Trevor, Trinity, as well as gifted and talented programs and other public and private school programs throughout the city.

Member. Child Care, Inc., ERB, ISAAGNY, Parents League.

The Calhoun School
Ages: 3–18 yrs

Nonsectarian Preschool and Comprehensive School

3s through 1st grade:
Robert L. Beir Building,
160 West 74th Street
Tel: 497-6550
   497-6575, Admissions Office
Grades 2 through 12:
Main Building
433 West End Avenue
   (at 81st Street)
Zip: 10024
Tel: 497-6500
   497-6542, Admissions Office
Website: www.calhoun.org
E-mail: robin.otton@calhoun.org

Established 1896
Kathleen Clinesmith,
Lower School Director
Robin Otton,
Admissions Director, 3s–1st grade
Jenny Eugenio,
Admissions Director, 2nd–12th grade
Total enrollment: 730
3s–1st grade enrollment: 210

School year. September through early June.

Ages	Hours	Days	Tuition
3s	9:00–12:00	Mon–Fri	$22,200
3s	9:00–2:30	Mon–Fri	$24,400
4s	8:45–2:30	Mon–Fri	$34,800
K, 1st	8:30–2:45	Mon–Fri	$36,100

Extended hours. Afterschool program for 4s–1st graders until 4:30, and extended care until 5 P.M., at an additional cost. Early dropoff at 8 A.M. at no additional charge.

Program. Developmental. The program is based on the principle that all children want to learn and that all children learn best when actively involved and when learning is relevant to their lives.

The 3s and 4s programs emphasize developing socialization skills, strengthening a child's sense of self, and laying the groundwork for a successful academic path. A team of teachers creates an environment, both physical and social, in which children can absorb information and then use it in their play. There are opportunities for open-ended play as well as directed activities and thematic studies. Each room features areas for block building, dramatic play, cooking, water and sand play, art, science, quiet reading, and perceptual/manipulative materials.

The kindergarten and first-grade programs emphasize an integrated curriculum in language arts, math, social studies, and science. Notable is the comprehensive language arts program and the extensive integration of music and Spanish into the curriculum.

There is a strong sense of community at the school, with visits between classrooms, school-wide assemblies, weekly sing-alongs, shared performances, visits from older Calhoun students, and, for first-grade students, trips to the ongoing building.

Admissions. The application fee is $65. Application can be done from mid-August on using the website www.calhoun.org/admission74. (The school frequently wait-lists applications received after a critical number has been received.) Most children enter at age 3 or in kindergarten. Open houses are held in April, May, September, and October. Interviews and school tours are arranged once the application is received. The child's interview consists of a small-group visit with a teacher. In a separate visit, parents attend an information session and tour followed by a meeting with the Lower School Director.

Notifications are sent in mid-February for kindergarten and late February for the 3s and 4s. The school seeks students with academic potential who bring diversity in talent and background.

Tests. ERB testing results may be submitted but are not required.

Class size. There are four classes at the 3s through 1st grade levels. Class size is ten to sixteen, with one teacher and one associate or specialist.

Staff. Calhoun teachers are experienced professionals, most with master's degrees in early childhood education. There are also specialists in music, theatre/movement, physical education, Spanish, media, and art. Calhoun maintains a strong professional developmental program. Many teachers are given grants for study leading to new curricula.

Facilities. A completely renovated five-story former school with spacious, light-filled classrooms, a library, gym, art room/wood shop, auditorium/theater, outdoor play terrace, and gardening terrace.

Summer program.   A full six-week program is offered to children enrolled at Calhoun. Part-time registration is available.

Separation.   Phase-in is gradual, beginning with brief classroom sessions with small groups of children. Parents and teachers work closely together to ease the home-to-school transition.

Parent involvement.   Parents are welcome in the classroom. They may, for example, share in holiday celebrations, cook with the children, offer their expertise in a curriculum area, or volunteer in the parent-run library. There is daily contact with teachers; formal conferences are scheduled twice a year and parents receive reports about their child's progress. The school offers workshops and monthly parent-education forums. There is a very active parents' association which sponsors social events and raises funds for special improvements.

Financial.   There is a registration fee of $170 for new students. A deposit of $3,000 is required on signing the contract. Tuition is normally paid in two installments: June and January. A ten-month payment plan is also an option. Limited tuition assistance is available at the kindergarten level.

Transportation.   Department of Education bus service information is available upon request.

Graduates.   Students are automatically admitted to Calhoun's ongoing school, which goes through 12th grade.

Chartered.   By the Board of Regents of the State University of New York.

Member.   Early Steps, ERB, ISAAGNY, NAIS, NYSAIS, Prep for Prep, The Oliver Program, A Better Chance.

Cathedral Parkway Towers Pre-School, Inc.

Ages: 2–6 yrs

Nonsectarian All-Day Care

125 West 109th Street, Suite
Three (between Columbus
and Amsterdam Avenues)
Zip: 10025
Tel: 749-0291

Established 1968
Sandra Hunt-Smith
Director
Enrollment: 35

School year. All year.

Ages	Hours	Days	Tuition
2–5	8:00–6:00	Mon–Fri	$278 weekly

Program. Eclectic. Cathedral Towers employs many Montessori teaching techniques and believes that its program is unique. Activities include arts and crafts; block building; sand and water play; prereading, prewriting, and premath activities; early science; play with puzzles, games and small play objects; music and dance; field trips; films; storytelling; and active outdoor play.

Admissions. There is no application fee. Inquire any time. Interviews are scheduled only when positions are open, and children are accepted on a first-come basis. Parents may visit to see the school in operation and meet the director, with or without their children. They are notified of acceptance as soon as possible.

Class size. There is one class of 2s/3s and a mixed group of 4/5s.

Facilities. The preschool is located in rooms on the third floor of a residential high-rise. It also has use of a backyard play space.

Parent involvement. Three evening seminars are given each year. Parents are involved in fund-raising and help with field trips. Conferences are twice a year or as requested. Parents may visit any time.

Financial. Tuition is payable monthly or weekly. A $100 deposit is required; parents sign a contract for the full year. Parents more than a month in arrears must withdraw their child until payments are up-to-date. No financial aid is available.

Transportation.   Parents bring their children directly to the classroom. No private bus service is available.

Graduates.   Have attended Cathedral and Manhattan Country, as well as neighborhood public schools.

Chabad Early Learning Center
Ages: 18 mos–5 yrs

Jewish Nursery School

(Toddler Location)
101 West 92nd Street
   (corner of Columbus)
(Location for 3–5 yrs)
160 W. 97th Street
Zip: 10025
Tel: 864-5010
Fax: 932-8987
E-mail: celec@chabadwestside.org
Website: www.chabadwestside.org/celc

Rabbi Shlomo Kugel,
Executive Director
Pearl Stroh,
Educational Director
Enrollment: 160

School year.   September through mid-June.

Ages	Hours	Days	Tuition
18 mo–2 yrs°	1:00–3:45	2–3 days	$6,600–$8,610
2s	9:30–12:30 or 9:30–2:30	2 days	$6,600–$10,650
3s	9:30–12:30 or 9:30–2:30	3 days	$8,310–$10,650
4s	9:00–12:30 or 9:00–2:30	Mon–Thurs	$9,870–$12,090
5s	9:00–12:30 or 9:00–2:30	Mon–Fri (until 12: 30 on Fri)	$10,950–$13,110

°Tuition includes daily hot lunch, except for afternoon toddler class, and field trips.

Program.   Activity-based. The program carefully balances structured play and free play throughout the day. The children become acquainted with many mediums to encourage proper growth in cognitive, physical, and social-emotional areas. Structured play includes group activities such as stories, music, movement, discussion, and dramatic play. Free play involves manipulative toys, sand and water tables, clay, and an outdoor and indoor gym. Jewish holidays are taught through hands-on preparation and participation throughout the year. Readiness and self-help skills are naturally integrated throughout the curriculum to prepare the children for school. Each child's unique style of living and learning is valued and nurtured.

The school provides a daily lunch program. Mid-morning and afternoon snacks are also served, usually crackers or fruit.

Admissions.   Inquiries begin at the end of October. Call for an application. Once an application is submitted the school will call to schedule an appointment to visit the school. Notification is usually within three weeks of school visit.

Class size.   There are three toddler classes of ten, three 2s classes of twelve, two 3s classes of fifteen and two 4s classes of twenty. Each class has three teachers.

Staff.   Each head teacher is certified in early childhood education and is usually a parent or comes from a large, close-knit family or both.

Facilities.   Both locations of the Chabad Early Learning Center are newly renovated. Each have bright classrooms and a mobile library. There is a covered play area and outdoor playgrounds with state of the art play equipment.

Separation.   Teachers encourage parents to visit and stay in our classrooms as long as necessary for a smooth transition.

Parent involvement.   The Parents Association is involved in fundraising activities and coordinates parent support groups. Formal conferences are held twice yearly. Parents are welcome to visit the classroom for special activities and holidays.

Financial.   Registration fee is $250
There is a $250 non-refundable registration fee payable upon enrollment and a one-time $1,000 Building Fund contribution pay-

151

able per family. Parents are required to pay an additional $720 for Chabad's annual dinner, which is held in May or June.

Transportation.   The school is happy to assist parents in forming carpools.

Graduates.   Have gone on to Abraham Joshua Heschel, Manhattan Day School, Ramaz, Solomon Schechter, and other local public and private schools.

Children's Center of John Jay College of Criminal Justice Inc.

445 West 59th Street   William Altham,
Zip: 10019   Director
Tel: 237-8310
Website: www.jjay.cuny.edu

For John Jay students' children only.
        All-day care. Check the website for current enrollment and tuition as well as other information. Ages: 6 mos–5 yrs, September through July. Parent education workshops are also offered.

Columbus Park West Nursery School
Ages: 2.8–5 yrs

Nonsectarian
100 West 94th Street   Established 1964
   (Corner of 94th Street   Elisabeth Matthews, Phd.,
   and Columbus Avenue)   Director
Zip: 10025   Sarah Morris,
Tel: 866-6720   Admissions Director
Website: www.cpwn.org   Enrollment: 25
E-mail: admissions@cpwn.org

School year.   Second week in September through the first week in June.

Ages	Hours	Days	Tuition
2.8–3.9	8:45–12:00	Mon–Fri*	$16,025
3.9–5	8:45–2:30	Mon–Fri	$17,800

*All children leave at 12:00 on Fridays.

Program. Progressive. The school was started by neighborhood parents over forty years ago. The program provides a warm environment which supports children's emotional, social, cognitive, and motor development. Children are encouraged to express their thoughts and feelings and to exercise their newly developing competence with the support and guidance of caring adults. They are helped in learning to maintain their own individuality while functioning effectively as part of a group. The program is designed to provide a child-centered environment which enables the child to move comfortably out of the home environment and move on with confidence after nursery school.

Admissions. The application fee is $35. Inquiries are from September on. Parents are required to attend an informal meeting and interview. The school schedules a brief playgroup for the child in January. The school follows ISAAGNY guidelines.

Facilities. A large sunny community room on the second floor of a high-rise residential building. Tables offer a variety of art materials, puzzles, and other manipulatives, Play-doh, and sand. There is also a generous block area, house and dress-up corner, painting easels, and a story corner. A large adjoining patio has outdoor play equipment. There is a full kitchen.

Summer program. Varies; call for information.

Separation. Over the summer children attend playdates at the school as well as home visits before school starts to ease the separation process. School starts in September on a staggered schedule and gradually increases.

Parent involvement. Parents take responsibility for organizing fundraising activities or social events, serving on committees, and attending parent education evenings.

Financial.   A tuition deposit of 25 percent of the year's tuition is due on signing the contract in March, and the remainder is payable in standard form. Expanded plans and financial aid are available. The contract is for the full school year. Some scholarship aid is available.

Transportation.   Most children come from within a ten-block radius, and are brought by parents or caregivers.

Graduates.   Have gone on to Bank Street, Calhoun, Cathedral, Dalton, Ethical Culture, Hunter, Horace Mann, Manhattan Country, Trevor Day School, and others; half go on to public schools.

Columbus Pre-School
Ages: 2.0–5 yrs
Nonsectarian nursery school

606 Columbus Ave.	Established 1988
(89th Street)	Joy Baum,
Zip: 10024	Director
Tel: 721-0090	Enrollment: 130
Website: www.columbuspre-school.com	

School year.   September through June.

Ages	Hours	Days	Tuition
2s	8:30–11:30	T, Th	$8,995
2–3s	8:30–12:00	M, W, F	$14,250
2–3s	1:00–4:00	T–Wed–Fri	$10,750
3s	8:30–12:00	Mon–Fri	$16,800
3/4s	1:00–4:00	Mon–Fri	$15,000
4s	8:30–2:30	Mon–Fri	$20,775

There is a nonrefundable application fee of $60.

Program.   Developmental/Progressive. Focuses on the whole child as an active learner. Children explore, manipulate, discover, question, make choices, problem-solve, and create as they participate in a variety of interactive play activities, music, science, and art experiences. The specialized gymnastic program offers every child the opportunity to develop physical strength and coordination as they learn a progression of basic gymnastic skills under the direction of qualified gymnastic instructors. Music and dance specialists enrich the schools arts program. There's ERB testing onsite.

Facilities. Classrooms are bright and spacious. Children also have access to the outdoor rooftop play area, which is equipped to safely meet the needs of the growing, energetic young child.

Parent involvement. Parents are actively involved both in the classrooms and the school community. Parents volunteer to go on school trips and run the annual coat, toy, and food drives.

Graduates. Go on to Bank Street, Caedmon, Calhoun, Cathedral, City and Country, Columbia Grammar, Dwight, Ethical Culture, Riverdale Country, Speyer-Legacy, St. Hilda's & St. Hugh's, Trevor Day, Trinity, Anderson, and other Gifted and Talented and charter public school programs.

Member. ERB.

Crèche du Monde

Ages: 3 mos–3 yrs

Nonsectarian Nursery

2 Locations on West 87th
Zip: 10024
Tel: (646) 592-5527
Website: www.psdumonde.org
E-Mail: info@psdumonde.org

Established in 2010
Robin Savage,
Co-Founder and Executive Director
Shauna Howard,
Co-Founder and Program Director
Enrollment: 24 (12 at each school)

School year. Twelve-month program.

Ages	Hours	Days	Tuition (monthly)
Infants	8:00–6:00	Mon–Fri	$2,275
		Mon Wed Fri	$1,925
		Tues Thurs	$1,475
Toddlers	8:00-6:00	Mon–Fri	$2,075
		Mon Wed Fri	$1,680
		Tues Thurs*	$1,425

*The program is flexible to accommodate parent's needs. Earlier start is available, as well as shorter schedules–the fees are revised accordingly.

Program. Crèche du Monde offers a childcare program for infants and toddlers. Each child participates daily in periods of group activity (exposing them to art, music, and science), individual play, outdoor play, and quiet times. All activities are developmentally appropriate and meet each child's physical, emotional, social, and cognitive needs. Children also engage in fine motor development through manipulative table toys, games, and other activities. A variety of small motor toys are offered and changed weekly to coordinate with the weekly theme and gross motor development. Children receive large muscle control through outside play, walking in the neighborhood, and indoor play in the classroom. Depending on the weather children are offered large muscle play. Children also participate in a number of weekly enrichment classes such as cooking, yoga, a foreign language, and live music circle time.

Admissions. The application fee is $100. Parents may call or email the school for information and to schedule a visit. An informal meeting with the Program Director for parents is provided along a tour of the school.

Class Size. Both schools have two classrooms, one room accommodating four infants and a second room allowing for eight toddlers.

Facilities. The school has 2 classrooms and 2 children's restrooms. Children go to the public playground which is 2 blocks away accompanied by their teachers.

Staff. Highly trained, experienced, and educated staff. Director holds a master's degree in early childhood education.

Facilities.   The schools are located in apartment buildings. Close to Riverside Park, one school is situated in a ground floor apartment with a private backyard where children spend much of their outdoor time (as well as taking walks to Riverside Park). The second school is located in an apartment building with a private playground (for apartment residents only) where children spend time daily.

Separation.   Depends on the individual needs of the child. Most children participate in a two-week phase-in process.

Parental involvement.   The schools have an open-door policy, and parents are welcome to visit any time. Parents are encouraged to attend and participate in parent meetings, parent/teacher conferences, and family social events. Parents are provided day sheets where they are informed of what their child did that day (includes nap times, what they ate, etc.). A monthly newsletter is sent to parents.

Financial.   A deposit of one month's tuition is required upon signing the contract and applied to the last month's tuition payment. Parents are required to provide a 30-day notice prior to leaving the school. Tuition is paid monthly.

Transportation.   Children come from the Upper West Side area and are brought by their parents or caregivers.

Affiliations.   NAEYC

The Day School at Christ & Saint Stephen's

Ages: 3–5 yrs

Episcopal Nursery School

122 West 69th
(between Columbus Avenue
and Broadway)
Zip: 10023
Tel: (212) 787-2755 ext. 8
Website: www.dayschoolatcss.blogspot.com
E-Mail: bparson@csschurch.org

Established in 2011
Brinton Taylor Parson,
Director
Sangeeta Singh,
Associate Director
Reverend Kathleen Liles,
Rector
Enrollment: 20 (60 maximum)

School year. September through May/June.

Ages	Hours	Days	Tuition
All	9:00–12:00	Mon–Fri	$16,000

Program. A traditional developmental curriculum is offered with a balance between indoor and outdoor activities, gross motor and fine motor control, individual activities, small group work and whole class activities, creative endeavors, and academic pursuits. The program is structured and teacher directed, yet child centered. Music, art, science, and cooking are offered. There is a weekly chapel service and several family chapel services throughout the year.

Admissions. The application fee is $50. Until a maximum of 60 is reached, there will be a rolling admissions policy. Thereafter, the ISAAGNY guidelines will be followed, with preferential consideration given to siblings and parishioners.

Class size. There is one "nursery" class for 15, 3–4-year-old children with a head teacher and an associate teacher. There is one pre-kindergarten class for 15, 4–5-year-old children with a head teacher and an associate teacher. Additional afternoon classes will be added to accommodate further increased enrollment.

Facilities. There are two spacious, newly renovated classrooms and an outdoor play garden. The students also enjoy a well-stocked lending library with a weekly after-school story hour that is open to the public.

Parental involvement. Parents visit and observe by appointment as frequently as they like. There are semi-annual conferences scheduled. All parents are invited to join the Parents Association and become as involved as their time and interest level permits.

Financial. Financial aid is available.

Family School West

Ages: 2.6–6

Nonsectarian Montessori Nursery School and Kindergarten

308 West 46th Street
  (between Eighth and
  Ninth Avenues)
Zip: 10036
Tel: 688-5950
E-mail: famschool@aol.com

Established 1989
Lesley Nan Haberman,
Founder and Headmistress
Enrollment: 40

School year. September through June. Optional vacation programs are available.

Hours. 8:15–3:00, extended day program until 6:00.

Tuition. From two half days to five full days: $6,300–$12,500.

Program. This Montessori school is a satellite of the Family School located at 323 East 47th Street. The school cites its cultural diversity and emphasis on independence, creativity, and tolerance. The Montessori-based program includes math, language, practical life, sensorial, science, and geography. Specials include music, art, foreign languages, physical education, martial arts, drumming, and yoga; violin and chess for older pre-primary students.

Admissions. See The Family School entry, pages 51–53.

Class size. Including part- and full-time students, there are approximately 40 students, with no more than 28 at a time, with 4 teachers and several part time specialists.

Facilities. Located in St. Luke's Lutheran Church, a landmark building, in a former basketball gym, with high ceilings which proves a large open classroom, and an attached outdoor play area.

Parent involvement. Parents are actively involved in the life of the school. Class parents are knowledgeable and accessible.

Graduates. Have gone on to many independent schools and selective public schools; see Family School.

Member. ERB, ISAAGNY, The Parents League.

First Friends Preschool
Ages: 2–4.11 yrs
Nonsectarian

245 West 74th Street
  (between Broadway and
  West End Avenue)
Zip: 10023
Tel: 769-1088
Website: www.ffpreschool.com
E-mail: admin@ffpreschoolnyc.com

Established 2001
Ruth Summer Keller,
Director
Enrollment: 90

School program. Mid-September through first week of June.

Summer program. June through early August.

Age	Hours	Days	Tuition (Monthly)
2–4.11	9:00–11:30 11:30–3:30 3:30–5:30	Tues Thurs or Mon Wed Fri or Mon–Fri*	$1,040–$1,930

*The school offers a variety of class sessions depending on the child's age and space availability.

Program. Developmental. Formerly, Ruthie's Toddler Time, this cozy and supportive nursery program offers children a variety of activities and materials that provide them with hands-on learning experiences in science, art, music, drama, movement, free play, cooking, and literature. The school fosters a strong sense of community in a low-key atmosphere where individual differences are appreciated.

Admissions. The application fee is $25. Parents may call the school to schedule a tour/information session, at which time they receive an application. An informal meeting for parents with the director is held along with a group tour of the school. Applicants are admitted on a first-come basis.

Class size.   There are two classrooms, the size of the group varies depending on the ages of the children. One morning class consists of young two-year-olds; three-year-olds comprise the other morning group. One afternoon class consists of two- and three-year-olds, while four-year-olds attend a pre-kindergarten program in the afternoon. The late session is for two- and three-year-olds.

Staff.   The school offers a high teacher to student ratio. Teachers are well trained and parents depend on their observations and judgements.

Facilities.   The school has two classrooms, a kitchen, and a resource room for small group activities. Children's artwork adorns the walls, there is age-appropriate furniture and play equipment. Children play at Riverside Park, two blocks away during the summer program.

Separation.   For most children this is their first school experience, the separation process begins with a very structured, phase-in period over five weeks.

Financial.   Limited scholarship aid is available.

Parent Involvement.   After the separation period, parents are welcome as visitors and observers; they are also encouraged to volunteer in classrooms, either reading or telling stories. Some take dictation from the children, others who have special skills or hobbies are invited to perform demonstrations.

Graduates.   Have gone on to a variety of private and public schools including Abraham Joshua, Bank Street, Heschel, Dalton, Calhoun, Columbia Grammar, Ethical Culture, West Side Montessori, St. David's, Marymount, Trinity, PS 87, PS 199 gifted and talented programs, The Anderson Program, and Hunter.

Affiliations: none.

43rd Street Kids Preschool, Inc.

Ages: 1–5 yrs

Nonsectarian Parent Cooperative

484 West 43rd Street
(between 9th and
10th Avenues)
Zip: 10036
Tel: 564-7496
Fax: 695-2027
Website: www.43rdstreetkidspreschool.org
E-mail: prekids43@aol.com

Established 1986
Nancy Lilienthal,
Director
Enrollment: 70

School year. September through early June.

Ages	Hours	Days	Tuition**
1–2* (with parent)	9:00–10:30	Tues Thurs	$1,800 yearly
2–3 (with parent)	9:10–11:00	Mon Wed Fri	$2,400 yearly
2.4–3	11:00–12:30	Tues Wed Thurs	$2,400 yearly
2.9–5	8:30–12:30	Mon–Fri	$6,500
	8:30–6:00	Mon–Fri	$13,400
	1:00–5:00	Mon–Fri	$6,500

*Children must be 1 by December 31st. Families are not required to join the co-op.

**The non-cooperative tuitions are 45 percent higher than those listed above.

Program: The school's director, Nancy Lilienthal, has given workshops on the Reggio Emilia schools in Italy,* and has been with the school from its inception. The Steps Classes, for one- and two-year-olds, offer an environment where parents can meet and discuss their children's milestones while their children play with blocks, sand and water, age-appropriate art materials and listen to music. Two-year-olds begin a separation process that takes about half the year for some and longer for others. The 2s classes are small and are supervised by a teacher and parent aide. The preschool group is larger with approximately 20 children per class, offering three- and four-year-olds the opportunity to learn from pretend play, block building, games, art, manipulatives, puzzles, and books.

---

*See page 7, *supra.*

The program is integrated and revolves around a social studies or science curriculum. Past projects have focused on fall harvest, families, celebrations, and fish. Children discuss the program, sing, and read stories, as well as talk about social and emotional issues every day. They help with cleanup and choose daily jobs that include caring for the school's pets and plants. Children swim twice a week and play outside every day, weather permitting.

Admissions. The application fee is $30. Inquire from January 1st on. Parents who apply are invited to visit a class with their child. There is no application deadline.

Class size. The parent/toddler groups each accommodate 13 children. The 2s program without parents accommodates 6. The preschool can accommodate twenty children, 2.9 to 5. There are three staff members in the preschool classes plus a parent aide. Music and creative movement are taught. A mental health consultant visits regularly and is available to parents and staff and to speak on parenting issues.

Facilities. The school's large, bright, and modern space is donated by the Manhattan Plaza complex, where many families live. It consists of two rooms: one class and an extremely large rehearsal space, outdoor play terraces, and a kitchen. Children swim at the health club in the complex.

Summer program. Summer program from mid-June through July, for 3s through 8s.

Separation. Separation is handled individually. Parents are in the classroom as long as they are needed and withdraw gradually.

Parent involvement. Co-op parents assist in the classroom once a month, work two hours on a "work day" once a year and join one of many school committees. All families participate in fund-raising and general business meetings three times a year.

Parents, some of whom have careers in entertainment, volunteer to perform in plays and concerts.

Financial. Families that are not residents of Manhattan Plaza pay a surcharge of $190. A deposit of 15 percent of tuition is required on signing the contract. The balance is paid in installments. Limited financial aid is available.

Transportation.   None.

Graduates.   Have attended Bank Street, Ethical Culture, and Hunter and UNIS, as well as public schools such as PS 9, Anderson, Midtown West, and NEST + M. Many children enter public school gifted and talented programs.

The Geneva School of Manhattan
Ages: 2.6–14

Classical and Christian Nursery to Eighth Grade

122 West 57th St. (West side)	Established in 1996
Zip: 10019	Rim An Hickley,
593 Park Ave. (East side)	Head of School
Zip: 10065	Preschool Enrollment: 60
Tel: (212) 754-9988	Total Enrollment: 160
Website: www.genevaschool.net	
E-Mail: admissions@genevaschool.net	

School Year. September through mid June.

Ages	Hours	Days	Tuition
Beginners* 2.6 by Sept. 1	8:30–11:30 or 12:15–3:15	Tues Thurs Fri (Mon optional 4th day)	$11,900– $13,270
Pre-Kindergarten 4 by Sept. 1	8:30–2:45	Mon Tues Thurs Fri (Wed optional 5th day)	$17,350
Kindergarten 5 by Sept. 1	8:20–3:10	Mon–Fri	$19,900

*Toilet training is required.

Program. Traditional. Program is composed of large learning blocks of time broken up with snack and play time. Learning centers allow children to explore their specific interests.

In the *Beginners* class, seven key developmental areas are explored including phonics, math and science, French, Bible

164

appreciation, music and rhythm, visual arts and motor skill development, and social development.

The *Pre-Kindergarten* program ensures readiness for Kindergarten, with phonics and reading readiness an important part of the daily schedule. Other classes include math, science, French, physical education, Bible, music, and art. Classes are slightly longer periods of time; learning centers play an integral role.

Admissions. The application fee is $100. Admissions begin after Labor Day. Applications are available online with electronic submission. Open houses are scheduled in September and October. Student assessments and parent interviews are part of the application process. Acceptances are mailed in February.

Class Size. Preschool classes are capped at 11 students for each Beginners class and 12 students for each Pre-Kindergarten class. Student-teacher ratio is approximately 6:1.

Facilities. The West Side preschool location is a three classroom suite on the second floor of Calvary Baptist Church. The classrooms, constructed in July 2010, are bright with wall-to-wall windows, new carpets, and bright colors. Student cubbies are located right outside the classroom, as is a dedicated, toddler bathroom. The East Side preschool location is a newly renovated space at 593 Park Avenue, with two classrooms, a large common play area, and an enclosed, rooftop play yard.

The JCC in Manhattan
The Saul and Carole Zabar Nursery School
Ages: 2.7–5 years

Jewish Nursery School

334 Amsterdam Avenue
  (at 76th Street); 2nd floor
Zip: 10023
Tel: 646 505-4400
Fax: 646 505-4388
Website: www.jccmanhattan.org/nurseryschool
E-mail: tekelman@jccmanhattan.org

Established 2001
Ilana Ruskay-Kidd,
  Director
Felicia Gordon,
Associate Director
Tara Ekelman,
School Administrator
Enrollment: 184

School year. September through beginning of June. Summer program from the end of June through August.

Ages°	Hours	Days	Tuition
2.7–2.11	8:45–11:30 or	Mon Wed Fri or	$14,700
		Tues Thurs	$12,900
	12:45–3:30	Mon Wed Fri	$13,250
3°°	8:45–12:00	Mon–Thurs	$14,925
	12:30–3:30	(Fri until 3)	
3.0–3.11	8:45–12:00	Mon–Fri	$18,125
4s/5s	8:45–2:45	Mon–Thurs	$22,675
		(Fri until 1:00)	

°Bridge Program for siblings only, 12:45–2:45 P.M., Tues/Thurs, $9,250
°°Extended 3s Program, $19,925.

Program. Connection is the philosophy of this nursery school housed in the newly built Jewish Community Center. Children are encouraged to learn ways to connect to one another, to their teachers, to Jewish life, and to their community.

JCC's parenting resource center offers parents and caregivers an opportunity to learn from one another, as well as from experts.

Admissions. The application fee is $75 Inquiries begin in September after Labor Day. The school offers tours during October and November. Applications are only given out on tours. Small group play sessions are scheduled on Sunday mornings in January and early February for prospective students. Acceptances are mailed at the beginning of March in accordance with ISAAGNY guidelines.

Class size.   There are four classes of 2s with twelve children, five classes of 3s with sixteen to seventeen children, and three classes of 4s/5s with eighteen to twenty children in each class. There are three teachers in each class.

Staff.   Each class has one head teacher with, or studying for, a master's degree in the field of education, and two associate teachers.

Facilities.   The JCC Nursery School is housed in an eleven-story building with a separate and secure entrance dedicated to nursery school. The learning areas are flooded with natural light. The school has the exclusive use of the facilities of the Jewish Community Center, which include the gym and rooftop playground, during school hours.

Separation.   The separation process at the beginning of the year is gradual and individual. During the first week of school parents stay in the classroom building. A parent or caregiver is expected to be available if needed for the first few weeks of school.

Afterschool programs.   There is an extensive afterschool program, available to children ages four through thirteen, including homework help. Check website: www.jccmanhattan.org/afterschool.

Parent involvement.   The nursery school welcomes parent involvement, both in the school and in the JCC. Parents serve on many committees, and attend birthday and other holiday celebrations at the JCC and in their child's classroom. There is an additional $350 in PA dues, payable with tuition.

Financial.   Once enrolled in the JCC Nursery School, the parents automatically become community members of the JCC. The school maintains a generous financial aid program.

Transportation.   The school does not provide transportation. Most children are accompanied to school by a parent or caregiver.

Graduates.   Former students have gone onto many private schools as well as selective public schools, gifted and talented programs, and Jewish day schools.

Member.　ERB, BJE.

La Escuelita

Ages: 2–5 yrs in the preschool program
12 mos to 6 yrs in the playgroups program
K–3rd grade in the afterschool program

302 West 91st Street
　(at West End Avenue)
Zip: 10024
Tel: 877-1100
Fax: 917-591-3023
Website: www.laescuelitanyc.org
E-mail: info@laescuelitanyc.org

Established 2003
Rosina Pichardo-Glean,
Educational Director
Jennifer Friedman,
Co-Founder and Director
Enrollment: 80
Playgroups: approximately 100
Afterschool program:
approximately 20

School year.　Early September to early June. Summer program for six weeks in June and July.

Ages	Hours	Days	Tuition
2s°	9–11:30 A.M.	Mon–Fri	$14,700
2s	9–11:30 A.M.	Mon Wed Fri	$8,820
2s	9–11:30 A.M.	Tues Thurs	$5,880
2/3s	2–4:30 P.M.	Mon Wed Fri	$8,820
3s	9–12 P.M.	Mon–Fri	$14,700
3/4s	1:30–4:30 P.M.	Mon Wed Fri	$8,820
4s	9–2:30 P.M.	Mon–Fri	$18,900

°New students must be two years of age by September 1st.

Program.　Developmental. The mission of La Escuelita is to support bilingualism in children from English and Spanish speaking families of one to eight years of age. The curriculum is based on an understanding of children's linguistic, social, physical, and cognitive development. Thematic units which emerge from children's interests

168

provide organization for activities and concepts; for example, classes have studied transportation, restaurants, outer space, and babies. A music teacher instructs children once or twice a week. Academic skills, including early literacy and mathematical concepts, are introduced in a developmentally appropriate way at a child's individual level of understanding. There is a wide variety of linguistic backgrounds among the families of La Escuelita, including English-only, Spanish/English bilingual, and families who already speak other languages and are adding Spanish to their child's repertoire.

Admissions.   Applications are available in September. Parents must plan to attend an information session in the fall to receive an application, which combines a tour and an open house. Dates for the information session are available at the end of August. Parents can sign up by phone or e-mail. A written application includes a page of contact information and short essays regarding what a parent is looking for in a preschool program. Upon receiving an application, a family meeting is scheduled with the director of admissions. Children are not observed or evaluated as part of the admissions process. Siblings are automatically accepted providing that the school meets their developmental needs. Legacies and children enrolled in La Escuelita's playgroups are given preference.

Class size.   In the 2s and 2/3s classes there are eleven children with one head teacher and two assistant teachers. In the 3s class there are sixteen children, one head teacher, and two assistant teachers. The 3/4s and 4s classrooms have 20 children each, with one head teacher, and two assistant teachers in each classroom. There is also a floater teacher, student teachers, volunteers, and other staff available to assist in the classrooms.

Staff.   All head teachers have bachelors degrees with certification in education or are completing certification in early childhood education. Assistant teachers have a variety of backgrounds, including decades of working with young children and bachelors degrees in education. All teachers are native Spanish speakers, and speak English as either a native or second language.

Facilities.   La Escuelita is located on the Upper West Side in the newly renovated basement of the Greek Orthodox Church of the Annunciation. The classrooms are spacious with high ceilings and plenty of light, but with limited windows. Classrooms have centers for art, blocks, dramatic play, books, manipulatives, water, sand, and music. The school is one block from the Hippo Playground in Riverside Park, which provides an area for outdoor activities. A large meeting room is used for parties and gross motor activities. An outside ramp and an elevator provide convenient access for strollers.

Summer program.   A six-week summer session is held in June and July. It is similar to the regular preschool program with an expanded outdoor and sports component. Often, the entire school works on one theme such as "water" or "sports" and participates in activities together. Preschool children are given priority for enrollment, but children from other preschools are also welcome.

Afterschool programs.   The afterschool program, which runs from 3:30 to 5 P.M., is aimed toward children in kindergarten through third grade who are already bilingual. Many of the afterschool program students are La Escuelita graduates. Conversational Spanish is emphasized, with Spanish literacy skills introduced for children who are ready.

Separation.   The separation process includes a teacher visit to the child's home in August, during which the teacher speaks to the child in his/her dominant language (Spanish or English). The first week of school has shortened days and smaller groups, and parents are expected to accompany children for the first few days at least. Thereafter, separation is discussed between a parent and the head teacher and proceeds at a pace appropriate for each child.

Parent involvement.   Parents are welcome to participate in a variety of ways, including organizing social events, serving on the Parent Advisory Board, leading classroom activities, or organizing the school library. As some parents work full-time, parent participation is not required. The school does encourage families to find ways to be involved in events and in their child's classroom.

Financial.   Tuition assistance is available based on need. Tuition reduction funds come from the school's budget, not fund-raising, in order to preserve an atmosphere of equity.

Transportation.   The 2/3 express and 1/9 local subway stop at 96th Street is three blocks from the school. The M104 Broadway bus and the 96th and 86th Street cross-town buses come within a few blocks of the school.

Graduates.   Students have gone to Dalton, Calhoun, Columbia Grammar, Cathedral, Ethical Culture, Heschel, Buckley, Studio School, Grace Church, Collegiate, Horace, Mann, Sacred Heart, Ramaz, Mandell, St. Lukes, Bank Street, Rodeph Sholom, St. Luke's, Manhattan Country School, The School at Columbia University, Special Music School, Hunter, Anderson, PS 199, PS 87 dual language program, PS 75 dual language program, PS 163 dual language program, PS 9 G & T, PS 199, Hunter, Anderson, Amistad, Manhattan School for Children, Special Music School, Hamilton Heights Academy, Central Park East II.

Member.   ERB, NAEYC, Institute for Language and Education Policy.

Le Jardin a L'Ouest (The Garden of the West) French-American Preschool

Ages: 2.6–5 yrs

French-American Preschool

164 West 83rd Street
    (between Columbus and
    Amsterdam Avenues)
Zip: 10024
Tel: 362-2658
Fax: 362-3419
E-mail: LJO@lejardinalouest.com
Website: www.lejardinalouest.com

Established 1972
John Arden Hiigli,
Dominique Bordereaux-Hiigli,
Co-Directors
Enrollment: 30

School year.   September through June.

Ages	Hours	Days	Tuition
2s and 3s	9:00–11:45	Mon–Fri	$19,000
4s and 5s	1–4	Mon–Fri	$19,000

171

Program. European Progressive. The teacher/directors, a husband and wife team, are Bank Street–trained and hold master's degrees in early childhood education. It is a French language immersion program. The children follow clear routines with plenty of time for free play as well as organized activities. Activities include pre-academic skills in math, science, writing, reading, and French. Above all, an early exposure to the French language and culture is offered to young children. Teachers are experienced and are native French speakers who also speak English fluently. Children discover that although they speak to teachers in English, teachers only respond in French; the environment is a bi-lingual one. Art is a special area that all the children are exposed to and participate.

Admissions.   The application fee is $100. Inquiries are from September until December. Applications can be downloaded from the website. Parents must return the application form before arranging an interview. These are interviews and play-dates scheduled beginning November 1st.

All applicants who have been interviewed will be notified by March 1st. The school maintains a waiting list for openings that may occur in mid-year.

Class size. There are 14–15 children in each class.

Staff. Two native French-speaking teachers to each class plus an assistant. The directors also participate in special projects throughout the year. Ms. Borderaux holds a New York State Permanent Certification.

Facilities. The school is located on the bottom floor of a townhouse with an enclosed backyard. (The directors live and have their offices directly above.)

Separation. Special attention is dedicated to making the separation process as smooth as possible.

Parent involvement. Parents are expected to attend all school-related functions and events, including scheduled conferences with a teacher, fund-raising events for Jardin Galerie Inc., a non-profit organization and annex to the preschool dedicated to portray children's art.

Financial. A non-refundable deposit of $3,000 is due on signing the enrollment contract. The remaining balance is payable in two equal installments, April 1st and September 1st. An alternative payment plan is available. There are no scholarships, financial aid, or sibling discounts.,

Graduates. Have gone on to Brearley, Dalton, Dwight, Calhoun, Collegiate, Columbia Grammar, Ethical Culture, Riverdale Country, Hewitt, Convent of the Sacred Heart, St David's, St. Bernard's, Cathedral, Bank Street, Horace Mann, Hunter Elementary, Lyceé Français, Marymount, Spence, Trevor Day, Trinity, UNIS.

Affiliations. ERB.

The Mandell School

Ages: 2–13 yrs

Toddler, Elementary and Preparatory Divisions

795 Columbus Avenue,
  (between 98th and 99th Streets)
103 West 96th Street; Pre-School Division
  (between Amsterdam
  and Columbus Avenues)
Zip: 10025
Tel: 222-2925
Fax: 316-1537
Website: www.mandellschool.org
E-mail: mandell.admissions@mandellschool.org

Established 1939
Gabriella Rowe,
Head of School
Meghan Losche
and Elkin Taylor,
Directors of Admissions
Enrollment: 80 Toddlers
130 Pre-Schoolers
(Nursery and
Pre-Kindergarten)
240 Elementary and
Preparatory Students

School year. Second week in September through beginning of June. There is a Summer Program for all classes through the third week in July.

Ages	Hours	Days	Tuition
Younger 2s°	8:45–10:45; 12:30–2:30	Tues, Thurs	$12,400
Older 2s	8:45–11:15; 12:30–3:00	Mon, Wed, Fri	$18,800
3s°°	8:30–11:30; 12:00–3:00	Mon–Fri	$21,750
Pre-Kindergarten	8:30–2:45 (Fri until 12:45)	Mon–Fri	$24,750
Junior Kindergarten	8:30–2:45	Mon–Fri	$32,500
Kindergarten°°°–4th grade	8:15–3:00	· Mon–Fri	$33,750

°Children must be 2 by October 1.

°°Children must be 3 by December 15 and must be toilet-trained.

°°°Children must be 5 by September 1st to enroll in kindergarten

Program.   Traditional, Structured, and Academic. The curriculum focuses on good citizenship, academic preparedness, and parental involvement. It includes social studies, reading and math readiness, music, art, cooking, science, technology, drama, and athletics.

In the 2s program the children are provided with an educational environment designed to support their physical and developmental needs and enable a smooth transition from home to school. The primary focus in the 3s program is to promote independence, community, and collaborative learning. The 3s classroom activities include block building, art projects, puzzles, manipulatives, and skill work.

The pre-kindergarten program focuses on the development of social, emotional, and academic readiness. For example, during Constructive Choice Time, children are provided access to several different types of educational activities and move freely from one learning center to another. The block and doll corners allow children to play and further develop their social skills. Art projects afford the children opportunities to experiment with different mediums and play with dough, as well as puzzles and table games, conduct science experiments, cooking, and more.

The Elementary Division consists of junior kindergarten through fourth grade. Students develop solid foundations in literacy and numeracy in small groups. In addition, students have classes in art, music, drama, wellness, physical education, foreign languages, library, and science.

Admissions. The application fee is $60. Requests for applications for the preschool can be made through the school's website from the first working day after Labor Day. Applications should be returned promptly. For the Elementary and Preparatory Divisions, applications are available on the school's website beginning in August. Once accepted, children are expected to remain enrolled through eighth grade. In January, the school hosts an open house for applicant parents to speak to teachers and other Mandell families. There's a strong sibling policy and early notification. The school follows the ISAAGNY calendar with respect to admissions notifications.

Facilities. The Preschool is housed on two floors at the 96th Street building. Classrooms are colorful, warm, and nurturing. There's a gym and music room. Pre-kindergarten children bring their own lunch; snacks are provided for the younger children. The Elementary and Preparatory Divisions are located one block from Central Park in a new state-of-the-art 50,000-square-foot facility. Classrooms are spacious, well-equipped, and extremely bright with oversized windows and high ceilings. There's a black box theater, cafeteria with a "living wall," gym, art, music and drama studios, music technology lab, invention lab, library, science lab, and an 8,000-square-foot terrace. Lunch is included in the tuition and is provided by a catering company that specializes in healthy, sustainable, locally grown food.

Separation. The Toddler Program focuses on separation. The 2s have a phase-in schedule. Children come for gradually longer periods of time at the beginning and build up. Parents and teachers work closely to ease the transition. There's a summer "bridge" camp, that although is not a separation program, is offered to help with the process.

Parent involvement. Parents serve on school committees and help with community-based activities, the library, scholarships, and field trips. There are conferences twice a year or as requested.

Financial. Depending on the program, between $6,500–$7,500 is due on signing the contract. The remainder is payable in mid-May and mid-August. Approximately 14 percent of the school receives some financial aid

Transportation. There is no private bus service.

Graduates. Have gone to Bank Street, Brearley, Browning, Chapin, Collegiate, Columbia Grammar, Convent of the Sacred Heart, Dalton, Ethical Culture, Hewitt, Hunter, Nightingale-Bamford, Riverdale, Spence, St. Bernard's, St. David's.

Chartered. By the Board of Regents of the State University of New York.

Member. ERB, ISAAGNY. For profit.

Manhattan Day School
Ages: 2–5 yrs
Orthodox Yeshiva

310 West 75th Street
(between West End
Avenue and Riverside)
Zip: 10023
Tel: 376-6800
Fax: 376-6389

Established 1943
Rabbi Mordechai Besser,
Principal
Aviva Yablok,
Assistant Principal and
Director of Early Childhood
Enrollment: 165

School year. September through June. Day camp, end of June until August.

Ages	Hours	Days	Tuition
2s	8:45–12:45	2, 3, or 5 days	$6,600–$14,700
3s	8:15–1:00 or	Mon–Fri	$15,000
	8:15–3:00		$17,900
4s, 5s	8:15–3:00	Mon–Fri	$19,470

Children must be 3, 4, or 5 respectively by December 1st.

Program. Eclectic. The school is bilingual. Hebrew is introduced as part of the daily routine. The curriculum revolves around the Jewish holidays and the secular calendar and includes both free and teacher-directed activities such as painting, collage making, cooking, storytelling, singing, dancing and movement, and dramatic play. Activities are often coordinated with a classroom study unit.

All children participate at their level in daily Tefila and Brachot. The development of social skills and the expression of feelings and ideas is also stressed. The children spend at least a half hour per day in the outdoor playground and forty-five minutes each day in the gym, and visit the library once a week. Fours have prereading, computers, math, and science skills. The preschool program is committed to learning by doing, and to recognizing the unique learning styles and interests of each child. The 5s program develops a firm pre-academic foundation in both Judaic and general studies.

Admissions. The application fee is $250. Inquiries are from mid-September on. The school will mail application forms and a parent visit and private tour can be arranged. After visiting the school an appointment may then be made to meet the principal who may arrange a time to observe the applicant in a small group.

Class size. There are typically two classes for each age level, varying between fifteen to twenty-two children in each class.

Staff. All head teachers have masters in early childhood education. Assistants are present in each classroom and work individually with each child.

Facilities. Built in 1972, the school has a separate early childhood area, a gym with adjoining cafeteria, an art room, a fully-equipped science laboratory, a library and Bet Midrash, classrooms, and offices. Wide corridors serve as assembly spaces and extra learning areas. The outdoor playground is equipped with a large, multi-purpose climbing apparatus.

The school has a hot lunch program; preschoolers eat in their classroom. Lunch is followed by Birkat Hamazon.

Separation. Children start school in small groups and in abbreviated sessions. Parents or other caregivers withdraw gradually.

Parent involvement. The Parents Association conducts social and fund-raising activities, coordinates the class-parents functions, and helps with extra-curricular activities. Conferences are twice yearly.

Financial. Tuition assistance is available, based on need for pre-K and kindergarten. For information regarding tuition call the executive director at: (212) 376-6800 ext. 800.

Transportation. The school participates with NYC Board of Education bussing for kindergarten and up.

Graduates. To Yeshiva High Schools.

Affiliations. Torah U'Mesorah, Jewish Education Project.

Metropolitan Montessori School
Ages: 3–12 yrs, Nursery to 6th grade

Nonsectarian Montessori Nursery and Elementary School

325 West 85th Street
 (between West End and
 Riverside Drive)
Zip: 10024
Tel: 579-5525
Fax: 579-5526
Website: www.mnsny.org

Established 1964
Brenda Mizel,
Head of School
Heidi Morrison,
Director of Admissions
Total enrollment: 200
Nursery enrollment: 90

School year. September through beginning of June. Five-week summer program.

Ages*	Hours	Days	Tuition
3–6 (Primary)	Half Day	Mon–Fri	$24,000
3–6	Full Day	Mon–Fri	$28,500

Children must be 3 in September. Toilet training is preferred but not necessary.

Program. Montessori. Metropolitan Montessori is a nursery school and an ongoing school rooted in the Montessori philosophy. Specific concepts, properties, and skills are explored at the nursery level. However, children here are not required to follow strict sequences for using materials, but the school has adapted other ways of teaching. Teachers are addressed formally and record the materials children are using in order to determine their skills levels. New materials are introduced in small groups or individually. Mixed-age groupings of children stay in the same classroom for three years. Sometimes teachers will ask an older student to demonstrate a material's use to a younger one. As the children move

178

through the curriculum, they will learn to write, read, and learn basic math skills using materials that demonstrate these in tangible ways. Children meet with specialty teachers for French, Spanish, art, music, physical education, science, health, violin, and library.

Nursery children exchange their shoes for slippers shortly after arrival. The children work alone, in pairs, or small groups, either at tables or on little floor mats, which they roll up and put away when they are finished. Playing with sandpaper letters gives youngest children a swift introduction to phonics. Opportunities for social exchanges come with circle time, outdoor play, and at lunch. Field trips supplement classroom learning. Metropolitan Montessori holds a schoolwide Book Fair in the spring. An onsite Learning Center is staffed by a full-time psychologist and teacher who work with teaching teams, review student issues, and plan individual and group remediation in conjunction with parents or outside professionals.

ERBs are given to students in grades two and above (but not to nursery or kindergarten age children) on the premises. About 10 percent of the children transfer to ongoing schools before graduation.

Admissions. The application fee is $40. Inquiries are accepted from early-September on. The applications deadline is December 15th for children who will be age 3 to 10 years old, with preference given to younger children. After receiving an application, the admissions office calls parents to schedule two appointments, one for the parents' tour and another for the child's visit with a teacher. (One parent can be present in the classroom during the child's visit.) Parents tour the school with the admissions director in small groups followed by a question-and-answer session. Notifications of acceptance are given the second week of February for 5s applicants and the first week of March for younger children.

Class size. Nursery children are grouped into four Primary mixed-age classes (3s through 6s) of about twenty-one to twenty-four children, each staffed with two teachers. Children remain in the same classroom for three years. Every head classroom teacher has Montessori training and a master's in education.

Facilities. The school's renovated carriage house is a well-equipped early childhood facility furnished with small tables, and chairs made of pastel painted wood or wickerwork. Baskets hold the children's rolled up mats. The white, immaculate floors reflect light flooding in through huge windows. There are plants and animals in each room.

The full-fledged kitchen provides an optional hot natural foods lunch for all-day students. There is also a gym, a ground-level playground with a climbing structure, and a rooftop play area and greenhouse. There is an appreciation for nature evident throughout the school, from the flower beds that grace the entrance to the tropical fish in the lobby. Classrooms have pets. Children plant bulbs, and grow herbs and vegetables. All students visit the Black Rock Forest Consorium in Cornwall, N.Y. for hiking, science, carpentry, and exploration.

Afterschool program. Children can join either before or after-school classes in physical education, music, foreign language, art, chess, and more. There is an additional charge for participation.

Separation. New children visit, one at a time, before the term begins to see the classroom and meet the teacher. During the first weeks of school, coffee is offered by the Parents Association. Parents may come to observe after six weeks. A few new children per week are introduced into each class of returning children, allowing teachers to focus on them.

Parent involvement. Parents are seen as important partners to the school; they organize social events and serve as fundraisers. There is a spring gala, a winter social, and a parent-run book fair.

Classroom observation and conferences are provided two times each year. A complete personal and academic profile for each child is prepared twice a year; parent/teacher conferences are held twice a year for nursery school children.

Transportation. Not available for nursery children; older children use public transportation.

Graduates. Have gone on to Allen-Stevenson, Brearley, Bronx Science, Browning, Buckley, Calhoun, Collegiate, Columbia Grammar, Convent of the Sacred Heart, Dalton, Delta Honors Program (a gifted and talented program), Ethical Culture, Fieldston, Friends Seminary, Horace Mann, Hunter College High School, Nightingale-Bamford, Riverdale Country School, Sacred Heart, Saint Ann's, Spence, Stuyvesant High School, Town School, and Trinity.

Member. AMI, AMS, ERB, Early Steps, ISAAGNY, North American Montessori Teachers Association, NYSAIS.

Montclare Children's School

Ages: 2–Pre-Kindergarten

Nonsectarian

747 Amsterdam Avenue
  (between 96th & 97th Streets)
Zip: 10025
Tel: 865-4020
Fax: 865-3435
Website: www.claremontschool.org
E-mail: info@claremontschool.org

Established 2001
Dianne Williams,
Director
Laurie Uffner,
Assistant Director
Rosie Finizio,
Assistant Director
Candida Gray,
Admissions Coordinator
Enrollment: 200

School year. Mid-September through mid-June. Summer program from mid-June through July.

Ages	Hours	Days	Tuition
2s*	8:45–11:45	Tues Thurs	$11,700
	8:45–11:45	Mon Wed Fri	$14,300
	12:30–3:30	Mon–Fri	$18,400
3s	8:45–11:45	Mon–Fri	$18,400
	8:30–2:30	Mon–Fri	$20,900
4s	8:30–2:30**	Mon–Fri	$27,500

*Children must be two years of age by September 1st.

Program. Traditional. This Upper West Side nursery school formerly known as Claremont Children's School, provides a comfortable setting, offers teacher-directed activities with an enriched curriculum, and is based on the philosophy that preschool-aged children can learn and therefore should be taught. The main goal of the program is to provide an atmosphere that fosters a sense of community, encourages participation, and is structured so that children can function independently. Children learn both individually and in

181

groups through activities that include block building, sand and water play, dramatic play, language arts, paint, clay, cooking, story time, outdoor play, and trips into the community. In addition, the school has seven specialists on staff to teach music, art, science, gymnastics, yoga, library, and computers.

Admissions.   The application fee is $75 Inquiries begin in September. Parents must apply before taking a tour of the school. Children are seen later in playgroups of five. The school maintains a sibling priority policy.

Class size.   There are six 2s classes with up to fourteen children and four teachers and four 3s classes of up to eighteen children with four teachers per class; the three 4s classes of up to twenty children have three teachers in each class.

Staff.   All head teachers have master's degrees in early childhood education. Many assistant teachers are working on getting their master's degree in education. The school uses specialists, who are trained in a particular field, to teach art, music, gymnastics, yoga, library, and computer. All teachers have previous experience working with children.

Facilities.   Montclare Children's School, formerly Claremont Children's School, is housed in a landmarked building that was formerly the East River Savings Bank. The renovated space has magnificent floor to ceiling windows, which provide natural light to the ten classrooms from both 96th Street and Amsterdam Avenue. In addition, there is a computer lab, a library, an art room, a gym/auditorium, a music room, and a rooftop play area. The classrooms are set up as centers so that children can easily navigate their way around. Each classroom has an area for dramatic play, an art area, and a carpeted area for floor activities, circle, and story time.

Summer program.   Camp Montclare, which runs from mid-June through July.

Separation.   For two-year-olds before the first day of school, children visit the school. A parent or caregiver is expected to be available and on the premises until children are fully separated. A typical separation takes three weeks.

Parent involvement.   The school encourages parental participation in the Parents Association. Each class has two class parents and parents are invited to celebrate holidays and cultural events in the school. Conferences are arranged twice yearly.

Financial.   Montclare is a for-profit school. Limited financial aid is available.

Transportation.   The school is convenient to public transportation; the cross-town bus route at 96th Street, the Seventh and Eighth Avenue subway lines, and the uptown M7 and M11 buses stop right in front of the school. The school does not provide transportation.

Graduates.   Attend approximately forty-two different private and public schools including Brearley, Cathedral, Chapin, Collegiate, Columbia Grammar, Dalton, Ethical Culture, Little Red School House, Riverdale, Sacred Heart, St. Bernard's, St. David's, Spence, Trinity, UNIS, Anderson, Hunter, and the Region 10 Gifted and Talented Program.

Member.   ATIS, ERB.

Morningside Montessori School

Ages: 2–5.6 yrs

Nonsectarian Parent Cooperative

251 West 100th Street
  (at West End Avenue)
Zip: 10025
Tel: 316-1555
Fax: 866-2128
Website: www.morningsidemontessori.org
E-mail: info@morningsidemontessori.org

Established 1966
Jorinda Moorhead,
Director
Deborah Gonzalez,
Assistant Director
Enrollment: 90

School year.   September through mid June. Summer Camp mid-June through end of July.

Ages	Hours	Days	Tuition
2.0–2.9	9:00–12:00	2 days	$9,060
2.9–5	9:00–12:00	3 days	$11,495
	9:00–12:30	Mon–Fri	$16,490
	1:30–4:30	Mon–Fri	$11,045
2.9–5	9:00–3:30	Mon–Fri	$19,485
2.9–5	8:00-6:00	Mon–Fri	$23,130

°Additional schedules are available.

°°Children must be toilet-trained by the time they are 3.

Program.　　Modified Montessori. Morningside offers a secure nurturing environment where children can develop according to their own pace and interests in an organized and stimulating environment. Important features of the mixed-aged classrooms include class pets, blocks, music area, and fantasy-play materials, as well as Montessori materials. Work areas are divided into science, sensorial, practical life, math, and language. Skills demonstrations are given to the entire class and are followed up individually or in small groups. Descriptions of recent class projects are mounted on a bulletin board and later put into a loose-leaf binder. Visitors are invited to look through this detailed record, impressive for the volume and variety of activities.

Admissions.　　　　　　　　　　The application fee is $40. Inquiries are from mid-September on. The deadline for applications is mid-December. Call for an applications package and arrange a time to observe activities in a classroom and take a tour. Parents may visit individually or in pairs. Once the application has been filed, parents call for an appointment for an interview. The child will be invited to participate in class activities with the parents present. Notifications are given by March. All children who apply are interviewed in January or February.

Class size.　　There is one toddler class of 12 children, one 3s class of fifteen children and four half-day mixed-age classes of twenty-five to eighteen children each, with a minimum of three teachers per class. Two classes share a Montessori teacher.

Facilities.　　Four old-fashioned classrooms on the sixth floor of Temple Ansche Chesed, reached by an automatic elevator. One is an extremely large room which has been divided into two separate classrooms. Two smaller rooms adjoin. Every classroom has building block areas. The toddler room has a high climbing loft. A teacher commented that a child's first task was to master climbing up and down the loft stairs. Two other preschools housed in the temple, Yaldaynu and the Purple Circle, share the large, well-equipped rooftop play area with Morningside.

Summer program.   Camp Morningside offers an optional, full-time program as well as half-day programs.

Separation.   For the toddlers, this takes a few weeks. Parents stay in the classroom for the first week then stay outside classrooms by cubbies, then in the near-by kitchen. New children in the mixed-aged program are in school for the first two days by themselves before the returning students join them. Parents may stay in the classroom for half an hour or so the first day or two, and can remain on the premises longer. New 3s can also join the summer program.

Parent involvement.   The school is a parent cooperative that is guided by a parent-elected and -run board of trustees. Parents are required to donate eighteen work hours (nine for a single parent) and sign a parent work agreement. Committees include work coordination, fund-raising, social, maintenance, communications, scholarship, admissions, and personnel; or the work assignment may consist of office assistance or help on field trips.

Financial.   A tuition deposit is required on signing the contract. The balance of the tuition is payable in two or eight installments. (There is an additional charge for the latter.) Limited financial aid is available. Parents are required to make a loan to the school upon enrollment.

Transportation.   No private bus service is available; parents bring their children to the classroom.

Graduates.   Have gone on to Bank Street, Brearley, Cathedral, Calhoun, Collegiate, Columbia Grammar, Dalton, Ethical Culture, Friends, Fieldston, Horace Mann, Hunter, Manhattan Country, St. Hilda's & St. Hugh's, Town, Trinity, and local public schools.

Member.   AMS, ERB, ISAAGNY.

The Nursery School at Habonim

Ages: 2.6–6 yrs

Jewish Nursery School

44 West 66th Street
  (Between Central Park West
  and Columbus Avenue)
Zip: 10023
Tel: 787-5347 x16
Fax: 595-3542
Website: www.habonim.net
E-mail: cgrebow@habonim.net

Established 1997
Cindy Grebow,
Director
Andrea H. Lefkovits,
Assistant Director
Enrollment: 70–75

School year. Mid-September through mid-June. No summer program.

Ages	Hours	Days	Tuition
2s	11:45–2:15	Tues Wed Thurs	$12,500
3s*	8:45–12:00	Mon and Fri	$15,500
	or 8:45–11:30	or Tues Wed Thurs	
4s	8:45–2:15	Mon–Fri	$18,250
		(Fri until 12:00)	

*There is an extended program begins in January; lunch bunch begins in January.

Program. Developmental. There is a strong sense of community in each classroom. The curriculum is child-centered and play based using age-appropriate materials and activities. There's a daily access to either two large indoor play spaces or an outdoor playground. Children also have specialists in music, library, movement, science, storytelling, and story acting. The nursery school is part of Congregation Habonim, a Conservative, egalitarian synagogue. Jewish holidays and Shabbat are observed.

    Children are introduced to Jewish traditions through weekly Shabbat and holiday celebrations, "Rock Shabbat" with the Rabbi and Cantor, and food. Children really connect with their Jewish identity.

Admissions. The application fee is $60. The application process begins after Labor Day. Applications are available online or by phone or at the conclusion of each tour. Tours are held in October and November and are held by the school's director and are required. Children are interviewed individually in

January and February. Admissions decisions are sent in accordance with ISAAGNY guidelines.

Class size. There are ten to twelve children in the youngest 2s class (2.6 to just under 3 years), and fifteen children in each of the 3s class with three teachers in each class. The two pre-K classes of 4s has up to eighteen children in the class with three teachers.

Staff. Each class typically has two co-head teachers, and an associate or assistant teacher. All head teachers have a master's degree in early childhood education and special education. Other teachers are working on their graduate degrees in education. There is a movement teacher and a music teacher, librarian, and a story acting specialist who meet with every class once a week. A school psychologist is on staff; a speech and language therapist and occupational therapist are available.

Facilities. Located in three bright classrooms on the ground floor of the synagogue. Each classroom has a child-sized bathroom. There is an outdoor play area with climbing apparatus, a climbing wall, large wooden blocks, and two large multipurpose rooms that are used daily as an indoor play space and for movement. The school also uses the sanctuary and the kitchen of the synagogue.

Separation. The separation procedure at the beginning of the school year is gradual and individual. Every year teachers make home visits before school starts. Pre-K and K children visit the classroom one at a time before school starts; parents or caregivers must be available during the first weeks of school.

Parent involvement. Parents work in the library and are involved with fund-raising events. There's a teacher-written weekly and monthly newsletter for parents. Formal conferences are scheduled in the fall and spring, and as needed. Daily messages are e-mailed. The school psychologist is available for consultation two days a week.

Financial. Financial Aid is available for children ages 3 and above.

Transportation. The school does not provide transportation. Most children are accompanied to school by a parent or caregiver.

Graduates. Have gone to a wide variety of public, private, and Jewish

Day Schools including, Abraham Joshua Heschel, Brearley, Calhoun, Chapin, Columbia Grammar, Dalton, Dwight, Ethical Culture, Little Red Elisabeth Irwin, Hewitt, Horace Mann, Hunter, Ramaz, Riverdale, Rodeph Sholom, Soloman Schechter, Stephen Gaynor, Trinity, as well as a wide range of public elementary schools, Hunter, Anderson, NEST + M, Lower Lab, Manhattan School for Children.

Affiliations. Congregation Habonim, membership required upon enrollment.

Member. ERB. ISAAGNY, and The Jewish Education Project.

The Poppyseed Pre-Nursery Inc.
Ages: 8 mos.–3.5 yrs

Nonsectarian Pre-Nursery School

424 West End Avenue	Established 1986
(corner of 81st Street)	Gail Ionescu,
Zip: 10024	Director
Tel: 877-7614	Enrollment: 120

School year. September through May; summer program June and July.

Ages**	Hours	Days	Tuition
8 mos.–3.5 yrs.	2 hours	2–3 days	$4,195–$5,995

*Semesters are: October through February and February through May.
**Children are grouped according to age.

Program. The program offers a gradual bridge between home and school with its small classes. Age-appropriate activities and a daily routine, include, music, art through brush and finger painting, collages, clay and Play-doh, waterplay, dancing, and singing. A mini gym that's fully equipped keeps kids fit rain or shine. Children also have a snack and story-time.

Class size. The center serves up to eight to twelve children in a class. There are two staff members per class (in addition to the parents and caregivers).

Admissions.   Call for an application in January; inquiries are ongoing.

Facilities.   A large carpeted play room with a variety of toys (train set, Duplo table, dolls, kitchen area, cars, trucks to ride in, books, puzzles, and puppets), a piano, guitar, and other musical instruments. There is also a well-equipped mini-gym (including a ball pit, foam mountain, and slide), a snack area, and an arts-and-crafts area.

Separation.   Parents or caregivers are required to remain with the children and participate in the program.

Financial.   Payment is made in two installments. There is a $50 registration fee. A deposit is required upon enrollment.

Summer program.   June and July, Tuesdays, Wednesdays, and Thursdays for two hours for children ages 1 year through 3.5 years.

Preschool du Monde

Ages: 2–5 yrs

Nonsectarian Nursery/Preschool

79th Street and Riverside Drive
Zip: 10024
Tel: (646) 592-5527
Website: www.psdumonde.org
E-Mail: info@psdumonde.org

Established 2010
Robin Savage,
Founder and Executive Director
Enrollment: 12

School Year. Twelve-month program.

Ages	Hours	Days	Tuition (monthly)
2–5	8:30–4:15	Mon–Fri	$1,860
	8:30–12:30	Mon–Fri	$1,455
	2:30–5:30	Mon–Fri	$1,265
	Afterschool	Mon–Fri	Varies

* The program is flexible to accommodate the parent's needs. Extended days are available, as well as attending fewer than 5 days a week—the fees are revised accordingly.

Program.   Progressive/Developmental. A dual language early child-hood education program. The program nurtures and prepares young children to become "lifelong learners" as well as dedicated and compassionate participants in the world around them while actively contributing to their cognitive, emotional, physical, and language development.

A hands-on inquiry program with studies organized weekly by theme, accompanied by educational learning centers, small group instruction, classroom "museum walks," and community walks (weather permitting) that bring together literacy, art, music, drama, science, math, and social studies topics. Outdoor playtime is incorporated into the program on a daily basis (weather permitting), meaning that children can spend the length of one class (around 45 minutes) outside in the school's enclosed backyard.

The dual program includes Spanish instruction from 30% daily, to 60% daily mid-mester, to 90% daily by May. By the end of the term, a 90/10 dual language model will be in effect, with periods of English designed to enhance vocabulary and strengthen concepts that were taught in Spanish. Children will also participate in a creative and dynamic music and movement environment.

Admissions.   The application fee is $100. Parents may call or email the school for information and to schedule a visit. An informal meeting with the Program Director and/or head teacher for the parents is provided along with a tour of the school.

Class size.   The mixed-age program allows to 12 children.

Staff.   All teachers have degrees in early childhood education and are certifies to teach in NYS. The head teacher also has his master's in early childhood education. One of the teachers is a native Spanish speaker.

Facilities.   Across the street from Riverside Park, the school is situated on a ground floor apartment with a private backyard where children spend much of their outdoor time (as well as taking a daily neighborhood walk and walks to the various play grounds inside Riverside Park). The children also walk to Central Park.

Separation.   Depends in the individual needs of the child. Most children gradually increase time spent at the school during a one-week transitions phase.

Parent involvement.   The schools have an open-door policy, and parents are welcome to visit any time. Parents are encouraged to attend and participate in parent meetings, parent/teacher conferences, and family social events. A monthly newsletter is sent to parents.

Financial.   A deposit equal to one month's tuition is required upon signing the contract and applied to the last month's tuition payment. Parents are required to provide a 30-day notice prior to leaving the school. Tuition is paid monthly.

Transportation.   Children come from the Upper West Side are and are brought by their parents or caregivers. Teachers can do pick-up for the afternoon program.

Affiliations.   International Baccalaureate (Primary Years Program).

Member.   National Association for Bilingual Education, New York State Association for Bilingual Education.

Purple Circle Day Care Center, Inc.

Ages: 2–6 yrs

Nonsectarian Parent Cooperative

251 West 100th Street
  (at West End Avenue)
Zip: 10025
Tel: 866-9193
Website: www.purple-circle.org

Established 1971
Eleni Karas,
Director
Enrollment: 60

School year.   Open fifty weeks a year.

Ages	Hours	Days	Tuition
2–5	8:30–1:50	Mon–Fri	$17,512
2–5	8:30–4:00	Mon–Fri	$21,357
2–5	8:30–6:00	Mon–Fri	$25,106
2–5	2:30–6:00	Mon–Fri	$13,474

Program.   Eclectic. A community-based diverse program within a nurturing environment, blending cognitive, emotional, social, and physical development. Teachers focus on individual interests and strengths using space, time, and materials that are geared for problem solving and investigating. Children explore their ideas through storytelling, blocks, sand, water, clay, books, drawing, writing, music, movement, neighborhood trips, dramatic play, painting, and cooking.

Admissions.   The application fee is $35. Inquire from September on. Tours are scheduled upon receipt of application. Children are not interviewed. Notifications are sent in early March, and parents are asked to reply within one week.

Class size.   There are four groups of 2s, 3s, and 4s. Each has three teachers.

Facilities.   Two sunny and spacious classrooms on the fourth floor and two on the fifth floor of Temple Ansche Chesed and a large playroof. Children also use local parks and library. They bring their own lunches; morning and afternoon healthy snacks are provided.

Separation.   Teachers make home visits with families before school starts, for a gradual and more positive separation process. New children are introduced over a two-to-three-week period in gradually lengthening sessions. Parents remain in the classroom for several days, then move to the hall, and then may leave the floor briefly for refreshments with other parents downstairs. From then on, the process is handled at whatever pace each child and parent seems to need.

Parent involvement.   The school sees itself as a close community. Parents contribute to the running of the school in a variety of ways. Opportunities include serving on the board of directors, participating in the physical upkeep of the school, fund-raising, or donating time or services to the school.

Financial.   A deposit of approximately 10 percent of tuition is required on signing the full-year contract. The balance is paid in ten monthly installments. There is limited financial aid. There is a tuition reimbursement of $700 each for teachers who are pursuing their undergraduate or graduate degrees. There is also about $2,000 available for general staff development.

Transportation.   Children come from 70th to 145th Streets on the Upper West Side, and are brought by their parents or caregivers.

Graduates.   Have gone on to Bank Street, Calhoun, Cathedral, Chapin, City and Country, Columbia Grammar, Dalton, Ethical Culture, Manhattan Country, Trevor Day, Solomon Schechter, as well as public schools including The Anderson Program, Central Park East, Hunter Elementary, Manhattan School for Children, PS 75, and PS 87.

River School
Ages: 2 months–5.6 yrs

Nonsectarian Nursery School

75 West End Avenue	Established 1989
(at 63rd Street)	Jane Kresch,
Zip: 10023	Director
Tel: 707-8300	Enrollment: 100
Fax: 707-8600	
Website: www.theriverschool.com	
E-mail: kidslearn@theriverschool.com	

School year.   All year.

Ages	Hours	Days	Tuition (monthly)
2 mos–18 mos	7:30–7:00	Mon–Fri°	$1,100–$2,375
18 mos –3.5 yrs	7:30–7:00	Mon–Fri°	$1,050–$2,235
3.5 yrs–5.5 yrs	7:30–7:00	Mon–Fri°	$1,025–$2,115

°Children may be enrolled for 2, 3 or 5 days per week.

Program.   Developmental. The program is highly nurturing and emphasizes creative participation in the learning process. Children explore their environment via active play involving art, music, dance, literature, drama, and sports. Frequent field trips enrich the regular curriculum. Age-appropriate literacy experiences and the encouragement of a relaxed social milieu are regarded as the essential foundation of the learning process.

193

Admissions. There is no application fee. Applications are accepted on an ongoing basis and admission is offered as space becomes available. Parents are welcome to stop in or make an appointment. Siblings are given priority.

Class size. There are eight infants, ten toddlers, and 10 to 20 preschoolers per individual class based on age.

Facilities. The school occupies a dramatic 7,000-square-foot, light-filled ground floor space with a park and playground directly adjacent. Creative design integrates library, computer areas, and an indoor amphitheatre with comfortable classrooms, each with its own bathroom. An active gym space in the building complement the convenient outdoor play space.

Summer program. The summer program for preschoolers includes field trips, sports, and special projects involving science, nature, art, and dramatic play.

Separation. The separation process is individualized to suit the needs of the child. It can range from just a few days up to two weeks. Parents are encouraged to stay until the child feels at ease with the environment.

Parent involvement. Parents are encouraged to volunteer as chaperones on class trips. Families come in to read stories, talk about their culture, or to participate in school activities. Parent workshops with guest speakers are offered throughout the year.

Financial. A deposit of one month's tuition is required along with the first month's tuition to reserve a space. Tuition is payable monthly. A ten percent discount is offered for siblings.

Transportation. The school is conveniently located near public transportation: the M104 bus and the 1/9 trains are located on Broadway along with the M57 on West End Avenue. The school does not provide transportation.

Graduates. Have gone on to Ethical Culture, Columbia Grammar, Chapin, Nightingale, Spence, Bank Street, Cathedral, Calhoun and Dwight, Trinity, Collegiate, Trevor Day, Hewitt and others. Children also attend parochial school or public schools, including

Anderson, Hunter, PS 199, PS 87, and various gifted and talented programs.

River-Park Nursery School and Kindergarten
Ages: 2.8–5 yrs

Family Cooperative
711 Amsterdam Avenue (at 94th Street)   Established 1967
Zip: 10025   Desiré J. Ford,
Tel: 663-1205   Director
Fax: 663-1205   Maria Nunziata,
Website: www.riverparknurseryschool.com   Co-Director
E-mail: riverparksns@verizon.net   Enrollment: 40

School year. September through mid-June.

Ages	Hours	Days	Tuition
2.8–3s	8:45–11:30	Mon–Fri	$11,073
3s	8:45–1:00	Mon–Fri	$12,898
3s–4s	8:45–4:00	Mon–Fri	$18,949
4s	1:00–4:00	Mon–Fri	$10,677
4s	11:30–4:00	Mon–Fri	$12,429

There is a $350 equipment and emergency fund fee; and a furniture moving fee of $50.

Program. Eclectic. The school's philosophy stresses "meeting each child where he or she is and helping them grow and develop from there," encouraging exploration at their own pace without undue pressure. With a strongly diversified student body, the staff particularly emphasizes a non-sexist, non-racist approach, the keystones of which are "trust, dignity, and respect for yourself," and also for other people. Self-expression in the creative arts as well as reading and math readiness anchor the curriculum. Teachers use the term "sciencing," which means learning through investigation. The staff encourages children to learn from each other's diverse backgrounds as well as from the formal program.

Admissions. The application fee is $50. Inquiries are from September on. After applying, parents tour the school with their child, who is invited to participate in that day's activities. Testing runs counter to the school's philosophy and is thus not required. The school is interested in families that will benefit from participating in a cooperative and that will contribute to this "extended family" (now extended to two generations). Families are accepted on a first-come, first-served basis, so parents are encouraged to send applications as soon as possible.

Class size.   The school day is divided into half-day sessions for 3s in the morning, half-day sessions for 4s in the afternoon, and full-time sessions for both groups, 3s and 4s. Lunch can be added to the half-day program for a slightly longer day. Approximately one-half of the students are in the full-day program. There are 20 to 28 children in the morning and afternoon sessions, with two teachers and two teacher directors working in the classroom.

Staff.   All teachers have a minimum of 30 years teaching experience, are certified early childhood educators and/or have a master's degree in early childhood education. The school also draws student teachers and teaching assistants from a number of New York City educational institutions.

Facilities.   The spacious ground-floor area (the size of three classrooms), is adjoined by a large, private outdoor play yard. The bright, airy classroom has high ceilings and two walls of floor-to-ceiling windows. It includes a full kitchen, which is used frequently for children's projects. Both the indoor and outdoor spaces permit even the most physically active child to use his/her energies constructively.

Separation.   A teacher visits each child's home before school begins to develop a one-to-one relationship. The first two weeks of school are adjustment weeks. As with all issues, the staff works closely with parents to allow the child to adjust at his or her own pace.

Parent involvement.   Each family contributes 35 hours of service during the school year. The River Park co-op has worked for over forty-four years, and many alums return to the annual International Dinner in May to meet and greet former teachers and friends. The school sponsors a bazaar in December, the proceeds of which benefit the school fund. There are at least two parent/teacher conferences annually and monthly parent-staff meetings.

Financial.   A deposit of 25 percent of the annual tuition is due upon signing the contract. The remaining payments are due August 1 and December 1. Limited scholarship assistance is available. The deadline for scholarship applications is December 15th. In addition, a non-refundable equipment fee of $350, and a $1,500 reservation which is deducted from the first tuition payment, is required.

Transportation.   Children come from many Manhattan neighborhoods and other boroughs. No private bus service is available, but the school is located at the junction of many city bus and subway lines.

Graduates.   Alumni are represented at a broad range of both public and private schools throughout Manhattan.

Chartered.   By the Board of Regents of the State University of New York.

Riverside Montessori
(Part of Twin Parks Schools)

Ages: 3 mos–5 yrs

Nonsectarian Montessori Nursery

Central Park Montessori

1 West 91st Street

Zip: 10024

Tel: 595-2000

E-mail: enroll@twinparks.org

202 Riverside Drive

  (South corner of

  West 93rd Street)

Zip: 10025

Tel: 665-1600

Fax: 665-1775

Website: www.twinparks.org

E-mail: admissions@twinparks.org

Established 1997

Candace La Douceur,

Director of Admissions (Riverside)

Shelly McGuire,

Director of Admissions

(Central Park)

Enrollment: 111

School year.   September through June. Summer Session from mid July through August.

(See pages 205–207 for more information)

The Rodeph Sholom School
Ages 2.6–14 yrs

Reform Jewish Nursery through Middle School

7 West 83rd Street	Established 1958
and 10 West 84th Street	Mr. Paul Druzinsky,
(between Central Park West	Head of School
and Columbus Avenue)	Ms. Susan Weiss Newman,
Zip: 10024	Early Childhood Division Director
Tel: (646) 438-8600	Ms. Erin Korn,
Fax: 874-0117	Admissions Director
Website: www.rodephsholomschool.org	Nursery enrollment: 178
Total enrollment: approximately 700	

School year. September through mid-June.

Ages	Hours	Days	Tuition
2s°	9:00–11:30	2, 3 days	$12,500–$14,500
2s	12:30–3:00	Mon Tues Wed Thurs	$15,500
3s	8:45–11:45	Mon–Fri	$19,850
3s	8:45–1:00	Mon–Fri	$21,850
4s (pre-K)	8:45–2:45	Mon–Fri	$32,420
5s (kindergarten)	8:15–3:05	Mon–Fri	$33,840

°All families in the school are automatically members of Congregation Rodeph
Sholom. Extended hours are available beginning in the 3s program.

Program.   Reform Jewish Day School. The school offers a program
that aims to foster both self-expression and cooperative behavior.
In the nursery division, children explore a wide variety of materials and activities such as block building, dramatic play, sand and
water, art, cooking, planting, manipulatives, and music. In pre-K,
students are offered a curriculum which includes math, writing,
and reading readiness. Each pre-K classroom has a computer with
age-appropriate software programs. Children are introduced to
Jewish traditions through weekly Shabbat and holiday celebrations, songs, games, and blessings. All classes, starting in nursery,
are taught about *tzedakah*° through citywide programs, such as
Common Cents, a penny harvest that collects coins for various
charitable organizations.

°charity

Admissions. The application fee is $60. Online applications are available September 1st. Call to schedule a group tour and parent interview. Inquiries are from Labor Day on. Call for an application package and to schedule a group tour. Twos are interviewed with their parents; 3s participate in play-group interviews. Once enrolled at Rodeph Sholom students matriculate through eighth grade. The school welcomes children of all faiths.

Class size. There are four to five 2s classes of up to ten, five to six 3s classes of up to fifteen, four to five pre-K classes of up to eighteen, and four kindergarten classes of up to eighteen. Each class has two teachers.

Facilities. The campus comprises three buildings: the Temple building at 7 West 83rd Street houses the 2s and 3s; 10 West 84th Street houses the pre-K, kindergarten, and 1st grade; 168 West 79th Street houses grades 2–8. In Nursery, there is a fully equipped roof playground and gym. Students travel outside their classrooms for specials, including physical education, yoga, music, and art.

Summer program. Summer camp, located in the 7 West 83rd Street building, runs from late June through mid-August.

Separation. Before school begins, teachers visit the family at home. School begins with small, staggered classes and shortened sessions.

Parent involvement. The school encourages strong communication among parents, teachers, and administration. An active PTA organizes fund-raising events and parent outreach programs. All parents are automatically granted membership in Congregation Rodeph Sholom, including reserved High Holy Day seats.

Financial. A $5,000 nonrefundable deposit is due on acceptance. Financial aid is available beginning in kindergarten.

Transportation. Private bus service can be arranged for all children. Elementary children can use Department of Education buses.

Graduates. Eighth-grade graduates go on to both private and public schools, including Bronx High School of Science, Collegiate, Columbia Prep, Dalton, Fieldston, Horace Mann, Spence, Saint

Ann's, LaGuardia High School of the Performing Arts, Riverdale, Stuyvesant High School, and Trinity.

Affiliations. Congregation Rodeph Sholom.

Member. ERB, ISAAGNY, NYSAIS, AISAP.

Stephen Wise Free Synagogue
Early Childhood Center
Ages: 1.6–5 yrs

Jewish

30 West 68th Street
  (between Central Park West
  and Columbus Avenue)
Zip: 10023
Tel: 877-4050. ext 224
Fax: 787-7108
Website: http://ecc.swfs.org

Established 1983
Lori Schneider,
Director
Miriam Kalmar,
Assistant Director
Enrollment: 125

School year. Parents contract for the school year, September through early June. The center also operates a summer camp through July. Toddlers and 2s attend 2 or 3 days per week. Threes to 5s attend five days a week.

Ages	Hours	Days	Tuition
18 mos–2 yrs	9:10–12:45	Tues Thurs	$11,500
18 mos–2 yrs	9:00–12:45	Mon Wed Fri	$14,800
3s–4s	9:00–1:00	Mon–Fri	$18,200
Pre–kindergarten	9:00–2:45 (Fri 1:15)	Mon–Fri	$21,000

Synagogue membership is required and billed separately. Second child in family receives a tuition discount. An extended day program is available for 3-year-olds for an additional fee.

Program. Developmental. The overriding philosophy at Stephen Wise is that learning does not occur in narrowly designated subject areas but is a process where the curriculum is integrated into all areas. This is accomplished in an environment in which children can explore, experiment, and interact with their peers and teachers in an age appropriate way. Play is an essential component of the developmentally appropriate curriculum. The program emphasizes Jewish values and traditions. The Early Childhood Center has been inspired by the Reggio Emilia approach to education. A significant number of teachers have attended Reggio Emilia study tours in Italy.

Admissions. The application fee is $60. After Labor Day, applicants can fill out a tour request form from the website. Applications are due in December. Contracts are sent according to ISAAGNY guidelines.

Class size. There are single groups of eight to nine young 2s, twelve older 2s, three or four groups of thirteen to fifteen 3s, and two or three groups of fourteen to sixteen 4s; all groups have three staff members.

Staff. All head teachers have or are working toward masters degrees. Teachers have attended conferences and workshops.

Facilities. Eight comfortable classrooms on the fifth floor of the synagogue building. There is an indoor play space with lofts and climbing equipment plus a rooftop play area with a garden, tricycles, and playground equipment. There is a separate play space for toddlers on the terrace with appropriate sized climbing equipment.

Separation. This is carefully scheduled and handled slowly. Small groups and abbreviated hours lead into the full program. Parents or a caregiver must be available for at least two weeks, sometimes longer.

Parent involvement. An educational consultant is available to work with parents. Conferences are held twice a year and as needed. Parents are involved in fund-raising, social and educational activities, as well as celebrations.

Summer program. A four-week and six-week program are offered. Prices range from $1,840 to $3,775, based on full-day or half-day schedules. Spaces are for 2.5s to 5 year olds who have been through the separation process.

Transportation.   None. Children come from about 54th Street through 120th Street on the East and West Sides.

Graduates.   Have gone on to Abraham Joshua Heschel, Allen-Stevenson, Bank Street, Brearley, Chapin, Columbia Grammar, Dalton, Ethical Culture, Fieldston Lower, Horace Mann, Lycée Français, Manhattan Country, Ramaz, PS 87, 163, 199, Hunter, Trevor Day, Riverdale Country, Rodeph Shalom, Solomon Schecter, Spence, UNIS, Anderson, and the Lab School.

Affiliations.   BJE, Early Childhood Education Council, ERB, ISAAGNY, Federation of Jewish Philanthropies.

The Studio School
Ages: 10 months–14 yrs

Nonsectarian Nursery, Elementary, and Middle School

117 West 95th Street
(between Columbus and Amsterdam Avenues)
Zip: 10025
Tel: 678-2416
Website: www.studioschoolnyc.org
E-mail: info@studioschoolnyc.org

Established 1971
Janet C. Rotter,
Head of School
Jennifer Tarpley,
Director of Admissions
Nursery enrollment: 60
Total enrollment: 125

School year.   Early September to early June.

Ages	Hours	Days	Tuition
Beginners/Toddlers (10–18 mos)	9:15–10:30	Mon	$2,950
2s–nearly 2s	9:15–11:15	2, 3, 4 mornings	$7,980–$15,960
3s–nearly 3s	9:00–12:00	Tues Wed Thurs	$13,100
Early childhood/ kindergarten (3s, 4s, 5s)	8:20–12:30/3:00	Mon–Fri	$19,600–$31,500

Program.   Developmental/Progressive. Children at Studio are given ample space and time for experimentation and investigation. Believing that play is a child's work the school offers children the opportunity to make sense of their internal and external worlds and prepares students for the larger world utilizing a varied curriculum. In work period, each student has the experience of taking a project from start to finish, with a teacher's guidance. Children learn to choose and plan projects, think about what materials they want to use in the process, and enjoy seeing the results of their own handiwork. Open-ended materials are available, as well as mural paper for large pictures or group work, to stimulate and inspire students' creativity and originality. Children work with both large outdoor blocks and wooden unit blocks daily. Trips are specially arranged for them to learn more about the world, and to bring their new experiences into their work.

Other aspects of the curriculum are music, movement, physical education, reading and telling stories, natural and social sciences, art, and problem-solving. Beginning in the early childhood program, a small, mixed-age group of children learn about food and nutrition and helps to prepare lunch for the school

Admissions.   The application fee is $65. Inquiries are from mid-June on. Children are accepted throughout the year if openings are available; tuition is pro-rated to the trimester. Parents are encouraged to attend an open house or tour. Morning tours are held during the months of October, November, and December. A family interview and a group interview are arranged after an application is submitted. Preference is given to siblings of students currently enrolled in the school.

Class size.   Beginnings class has six children. The 2s and nearly-2s class has ten children, and the 3s and nearly-3s has fourteen with a teacher and an assistant in each classroom. Early childhood and kindergarten classes have sixteen children with one teacher and an assistant.

Staff.   Head classroom teachers have a master's degree in early childhood education; assistant teachers are pursuing masters. There's a learning specialist and educational facilitator and ongoing professional training and curriculum development for teachers.

Facilities.   The Studio School moved into its home at 117 West 95th Street in the fall of 2006. Some highlights of the building are spacious classrooms, a multi-media library, gymnasium, science lab, art and music studios, a kiln, a fully-equipped kitchen, and a rooftop garden.

Summer program.   The program runs from mid-June through mid-July for children ages two and up; open to children from other schools.

Separation.   Every young child receives a home visit from teachers before the new school year begins. Depending on each child's age and stage of development, a gradual plan is worked out.

Parent involvement.   Individual parent/teacher conferences are held three times each year. There are also monthly group meetings with classroom teachers and the head of each program. In addition, the head of school, Ms. Rotter, leads an ongoing bi-weekly series about children and parenting. A group of Studio parents, called Parent Connection, sponsors programs and events to welcome new parents and support returning ones. Parents are also involved in family events and fund-raising activities.

Financial.   Tuition is non-refundable and is to be paid in full by September 1st. For students admitted during the school year, tuition may be prorated to the trimester. There's a monthly payment plan and tuition assistance is available for children in kindergarten and above.

Transportation.   Children come from as far away as Brooklyn, Greenwich Village, Inwood, and the East Side, with the majority of students coming from the Upper West Side. Eligible kindergartners and elementary-grade students receive MTA MetroCards. The school will help arrange a private van or bus service.

Graduates.   Have gone on to Bard, Beacon, Bronx Science, Brooklyn Latin, Brooklyn Tech, Calhoun, Fieldston, Friends Seminary, Horace Mann, Hunter, Lab School, LaGuardia, Riverdale, Saint Ann's, School of the Future, Stuyvesant, and Trevor Day.

Chartered.   By the Board of Regents of the State University of New York.

Member.   Early Steps, ERB, ISAAGNY, NASAIS, Parent's League.

Twin Parks Park West Montessori School
(part of Twin Parks Schools)
Ages 3 mos–6 yrs

435 Central Park West
(between 103rd and
104 Streets)
Zip: 10025
Tel: 678-6072
Fax: 678-1998
Website: www.twinparks.org
E-mail: pwadmissions@twinparks.org

Dr. Kathy Roemer,
Director
Jessica Anub,
Director of Admissions
Enrollment: 150

School year. September through June. Summer program, July and
August.

Ages	Hours	Days	Tuition
3 mos–1.5 yrs	8:00–6:00	Mon–Fri°	$26,100–$28,380
2.9–5 yrs	8:00–6:00	Mon–Fri	$21,940–$24,980
1.6–2.8	8:00–6:00	Mon Wed Fri	$18,340–$19,900
1.6–2.8	8:00–6:00	Tues Thurs	$13,740–$14,920
1.6–2.8	8:30–3:30	Mon–Fri	$18,260–$20,860

Birthday cut-off is September 1st. Additional scheduling options available.
°School closes at 5 P.M. on Fridays.

Program. Developmentally based accredited Montessori program.
Twin Parks Montessori schools offer a flexible curriculum in a home-
like setting that is tailored to meet the individual needs of each
child. Activities are chosen to foster the joy of learning, as well as
cooperation. Children work at their own pace, alone, or with others.

In the infant program, babies learn by responding to gentle
touch and move freely as they interact with their environment.
Materials are displayed on low, open shelves and on floor mats, all
within reach of even the youngest child.

The toddler class focuses on trust, separation, independence,
and self-control. Toddlers learn to use verbal and non-verbal skills
to resolve social conflicts as well as to facilitate toilet training.

In the early childhood class the aim is to cultivate the child's
natural desire to learn. Children use manipulatives and are encouraged to make choices, work independently, and become capable
and confident learners. Music and physical education are sched-

uled daily; for art, children use paint, clay, paste, and colors. Although the school offers individualized instruction, cooperative learning is also encouraged.

Admissions. The application fee is $25. After a completed application is received, the director of admissions will call to schedule an appointment to tour classes and discuss the program. There is a meeting/interview for three- and four-year-old applicants.

Class size. Infant classes have eight children, toddler classes have twelve children, and early childhood classes have up to twenty children. The teacher to child ratio is 1:3 for infants; 1:4 for toddlers, and 1:7 for early childhood.

Facilities. Twin Parks schools are located directly across the street from Central Park and Riverside Park which the children use for outdoor playtime. Each school also has an indoor gym(s).

Summer program. There is a summer program during July and August.

Separation. During the first week of school, parents/caregivers are expected to remain nearby until their child has adjusted comfortably.

Parent involvement. Parents are invited to read in the classrooms and share their skills and family traditions and attend field trips. A "peek-at-the-week" is posted on the website weekly to keep parents informed of the events of the week. There are two parent/teacher conferences each year. Social events include pot-luck dinners, PJ night, coffee chats, parent education nights, grandparents day, and pick-up-in-the-park days. Parents Voice, made up of parent representatives from each class, meets monthly with the director.

Financial. There is a $500 nonrefundable annual tuition deposit, which also serves as a materials fee. Quarterly payment schedules are available.

Transportation. No private bus service is available.

Graduates.   Have gone on to public school gifted and talented programs and independent schools.

Affiliation.   AMS, Middle States Commission on Elementary Schools, NYAIS, and are affiliate schools of Columbia University.

West Side Preschool
Ages: 2.9–4.9 yrs

Teacher–parent cooperative

165 W. 105th Street	Established 1988
Zip: 10025	Denise LaMagna,
Tel: 749-4635	Director
Website: westsidepreschoolny.org	Enrollment: 30

School year.   Monday after Labor Day through third week in June. No summer school.

Ages	Hours	Days	Tuition
2.9–4.8	9:00–1:00	Mon–Fri°	$12,582
2.9–4.8	9:00–3:15	Mon–Thurs	$15,578

°Includes one afternoon to 3:30.

Program.   Developmental/Eclectic. The curriculum is play-based, but balances planned activities and free play, which encourage independent thinking. The mixed-age group setting is intended to allow children to work in small groups where peer education, social learning, problem-solving strategies, and cooperative learning may take place.

Admissions.   There is an application fee of $35. Parents can sign up for a school tour on the school's website, as well as download an application. Parents can tour before applying. The application deadline is mid-January, but may vary slightly each year. Interviews are held during the fall and winter. Tours last about one hour, and are only for parents and are held in the morning. Acceptances are sent according to ISAAGNY guidelines.

Class size/Staff.   There are places for fifteen 3s and fifteen 4s and some 5s. Many children remain in the school for two or three years. Director, Denise La Magna, holds a master's degrees in early childhood education as does the class teacher. There are four assistant teachers in the classroom. There's also a weekly music specialist.

Facilities.   The classroom is bright and spacious and has a high ceiling, walls with low banks of shelves and cubby-holes, as well as appropriate furniture. Children's artwork and projects decorate the walls. Special areas in the classroom contain a sand table, water table, painting, blocks, and library, and are well organized as well as rich in materials. Dramatic play is also encouraged. Directly across the street is a newly refurbished playground where the children go every morning (weather permitting). Otherwise, children meet on the third floor in the gym (a basketball court), which is stocked with balls, hoops, building blocks, wagons, and a trampoline.

Separation.   Children are introduced to school over a one-week individualized phasing-in schedule.

Parent involvement.   Parents assist in fund-raising, and volunteer for school activities, such as pot luck dinners, street fairs, school tours, the auction.

Financial.   Tuition is paid monthly through December. At this time, no financial aid is available.

Transportation.   Many children come from a twenty to twenty-five block radius and are brought by a parent or caregiver; others take a bus, or train.

Graduates.   Children have gone on to Bank Street, Cathedral, Columbia Grammar and Prep, Dwight, Ethical Culture, St. Hilda's & St. Hugh's, The School at Columbia, Riverdale, Manhattan Country, and local public schools gifted and talented programs, and Hunter.

Member.   ISAAGNY, ERB.

West Side Family Preschool
Ages: 18 mos–5 yrs

Nonsectarian Nursery School

63 West 92nd Street (between
  Central Park West and
  Columbus Avenue)
Zip: 10025
Tel: 316-2424
Fax: 932-8265
Website: www.westsidefamilypreschool.com
E-mail: westsidefamilypreschool@gmail.com

Established 1987
Elaine Rosner–Jeria,
Director
Enrollment: 30

School year. September through August.

Ages	Hours	Days	Tuition (monthly)
all ages	8–6	Mon–Fri	$1,075–$1,895

7:30 A.M. drop off by request; modified two- or three-day-a-week, half- or full-time schedules, including half-day afternoons are available for a lower fee, check website or e-mail.

Program. Developmental. The school hopes to serve as an extended family. The program is multicultural and includes small group work with children of the same age, as well as mixed-age activities. There are four small groups and hands-on learning is encouraged. Activities centers include a library and reading area. There are small play objects, musical instruments, dramatic play, puppetry, large hollow blocks, arts, cooking, singing, movement, biking and sand and water play.

Music and art classes are available in the afternoons on weekdays. Weekend classes are available at an additional fee.

Admissions. The application fee is $35. Inquire at any time, admissions are ongoing. Parents may fill out an application online, then may arrange to tour the school. Children visit at another time. Check website for specific dates for Open Houses.

Class size. The school is designed to accommodate twenty-seven children at any one time. One large mixed-age group of 10 to 14 is divided appropriately by age for small group activities.

Staff.   Staff members have backgrounds in early childhood education, as well as in theater, dance, art, and music. All staff members have a working knowledge of Spanish.

Facilities.   Housed on the ground floor of a brownstone, the center has a kitchen and a sunken, closed sandbox. The rooms have been designed around the children's activities centers. Snacks are provided; children bring their lunches.

Summer program.   A summer program runs through the week before Labor Day. The monthly cost is the same as the regular program for enrolled students.

Parent involvement.   Parents are encouraged to participate on school committees, help with fund-raising and in the classroom, join in special projects, and accompany the children on field trips. Conferences are twice yearly and whenever staff or parents feel the need. Parents visit by appointment.

Financial.   There is an annual registration fee of $500 per child. Contracts are generally for ten or twelve months. A deposit equal to one month's tuition plus an annual materials fee is required on registration, and tuition is payable monthly prior to the next month. Financial aid is available on a limited basis.

Member.   Early Childhood Education Council. Proprietorship.

West Side Montessori School
Ages 2.10–6 yrs

Nonsectarian Montessori Early
Childhood School and Kindergarten

309 West 92nd Street
  (between Riverside Drive
  and West End Avenue)
Zip: 10025
Tel: 662-8000
Fax: 662-8323
Website: www.wsms.org
E-mail: sday@wsmsnyc.org

Established 1963
Mimi Basso,
Head of School
Suzanne Day,
Admissions Director
Enrollment: 210

School year.   September through June.

Ages	Hours	Days	Tuition
3–6	8:30–12:30	Mon–Fri	$19,784
3–6	1:00–5:00	Mon–Fri	$19,784
3–6	9:00–3:00 (12:30 Fri)	Mon–Fri	$24,480
3–6	8:30–5:30	Mon–Fri	$30,240

Children must be 3 by November 1st.

Extended hours.   Children may arrive at 8:00 and leave at 6:00, at an additional cost.

Program.   Montessori. The school was founded in 1963 by five West Side families and a Montessori teacher. The multicredentialed Head of School, Mimi Basso, greets children every day and spends time in each classroom regularly.

In addition to Montessori activities, the classrooms are richly equipped with open-ended materials such as blocks, Legos, and dramatic play items. Their aim is to support each child's development in reading, math, science, the arts, and, most important, problem-solving strategies. Classroom practices include mixed-age groupings, hands-on active learning, valuing teacher observations and classroom research, and the careful design of the environment and materials. They expose children to a wide range of developmentally appropriate intellectual, physical, and social activities. Their goal is to create communities in which "everyone learns, works/plays, shares, has fun, and celebrates together."

ERBs are given on the premises, and admissions directors from ongoing schools visit the classrooms each year. Parents meetings are held on "exmissions," with multiple workshops and meetings.

Admissions.   Applications are available on the school's website. There are four steps to the admissions process: First, parents must submit an application. Second, they observe a classroom and attend an information session. Third, they meet with a member of the admissions committee, and fourth, the child visits the school, typically on a Saturday morning in December, January, or February.

The head of school hosts several evening open houses. It is not necessary to submit an application before attending an open house.

The deadline for applications is early January, and notifications are sent in March, according to ISAAGNY guidelines.

Class size.   There are up to 22 children per classroom. Each classroom has two or three teachers, at least one of whom is NYS-certified and Montessori-certified. Student teachers are from WSMS-TEP, the school's Montessori accredited teacher education program.

Staff.   Two social workers or psychologists are available to parents and teachers on a daily basis. Student teachers from New York University, various Montessori teacher education programs, and Teachers College assist. Movement and nature specialists work with the children on a scheduled basis. There are extensive professional development opportunities for the staff. Head of School Marlene Barron is head of NYU's Montessori teacher-education program and co-director of the school's accredited Montessori teacher-education program (WSMS-TEP).

WSM has five programs for staff development: there's a tuition grant of $1,500 yearly toward credit-bearing courses, free credits at NYU, a study/travel grant for $2,500 for teachers who have taught at the school for five years, a $150 cultural fund allowance and funds for workshops, and conferences on education.

Facilities.   A six-story air conditioned, renovated townhouse. The spacious classrooms, running the length of the building, have large windows at the front and back. There is also an institutional kitchen, staff lounge, a variety of small meeting rooms, an informal Parents Room, and administrative offices. The school is "very vertical"; there are no elevators. A well-equipped gym occupies the entire sixth floor. The building is topped by a rooftop play area.

The school provides lunch or supper for a fee or children may bring their own. Lunch/supper is eaten in the classroom.

Summer program.   There is an optional 8-week program.

Separation.   In the fall, families visit the school and meet the teacher before school begins. Teachers also make a home visit before the child begins school. Returning children begin classes earlier; new children attend shortened sessions during their first week. Parents or caregivers stay as long as necessary.

Parent involvement.   The parent body is very diverse; although most families live on the Upper West Side, some families live on the East Side or in Brooklyn, the Bronx, Queens and, some years, New Jersey. The school is a dynamic, interactive bustle of adult/child, parent/teacher, social/educational, formal/informal happenings. Activities range from evening workshops led by a social worker, to class events, such as early morning breakfasts, to family weekend events. Many West Side Montessori School parents are "super-volunteers." Parents are encouraged to involve themselves in their child's school life by participating in events as their time allows. Every year the Parents Association raises significant monies for the WSMS Financial Aid Fund—through the child-oriented street fair (the Saturday before Mother's Day), auction, and other smaller events.

Financial.   Twenty percent of the children enrolled receive tuition assistance either from the WSMS Financial Aid Fund or from the Agency for Children's Services (ACS).

Graduates.   Graduates attend over 38 different independent schools and various public schools including multiple gifted and talented programs.

Chartered.   By the Board of Regents of the State University of New York.

Members.   ACS, AMS, ERB, ISAAGNY, NAIS, NYSAIS, Early Steps, Middle States Association of Colleges and Elementary Schools.

West Side YMCA Co-op Nursery School
Ages 2.5–5 yrs

Nonsectarian

5 West 63rd Street (between
  Central Park West and
  Broadway)
Zip: 10023
Tel: 912-2652
E-mail: bsieling@ymcanyc.org;
arobarge@ymcanyc.org; scussen@ymcanyc.org

Established 1967
Shannon Cussen,
  Director
Abbey Robarge and Bridget Sieling,
  Admissions Directors
Enrollment: 130

School year.   Mid-September through early June. Summer program available from June through August (Kinder Camp).

Ages	Hours	Days	Tuition
2s	9:00–11:45/ 1:15–4:00	Tues Thurs/ Mon Wed Fri	$9,000–$10,500
3s/4s	9:00–12:00/ 1:00–4:00	Mon Wed Fri Mon–Fri	$10,500–15,000
4s	9:00–2:00	Mon–Fri	$17,000

Program.   The school would prefer to be known as "play-based," not "traditional," despite its emphasis on skills development. Children explore many areas of study in an informal way. Much attention is paid to social development. Activities include block building, dramatic play, sand and water play, cooking, storytime, manipulatives, art, music, and science. Children have access to the facilities at the YMCA which include weekly swim classes. Many classes use Central Park for outdoor playtime as an important resource for learning. Group problem solving, collaborative work, and critical thinking skills are emphasized. Teachers work with children individually in various skills areas, evaluating their current level and trying to improve their skills. In prekindergarten children begin more formal work in reading, math, and social studies. Careful records are kept of their progress.

ERB testing is offered on site to enrolled students at the nursery school.

Admissions.   The application fee is $65. Inquiries are from September on. During October and November parents may tour the school before submitting an application. After applying, children are seen in January and February in small play-groups with the admissions director, a teacher, and one parent present. The school is interested in finding families who will enjoy the cooperative and make a strong contribution to the school. Notifications are sent according to ISAAGNY guidelines, with optional early notification for siblings and legacies.

Class size.   There are three 2s classes of 12 children, three 3s classes of 12–16 children, a 3s/4s class with 16 children and two 4s classes with 18 children. Each class has two to three staff members and a daily "helping parent" volunteer.

Staff.   All teachers are licensed with most holding advanced degrees. Specialists in science, music, swimming, and creative movement, and gym work with the children. Two social workers are also available.

There are three staff development training days as well as regular weekly staff meetings at which the director meets with the teaching teams and the children are discussed in depth.

Facilities.   The classrooms are spotlessly maintained by the Y, and special classroom maintenance is done by parents as well. Parents bring children directly to their classrooms.

The Co-op Nursery is located in a renovated building adjacent to the original West Side YMCA. The nursery is accessible through a security-coded, stroller-friendly entryway. The classrooms are bright and sun-filled, with one classroom on the ground floor, and five more classrooms on the third floor. The children use the Y's pool; the 4th floor gym; additional facilities include a rooftop playground, a newly renovated indoor playspace, a library/resource room, and a family lounge. Large rooms are available for parent meetings and special events.

Summer program.   Kinder Camp serves children 3.6–6 years of age during the months of June, July, and August. The camp program includes swimming, sports, arts and crafts, and weekly trips. There is a registration process and additional fees are required. All campers must be fully toilet-trained.

Separation.   Both teachers visit each child before school begins. A schedule of short, staggered sessions for small groups lasts about two weeks. Much attention is paid to easing into separation. An orientation evening for parents is scheduled before the start of the school year to introduce parents to each classroom's procedures.

Parent involvement.   The director notes that the co-op aspects of the school provides a strong sense of community, and that parents have the opportunity to learn about their children in a new way, and often develop new parenting skills.

Parents must contribute time to committees such as fundraising and playground. They also participate in the classroom on a rotating basis, provide regular help with field trips and swimming, and initiate special classroom projects. Their attendance is required at several meetings per year, including "curriculum night" and a "helping parent" training session. Parents serve on the school's executive committee. Conferences are held twice a year.

Financial.   A deposit is due on signing the contract; tuition is payable in June, September, and November. Need-based financial aid is available.

Transportation.   Children come mostly from the West Side between 48th and 96th Streets. No bus service is available.

Graduates.   Have gone on to independent and public schools, with about one-half of the children choosing private schools such as Allen-Stevenson, Calhoun, Cathedral, Dalton, Ethical Culture, and Spence.

Affiliations.   YMCA. Chartered by the Board of Regents of the State University of New York.

Member.   ERB, ISAAGNY.

Tender Care
(at the Westside YMCA)
Ages: 6 mos–5 yrs

5 West 63rd Street
Zip: 10023
Tel: 912-2652
Website: www.ymcanyc.org/westside
E-mail: arobarge@ymcanyc.org
scussen@ymcanyc.org; bsieling@ymcanyc.org

Shannon Cussen,
Director
Admissions Director
Enrollment: 85

School year.   Twelve-month program.

Ages	Hours	Days	Tuition (monthly)
6 mos–2.6 yrs	8:00–6:00	Mon–Fri	$1,900
2.6–5 yrs	8:00–6:00	Mon–Fri	$1,500–$1,800

Flexible days and half days available.

Program: Tender Care is a child care center which provides a safe, nurturing, and challenging learning environment for young children. The emphasis of this program is on social development with

216

skill development attended to through the use of open-ended, creative materials, and age-appropriate, organized activities. Specials include music, movement, science, and swimming for the older children. There are five bright spacious classrooms on the second floor of the new McBurney Annex of the West Side YMCA.

Admissions: Parents call for an application and are given a small group tour of the facilities. After the application is received, the child's name will be placed on a waiting list and the parent will be contacted as soon as there is an available space in the program. (There are periods throughout the year when applications will not be provided because of the length of the waiting list.) Applications are typically available from late September through mid-January.

Woodside Preschool
The Early Years Program of the Dwight School
Ages: 2–5 yrs
Nonsectarian

144 Riverside Boulevard

Zip: 10069

Tel: (212) 362-2350

Fax: (212) 362-2377

Website: www.woodsidepreschool.org

E-Mail: admissions@woodsidepreschool.org

    rmiller@woodsidepreschool.org;

    callen@woodsidepreschool.org

Established 2005

Rochelle Miller,

Director

Chris Allen,

Admissions Director

Enrollment: 235

School year. Early September through early June. Summer program from mid-June through mid-July.

Ages	Hours	Days	Tuition
2s	8:45–11:30 or 12:30-2:30	2,3, or 4 days	$12,300–$15,600
3s	8:30–11:30, 12:30-3:30, or 8:30-2:30	Mon–Fri	$21,400–$27,900
4s	8:30–2:30	Mon–Fri	$27,900

Program.   Developmental. Woodside program promotes the emotional development of children in order to develop a strong sense of self-esteem. A team of highly qualified teachers who are trained in early childhood development apply the best techniques within a nurturing environment. The Primary Years Program (PYP) of the International Baccalaureate to teach the children in a fun, playful environment utilizing the best of traditional and inquiry based methodologies.

Admissions.   Woodside Preschool follows the guidelines set forth by the Independent Schools Admissions Association of Greater New York (ISAAGNY). Applications are accepted beginning the day after Labor Day of the year prior to the desired enrollment. The deadline for application submissions is posted on the website. After applications are received, the families will complete the admissions process by attending an Open House, a parent interview, and a child school visit.

Class size.   The 2s classes have groups of 10–12 children with 2–3 classroom teachers. The 3s classes have a group size of 14–15 children with 2–3 teachers. The 4s classes have 16–18 children with 2–3 teachers

Staff.   All head teachers, as well as many assistant teachers, at Woodside Preschool have advanced degrees in early childhood education or related fields. Additionally, there is a strong team of specialist teachers that includes music, art, Chinese, Spanish, physical education, as well as a staff psychologist and a consulting occupational therapist.

Facilities.   Woodside Preschool is situated off the Hudson River on Riverside Boulevard between West 66th and West 68th Streets. Woodside is a state-of-the-art facility designed by a team of experienced, international educators and architects. The buildings are comprised of bright, spacious classrooms with an enriching and nurturing environment for children. There are two indoor gyms, a library, and a wonderful playground in nearby Riverside Park.

Summer program.   During the Summer Discovery Program, designed for children ages three through five, children have the opportunity to take part in a range of sports, arts, and creative activities. The program offers a warm, nurturing environment for students while emphasizing fun and friendship. Each week features a special theme and children enjoy both indoor and outdoor activities in fully air-conditioned facilities and nearby Riverside Park. All programs are led by the school's experiences and enthusiastic teachers.

Afterschool program.　The Woodside Jr. Passport After-School Program is designed for students ages three to six to help students develop their abilities and talents in a variety of activities, as well as broaden their interests, build their self-esteem, cultivate their imagination, and reinforce what they have learned in their daily school program. The classes occur at the end of the school day and are also open to children who are not enrolled at Woodside Preschool.

Classes include drama, music, art, dance, yoga, soccer, ballet, foreign languages, cooking, and golf. The classes, which are offered weekly, are taught by a very talented and experienced group of teachers from the Woodside Preschool and organizations such as Super Soccer Stars, Drama Zone, Yogi Beans, and Urban Golf Academy.

Separation.　Home Visits are offered for all those entering the 2s program. This allows children to meet and develop a rapport with his/her new teacher in familiar surroundings. The school year begins with a gradual separation and a phase-in schedule, working up to a full session over the course of a few weeks. Children entering the 3s and 4s programs are invited to visit the class and meet their teachers prior to the beginning of school. Home visits may be organized upon request. For 3s and 4s, phasing into the full school day takes place gradually over the course of one week.

Parent involvement.　Woodside parents are a great resource in supporting and extending the curriculum and community. The Parents Association (PA) works to further communication between parents, teachers, and administrators. The PA brings the community together to participate in events like a book fair, toy drive, food drive, clothing sale, Spirit Day, and Spring Fair.

Financial.　A $5,000 non-refundable deposit is due upon signing the contract. The remaining balance can be paid in either one payment (due July 1st) or two payments (due July 1st and December 1st). Scholarships are available based upon financial need and will be re-evaluated annually.

Transportation.   Transportation is not provided by the preschool. There are several subway and bus stops located within walking distance of the school.

Graduates.   A large percentage of the preschool students continue onto the Dwight School. Some of the other schools graduates attend include: Buckley, Chapin. Dalton, Ethical Culture, Fieldston Lower, Horace Mann, Nightingale, Riverdale, and Trinity as well as local public schools and gifted and talented programs.

Affiliations.   The Dwight School.

Member.   ERB, Parent's League, ISAAGNY, NYSAIS, IBO.

Yaldaynu Center
Ages: 2–5 yrs

A Jewish Preschool

251 West 100th Street (corner of West End Avenue)
Zip: 10025
Tel: 866-4993
Fax: 866-1346
Website: www.yaldaynu.org

Established 1981
Elaine Anshen Bloom, Director
Enrollment: 50

School year.   Ten-month program. School is closed in August.

Ages	Hours	Days	Tuition
2s/young 3s	8:45–12:15	2 or 3 days	$5,025–$7,475
3s/young 4s	8:30–12:30	3, 4 or 5 days	$9,990–$14,900
4s/5s	8:30–12:30	5 days	$14,900

Afterschool enrichment or extended hours and other groups are available for an additional fee until 2:30.

Program.   Developmentally oriented. According to the director, "We offer challenging activities, but no child is pushed." Activities include block building, sand and water play, music, cooking, storytelling, dictation, art, vigorous outdoor play, and play with puzzles and small play objects.

Jewish holidays and Shabbat are celebrated.

Admissions. The application fee is $100. Inquiries may be made in the fall and winter. Group tours are offered in November and December. Children come for a small play group in January and February. Acceptances are sent in March.

Class size. Ranges from 12 to 17 children with three teachers in each classroom. A social worker is available regularly.

Facilities. The center occupies two rooms on the second and third floor of Temple Ansche Chesed. Children use the rooftop play area, equipped with a sandbox and climbing and riding toys. There is access to an indoor playroom for games in inclement weather.

Separation. A parent or caregiver is expected to be available during a phasing-in period which is both gradual and individual.

Parent involvement. Parents are welcome to participate in the class-room. The parents association is active and enthusiastic, and the board consists of parents. Conferences are arranged twice yearly; others are arranged as needed. Family events are planned.

Financial. There is a deposit of $2,000 on signing the contract. Tuition is payable semiannually in May and December. Financial aid is available.

Graduates. Have gone on to a variety of private and public schools, including Bank Street, Beit Rabban, Calhoun, Ethical Culture, Heschel, Manhattan Country, Ramaz, Rodeph Sholom, and Trinity.

Affiliations. ISAAGNY, ERB, BJE, Jewish Board of Family & Children's Services.

UPTOWN

A.C.T. Program at the Cathedral Church of Saint John the Divine

Ages: 2.3–5 yrs

Nonsectarian

1047 Amsterdam Avenue (112th Street)
Zip: 10025
Tel: (212) 316-7530
Fax: (212) 316-7407
Website: www.actprograms.org

Established 1971
Jose V. Torres, MSW,
Executive Director
Marie Del Tejo,
Director of Programs
Enrollment: 62

School year.   Early September through early June.

Ages	Hours	Days	Tuition
2.3–3.3	9:30–12:00	Tues Thurs	$3,655
2.9–4.0	9:00–12:30	Mon Wed Fri	$6,710
3.5–5.0	12:30–3:30	Mon–Fri	$1,500
3.5–5.0	8:30–2:30	Mon–Fri	$10,880

Extended hours: separate registration for aftercare program for the full-time preschoolers until 6:15 P.M. is available for additional cost.

Program.   Child-Centered. Children learn to master basic school skills and rituals. Academic readiness is pursued in a relaxed atmosphere of play that is effective in early learning. Teachers use the ACT outdoor garden as well as indoor growth tables when developing Natural Science lesson plans. Preschoolers help harvest the garden in the fall, clear it for winter, and plant new seeds for spring. The power and usefulness of the written word and number are experienced firsthand. Throughout each day, children's discoveries, thoughts, and insights are recorded. Graphs and charts provide chances to predict, compare, count, and measure. Printed words and pictures are seen throughout the class. It is our mission to prepare children for a successful road into kindergarten. Children perform at assemblies, parents are invited to family dinners and classes collaborate in theme activities.

Facilities.   The location on The Cathedral Church of Saint John the Divine's 11 idyllic acres makes a unique environment for preschoolers. Children remain on the grounds when observing and identifying the changes of the seasons, animal activities, as well as using the fully equipped playground. During the winter months, children use one of two full size gyms equipped with indoor climbing equipment, slides, and tricycles. There is a kitchenette designed for children to work on cooking projects as well as have their snack or lunch.

Separation. Teachers work with each family individually to help ease the home-to-school transition.

Staff. Head teachers are Board of Education certified and most hold a master's degree. Most staff is CPR/first-aid certified. Talented teachers share their artistic and musical talent as well as attend educational workshops and conferences each year to keep informed of new educational techniques and materials.

Admissions. There is no application fee. Inquire at any time. Monthly tours are offered September through January. Priority registration is offered to currently enrolled families in the fall, and open enrollment to the general public in January. Committed to a first come, first served admissions policy, A.C.T. accepts registrations until classes are full. Plan to come for a group tour. Parents are welcome to arrange an in-class visit before signing up. Testing is not required. Registration fees are not refundable.

Financial Aid. There is limited financial aid used to promote economic diversity and only applies to part-time and full-time preschool candidates. Awards are made on a first come, first served basis; the registration fee ranges from $750 to $1,430.

Graduates. Children have gone onto The Cathedral School, Hunter Elementary, Columbia University's The School, Bankstreet, and other neighboring private schools as well as neighboring gifted and talented public schools, public charter schools, and neighboring public schools. The director of programs assists parents individually with the ongoing school process.

Bank Street Family Center

Ages: 6 mos–4.9 yrs

Nonsectarian All-Day Care

610 West 112th Street (between
  Broadway and Riverside Drive)
Zip: 10025
Admissions Tel: 875-4412
Centerbased Early Intervention
  and CPSE° Tel: 875-4418
Homebased Early Intervention
  and SEIT
Tel: 875-4418/4714
Fax: 875-4759
Website: www.bankstreet.edu
Click on Family Center link.

Alexis Wright,
  Dean of Children's Programs
Mary Ellen Markman,
  Director/Admissions
Heather Prine-Clarke,
  Special Education Centerbased
Murray Kelley, Judith Gentry,
  Takima Levine,
  Homebased Early Intervention
  and SEIT
Enrollment: approximately 45

School year. September through July.

Ages	Hours	Days	Tuition
All	8:00–6:00	Mon–Fri	$30,000

Tuition is pro-rated for 2, 3, or 4 days.

Program. Developmental/interactive. The Family Center is not formally a part of The Bank Street School for Children, although there are overlapping programs, personnel, and history. The Family Center and the School for Children make up the Children's Programs within the Bank Street College of Education. The Family Center is designed to provide developmentally oriented, culturally sensitive day care, and support for families with children six months to four years. The philosophy, and therefore the curriculum, is based on their understanding of how young children learn best. A critical component of the program is providing the opportunity to explore the diversity of the community. Families with alternative lifestyles will feel comfortable here. Family members are encouraged to visit and participate throughout the day. The Family Center strives to create a welcoming, homelike environment to ensure that both children and adults feel comfortable.

Special education services. The Family Center also provides early

---

°Committee on Preschool Special Education

intervention, preschool special education, and evaluation services. Children with developmental delays or disabilities are integrated into the classroom. Children with special needs are provided with all appropriate therapeutic services and transportation. In addition, the Family Center provides home and community-based special education services and evaluations. All approved special education services are funded by the New York State Department of Education and Department of Health.

Admissions. The application fee is $60. Call in September or go online for an application; submit it promptly. Open houses are held in November, December, and January. Interviews with the director are held in January and February. Notifications for the general education program are sent typically in late February. Play sessions are held in March for children applying to the special education program. Admittance to the special education program is based on approval by the Early Intervention System (EIS) or the Committee on Preschool Special Education (CPSE).

Class size. There are four classrooms. Two are mixed-aged groups of children that range from 2.9 to 5 years old. Children in the Special Education Program range in age from 6 months to 4.9 years in September of the year of admittance.

Staff. Each room has a head teacher, assistant teacher, interns, and student teachers. There is a music teacher, a librarian, and a nurse all available through the Bank Street School for Children.

Facilities. The Family Center is located in the main building of the Bank Street College of Education. It has four fully equipped classrooms with kitchenettes and bathrooms for infant and toddler needs. There are indoor and outdoor play spaces and a library. Individual rooms are available for therapeutic services and napping.

Separation. There is a gradual phase-in process at the beginning of each school year, and the first-week schedule is abbreviated. Parents or others close to the child are expected to take part in the phase-in process.

Parent involvement. Parents are expected to participate on the varying committees and take part in fund-raising events. The director says, "We're here as a support and a resource for parents, and they stay in constant touch with us. We're an extension of the family, and we feel strongly that developing partnerships with families is essential to providing quality childcare and education for all children." In addition to daily conversations and written communications, parents and staff meet at least three to five times a year to discuss such issues as siblings, discipline, anti-bias education, etc. Conferences are arranged twice yearly or as needed.

Financial.   A $1,500 deposit is requested depending on schedule and financial aid. A monthly payment plan is optional. Limited scholarship assistance is available.

Transportation.   Transportation is available for children in the special education program.

Graduates.   Graduates go on to a variety of programs, other independent schools as well as public pre-K and kindergarten programs, including Bank Street. However, the Family Center operates independently of the Bank Street School for Children and you must apply separately to each; admission is not automatic.

Affiliations.   Bank Street College of Education—Children's Program. Bank Street College graduate students and Liberty Partnership teenagers observe and work with children at the Family Center as part of their professional training.

Bank Street School for Children
Ages: Nursery 3s–8th grade

Nonsectarian Nursery and Elementary School

610 West 112th Street
(between Broadway
and Riverside Drive)
Zip: 10025
Tel: 875-4420
Admissions tel: 875-4433
Website: www.bankstreet.edu

Established in 1918
Alexis Wright,
Dean of Children's Programs
Marcia Roesch,
Director of Admissions
Nursery and Kindergarten
Enrollment: approximately 100
Total Enrollment: approximately 430

School year. September through early June.

Ages	Hours	Days	Tuition
3s half day	8:45–11:45	Mon–Thurs, Fri until 1:00	$33,550
full day	8:45–3:00	Mon–Thurs, Fri until 1:00	$34,385
4s	8:45–3:00	Mon–Thurs, Fri until 1:00	$34,385
5s	8:45–3:00	Mon–Thurs, Fri until 1:00	$34,385

Applicants must be 3 by September 1st.

Extended hours. Full-day children, age 4 years and older, may join the after-school program, "Kids Club" which meets Monday through Friday from 3:00 to 6:00. A session on Friday, 1:00 to 6:00, is available for an additional fee.

Program. Bank Street, a progressive school, has had a profound effect on American education. The school's history is closely connected with the development of this approach. In 1916, Lucy Sprague Mitchell founded the Bureau of Educational Experiments to conduct research into child development. In 1918, the bureau opened its own nursery. It later found a home on Bank Street, expanded its nursery to an elementary school, and took a new name, the Cooperative School for Teachers. In 1950 it was renamed the Bank Street College of Education. The College and the School for Children moved to the Upper West Side in 1970. Bank Street

230

College helped design the national Head Start program and create guidelines for Title IV of the Civil Rights Act of 1965. Its research division is an Early Childhood Education and Research Center for the federal government's Office of Economic Opportunity.

Monitoring the work of New York's Associated Progressive Schools and incorporating the research of psychologists such as Piaget and Anna Freud, the bureau evolved the developmental-interaction approach, now sometimes called "the Bank Street approach." Considered revolutionary in the 1920s, this approach gained broad acceptance. Basically, the child's development is seen as a complex process. The progressive approach recognizes and values each child's unique learning style. Most basic is its conviction that young children learn by doing, and that their most important activity is free-choice play.

Play is seen as each child's method for exploring and integrating his or her rapidly expanding knowledge of properties, connections, and relationships, social experience, notions about reality, and the inner world of fantasy and feeling. Children are not seen as receivers of a curriculum determined by adults, but as discoverers of the value and meaning of their own activities, and as people with strong agendas of their own.

In a Bank Street classroom children are given materials that are flexible and open-ended, able to be used in a variety of ways. The staples are blocks, water, sand, and clay. Generous amounts of work/play time allow the child to choose the kind of play, how it will proceed, where it will lead, when it will stop, and what it will include or exclude. It is the teacher's role to understand the implications of the child's play and to facilitate it.

The core of the Bank Street developmental-interaction curriculum is called social studies (not to be confused with the high-school variety) and is firmly rooted in the child's experience. That is, through various activities, the child explores his or her own experiences of self, family, and neighborhood, re-creating and dramatizing these discoveries through block building, the arts, dramatic play, and other media. A visit to a firehouse may be examined by talking about it, dictating a story about it, drawing a picture, constructing a replica in blocks, or playing firehouse.

The curriculum responds to and includes the children's interests and daily experiences. Reading, writing, and math are seen as part of the process of finding, organizing, recording, and communicating information. Science and math are presented as methods of inquiry. Music and the arts are also emphasized.

Children's responses to one another are a vital part of the curriculum, and classroom activities are arranged to facilitate these. Children will construct elaborate buildings in teams, learning to plan, to negotiate, to make decisions, to do research, to compromise, and to work cooperatively on projects.

One 4/5s class, for instance, decides to do a "study" of shoes. They dictate to the teacher a list of various kinds of shoes. Some children are making, and attaching to a chart, cards describing how their shoes opened or closed, with velcro and shoelaces. In one corner of the classroom others set up a shoe store, using their shoes as stock, and busily wait on customers. One child is carefully copying out the word "velcro" for her chart card. Others trace their shoe sizes.

In the developmental-interaction classroom, important work centers around block building. Blocks are seen as remarkably versatile and vital. And they are the major focus for social studies work. By the age of 5, children's dramatic play with blocks is intricate and sophisticated. They have progressed from creating patterns and simple structures, to creating whole cities that mirror their understanding of the world. The cities remain up for a full week or more and become the focus of other activities, such as making signs or props for the buildings, or taking field trips to research and observe. Work with blocks continues until the 6s/7s.

Admissions. The application fee is $60. Inquiries should be made from September on. The application deadline is mid-November for all ages through 6. Since there are a limited number of spaces at each grade level, the admissions office cannot always process all applications received by the deadline.

Once the application has been submitted, the school will arrange an interview for the child. Parent interviews are scheduled after this. Notifications are sent according to ISAAGNY deadlines.

Class size. There is one 3s class of sixteen children, two 4/5s classes of about twenty-one children each, and two 5/6s with about twenty-three children each. The 3s have three teachers, and a part-time graduate student. Older children have two teachers and one or two graduate students. Classes frequently divide in half for specials, including music (they use Orff instruments), movement, gym, or visits to the library. An art specialist visits once a week, and the Spanish teacher is in each lower school classroom several times a week.

Staff. The lower school coordinator observes classroom teachers at work and meets with them weekly. The classroom teachers, in turn, supervise assistant teachers who are Bank Street graduate students and student teachers who work with them. Parent conferences are held twice a year in fall and spring; written reports are sent in as well.

Summer program. Extended day, holiday, and summer day camp programs are open to the community.

Facilities. The lower school, 3s through 5/6s, is housed on the second floor of the college's handsome, modern building, constructed in 1970. Spacious classrooms with indirect lighting line either side of a wide corridor, often used as additional work space. Puzzles, games, small play objects; books, blocks, woodworking, and cooking equipment; art materials and natural objects; and pets fill up low shelves. Sand and water tables are popular. The block building space is large, and the constructions are impressive. Ceilings are sound-proofed. Sinks and toilets are child-sized. The school is well designed and beautifully maintained. The inner classrooms look out to an extremely large, safety-surfaced play terrace, and their doors open out onto it. It is full of large, hollow building blocks and planks for constructions, as well as a high wooden climbing apparatus.

Lower school children bring their lunches and eat them in their classrooms.

Separation. Separation is considered part of the curriculum, and parents will need to commit themselves to the phase-in process. The school believes that even children who may have been in child care from birth will be confronting separation issues in a new way when they enter school as 3s.

Parent involvement. There is an active Parents Association and parents are encouraged to participate in fund-raising, organizing lectures, and to join school committees. Scheduled parent visits related to the curriculum and contributions to the classrooms are welcome.

Financial. 33 percent of the student body receives tuition assistance.

Affiliations. Bank Street College of Education.

Member. ERB, ISAAGNY.

Barnard College Center for Toddler Development

Ages: 1.7–3.0 yrs

Nonsectarian Nursery and Pre-Nursery Program

3009 Broadway
  (at 120th Street)
Zip: 10027-6598
Tel: 854-8271
E-mail: tklein@barnard.edu
Website: www.barnard.edu/toddlers

Established 1973
Dr. Tovah P. Klein,
Director
Patricia Shimm,
Associate Director
Enrollment: 48

School year. September through April. Spring program: May–June.

Ages	Hours	Days	Tuition
1.7–2.5	9:30–11:45	2 mornings or 1 afternoon	$4,500–$7,500
2.6–3.0	1:30–3:45	2 afternoons	$5,000

Program. The school is affiliated with the Psychology Department at Barnard College. Director Dr. Tovah Klein is trained in psychology and Patricia Shimm, Associate Director, is an early childhood expert and author of *Parenting Your Toddler: The Expert's Guide to the Tough and Tender Years*. The school's aim is to serve the Barnard/Columbia and neighboring communities, to provide Barnard and Columbia students opportunities to observe and work with children, to conduct research in early child development, and to provide a forum for parents to discuss the development of their toddlers. The highly individualized program is based upon active learning through self-discovery. Educational experiences are adjusted to the developmental level of the child to encourage cognitive and socio-emotional development. Activities include sand and water play, puzzles and small play objects, dramatic play, musical instruments, storytime, block building, arts and crafts, and active play.

Admissions. The application fee is $40. Inquiries begin October 15. All information is online at www.barnard.edu/toddlers. Admission is based on age and gender. Preference is given to siblings and children of Barnard College and Columbia University faculty and staff. The school welcomes applications from children with developmental disabilities.

Class size.   There are two morning groups and two afternoon groups, each with twelve children and six teachers. Each class has a head teacher and five assistants. The child/teacher ratio is two or two and a half to one.

Separation.   A parent must accompany the child to the program and stay with him or her for the first month, 8 sessions.

Financial.   Parents pay a $1,500 nonrefundable deposit on signing the contract. Tuition is payable in June. Financial assistance is available.

Affiliations.   The Center is affiliated with the Barnard College Department of Psychology.

Broadway Presbyterian Church Nursery School
Ages: 2.9–4.9

Nonsectarian Nursery School

601 W. 114th Street (at Broadway)
Zip: 10025
Tel: 864–6100, ext. 130
Fax: 864-4931
Website: www.greatlittleschool.com
E-mail: admin@greatlittleschool.com

Established 1991
Amy Webb, Director
Enrollment: 20

School year.   September through early June, with a six-week summer program.

Ages	Hours	Days	Tuition
2.9–4.9	9:00–12:30	Mon–Fri	$9,255
2.9–4.9	9:00–2:30	Mon–Fri	$12,065

Applicants must be 3 years old by December 31st.

Program.   Developmental Interactive. The children are not separated by age, allowing each to reach up or down depending on ability. "We try to address where each child is developmentally." The program is very individualized and very child-directed. Play is at the heart of the curriculum. There's lots of hands-on experiences with loads of materials. Teachers are highly experienced and trained, and facilitate learning through play to build basic and problem solving skills. Outdoor play is offered daily along with yoga, cooking, music, and movement.

Admissions. There is an application fee of $40. Parents may download applications from the school's website beginning September 1st. Tours are given October through December. A second visit with the child for an interview is scheduled in January or February. Notifications are sent in early March. The school gives priority to members of the church.

Class size. Twenty places are available. The ideal class size is 18. The children are not divided by age.

Staff. The Director and Head Teacher hold master's degrees in early childhood education. Assistant teachers hold a bachelor's degree and are working toward a master's in early childhood. The school also trains intern teachers from local colleges. There are extensive professional development opportunities for all staff.

Facilities. Housed on the second floor of Broadway Presbyterian Church. There is a large, open classroom arranged in learning areas: pretend play, blocks, art, science, games, puzzles and manipulatives, sensory exploration, books. A second, smaller room is available for large motor play and small group experiences. There is a gymnasium in the basement. Children bring their lunches. Plans are in development to open a second classroom for younger 3s who will attend two or three days a week.

Summer Program. The optional camp is offered in late June and July. Enrollment can be weekly.

Separation. Home visits and a parent meeting about separation are held the week before school starts. There is a two-week phase-in period building up to a full school day. By the beginning of the second week, they have begun full classes. Parents or caregivers are asked to be available for the entire two weeks for their child.

Parent involvement. Every parent must serve on a school committee, and two parents serve on the supervisory board. Involvement includes working in the school, fund-raising, special projects, maintenance, and gatherings.

There are two parent/teacher conferences, one in the fall and the other in the spring. Scheduled parent visits and contributions to the classroom are welcome. Parent education classes are held a few times a year in the evenings.

Financial. A 25 percent non-refundable deposit is due with the contract, with the balance due in June, September, and November. Other options are available. Approximately 20 percent of students receive financial aid.

Transportation. N/A.

Graduates. Children go to gifted and talented programs, dual language programs, Anderson, or other selective public school programs such as CPE1, CPE2, Hunter, NEST, Manhattan School for Children, and many others. Private schools include Bank Street, Birch, Brearley, Cathedral, Metropolitan, Montessori, St. Hilda's & St Hugh's, The School at Columbia.

Member. Broadway Presbyterian Church, NAEYC.

Children's Learning Center

Ages: 6 mos–5 yrs

Nonsectarian Child Care Cooperative

90 LaSalle Street

Zip: 10027

Tel: 663-9318

Fax: 663-9326

Website: www.clcnyc.org

E-mail: molly@clcnyc.org

Established 1976

Renee Bock,

Director

Enrollment: 50

School year. September through June, with an optional July program for the Center's children. Closed in August.

Program hours. Many other schedules are available in addition to those listed below. A minimum of three days a week is required.

Ages	Hours	Days	Tuition°
Infants	8:30–2:00	3–5 days/wk	$10,900–$16,750
	8:30–3:30	3–5 days/wk	$13,430–$20,080
	8:30–5:30	3–5 days/wk	$16,510–$23,710
2s/3s	8:30–2:00	3–5 days/wk	$9,120–$14,000
	8:30–3:30	3–5 days/wk	$11,230–$16,790
	8:30–5:30	3–5 days/wk	$12,800–$19,820
3/4s	8:30–2:00	3–5 days/wk	$7,400–$11,370
	8:30–3:30	3–5 days/wk	$9,120–$13,630
	8:30–5:30	3–5 days/wk	$11,200–$16,090

°For ten months, varies depending on number of days contracted for.

Program.   Developmental. The Children's Learning Center was founded in 1972 by a group of Union Theological Seminary students who wanted to share the responsibility of caring for one another's children in a Seminary apartment while they attended class. In the summer of 2000, the Children's Learning Center moved to Morningside Gardens and is no longer affiliated with Union Theological Seminary. The school believes that children learn best through play, at their own individual rates in a mixed-age group. Teachers encourage children to discover and interpret their world through cooperative and independent play. Art, science, music, social studies, cooking, sand and water play are some of the activities in all three classrooms. A music specialist works with children each week and an educational psychologist is available to teachers, children, and parents throughout the year.

The Center places a strong value on the social and emotional development of young children. Language development is one of the Center's strengths; children tend to score far above their peers on verbal assessments.

Admissions.   The application fee is $50. Inquiries are accepted throughout the year. Families tour the Center after submitting an application. Notifications are sent out the second week in March with preference given to siblings and affiliates of Morningside Gardens, Jewish Theological Seminary, and Barnard College. The center seeks a balance of ages and sexes. It is multicultural and multiracial.

Class size.   The children meet in three classes. The infant room has a maximum of 10 children. The 2s room has a maximum of 12 children, and Pre-K has a maximum of 18 children.

Three full-time teachers and an additional college work-study teacher are assigned to each group. A music teacher also works with the children once a week.

Staff. The Center fosters and supports many programs geared to the teachers' professional development. Twice a month the entire staff meets in order to discuss curriculum-building and the teachers participate in out of school or in-house workshops.

Facilities. The Children's Learning Center is located on the ground floor in one of Morningside Gardens' tenant cooperative buildings. The children enjoy the use of two large playgrounds which are located on the premises. The rooms are divided into activity areas with blocks, dramatic play, art activities, table toys, and a library. Each room is carpeted and the school is equipped with a full kitchen. Children bring their own lunches; the school provides snacks.

Separation. Children begin the year with an abbreviated school schedule. Parents are asked to remain in their child's classroom for the first few sessions and then leave the classroom for gradually increasing time periods. The transition period is essential to a successful integration into the life of a classroom.

Parent involvement. The Center is a parent cooperative which depends on parent participation. There is a Parent Board. In addition to a fund-raising commitment, parents must work on a school committee. Two maintenance work days are required each year. Parents are encouraged to bring any special interest or skill to the classroom. There are two parent conferences a year.

Financial. One month's tuition is required at enrollment, along with insurance fees, and an additional month's deposit is due in June. Monthly tuition is payable on the first of each month. There is limited scholarship assistance available.

Transportation. Parents bring their children directly to the classrooms.

Graduates. Have gone on to Bank Street, City and Country School, Dalton, Manhattan School for Children, and PS 25.

City College Preschool

Ages: 2–6 yrs.

Nonsectarian Preschool

Schiff House
133rd and Convent Avenue
Zip: 10031
Tel: 650-8616

LaTrella Thornton,
Director
Enrollment: 45

Tuition is $55 per week. The center is open from 7:45–5:30 with evening hours from 4:00–9:00 P.M.. The school follows the City College calendar, and all students are offspring of City College students. The program is developmental. Children are not assigned to a particular room, and they self-select the rooms in which they are to engage in activities.

The Columbia Greenhouse Nursery School

Ages: 2–5 yrs

Nonsectarian Nursery School

404 West 116th Street and
424 West 116th Street
  (between Amsterdam Avenue
  and Morningside Drive)
Zip: 10027
Tel: 666-4796
Website: www. columbiagreenhouse.com
E-mail: info@columbiagreenhouse.com

Established 1919
Vicki Aspenberg,
Director
Enrollment: 105

School year. Second week in September through early June. Summer program available through July.

Ages	Hours	Days	Tuition
2s	9:00–11:30	2 or 3 days	$6,500–$9,800
2s	12:45–3:15	Mon Tues Thurs	$9,800
2s/3s	9:00–12:00	Mon Wed Thurs	$10,300
3s	1:00–4:00	Mon–Thurs	$11,500
3s–5s	9:00–1:00	Mon–Fri°	$14,900
3s–5s	9:00–3:45	Mon–Thurs° (Fri until 1:00)	$19,000

°Option of an extended day: Monday through Thursday, from 2:45 to 3:45.

240

Program.   Developmental Interaction. The school emphasizes a play-based approach through concrete learning and exploration of age-appropriate materials. Activities like cooking, collaging, block building, and water play tie in with the rudiments of arithmetic, writing, and reading. Other activities include dramatic play, science, singing, music and movement, active play, storytime, art, and play with small objects, puzzles, and games. The curriculum evolves according to the child's interests and growing skills.

Admissions.   The application fee is $30. Inquiries are from mid-September on. Applications are available on the school's website. Parents will be scheduled for a group tour and a classroom visit after applying. Tours begin in October. Notifications are sent in early to mid-March. Children are not interviewed. There are openings for 2s, 3s, and 4s. Priority is given to parents affiliated with Columbia and siblings.

Class size.   There are three 2s classes of ten, a morning 3s class of fifteen, an afternoon 3s class of twelve, a 3/4s class of seventeen, and a 4/5s class of twenty-one. Each class has two or three staff members; the 4/5s class has three staff members. Interns also assist, so there are three or four adults in each room.

Staff.   Faculty supervision and school operation are in the hands of the director. Five teachers have master's degrees in early childhood education. Most teachers and assistants have been working at the school anywhere from ten to thirty-three years.
A specialist teaches music and movement.

Facilities.   The school has two locations: a brick townhouse on West 116th Street and the first floor of a nearby residential building also on West 116th Street. Both locations have comfortable classrooms, each well-equipped with sand, water, clay, playdough, blocks, puzzles, games, paints and art materials, books, and musical instruments. The school has two outdoor play yards, one with a slide, climbing apparatus, tricycles, large building blocks, and sandboxes.

Summer program.   Six weeks for 3s–5s. Children need to be previously enrolled in the school.

Separation.   A parent/faculty meeting takes place before the school year begins with special attention given to the first weeks of school.

Small groups attend shortened sessions at the beginning of the year with parent or caregiver present as needed.

Parent involvement.   Each parent is expected to participate on a committee or project, such as the school's newsletter. Parents frequently contribute their talents to the classroom and are invited to observe at any time.

Parent/teacher conferences are held twice yearly. There is an active Parent Association. Seminars on child development issues and ongoing school placement and parenting are offered.

Many of the parents are university students, teaching assistants, professors, and administrators.

Financial.   A deposit of 20 percent of the tuition is required upon signing the contract. The deposit is a nonrefundable part of the total tuition. The remainder of the tuition is payable on the 1st of June, September, and January. Other payment schedules are available upon request. Roughly 10 percent of students receive tuition assistance.

Transportation.   None provided.

Graduates.   Have gone on to such schools as Bank Street, Cathedral, Columbia Grammar, Dalton, Ethical Culture, Fieldston, Manhattan Country, Riverdale, Speyer-Legacy, The School at Columbia, St. Hilda's & St. Hugh's. Approximately a third of the children attend public schools, including Hunter and Anderson, PS 166, PS 163, PS 87, PS 75, PS 89, and other specialized public schools.

History.   The Greenhouse evolved from a playgroup for children of Columbia faculty established in 1919. In 1922 it was offered quarters in a botanical greenhouse belonging to the university. In 1950 parents took responsibility for the school's administration. The program was assessed by consultants from Bank Street and revamped according to the latest research and approaches in the mid-fifties and moved into its present home in 1958.

Affiliations.   Columbia University, which supports the school.

Member.   ERB, ISAAGNY, NAEYC.

Family Annex

Ages: 19 mos–5 yrs

Nonsectarian Parent Cooperative Day Care Center

560 West 113th Street   Established 1980
  (between Broadway and   Nancy Drescher,
  Amsterdam Avenue)   Director
Zip: 10025   Enrollment: 45
Tel: 749-3271 or 3540
Website: www.thefamilyannex.org
E-mail: Thefamilyannex@yahoo.com

School year. September 6th through end of July. Parents contract for the full year.

Ages	Hours	Days	Tuition°
19 mos.–5	8:00–5:45	Mon–Fri	$16,000–$22,000 (depending on age and schedule)
19 mos.–5	8:00–12:45 or 1:00–5:45 (8:00–3:30 also available)	2, 3 or 5 days	$8,596–$22,000

°Two or three-day schedules are also available.

Program. The school offers a Reggio Emilia approach, an open classroom curriculum with structured and free time and individual and small group work. Activities include meeting time (discussions, stories, games, and singing), art, learning with small play objects, and physical play. There are also frequent neighborhood outings, a studio teacher, and in-house music, movement teachers.

Admissions.   The application fee is $50. Inquiries are from September on. The director arranges tours for parents. Notification of acceptance is sent according to ISAAGNY guidelines. Children for whom places are not available may be put on a waiting list. Preference is given to children of employees or students at Columbia.

Class size. There is a toddler room for ten children 19 months to 2.7, a nursery room of fourteen children from 2.8–3.8, and a prekindergarten room with fourteen children 3.9–5. Each room has a teacher and an assistant. The toddlers have three staff members in the morning.

Facilities.   Three floors of a brownstone owned by Columbia University. The spacious toddler room opens into a backyard with a sandbox and climbing equipment. The nursery classrooms are on the second floor. The third floor has the prekindergarten room and a full kitchen, and an art studio. Children also use Riverside Park, the grounds of Columbia, and those of St. John the Divine.
Children bring their lunches.

Separation.   Parents and teachers have the option to work out a schedule to accommodate children's needs.

Parent involvement.   The director is in charge of the staff and the school's day-to-day functions. Parents elect the board of directors and participate through committees in admissions, hiring, fundraising, budget, and curriculum decisions. Formal parent/teacher conferences are scheduled twice yearly.

Financial.   A deposit of one-ninth of the year's tuition is due on signing the contract. Parents contract for the full year. Tuition is payable from September through May.

Transportation.   Most children come from the Columbia area. No private bus service is available.

Graduates.   Have gone on to private schools such as Bank Street, Ethical Culture, Heschel, and Manhattan Country, as well as to public schools such as Hunter, Anderson, Manhattan School for Children, PS 87, and the Lab School as well as Gifted and Talented programs.

Affiliations.   Columbia University, ISAAGNY, NAEYC.

Hollingworth Preschool of Teachers College, Columbia University

Ages: 3–5 yrs

Nonsectarian

Box 170
Teachers College
Columbia University
Zip: 10027
Tel: 678-3403
Website: www.tc.columbia.edu

Established 1983
Dr. Lisa Wright,
Executive Director
Heather Pinedo Burns,
Administrative Director/
Admissions Director
Enrollment: 36

School year. Second week in September through beginning of June.

Ages	Hours	Days	Tuition
3s/4s	8:30–11:30	Mon–Fri	$15,985
3s/4s	11:30–1:00	Mon–Fri	$5,440
	(optional extended morning)		
4s/5s	11:45–4:00	Mon–Fri	$17,176

Children must be 3 or 4 at the start of the year.

Program. Eclectic. Founded in 1984, Hollingworth Preschool is most often described as a hybrid program that is influenced by a variety of educational theories and approaches. The most prevalent is progressive. The children are encouraged to learn through play, inquiry, and experiences in a developmentally appropriate and responsive environment.

The school is a program of Teachers College at Columbia University and has a distinct reputation serving bright, gifted children. The Hollingworth center is an integral component of the Department of Curriculum and Teaching and the Program in Gifted Education at Teachers College. As a demonstration school, graduate students may observe and research the children. Parental permission is obtained for any study carried out in the preschool.

Admissions. The application fee is $100. All applicants must be at least 3 years old by the first day of the academic year which falls on the Tuesday after Labor Day. All applicants for the afternoon class of 4s and 5s must be at least

245

four-years-old by the first day of school. The school welcomes calls if there's a question regarding the birthday cut-off.

The application process consists of four phases: 1) submitting the application, 2) the individual activities session, 3) responses to the observational questions, and, 4) the small group observational session.

Class size.   There is one 3s and one 4s class. Each has seventeen to eighteen children and three teachers.

Staff.   The Hollingworth Center is directed by Dr. Lisa Wright and Heather J. Pinedo-Burns is the Director of Hollingworth Preschool. The faculty includes two head teachers, associate teachers, assistant teachers, and administrative assistants. All members of the faculty are, or have been graduate students in various programs of Teachers College at Columbia University. In addition, there are qualified student teachers and interns. There are extensive internships, research opportunities, seminars, etc. available to graduate students through the Hollingworth Center.

Facilities.   The Hollingworth Preschool occupies two sunny classrooms in the Horace Mann building at Teachers College.

Separation.   The preschool offers several ways that families begin to connect with the school, starting with a home visit, pictures of teachers, CDs of songs and stories, postcards, and a classroom open house. The youngest children in the morning class follow a gradual entry schedule that allows for the children to begin school slowly and in small groups. By the first Friday of school all gather for a shortened school day. On the first full day of school, the following Wednesday, everyone has built up the stamina to attend a full day, 3½ hours. The afternoon class follows a brief gradual entry schedule.

Parent involvement.   There is a mutually supportive collaboration between home and school. Families are included in daily classroom events through head teachers and the director. There are scheduled parent/teacher conferences and general meetings for parents. Families gather for special events and celebrations throughout the year.

Financial.   Tuition can be paid in three installments. A nonrefundable deposit is due on acceptance, which is applied toward the tuition. Scholarship aid is limited.

Transportation.   Transportation is provided by parents. The Preschool is located on the Columbia University, Teachers College campus on the corner of 120th Street and Broadway. It is accessible from the #1 subway and the M104, M4, and M11 buses.

Graduates.   Have gone on to Brearley, Cathedral, Chapin, Collegiate, Dalton, Ethical Culture, Fieldston, Horace Mann, St. Bernard's, St. Ann's, Spence, The School at Columbia, Town, Trinity, UNIS, and to public school programs for the gifted such as Anderson, Hunter, NEST + M and PS 6, 9, 87, 163, 166, and 199. An admissions folder is set up for each child and advice as to ongoing school placement is provided by the Director.

Affiliations.   Hollingworth Preschool is part of Teachers College, Columbia University. However, enrollment is open to all, and college affiliation is not necessary.

The Medical Center Nursery School
Columbia University Medical Center Campus
Ages: 2–5 yrs

Nonsectarian

60 Haven Avenue (between 169th and 170th Streets)
Zip: 10032
Tel: 304-7040
Fax: 544-4243
Website: www.mcns.org
E-mail: mcns@mcns.org

Established 1957
Howard E. Johnson, Director
Linda P. Soleyn, Assistant Director
Enrollment: 75

School year.   September through late June. Summer program available through August.

Ages	Hours	Days	Tuition
2s/3s	1:30–5:00	Mon–Fri	$11,200
2s/3s/4s/5s	8:30–12:30	Mon–Fri	$12,400
2s/3s/4s/5s	8:00–5:30	Mon–Fri	$22,400

Program.   The school provides a secure setting in which children can explore materials, develop relationships with peers and non-parental adults, and participate in learning activities. It cooperates with various departments of Columbia University to permit carefully screened research projects and regular observation of healthy, normal young children.

ERBs are given on the premises.

Admissions.   There is a $50 application fee. Inquiries are from September 1st on. Preference is given to children of parents affiliated with New York Presbyterian Hospital or Columbia University. Parents will be called after November 1st to schedule a visit between late November and late February to see the school, and observe a classroom. Notifications are sent in early March.

Class size.   Class size ranges from 16 to 25 with four teachers per room. The school has a consulting psychologist, developmental pediatrician and occupational therapist, as well as an educational consultant.

Facilities.   The three fully equipped, air-conditioned, spacious classrooms all have expansive views of the Hudson River. There is an additional space for indoor play, a small library, and a kitchen. The outdoor, fenced play area on the terrace, one floor above the school, is equipped with a challenging and dramatic climbing and play structure.

Summer program.   End of June through end of August; morning and extended-day programs. Enrollment is by the week.

Parent involvement.   Conferences are scheduled regularly, as are schoolwide and classroom parent meetings. Parents are invited to visit the school at any time. Parents voluntarily raise funds for equipment, trips, and other projects through a parents association.

Financial.   A deposit of the first tuition payment is due on signing the contract. The balance of the tuition is payable monthly, April through February.

Financial aid is available and must be applied for before February 1st.

Graduates. Have gone on to Bank Street, Calhoun, Cathedral, Dalton, Ethical Midtown, Fieldston, Manhattan Country, Riverdale Country, Hunter, and District 3 public schools.

Affiliations. Columbia University. Medical Center, Chartered by the Board of Regents of the State University of New York. Accredited by the NAEYC.

Member. ERB, ISAAGNY, Parents League, NYCAEYC, NAEYC.

The Red Balloon Community Day Care Center
Ages: 2–5 yrs

Nonsectarian Learning Center

560 Riverside Drive   Established 1972
  (between Tiemann Place   Norma Brockman,
  and 125th Street)   Director
Zip: 10027   Enrollment: 45
Tel: 663-9006
Fax: 932-0190
E-mail: rbdcc@aol.com
Website: redballoonlearningcenter.com

School year. All year/12 months.

Ages	Hours	Days	Tuition
2s	8:00–6:00	Mon–Fri	$2,000 monthly
3–5	8:00–6:00	Mon–Fri	$1,750 monthly

Program. Eclectic. The environment is designed to nurture exploration, independence, self-esteem, and active participation. Teachers prepare a variety of interesting choices which challenge the children and help them develop problem-solving techniques and develop skills. The program encourages hands-on learning through play. It also nurtures the children's social and emotional sides; the children learn to value themselves as individuals and as part of a community in small or whole groups. According to the director, "When children leave the Red Balloon they are confident, curious, and happy, open to the many possibilities the world has to offer."

Admissions.   The application fee is $25. Inquire at any time. The center has a waiting list, so parents should apply and arrange to visit with their children. Preference is given to members of the Columbia University community.

Staff.   The director, three certified head teachers, six assistant teachers, a cook, and a part-time bookkeeper.

Facilities.   Columbia University donates the school space in a faculty building. In addition to three large classrooms arranged into activities areas, there is a large indoor gym, a music room, a small library, a safety-surfaced outdoor play deck, and a built-in wading pool. Breakfast, a hot lunch, and snacks are served.

Parent involvement.   The school has an open-door policy and invites parents to spend time in the classroom. An elected Parent Board meets about ten times a year to discuss school policies and daily school functions. Parents are encouraged to join all trips and participate in fund-raising events.

Financial.   A deposit of one month's tuition is required on acceptance. Tuition is payable monthly. One-third of the children are funded by ACS.

Transportation.   No private bus service is available.

Graduates.   Go to public, private schools and gifted and talented public school programs.

Affiliations.   ISAAGNY.

Rita Gold Early Childhood Center
Ages: 6 wks–5 yrs

Box 98, Teachers College
Room 246, Thorndike Hall
525 West 120th Street
Zip: 10027
Tel: 678-3013
Fax: 678-3048
E-mail: ritagoldcenter@tc.edu

Dr. Susan Recchia,
Faculty Co-Director
Patrice Nichols,
On-site Director

Services are available only to those associated with Columbia University.

The Riverside Church Weekday School
Ages: 2.0–6 yrs

Nursery School and Kindergarten

490 Riverside Drive (between
    120th and 122nd Streets)
Zip: 10027
Tel: 870-6743
Fax: 870-6795
Website: www.weekdayschool-nyc.org

Established 1930
Ms. Jennifer A. Grogan,
Head of School
Dr. Peter A. Mutarelli,
Associate Head of School
Ms. Jean Monaco,
Admissions Director
Enrollment: 143

School year. September through June. Summer camp, mid-June through late July.

Ages	Hours	Days	Tuition
2s	9:00–11:30	Mon Wed Fri	$9,970
2s	9:00–11:30	Tues Thurs	$6,680
3s	8:45–2:30	Mon–Fri	$19,350
3s	8:45–12:30	Mon–Fri	$15,475
3s	8:45–5:30	Mon–Fri	$22,715
4s	8:45–12:30	Mon–Fri	$15,475
4s	8:45–2:30	Mon–Fri	$19,350
4s	8:45–5:30	Mon–Fri	$22,715
Kindergarten	8:45–2:30	Mon–Fri	$19,350
Kindergarten	8:45–5:30	Mon–Fri	$22,715

Extended hours.   Early Room (8:00–8:45) and Late Room (2:30–5:30) are available for an additional fee.

Program.   Progressive/academic. The program is child-centered and within a broad framework allows children to explore and experiment with materials and to discover their own potentials and strengths. The play-based curriculum focuses on facilitating social and emotional growth in children as well as on language development and the arts. The "whole language" approach is integrated across the curriculum, with beginning phonics introduced in the 5s program. Children are encouraged to use art to express their thoughts. An art specialist and the children work in a stimulating art studio. A movement specialist helps develop physical skills through music and movement activities conducted in a spacious movement room. A music specialist develops the children's awareness of sounds, rhythm, and different kinds of musical instruments. Block building is a significant activity, and every classroom offers a large block area with a spectacular collection of unit blocks.

The school strives to bridge home and school experiences for each child. The basic assumption is that learning occurs best within a context, and new information is best assimilated when based on a child's prior knowledge and experiences. The school's mission reflects the all-inclusive philosophy of Riverside Church and is manifested in the celebration of holidays significant to member families such as: Christmas, Easter, Succoth, Passover, Hanukkah, Lunar New Year, Kwanzaa, Thanksgiving, Martin Luther King Day.

A hot lunch, prepared on site, is served at noon in each classroom. The children eat lunch with their teachers.

Admissions.   The application fee is $75. Inquiries are from Labor Day on. Tours are scheduled between September through the end of November. After touring, parents schedule a play date for their child during January. Notifications are sent in accordance with ISAAGNY guidelines. Preference is given to legacies, church members, and siblings. The school strives for a racial, cultural, gender, and economic balance in the classrooms.

Class size.   There are ten classrooms: twelve children in the 2s group, fifteen in the 3s, up to twenty in the 4s, and up to twenty-five in the 5s.

Staff.   Each classroom has one head teacher and one assistant teacher. Each head teacher has a master's degree in early childhood education; all assistant teachers hold a bachelor's degree. There are a number of opportunities for professional development.

Facilities.   The school's spacious, well-lit, and beautifully maintained classrooms, on the sixth and seventh floors of the church, have breathtaking views of the Hudson River on the west and Morningside Park on the east. There are two large rooftop playgrounds and a full-size gym. The school also has an art studio, movement room, indoor play area, and a charming library.

Separation.   The process is gradual. All families meet teachers before school starts either during a home visit or individual classroom visit and discuss a plan. There is an orientation schedule for each group. In the 2s program, a parent or caregiver stays with the child until both are comfortable separating. 3s begin school in small groups and small sessions which gradually lengthen during the first two weeks. 4s and 5s take only a few days to work up to a full session.

Parent involvement.   Parents serve on the advisory administrative board and school committees, and help with social and fund-raising events during the school year. They are encouraged to share their skills and talents, or to read a story, or join the class on field trips.

Financial.   A non-refundable deposit of approximately 30 percent is due on signing of the contract. Tuition is payable in five installments. Income from a small endowment fund and from annual fund-raising events enables the school to offer limited, need-based tuition assistance.

Transportation.   More than half the students come from the Upper West Side, from the 70s through the 120s. Several families come from Washington Heights, the Bronx, and New Jersey. No private bus service is available.

Graduates.   Children have gone on to a variety of private and public schools such as Bank Street, Brearley, Calhoun, Cathedral, Chapin, Collegiate, Columbia Grammar, Dalton, Ethical Culture, Fieldston, Horace Mann, Manhattan Country, Nightingale-Bamford, Riverdale, Sacred Heart, Spence, St. Hilda and St. Hugh's, Trevor Day, Trinity, UNIS and the Lab School, Manhattan School for Children, PS 9, PS 163, PS 166, PS 75, PS 87, PS 84.

Affiliations.   Riverside Church.

Saint Benedict's Day Nursery
Ages: 2.11 to 5.11 years

Catholic Nursery School

21 West 124th Street	Established 1923
Zip: 10027	Ms. Doris Furtuna-Moore,
Tel: 423-5715	Administrative and
Fax: 423-5917	Admissions Director
E-mail: st.benedictdaynursery@verizon.net	Sr. Patricia Marie, FHM,
	Education Director
	Enrollment: 55

School year. The center is open 48 weeks a year.

Ages	Hours	Days	Tuition (monthly)
2.11–5.11	7:30–6:00 only	Mon–Fri	$600/$700/$800°

Children must be toilet-trained.
°Depending on income.

Program. Traditional. All children participate in daily prayers. The program is highly structured and has a strong skills orientation. Scheduled activities for 4s, for example, include prayers, religion, phonics, math, circle time, free play, storytime, music, social studies, science, holiday shows, and free play indoors and outdoors. Art and musical instruction are included in the curriculum.

Admissions. There is a $460 registration fee. Call for an application and to arrange a talk with the director and a visit to the nursery school. Afterward an interview will be arranged for the child. Children are accepted on a first-come basis; parents register in the spring for the following September. The school maintains an active waiting list.

Class size. There are four classes: two classes of thirteen 3s, one class of thirteen 4s, and one kindergarten bridge class of eighteen. Each class has two in staff.

Facilities. There are six classrooms, four in use and two more pending approval by 2012. A kitchen, office, storeroom, and a well-equipped outdoor playground.

Breakfast and a hot lunch are provided for children in the St. Benedict's Day Nursery and two snacks.

Parent involvement. Parents are active in fund-raising, on school committees, and help on field trips, and assist with plays and graduation exercises. Conferences are twice yearly, and class parents meet twice yearly. All communications with parents pass through the director's and/or administrative assistant's office.

Financial. A registration fee of $460 is required on signing the full-year contract. Payment arrangements vary with parent's income.

Transportation. Children come from Harlem, the Bronx, Queens, and Pennsylvania. No private bus service is available.

Graduates. Attend All Saints, St. Aloysius, St. Charles, St. Ignatius, St. Mark, St. Joseph's of Yorkville, as well as independent schools.

Affiliations. The school was founded by the Franciscan Handmaids of the Most Pure Heart of Mary and is affiliated with the Archdiocese of New York and Catholic School Board.

St. Hilda's & St. Hugh's School
Ages: 2–13 yrs

Episcopal Early Childhood Program and Primary School

619 West 114th Street
(between Broadway and
Riverside Drive)
Zip: 10025-7995
Tel: 932-1980
Fax: 531-0102
Website: www.sthildas.org

Established 1950
Virginia Connor,
Head of School
Kate Symonds,
Admissions Director
Early Childhood enrollment: 116–118
Total enrollment: 374–380

School year. The week after Labor Day through first week of June.

Ages	Hours	Days	Tuition
°2s (Beginners)	9:00–11:00	°Tues Thurs or Mon Wed Fri	$6,500–$8,500
	8:25–12:30	Mon–Fri	$19,000
3–4s	8:25–2:50	Mon–Fri	$23,000
5s	8:25–2:50	Mon–Fri	$25,000

°Children must be 2 as of September 1st for the beginner program.

Extended hours.   Parents can arrange for an extended day until 6:30 at an additional cost of $3,500 for the year. Parents may also arrange for an extended day on any afternoon without notice. Costs are pro-rated.

Program.   Traditional. The school is structured and offers a clear academic program. There is a blending of faiths among the students, and concepts of the spiritual and moral world are explored. Daily chapel service begins in first grade.

The curriculum is planned around units of study based on themes. Music, drama, art, foreign language, and physical education are emphasized. The beginner program focuses on language development, socialization, and separation in a secure and nurturing environment. Beginning in nursery, students are taught by specialists twice a week for art and music, library, physical education, and foreign language. The school offers Spanish, French, and Mandarin beginning in nursery.

Junior kindergarten students go to nearby art studios for lessons in technique. Senior kindergarten students have physical education daily in the gym, and go to science lab twice a week. Computer begins in second grade.

Children begin wearing uniforms in first grade.

Admissions.   The application fee is $60. Inquiries may be made at any time by phone or via website, but the school requires parents to submit an application before arranging a tour. After the school receives the application, the admissions office contacts parents to arrange a parent tour and an appointment to meet children individually or in small groups. Older children spend either a full- or half-day in a classroom. Applicants to junior kindergarten (4s) and senior kindergarten (5s) must take the ERB. Notifications are sent in February and March.

Class size.   The early childhood division includes beginners, nursery, junior, and senior kindergarten classes. Each has two staff members. Beginner classes have three teachers. Children work with specialists in art, music, movement, foreign language, science, and library. A full-time nurse is on staff.

Facilities.   The school is modern, fully-air conditioned, and beautifully designed. Its centrally located chapel (sometimes used for theater-in-the-round presentations) has a Reiger organ. There are spacious classrooms, a floor of art studios and music studios, three science labs, two technology centers, a full-sized gymnasium/auditorium, a 2,600 sq ft library with three rooms and 25,000 volumes, a new rooftop greenhouse, a large cafeteria where the children eat, and, off the second floor, an enormous outdoor play deck with a slide and swings.

Separation.   Varies according to the individual child. The process is not rushed.

Parent involvement.   The Parents Association meets monthly. It is active and coordinates fund-raising events and classroom projects; many share special talents, interests, or their cultural heritage both in the classroom and with the school as a whole. Conferences are held twice yearly.

Financial.   There is a $3,000 deposit due on signing the contract. Tuition refund insurance (at a cost of 7.5 percent of tuition) is recommended. Financial aid is available based on need.

Transportation.   Children come from the Upper West Side and various other neighborhoods.

Affiliations.   St. Hilda's & St. Hugh's is a member of the National Association of Episcopal Schools. The school has a full-time chaplain on staff.

Member.   ERB, ISAAGNY, NAIS, NAES, NYSAIS.

Tompkins Hall Nursery School and Childcare Center

Ages: 3 mos.–5 yrs

Nonsectarian Parent Cooperative

21 Claremont Avenue
(near 116th Street)
Zip: 10027
Tel: 666-3340
E-mail: TompkinsHall@earthlink.net
Website: www.tompkinshall.org

Established ca. 1935
Cynthia Pollack,
Director
Nursery enrollment: 28
Toddler enrollment: 13
Infants: 12

School year. September through July 31st.

Ages	Hours	Days	Tuition
Infants	8:30–5:30	Mon–Thurs (Fri until 12:30)	$25,200
Toddlers*	8:30–5:30	Mon–Thurs (Fri until 12:30)	$25,200
3s	8:30–12:30	Mon–Fri	$14,800
3s and 4s	8:30–2:30	Mon–Thurs (Fri until 12:30)	$16,000
3s and 4s	8:30–5:30	Mon–Thurs (Fri until 12:30)	$22,400

*Less than full-time available.

Parents who volunteer one morning per week in the classroom receive reduced tuition. Extended days are available for 3s and 4s at an additional fee. Many scheduling options are available at a prorated fee. Visit the website for more information.

Program. Developmental. The school focuses on social skills and emotional development, identifying and talking about feelings, conflicts, choices, relationships, and activities. The day begins with free play, block building, art, and imaginative play. Other activities include circle time, music and movement, cooking, and outdoor play. The afternoon program includes more complex activities and field trips.

Admissions. The application fee is $45. Applications begin in October for following year. Applications are available online and parents can register for an Open House. Notifications are sent in March. Priority is given to Columbia faculty or staff.

Class size. There is an infant program with 12 babies, a 2s program of 13 children; the preschool is a mixed-age grouping of 28 children in the morning, which is divided by age in the afternoon, twelve in one group, thirteen in the other. After 2:30 all combine into one group.

Facilities. The nursery school occupies two apartments on the ground floor of a Columbia-owned residential building. Visitors are buzzed into a white marble foyer. The door to the nursery school is at the far end. A small room is filled with cubbies and strollers. There is a well-furnished dress-up room, kitchen and snack room, bathroom, office, library, and activities room filled with blocks, toys, a sand table, small climbing structure, small play objects, and a space for large motor activities; a nature and science room, easels, art table, and reading and small motor areas. All the rooms have windows. Half the roof has been fenced in and carpeted to form a play yard. It is equipped with a play house, wooden climbing structures, slides, and a toy shed full of tricycles, wagons, blocks, and other toys. Children bring their lunches; the school provides snacks. There's an organic roof-top garden, complete with composter and greenhouse. The rest of the ground floor occupies the new infant center and the 2s program. Both areas are newly renovated and well-equipped.

Parent involvement. Parents can elect to work in the classroom. They are obliged to attend monthly parent/staff meetings to discuss curriculum and developmental issues, participate in fund-raising, and to contribute two work days each year, and to serve on a committee, or take on a school job such as food shopping.

Transportation. No private bus service is available.

Graduates. Have gone on to public and private schools, most recently Bank Street, Dalton, Manhattan School for Children, PS 75, PS 87, and The Anderson Program.

Affiliations. Columbia University.

Washington Heights
and Inwood YM-YWHA

Ages: 2.9–5 yrs

Nursery School and Kindergarten

54 Nagle Avenue
Zip: 10040
Tel: 569-6200
Website: www.ywashhts.org
E-mail: sherman@ywashhts.org

Established 1955
Susan Herman,
Director
Enrollment: 120

School year. September through June.

Ages	Hours	Days	Tuition (monthly)
2.9–5	9:00–11:30 or	Mon–Fri	$695
	1:00–3:30	Mon–Fri	$495
2.9–5	9:00–3:30	Mon–Fri	$1,045(4s)–$845(3s)
2.9–5	9:00–6:00	Mon–Fri	$1,295

°Children must be 2.9 by September 1st; family membership is $200 yearly for one child in the nursery program; $225 for more than one child.

Program.   Developmental. The curriculum supports each child to learn how to make choices, solve problems, socialize, and express themselves. Project-based units of study are based on children's interests.

Admissions.   Y membership fee. Inquiries are from October on. Parents call to arrange to visit the school with their child. Children are accepted on a first-come basis, and parents are notified as soon as possible. Membership in the Y is a prerequisite for nursery school enrollment.

Class size.   There are six classes of 3s and/or 4s. Each class has two staff members; art, music, and rhythm and dance specialists visit weekly. A social work consultant is available weekly and for consultations with staff and parents.

Facilities.   The school is located in a three-story community center. The children meet in five large, well-equipped classrooms on floors one through three. There is a large indoor play space, a gymnasium, a well-equipped rooftop play area, and a smaller outside playground.

Summer program. Day camp and Nursery camp operates in July and August. Those interested should register between January and March.

Separation. Children are brought into the program in small groups for short periods of time. The orientation takes about a week. Parents remain in the building until children are ready to remain on their own. Separation is handled individually.

Parent involvement. Parents may visit any time, often joining classroom activities, or accompanying a class on a field trip. The school has a parent committee, which meets every 4-6 weeks with various staff members to discuss special programming, fund-raising, and other relevant issues. Fund-raising events take place in the building. Parents raise roughly $20,000–$30,000 for the school each year. Occasional workshops on parenting issues are organized by a school consultant. Conferences are held twice a year and at parents' request.

Financial. There is a registration fee of $250. After an initial deposit, parents pay three months' tuition and sign a contract for the school year. Tuition is payable quarterly. Financial aid is available.

Transportation. The school provides door-to-door transportation for a cost of $275 monthly for round trips, and $175 monthly for one-way trips.

Graduates. Attend community public schools and private schools, including Fieldston, Bank Street, Solomon Schecter, JCC, and PS 187, and 178, Anderson, The Special Music School.

Affiliations and Memberships. Federation of Jewish Philanthropies, YM and YWHA.

DOWNTOWN

The Acorn School

Ages: 2–4 yrs

Nonsectarian Preschool

330 East 26th Street (between
First and Second Avenues)
Zip: 10010
Tel: 684-0230
Fax: 696-0514
Website: www.acornschoolny.com

Established 1966
Jill Axthelm,
Director
Helene Daub,
Administrator
Enrollment: 108

School year. Early September through early June, with optional June program for enrolled students.

Ages	Hours	Days	Tuition
2s	8:45–11:30	2 days	$7,150
2s/3s	8:45–11:30	3 days	$9,200
	or 1:00–3:45		
3s/4s	8:45–11:45	5 days	$12,750
	or 12:45–3:45	2 days	$2,675–$5,325

Extended hours. There is an early drop-off at 8:30 for $3.00 per day. In addition, an optional extended-day program for 4s is available. A June program for two extended weeks is also available at an additional fee.

Program. Eclectic. The 2s: Encourages creativity, exploration, and interaction with a variety of materials (easel, water table, blocks, kitchen area, and many manipulatives) in a nurturing, cheerful, and stimulating environment. The arts are introduced through active participation in singing, listening to stories, cooking, and group art projects. Many children discover the rewards and responsibilities of friendship for the first time. Teachers encourage each child to grow at his or her own pace as they build confidence and independence.

In the 3/4s: The emphasis is on self-teaching through independent, active learning planned but not dominated by the teacher. Through an organized, diverse environment, the program seeks to stimulate the child to discover, test, and experience independently his or her rapidly expanding world. All learning experiences encourage each child's cognitive, physical, and socio-emotional development. Three large, attractively designed, and colorful classrooms contain a wide variety of materials. The

265

children are free to choose their own activity and pursue it alone or with others, whether the area be socializing, the sand table, block building, books, painting. In the large group, each child is encouraged to participate, whether it be the presentation of new materials, the sharing of his/her experiences, singing, or listening to stories. Art, cooking, language arts, and music are all integral parts of the program, encouraging the children to express themselves creatively.

ERBs are given on the premises. The director helps parents choose appropriate ongoing schools for their children.

Admissions. The application fee is $40. Call for an application and to schedule a visit. Parent observations begin in the fall, children visit in January or February. The children play, usually in small groups and with parents present. Preference is given to siblings. Notifications are sent by March.

Facilities. The school occupies the ground floor of an apartment building and has several doors opening onto a courtyard through which parents and children enter. The interior is ingeniously divided into classroom areas. There are four main classroom spaces and an indoor play space for music, movement, and rainy-day play. Acorn uses outside, age-appropriate climbing equipment in an enclosed playing area. Weather permitting, all children spend approximately forty minutes a day climbing, running, and playing freely. On cold, rainy days, the children use the all-purpose room for free play. A climbing apparatus, rocking boats, and a slide are provided. Acorn has won over 30 awards for architecture and design and has been chosen by various companies as a testing site for child-related products.

Separation. New children come in small groups for shortened sessions during the first few weeks. Parents may stay in the classroom for this time. The separation program is gradual and flexible.

Parent involvement. Parents serve on the board of directors and are encouraged to become class parents, observe and participate in class activities, join the Garden Committee, and support local fund-raising endeavors such as Room to Grow, Reach Out and Read, Educare's Childcare Center, and God's Love We Deliver. Parent/teacher conferences are scheduled in November and March.

266

Financial.   A one-time, $500 nonrefundable reserve fund contribution is required of all new families (the reserve fund is used for capital improvements, e.g., new indoor and outside playground equipment, air-conditioning system, office equipment).

Graduates.   Have gone on to a variety of public and private schools, including Allen-Stevenson, Birch Wathen-Lenox, Brearley, Chapin, Dalton, Friends Seminary, Grace Church, Riverdale, Spence, Trevor Day, UNIS, Village Community School, and PS 40, PS 116, and NEST + M.

Chartered.   By the Board of Regents of the State University of New York.

Member.   ISAAGNY, Parents League.

Avenues: The World School

Ages: 3–5 yrs
Nursery–12th grade

259 Tenth Avenue (at 26th Street)
Zip: 10001
Tel: (212) 935-5000
Website: www.avenues.org

Established 2012
Nancy Schulman,
Head of Early Learning Center
Susan Robinson,
Director of Admissions
Soraya Diaz Tamayo,
Director of Early Learning Center
and Lower School Admissions
Enrollment: 125
(maximum approximately 220)

School year.   September through mid June.

Ages	Hours	Days	Tuition
3.0–3.11	8:30–2:45	Mon–Fri	$39,750
4.0–4.11	8:30–2:45	Mon–Fri	$39,750

Extended hours. Early drop off – 8:00.

Program.   The educational philosophy of Avenues' Early Learning Center focuses on the child and provides an environment rich in opportunities to grow in the understanding of language and to learn how to work with others. Communication skills, reading, writing, and effective speaking are central components of the Avenues' educational plan, so Early Learning Center students will be encouraged to begin to develop good habits in these areas in preparation for more formal language instruction in later years.

When fully developed, Avenues plans to be a system of schools—one school with campuses in 20 or more cities around the world.

In the Early Learning Center, students will be exposed to stories, songs, and traditions from many parts of the world in order to build a base for future understanding. holidays from around the world will be celebrated, and there will be plenty of projects dealing with other lands and people.

All students at Avenues will be expected to become fluent in a second language, a process that will begin in the Early Learning Center. Children will begin in the Early Learning Center with a 50 percent immersion program in either Spanish or Mandarin.

An important part of Avenues' educational mission is to help students learn healthy habits of behavior. It is important to begin this education in the earliest years, when so many habits of diet, exercise, and sleep are formed. The Early Learning Center sees this as an important part of its curriculum, and parents will be encouraged to discuss these issues with faculty. Physical play—both as a healthy stimulus for growth and as a means of learning to work with others— will be an important part of the day, utilizing exceptional facilities such as the rooftop playground, gardens, and gymnasium.

The Early Learning Center, as the school in general, is a technologically rich environment. Teachers will introduce technology in the Early Learning Center classroom in an age-appropriate way.

Students will be exposed to regular instruction in music, art, and movement. The gymnasium and playground facilities in the school will be available for indoor and outdoor play. While students will generally eat lunch in their classrooms, the dining halls will be available for special functions.

Admissions.   Applications are available through the website only. Parents are encouraged to come to an information event prior to parent interview. Children are assessed in small playgroups, with one parent present, for thirty minutes. Children must be 3 by August 31st.

Class size.   Nursery (3 year olds) and Pre-K (4 year olds) each have eight classes with 15 children each.

Staff.   The Early Learning Center's Head, Nancy Schulman comes to Avenues with over 25 years experience and former head of the 92nd Street Y Nursery School. Her expertise in the field of early childhood development guarantees a fabulous program.

Each class will have two teachers, a head teacher with a master's degree and an experienced assistant teacher. There will be specialists for movement, science, music, and physical education. In addition to the Head of the Early Learning Center, there will be a Head of Grade for nursery (3 year olds) and pre-K (4 year olds). The student/teacher ratio is 6:1.

Facilities.   Avenues' Early Learning Center for nursery and pre-kindergarten grades will occupy the first two floors of Avenues' flagship Chelsea campus and have access to other special floors in the building, such as the playground on the roof. A separate entrance on 26th Street will provide families and small children a quiet and secure entrance to the Early Learning Center lobby and floors. As an added convenience, there will be a small café and waiting area on the first floor for parents who have come to pick up children or see faculty and staff.

The ten-story building allows the divisions of the Early Learning Center, Lower, Middle, and Upper Schools into two-floor units and gives each its own identity. All the school's divisions are connected with vertical openings in the floor to allow improved light transmittance through the floor plate and to establish a visual connection between like floors. High ceilings and an abundance of tall clear glass windows fill spaces with natural light.

A beautifully designed rooftop recreation and play space with views to many areas of the city. The school's roof area has been designed with students in mind; the south roof will feature playgrounds for Early Learning Center and Lower School students, with the north side of the roof reserved for Middle and Upper School students.

Summer programs.   A summer camp program is being planned.

Separation.   New students will visit before school starts, and there will be meetings for parents to share information regarding separation and how parents can work with the school to facilitate the transition to school. The schedule is phased in gradually for the beginning weeks of school. A parent or caregiver needs to be available during phase-in.

Parent involvement. Parents will often be invited to participate in Early Learning Center programs. There will be many opportunities for parents to help facilitate events and to be involved—to the degree they are able—in the day-to-day life of their children in school. Parents will be encouraged to take an active role in the children's life at school. Parent education and participation in classroom activities will be part of the Early Learning Center curriculum.

Financial. Avenues seeks to build a student body that reflects the diversity of New York City. Students of all backgrounds will find that the Avenues environment embraces the tents of mutual understanding and creativity as a method of promoting the highest levels of student achievement. To this end, Avenues will offer financial assistance to the parents of admitted students through the School and Student Service for Financial Aid (SSS). SSS, a nationwide service, assists independent schools in processing requests for financial assistance. All financial information and all financial assistance decisions are confidential.

The Barclay Street School
Ages: 2–5 yrs

6 Barclay Street – 2nd Floor
Zip: 10007
Tel: (212) 571-2715
Fax: (212) 732-0246
Website: www.thebarclaystreetschool.org

Established 2008
Ellen Offen,
Director
Kevin Artale,
Director
Enrollment: 63

Ages	Hours	Days	Tuition
All	8:30–5:30	2,3,5	$9,600–$20,900
All	8:45–3:30	2,3,5	$9,000–$19,400
All	8:45–12:45	2,3,5	$7,800–$16,500
2–3.5	8:45–11:45	2,3,5	$7,200–$15,100
All	1:00–4:00 or 5:30	2,3,5	$7,200–$16,500

There is an enrollment fee of $150 and a supply fee ranging from $175–$300.

Program.   Progressive. The school has a relaxed, welcoming atmosphere. Teachers help children develop social skills, independence and self-esteem. Learning is tailored to each child's developmental level and emotional needs. The program gives them opportunities to experiment, discover, and express their original ideas. "We give them freedom, let them try, let them fail, encourage them, let them succeed, and rejoice with them," says the Director. Groups are mixed age; younger children model appropriate social and academic strategies by watching the older children; the older children reinforce concepts they have already learned by teaching the younger ones.

Each room has areas for science, math, language arts, art, manipulative, and puzzles with a a library and a listening center. Children's artwork is on display.

Admissions.   All applicants to the school need to begin the process one academic year prior to entry. Applications are not mailed or handed out. Interested families must call (212) 571-6191, The Park Preschool, beginning at 9:00 A.M. the Thursday after Labor Day to schedule an appointment to tour the school. Tours are scheduled from October until January and filled on a first-come, first-served basis. Tours are scheduled at a time when you can usually see the classes in action, at 9:30 A.M. and 10 A.M. and last about an hour.

Applications for the upcoming school year are typically mailed in late January. Available spaces will be filled on a first-come, first-served basis with priority being placed on age and gender.

Class Size.   There are three mixed-age classrooms, including two 2–3 year old classrooms with 12 students with two teachers and one 3–5 year old class with 18 students and two teachers.

Staff.   Music and movement specialists visit once a week.

Facilities.   Entry at street level takes you past the Director's office and into a large room with storefront windows. The older children occupy this space. Downstairs, there is a gym, and the two classrooms are windowless but brightly lit with off-white walls. Here, the 4's were observed with their Movement Teachers dancing with colored scarves. Children use the playground on Washington Market Park, a half block away.

Summer Programs.   A summer program is offered from the end of June to early August.

Separation.   All students are phased in. Phase-in takes about a week, after which separation is tailored to the individual child's needs.

Financial.   A non-refundable deposit is required to ensure a space. Financial aid is not available.

Transportation.   Most families come from walking distance in Battery Park City, the Financial District, and Tribeca.

Graduates.   Have gone to Allen-Stevenson school, Berkeley Carroll, Brearley, Chapin, City and Country, Claremont School, Columbia Grammar, Grace Church, Packer Collegiate, Sacred Heart School, St. Luke's, UNI, Village Community School, PS 89, PS 234, PS 150, The Anderson Program (PS 334), Hunter Elementary School, and NEST.

Barrow Street Nursery School/ Greenwich House

Ages: 2–5 yrs

Nonsectarian

27 Barrow Street	Established 1984
(at Seventh Avenue)	Nancy Glauberman, Ed.D,
Zip: 10014	Director
Tel: 633–1203	Nicole Ferrin,
Fax: 633-1209	Admissions Director
Website: www.barrowstreetnurseryschool.com	Enrollment: 130

School year.   Second week in September through mid June. Camp available in the summer.

Ages	Hours	Days	Tuition*
2s	9:10–11:40 or 1:00–3:30	Mon Wed Fri	$11,868
2s	9:10–12:30 or 1:00–3:30	Tues Thurs	$9,494
2s	9:10–11:40 or 1:00–3:30	Mon–Fri	$15,429
3s	9:00–12:00 or 1:00–4:00	Mon–Fri	$16,660
4–5s	9:00–3:00	Mon–Fri	$19,581

Program.   Developmental. The curriculum is designed to support individual children's interests and abilities through a variety of hands-on activities such as, block building, cooking, playing with sand, and art materials. The environment promotes self-expression, problem solving which helps children develop positive self images, confidence, and basic social skills. Language skills are taught through literature, conversation, and dramatic play.

Admissions.   The application fee is $60. Applications can be downloaded from the school's website beginning Labor Day and must be submitted by mid-November. Tours for parents only after an application is received are scheduled from late-September until mid-December. Small group play sessions are held in January. Regular ISAAGNY notification dates are followed.

Class size.   There is a class of 2s with ten children and three teachers, a class of 3s have 12–15 children and three teachers, and the 4s/5s have 10–13 children with two teachers.

Facilities.   The school is located on the second and third floors of Greenwich House, a Village landmark. There are 6 bright classrooms, a children's library, and offices. There is also a music room on the 6th floor. The school has use of Greenwich House's gym and running track (a great runway for tricycles and wheeled toys) and its roof playground, equipped with a climbing structure, toys and blocks, and a small garden.

Separation.   In the spring, the school holds a separation workshop for incoming parents. In the fall, after children and parents have one-on-one visits in the classroom with the teachers, the separation period begins with half of each class meeting for a short time for several days. For the following 2–4 weeks, children work up to the full program. Parents may remain in the classroom until their child has made a comfortable adjustment.

Parent involvement.   The Parents Association acts as a formal liaison between staff and parents and organizes many fund-raising events and social functions each year. Parents are welcome into the class at any time to participate in special projects, as well as hold special readings in the library or their child's class. Formal conferences are held twice each year. Throughout the year, the school and PA also work together to conduct 7–10 workshops for parents on various topics, such as children's literacy, sleep habits, limit setting, sibling rivalry, and nutrition.

Financial.   Upon enrollment, a deposit of 25% of the total annual tuition is required. The rest of tuition is paid in installments. Scholarship aid and payment plans are available.

Transportation.   All students are brought and picked up by parents or caregivers, most of who come from the East and West Village, Greenwich, Chelsea, Tribeca, and Soho.

Graduates.   Have been accepted at: Allen-Stevenson, Bank Street, Blue School, Calhoun, Chapin, City & Country, Corlears, Dalton, Ethical Culture, Friends Seminary, Grace Church, Hunter, Little Red School House, Packer Collegiate, Poly Prep, Riverdale, Rudolph Steiner, Spence, St Ann's, St. Luke's, Trevor Day, UNIS, Village Community School, and PS 3, 41 & 234.

Member.   ERB, DECA, NAEYC, NYSAIS, Parent's League.

Battery Park City Day Nursery

Ages: 1–5 yrs

Nonsectarian

215 South End Avenue,
  Battery Park City
  (between Albany Street
  and Rector Place, south of
  World Financial Center)
Zip: 10280
Tel: 945-0088
Fax: 786-1673
Website: www.bpcdaynursery.com

Established 1986
Denise Cordivano,
  Head of School
Darrlene Rosete,
Education Director
Enrollment: 150

School year.   September through June.

Ages	Hours	Days	Tuition (monthly)
1–2.11	8:00–6:00	Mon–Fri	$2,100
3–5	8:00–6:00	Mon–Fri	$1,925
1–2.11	8:00–12:00/2:00–6:00	Mon–Fri	$1,395
3–5	8:00–12:00/2:00–6:00	Mon–Fri	$1,245

Two and three full- and half-day a week schedules are also available at proportionate rates.

Program.   The developmental-interaction model is a primary influence. Activities include dramatic play, painting, drawing, cooking, working with puzzles and small play objects, music and dance, poetry, storytelling, block building, active outdoor play, and reading- and math-readiness for older children.

Admissions.   The application fee is $50. Currently parents may call at any time to see if positions are open and to arrange to see the school with their child and talk with the director. The child is invited into a classroom with a parent. Notification of admissions is continuous.

Class size.   Student/Child–Teacher ratio: Toddlers are 10 to 3; preschoolers are 15 to 3; and prekindergarteners are 20 to 3.

Staff.   Degreed head teachers and early childhood professionals as

275

assistant teachers make up the staff. The schools also trains interns from local colleges.

Facilities. Seven classrooms on the main floor of a residential building. Each is equipped with a bathroom and learning and play items. There is a backyard with a playhouse, climbing equipment, play cars, carts, etc.

Children bring their lunches. Snacks are provided.

Summer program. A summer program is available in July and August. Enrollment can be weekly or monthly.

Separation. Parents are asked to stay until both child and parent are comfortable.

Parent involvement. Parents may drop in any time. Formal conferences are arranged three times per year. Informal conferences are held as needed.

Financial. A deposit of one month's tuition is due on signing the contract. Tuition is payable monthly.

Transportation. Most children come from Battery Park City, the financial district, and Tribeca, or have parents working in the financial district. No private bus service is available.

Member. NAEYC.

Beginnings, A Toddler Program and Nursery School

Ages: 18 mos–5 yrs

Nonsectarian

130 East 16th Street
  (between Irving Place
  and 3rd Avenue)
Zip: 10003
Tel: 228-5679
Fax: 228-9907
E-mail: info@beginningsnursery.net
Website: www.beginningsnursery.net

Established 1983
Sheila Wolper,
Founder
Jane Racoosin,
Director
Claudine Zamor,
Admissions Director
Enrollment: 215

School year.   Mid-September through May; June and July Programs available for children enrolled in the school.

Ages	Hours	Days	Tuition
2s/Toddlers	2:30–4:30	2 days	$8,455
2s	9:30–12:30	2 days/3 days	$14,175
3s	8:45–12:45; 2:00–5:00	3 days	$12,170–$15,665
3s	8:30–12:30; 2:15–5:15	3, 4 days	$12,170–$17,655
4s	8:30–12:30; 1:45–5:15	3, 4 days	$13,050–17,655
4s–5s	8:30–12:30; 1:30–5:00	3, 4, 5 days	$13,050–$19,040

Extended hours.   For morning 4s and morning 4/5s, an extended day is available from Monday through Thursday at an additional cost.

Program.   Developmental. The school's goals for children are simple: to create a nurturing and stimulating environment, promote community and personal awareness within a group, encourage cooperation and problem-solving, and develop within each child a love of learning. The partnership between teachers and children—through careful attention to listening and observing—provides a collaborative environment which is rich in possibilities and responds to the unique wonders of each individual child.

Children work together in small groups and develop critical thinking skills and an awareness of the world around them. Creativity is fostered through the vast array of materials available along with a virtual artist-in-residence-type preschool teacher.

Admissions. The application fee is $75. Applications are available mid-August through mid-October. There's a lottery for applications dependent on space availability. Tours for families selected in the lottery begin the first week in November. Children visit in small groups in December and January. Notifications are sent in early March.

Class size. Children are grouped both chronologically and developmentally. Class size varies with age group. Each class has three or four staff members.

Staff. Head teachers have master's degrees in early childhood education. The school has a part-time child development consultant, available one day each week, as well as a music specialist and yoga teacher.

Facilities. The school occupies an entire commercial brownstone with classrooms on the ground, first, and second floors. There's an art studio on the second floor, and an incredibly stocked materials center on the top floor. The classrooms have access to a sunny play area with a wide range of equipment. Flower gardens and trees provide a welcome respite from city streets. Children bring their lunches and are served healthy and varied snacks (seasonal fruits, cheese, rice crackers, and pretzels).

Separation. The process includes home visits, a separation workshop for parents and caregivers, as well as a modified schedule that gradually builds to the full session. A parent or caregiver remains in the classroom until the child is comfortable.

Parent involvement. Parents coordinate fund-raising events, act as class parents, assist on field trips, participate in classroom activities, and help with the school library. Parenting workshops and seminars are offered throughout the year; topics include toilet training, limit setting, and sibling issues. Two parent/teacher conferences are scheduled yearly. Parents may visit at any time, join the group to read stories or share a project.

Financial. A deposit of $3,000 is due on signing the contract; tuition is payable in eight installments. Partial financial aid is available.

Transportation. Parents or caregivers bring the children, most of whom come from the East and West Village, Gramercy Park, Tribeca, and Soho.

Graduates. Have gone on to Allen-Stevenson, Berkeley Carroll, Blue School, Brooklyn Friends, Brearley, Browning, Buckley, Calhoun, Chapin, City and Country, Claremont, Collegiate, Columbia Grammar, Corlears, Dalton, Dwight, Ethical Culture, Epiphany, Friends Seminary, Grace Church School, Heschel, Hewitt, Horace Mann, Hunter Elementary, Little Red, Lower Lab School, Packer-Collegiate, Riverdale, Rudolf Steiner, Saint Ann's, Spence, Town, Trevor, Trinity, St. Luke's, UNIS, Village Community School, NEST + M, The Anderson Program, BISNY.

Bellevue Educare Child Care Center
Ages: 6 mos–4 yrs

Nonsectarian All-Day Care

462 Second Avenue
(at 27th Street)
Zip: 10016
Tel: 679-2393
Fax: 679-7366

Established 1971
Sarah J. Maldonado, EdD,
Executive Director
Dolores McCullough,
Client Services Coordinator
Enrollment: 41

School year. All year.

Ages	Hours	Days	Tuition (monthly)
6 mos–4 yrs	7:30–5:45	Mon–Fri	°

°Parents must call to inquire about the current fees.

Program. Children and staff are multilingual and multicultural, and emphasis is placed on interpersonal, self-evaluation, and verbalization skills. The curriculum is based on the High/Scope Educational Approach. The center uses a variety of preschool key experiences that allow a child to assess a situation and make independent choices. The school has an open classroom setting which incorporates different areas that include a library, blocks, music, house corner, science, art, and computers.

Admissions. The registration fee is $100. Inquire at least six months in advance. Admission availability is based on the age of the child. Tours are arranged at a mutually convenient time.

Class size. The class size is presently 10 infants, 10 toddlers, and 21 preschoolers. Due to the extended hours option, sometimes the center can accommodate more children.

Staff. Volunteers and interns occasionally augment the staff. Nurses, pediatricians, and social workers are available through Bellevue Hospital.

Facilities. Located within Bellevue Hospital Center, accessible through a staircase and elevators. Educare consists of one large area, divided imaginatively into three classrooms with interconnecting activities areas. Lockers are available for belongings. Activities areas include block building, library, dramatic play, music and movement, science, art, and table toys. The facilities are modern and inviting, imaginatively designed, and well-maintained and equipped.

Children are given breakfast, lunch, and an afternoon snack.

Separation. Parents bring the children and stay for the first day. Parents are asked to be accessible when it is felt the children need them. There is an open door policy.

Parent involvement. Many parents are on the staff of Bellevue Hospital. There are monthly evening meetings of the board, staff, and parents (child care is provided) on subjects chosen by the parents. Parents are members of the board of trustees. Parents also help with fund-raising and assist in the classroom. Field trips are organized by the parents association. Parents may visit whenever they choose, but they should call if they plan to spend a half or full day. Parent/teacher conferences are twice yearly or at the parents' request.

Financial. There are different measures of eligibility for enrollment. Parents can call the center for specific information.

Transportation. Parents are required to escort their children to and from the center.

Graduates. Attend both private and public schools.

Affiliations. Bellevue Hospital Center.

Bellevue South Nursery School
Ages: 2.10–5 plus yrs

Nonsectarian

10 Waterside Plaza (at 25th
Street and East River)
Zip: 10010
Tel: 684-0134
Website: bsnurseryschool.org
E-mail: bsns10@aol.com

Established 1970
Estelle Hofstetter,
Director
Enrollment: 30

School year. Early September through Early June.

Ages	Hours	Days	Tuition
2.10–3.8	8:45–11:45	Mon–Fri	$11,300
3.9–5	12:45–3:45	Mon–Fri	$11,300

Program. Eclectic. At Bellevue South Nursery School, the children are given a great deal of freedom to explore in a noncompetitive atmosphere. Teaching is informal and based on the child's interest. The director plays the piano and sings with the children daily. There is a combination of full group, small group, and individual activities which include art, water and sand play, block building, dramatic play, small play objects (beads, puzzles), daily music and movement, art projects, cooking, science and nature, reading, math, and computer-readiness.

Admissions. The application fee is $50. Inquiries are from mid-September on. Parents should call for information. They will be invited to attend the school's open house. A parent guide will answer questions. Parents are active in the school's operation and can serve in the classroom once a month. The school wants prospective parents to have a clear idea of what is involved. Interested parents are given an application form after the open house.

An appointment is made to meet the child, usually in a group with four other applicants, while school is not in session. During this time, the director will talk with the parents individually. Parent guides are also available to answer more questions about parent involvement in the school.

The school tries to balance the age range in the classes. Notifications are sent in March.

Class size. There are usually fifteen children in the morning class and fifteen children in the afternoon. There are two head teachers, the director, and a parent in the classroom. The afternoon program offers young 5s a chance to mature for kindergarten.

Facilities. The school is on the plaza level of the southernmost Waterside Plaza building. The 25th Street pedestrian bridge goes right to its door. One large, well-windowed room is divided into activities centers by low bookshelves filled with brightly colored plastic baskets containing small play objects and blocks. An adjoining room contains a climbing loft, workbench, a slide, a play kitchen, dress-up, and puppet theater. There is a child-sized bathroom. The children also use the playground in the Waterside complex.

Separation. Seen as a developmental process and a great deal of attention is paid to it. Parents are informed during the application process that they or their caregiver will need to make a two-week commitment when school starts and they are encouraged to stop by before school opens to familiarize their child with the location. Teachers visit new children at home; there is a parents' orientation meeting to explain the phasing-in process.

The children start in small groups with shortened hours, leading up to the full session and full group. Parents or caregivers remain in the classroom during this period, and their withdrawal is gradual.

Parent involvement. Parents are active in nearly every facet of the school. They constitute the board of directors, handle the school's payroll, bookkeeping, communications, and legal matters, and help coordinate admissions, oversee fund-raising, and serve as parent of the day. Parents organize a dinner with a silent auction in the spring and in the fall. In addition, there are frequent workshops on such issues as reading- and math-readiness, child development, and ongoing schools.

Financial.   A $3,500 nonrefundable deposit is due on acceptance and applied toward tuition. Tuition is payable quarterly.

Transportation.   No private bus service is available.

Graduates.   Have gone on to Collegiate, Brearley, Browning, Dalton, Friends Seminary, Hewitt, Horace Mann, Manhattan Country, Town, and UNIS, Village Community School, as well as local public schools and Gifted and Talented programs, including PS 158, and PS 116, NEST + M, and Hunter.

Member.   The Early Childhood Education Council, ERB, ISAAGNY, ATIS.

Blue School

Ages: 2–10 yrs

Nonsectarian Nursery and Elementary School

241 Water Street (between Peck Slip
   and Beekman Street)
Zip: 10038
Tel: (212) 228-6341
Admissions: 212-228-6341 x110
Website: www.blueschool.org

Established 2006
Don Grace,
Interim Head of School
Jeni Ardizzone-West,
Executive Director
Nursery and Kindergarten
Enrollment: 142
Total Enrollment: 200

School Year.   September through early June.

Ages	Hours	Days	Tuition
2s	8:45–10:30 or 11:00–12:45	Mon Wed Fri or Tues Thurs	3-day: $7,950 2-day: $5,300
3s	9:00–12:00 or 1:00–4:00	Mon–Thurs	$15,890
4s	8:45–1:00	Mon–Fri	$21,750
4s Extended Day (optional)	8:45–3:00 8:45–1:00 (Fri)	Mon–Fri	$29,820
Elementary (K–3rd)	8:45–3:00 8:45–1:00 (Fri)	Mon–Fri	$29,820

Program.   Blue School's curriculum is inspired by Co-Constructivist theory and the Reggio Emilia Approach. A whole-child approach recognizes that everyone is a part of the curriculum development process. Each child develops social-emotional, cognitive, and physical skills in individualized ways.

A child-centered curriculum where the content areas are both integral and interdependent. Curricular threads emerge from the interests of the children and are used to develop projects that will meet grade-level benchmarks. For example, while engaged in a single class project, the children develop literacy skills through problem-solving, reasoning, and comprehension skills, and extend their vocabulary while exploring the use of language. Through this same project children develop social skills such as turn-taking and building self-confidence. They also use observation, prediction, and reflection, as well as science and math skills.

Teachers use observation, reflection, and assessment to iden-tify each child's developmental profile. The developmental profiles then drive curricular content, teaching strategies, and differentia-tion of instruction.

Social and emotional learning are the key elements of a Blue School education and tie the entire curriculum together.

Admissions.   The application fee is $60. Online application requests are accepted beginning in mid August. Application deadline is December 1st for all grade levels. Once an application has been received, a tour, playgroup, and parent inter-view will be scheduled starting in September. Notifications are sent according to ISAAGNY deadlines.

Class size.   All classes have at least two teachers. The lead grade in

2012–13 will be 4th grade, and we will be adding one grade per year until 5th grade. There are four sections of 2s with a maximum of 10 children each, three sections of 3s with a maximum of 13 children each, two sections of the 4s–5th grade with a maximum of 18 children each.

Facilities. Located at 214 Water Street, in Manhattan's oldest commercial district, the newly redesigned, 33,168 sq. ft. six-story building will house the programs from the 2s through the 5th grade. Fourth grade will begin in 2012 and a fifth grade will begin in 2013. The school has multiple class sections and generous common spaces for a library, labs, studios, multipurpose/common space, small gymnasium, and play space.

Separation. The supported autonomy process begins in the 2s class, a parent participation class, when children are given activities individually and in small groups independent of their parent or caregiver. Children and parents or caregivers continue the process of building confidence and independence at the beginning of the 3s class. The goal is to meet each child's and parent/caregiver's need in a process that establishes a strong partnership between parents/caregivers and teachers.

Parent involvement. At Blue School, parent and family participation are critical components. In keeping with community as one of the school's core values, the presence of parents is welcome in the classrooms. It is a central goal to involve families in intentional projects that are linked to classroom initiatives.

Member. ERB, NAIS.

Borough of Manhattan Community College
Early Childhood Center

199 Chambers Street
Zip: 10007
Tel: 220-8250
Fax: 748-7462
E-mail: cscottcroft@bmcc.cuny.edu

Cecilia Scott-Croft,
Executive Director

For BMCC students' families only. Serves children ages 2 years through kindergarten. The family day care network serves children from two months through 12 years of age.

The British International School of New York
Ages: 3–14 yrs

20 Waterside Plaza (25th Street and
   the East River)
Zip: 10010
Tel: (212) 481-2700
Website: www.bis-ny.org

Established 2006
William T. Phelps,
Headmaster
Shehla Ghouse,
Deputy Head and
Curriculum Coordinator
Kristin Geiger,
Director of Admission
Enrollment: 255

School year. September through mid June.

Ages	Hours	Days	Tuition
3.0–3.11	8:40–3:20	Mon–Fri	$35,650
4.0–4.11	8:40–3:20	Mon–Fri	$35,650

°Extended hours: Early drop off: 8:15 A.M., after school supervision available until 5:30 P.M.; children must be toilet trained.

Uniforms are required for all students.

Program. Traditional/Developmental. The English National Curriculum and the International Baccalaureate's Primary Year's Program form the basis of the Nursery and Pre-K curriculum.

Each student's developmental level is considered and accommodated. "Learning through doing" is central to the school's philosophy. Work and play are interchangeable.

Units of Inquiry form the core of the program. These are an in-depth study of a topic that is significant, relevant, engaging, and challenging to the students. recent Units of Inquiry have included *Who Am I, People Need People, Let's Pretend, I Wonder, Our World,* and *What Can I Wear Today.* An atmosphere that encourages all students to engage in intellectual activity and independent thinking, going on field trips, meeting professionals, constructing play areas, and conducting interviews or surveys. Culminating experiences include sharing what has been learned with the parents or other classes.

The language arts program begins in pre-K. Students are encouraged to express their thoughts and feelings in words or pictures; this begins with creating non-representational art. In pre-K phonics, initial and final sounds as well as high frequency words are taught to enable independent reading and writing skills.

Students of The British International School of New York have the opportunity to study world languages such as French and Spanish from the age of three. The school believes that language is at the heart of student learning and is fundamental to thinking. As children progress, Latin and Mandarin are also incorporated into the curriculum.

Math in the early years is experimental. Children develop an understanding of basic math concepts through manipulating, counting, and sorting objects. They have the opportunity to experience mathematical concepts in their world by collecting data for graphs, learning about the calendar, and exploring patterns.

In music and art, children are exposed to another language. they work with specialist teachers twice per week. Students in Nursery and above exhibit their musical accomplishments during a winter and summer performance for their families.

A physical education specialist provides lessons twice per week, focusing on movement, body awareness, and team work. Weekly visits to the onsite swimming pool (starting in pre-K) give students the opportunity to learn and hone vital swimming skills from professional instructors.

The use of personal laptops and tablets allow seamless access in the classroom and everywhere around the wireless campus. ICT (Information Communication Technology) is introduced to BIS-NY students in pre-K; at this age they learn the basics of the computer and are encouraged to start exploring typing and using their mouse as well as playing educational games.

BIS-NY has 3 Houses that its pupils are assigned to from pre-K; the House system is designed to encourage and increase collaboration between students and to create a supportive environment among all age groups. House events range from academic to athletic competitions.

Once classes have ended at 3:20 P.M., students in Pre-K and above can choose from a wide range of after school activities or register for after school care from 3:30 to 5:30 P.M. After school activities change per term but may include yoga, music lessons, additional foreign language instruction, cooking, modern dance, chess and sports.

Admissions. The application fee is $125.

Application material and requirements are available on BIS-NY's website or by phone. Parents are encouraged to visit for a spring tour and attend the Open House in October. Children are assessed in small groups, for thirty to forty five minutes. A school report and teacher's recommendation is required if a child has previously attended school; applicants must have turned 3 by September 1st and be toilet trained in order to be eligible for Nursery. If space is available, BIS-NY offers rolling admissions to families who might need to apply outside of the normal admissions season.

Class size. The Nursery (3 year old) program averages 9 children per section with 2 teachers each. The pre-K (4-year-old) program averages 17 children per class with 2 teachers each.

Staff. Each class is led by a head teacher, with a graduate degree in education, and supported by an experienced assistant teacher. BIS-NY's teachers are selected for their international teaching experience as well as their passion for children and learning. The students in the Nursery and pre-K also work with specialist teachers for music, physical education, world languages, library, and art.

Separation. New students visit for a "tester morning" before school starts. There is a gradual phase in process for all Nursery students over the first 2 weeks of school.

Parent involvement. At BIS-NY, an active dialogue between the school and parent body is strongly encouraged. Parent involvement comes in various forms; be it structured involvement through the Parent's Association or individually by sharing a relevant area of expertise with a particular class. The school does not fund-raise or hold fund-raising events, so the Parent's Association focuses its efforts on "friend-raising" and building its community through events such as BIS-NY's Book Week, International Fair, and Parent's Night Out. The parent body is diverse, over 30 countries are represented.

Facilities.   The school is situated on the banks of the East River at Waterside Plaza (23rd Street) in Manhattan.

BIS-NY's modern facilities are custom built with floor to ceiling windows in many of the classrooms that provide an abundance of natural light and views of the East River. In the Nursery and pre-K classes children learn in large spacious classrooms and have access to a riverside private playground specifically designed for 3–5 year olds. Swimming is introduced in pre-K, with professional swim instructors teaching the children in a private pool. BIS-NY's state-of-the-art music, art, library, and PE facilities are utilized on a daily basis.

Brotherhood Synagogue Nursery School
Ages: 2.4–5 yrs

Jewish Nursery School

28 Gramercy Park South
(at 20th Street)
Zip: 10003
Tel: 995-9867
Fax: 505-6767
Website: www.brotherhoodsynagogue.org

Established 2001
Merril Feinstein,
Director
Enrollment: approximately 45

School year.   September through June.

Age	Hours	Days	Tuition
2.4–3.0	9:00–11:45	Mon Wed Fri	$11,150
3s	8:50–12:30	Mon–Fri	$14,300
4's	8:50–2:00 (Fri until 12:30)	Mon–Thurs	$16,000

Program.   Developmental. Special attention is paid to a child's individual needs by teachers and the director. Children are encouraged to participate in both large and small group activities that include language development, social skills, free play, circle time, science, snack, outdoor play, storytime, music, dramatic play, block building, art, and sand play.

Jewish traditions, values, and experiences are central to the program, through the celebration of Shabbat and other Jewish holidays.

Admissions. The application fee is $75. Parents may call the school the day after Labor Day to schedule a tour, and meet with the director. Applications are given out on the tours. An informational meeting for parents with the director is held along with a tour of the school.

Class size. In the 2s' group there are approximately twelve children to three teachers, the 3s' and 4s' will have roughly fifteen children and three teachers.

Staff. Teachers hold master's degrees in early childhood education and/or have extensive experience working with young children. Regular workshops are held with teachers and outside professionals. There is an early childhood consultant on staff along with a music and movement specialist, an art teacher, and a yoga teacher. Membership to a variety of early childhood organizations and associations is also provided. The director meets weekly with the staff.

Facilities. Located in a historic former Friends Meeting House, the new addition has three large classrooms and a private outdoor playground on the premises. The school is located adjacent to Gramercy Park.

Separation. Children are gradually expected to separate from their parents or caregivers. The school provides support to families throughout the process and does home visits and maintains frequent communication between home and school.

Parent involvement. The Parents Association is an active group of parents who volunteer for a variety of activities. There's a bookclub moderated by parent volunteers.

Graduates. Attend a variety of independent, public, and Jewish day schools including: Village Community School, Heschel, Solomon Schechter, Buckley, Dalton, Ethical Culture, Grace Church, Little Red School House, Rodelph Sholom, Birch Wathen-Lenox, PS 116 gifted and talented Program, NEST + M, PS 40, and PS 41.

Affiliations. Brotherhood Synagogue.

Buckle My Shoe Nursery School

Ages: 3 mos–5 yrs (Worth Street)
21 mos–5 yrs (West 13th Street)

40 Worth Street (at the junction
   of Church and Thomas Streets)
Zip: 10013
Tel: 374-1489
Fax: 577-9678
Website: www.bucklemyshoe.org
E-mail: lensko@bucklemyshoe.org

Linda Ensko,
Director
Preschool enrollment:
approximately 125

230 West 13th Street (between
   Greenwich Street and Seventh
   Avenue)
Zip: 10011
Tel: 807-0518
Call 374-1496 for inquiries

Preschool enrollment:
approximately 40

School year. Parents contract for September through June. A summer
program is offered for July and August. Full- and part-time programs
are offered for 3-month-olds through Pre-K at the Tribeca location,
and from 2 years to Pre-K at the 13th street school.

Ages	Hours	Days	Tuition (monthly)
Infants/toddlers	8–6	Mon–Fri	$2,000
2s		Mon–Fri	$1,950
3s–5s		Mon–Fri	$1,800

Toilet training. Not required for admission. Regular toileting time is
incorporated into the day's schedule, and children between 2 and 3
are encouraged to sit on the child-sized toilets as they are ready.
Students of all ages have a change of clothes on hand.

Program. The school follows a developmentally appropriate approach
in accordance with the Reggio Emilia philosophy. This includes
strong parental involvement and documentation of learning experiences. Children learn through hands-on, inquiry-based methods
with an emphasis on decision-making and socialization. Activities
include circle and storytime, art, science, math with manipulatives,

291

dramatic play, sand and water play, music, block building, computer, cooking, and gymnastics. Specialists offer French, Italian, movement, music, yoga, art, and theater. Children from the 3s on take monthly field trips to farms, museums, zoos, parks, and other destinations. The school also emphasizes community involvement, diversity, environmental responsibility, and nutrition.

Admissions. The application fee is $100 Parents attend a scheduled tour and meet with the director. Parents are interviewed by the administrative faculty.

Class size. The child to adult ratio for infants and toddlers is 3:1; for 2s, 5:1; for 3s, 6:1; and for 4s, 7:1. There are three groups: 2s, 3s, and 4s at the West 13th Street location.

Staff. Head teachers hold or are working toward a master's degree in early childhood education and have Reggio Emilia training.

Facilities. *Worth Street:* The vast (10,000 square feet) ground-floor space boasts high ceilings and light streaming in from two walls of windows. Low partitions divide the space into individual classrooms and play areas. Surfaces are colorful and clean, and the equipment is up-to-date. A roomy, cushioned gym is equipped with apparatus for tumbling and climbing as well as swings. A dedicated art space, or atelier, offers children a hands-on creative arts experience. Children use nearby Washington Market Park and Hudson River Park; as well as other community venues such as theaters, libraries, etc.

West 13th Street: The school has three rooms on the ground floor of a carriage house. While the classes rotate to share certain facilities such as the sandbox, water table, and mat-lined climbing area, each group is based in a classroom of its own. Books, math manipulatives, art materials, and puzzles are available on accessible shelves in activity areas. A large carpeted room that includes an upstairs loft playhouse and a piano is available to the 4s. The children use nearby playgrounds.

Separation. Depends on the individual child. Parents of 2s are encouraged to stay until the child is comfortable. To ease separation, parents may schedule play dates at the school for their child before school begins.

Parent involvement.   The school has an open door policy; parents are welcome in the classrooms. Potluck dinners at the beginning and end of the year; a parents' advisory board addresses school-wide issues, planning, and fund-raising. Parents volunteer for class trips and parent/teacher curriculum evenings are held once a month. Two parent/teacher conferences are scheduled yearly, more if requested.

Financial.   Tuition depends on the program and is payable in four yearly installments.

Graduates.   Have gone on to private and public schools including, City and Country, Corlears, Ethical Culture, Friends Seminary, Hunter Elementary, Little Red School House, Packer Collegiate, Trinity, Village Community, and PS 6, 124, 234, 41, and 3 as well as NEST + M, Hunter and other gifted and talented programs.

Member.   NAEYC.

Chelsea Day School

Ages: 2–5 yrs

Nonsectarian Nursery School

319 Fifth Avenue
  (32nd and 5th Ave)
Zip: 10016
Tel: 675-8541
Fax: 675-8385

Established 1981
Jean Rosenberg,
Director
Enrollment: 136

School year.   Second week in September through second week in June.

Ages	Hours	Days	Tuition
2s/3s	9:00–12:00	3 days	$12,000
3s	9:00–12:00	Mon–Fri	$17,500
3s–5s	9:00–3:00	Mon–Fri	$23,900

Extended days available weekly to 3 P.M., at an additional fee. There is an insurance fee of approximately $500. Toilet training is not required.

Program.   Developmental. Chelsea Day School was founded by its current director, Jean Rosenberg, who has taught children two to eighteen years of age. The school prefers to be known as the one that follows "the principles of child development." The curriculum stresses play and uses projects to encourage learning, intellectual growth, and build community. Ongoing projects are planned to bring families together. Religious rituals are not observed, but the "Celebration of Light" is. "The yearbook is a particular favorite of mine," says Mrs. Rosenberg. "The children's photographs and pictures are a fine example of preschool art work."

Staff.   The 2s/3s classes have twelve children in each session with two teachers; the 3s have fifteen each with three teachers; the 4s have sixteen with two teachers. Each class has specialists in art and music twice a week. There are two classes at the entry and three classes of 3s and 4s each. There is a teacher's enrichment fund that is used for conferences, staff development workshops, and study in Reggio Emilia.

Facilities.   The school moved in 2007 to a newly designed facility on the second and third floor of a four-story building on Fifth Avenue at 32nd Street. There are eight classrooms, a large central meeting room, and a roof playground and garden above the fourth floor.

Summer program.   Runs for six weeks; from 9 A.M. to 1:00 P.M. or 3:00 P.M. for an additional fee.

Parent involvement.   Parents may visit at any time without an appointment. They serve on school committees, run the library, create the yearbook, tend the garden, and run the Auction and Winter Fair. The school is closed twice a year for parent/teacher conferences, and parents are encouraged to request additional conferences whenever they feel the need.

Financial.   A non-refundable deposit of $2,000 is required upon signing of contract for the school year. Half of the remaining tuition is due on June 1st, the balance on November 1st. A non-interest bearing loan of $1,000 per family is required. Financial aid is available.

Transportation.   Children come from Murray Hill, Tribeca, Brooklyn, the Chelsea and upper Greenwich Village neighborhoods. Public bus service is available. No private bus service is available.

Graduates.   Have gone on to Brooklyn Friends, Chapin, Convent of the Sacred Heart, Dalton, Ethical Culture, Friends Seminary, Hewitt, Grace Church, Little Red School House, Midtown West, Saint Ann's, St. Luke's, Spence, Village Community School, as well as PS 3, 11, 41, 89, 116, and 234.

Chartered.   By the Board of Regents of the State University of New York.

Member.   Downtown Early Childhood Association, NAEYC and ISAAGNY.

The Children's Garden at General Theological Seminary

Ages: 2 mos–4 yrs

440 West 21st Street (between
  9th and 10th Avenues)
Zip: 10011
Tel: 243-5150, ext. 346
Fax: 727-3907
Website: www.gts.edu
E-mail: stein@gts.edu

Susan Stein,
Director
Nursery enrollment: 32

School year.   Year-round.

Ages	Hours	Days	Tuition (monthly)
Infants to 2.0	8:00–6:00	Mon–Fri/ 2 or 3 days	$1,155–$1,875
Preschool	8:00–6:00	Mon–Fri/ 2 or 3 days	$1,105–$1,825
(2s, 3s and 4s)			

Program.   Developmental. The child's interests, abilities, and experiences determine the curriculum for all age groups, with a special emphasis on encouraging social and verbal skills in an age-appropriate way. The twos and preschoolers daily activities are open-ended and include art, music, dramatic play, block building, sand, water play, pre-reading, math-readiness, and cooking projects. A musician often comes once a week to work with both classes and there is a strong emphasis on daily outdoor activity.

Admissions. There is no application fee. Inquiries are at any time; admissions are rolling. Parents should call the director to arrange to visit the school. Families of all religious traditions are welcome. Siblings and seminarians have priority admissions.

Class size. The infant room has eight children, and the preschool has thirteen. Each classroom has three full-time teachers, one of whom is licensed, and part-time assistants.

Facilities. One of the best-kept secrets in Chelsea, this small preschool nestles on the grounds of an 1830s seminary, its stone and brick church and buildings set amid grassy, tree-shaded lawns. The school has a large playground with swings, slides, a sandbox, and wooden climbing equipment. Children also ride trikes and scooters on the enclosed paths. They cultivate a garden along the playground fence. The preschool feels like a little house filled with amiable clutter. On campus, there is one small and one large room joined by a long bathroom and child-sized facilities.

Separation. Parents remain in the classroom as needed, leaving for increasing periods of time. Separation is an individualized process. Children usually take a week or two to fully separate.

Parent involvement. Parents can visit at any time, and come along on trips. Two parent/teacher conferences a year are supplemented by informal monthly meetings of parents and teachers where developmental issues and classroom activities are discussed.

Financial. Upon admission, there is a non-refundable registration fee of $250, along with a non-refundable deposit equal to one month's tuition payment, which is applied to the last month's tuition. There is a separate monthly fee for the music program.

Affiliations. General Theological Seminary.

Member. Downtown Early Childhood Association (DECA), National Association of Episcopal Schools (NAES).

The Children's International Workshop at Union Square

Ages: 2–5 yrs

17 East 16th Street (between Union Square West and Fifth Avenue)
Zip: 10003
Tel: 691-8964

Established 1976
Jacquelyn Marks,
Director
Enrollment: 60

School year. September through June. A summer program is available in July and August.

Ages	Hours	Days	Tuition (monthly)
All	8:30–12:00	3 days	$800
	8:30–12:00	Mon–Fri	$1,200
	12:30–5:30	3 days	$800
	12:30–5:30	Mon–Fri	$1,200
2s/3s/4s	8:30–5:30	Mon–Fri	$2,000
2s/3s/4s	8:30–5:30	3/4 days	$1,400–$1,800

There is an added charge for diapers. Flexible hours available for full-day program.

Program. The main emphasis is on the arts (painting, drama, music), along with a full readiness program for the 3s, which introduces children to the alphabet and numbers from 1 to 20. The readiness program relies on manipulatives as well as games and stories. Group play is also important, allowing young children to learn how to work out their fears and anxieties by role playing. Every other week the children take trips. The 3s visit the neighborhood police and fire stations, the deli, park, and farmer's market. Threes and 4s go to locations that complement their art and readiness programs, such as museums, the Empire State Building, the Fashion Institute of Technology, and parks. There is an annual exhibit of the children's artwork to which parents and friends are invited. There are no computers in school in accordance with the school's philosophy.

Admissions. The application fee is $35. Applications are on a rolling basis. Parents are asked to tour the school and the children are observed informally.

Class size. The student-teacher ratio is 5:1 for 2s, 6:1 for 3s to 5s.

Staff. The teachers have degrees in the fine arts and/or early childhood.

Facilities. According to the director, "We feel that nursery school children, especially those living in Manhattan, need space, light, and a warm feeling in their environment. The Children's Workshop is situated in a 2,000-square-foot loft with an emphasis on light and space. We purposely keep a home-like atmosphere and stay away from the classroom-like environment which your child will have from kindergarten through college."

Separation. Handled on an individual basis. Usually the child begins with an abbreviated schedule and parents stay on the premises as long as necessary.

Financial. Tuition is due yearly or in monthly payments.

Graduates. Have gone on to Friends Seminary, Grace Church, Little Red School House/Elizabeth Irwin and UNIS.

Chinatown Day

Ages: 2–5 yrs

35 Division Street
Zip: 10002
Tel: 431-3845

Gary Wen,
Director
Serves 150 children

City and Country School

Ages: 2–13 yrs

Nonsectarian Nursery and Elementary School

146 West 13th Street
   (between 6th and 7th
   Avenues)
Zip: 10011
Tel: 242-7802
Total enrollment: 360
Website: www.cityandcountry.org

Established 1914
Kate Turley,
Principal
Elise Clark,
Director of Admissions
Nursery enrollment
(IIs, IIIs, and IVs): 112

School year.   Second week of September through mid-June.

Ages	Hours	Days	Tuition
2s A.M.	9:00–11:30	Mon–Fri	$19,320
2s P.M.	1:00–3:30	Mon–Thurs	$16,590
3s A.M.	9:00–12:50	Mon–Fri	$22,890
3s P.M.	1:30–4:50	Mon–Fri	$20,580
4s	9:00–3:00	Mon–Fri	$27,620
5s	9:00–3:00	Mon–Fri	$29,700

By 3, children should be toilet-trained.

Extended hours.   3:00–5:45 for 4s–7s, at an additional cost. Children may be dropped off at 8:40. Early morning drop-off begins at 8:00 A.M. for an additional fee.

Program.   Progressive. One of the city's leading progressive schools, it was founded by Caroline Pratt in 1914. Her brilliant work and that of innovative educators associated with her was closely studied by the Bureau of Educational Experiments (later Bank Street) and was influential in the development of progressive education. Pratt's book, *I Learn from Children,* describes the experimenting through which the programs originated and reflects the respect for children that the method embodies.

The core of the preschool program is block building and dramatic play. Children create increasingly complex structures out of blocks that represent their world. Then they explore the social roles connected with the world they have created. Preschool activities include painting, collage and clay work, science, library and story time, music, woodworking (3s–5s) and movement, play with small objects, and vigorous outdoor play.

Another distinctive feature of City and Country is the absence of the usual dramatic play (housekeeping or dress-up corner) that most nursery schools have. C&C maintains that props channel a child's imagination too narrowly and often separate the boys and girls.

Both boys and girls participate equally in block building. Children do not congregate around "boys" or "girls" activities, commonplace behavior in many nursery schools, where boys monopolize the blocks, Legos, and the workbench, and girls use the housekeeping corner. A C&C member noted that both sexes show equal interest in blocks and woodworking. Teachers assist children to discover how to work as a group.

Admissions. The application fee is $50. Inquiries are from Labor Day on. The admissions process is informal. Parents observe the school in operation, escorted by the admissions director. Then 2s and 3s, accompanied by parents, are seen in small groups in a play setting. Notifications are sent by March, according to ISAAGNY guidelines.

Class size. There are two 2s classes of ten each, and two morning classes each of 3s, 4s, and 5s, and an afternoon class of 3s, each with at least two staff members. Teaching assistants are usually graduate students in early childhood education who come to this unique school for training. Specialists working with the children include a psychologist, art, music and rhythms teacher, a learning specialist, and librarian.

Facilities. Children and parents are buzzed through a windowed door into an airy reception room directly on street level. The school takes up a total of seven remodeled brownstones that have been sound-proofed and child-proofed. The buildings straddle 12th and 13th Streets and include the outdoor courtyards in between. As the school has grown, City and Country also occupies a three-story building joined by the school's outdoor yards, on West 12th Street. The rooms are large and many windowed, with high ceilings. They have open central spaces available for block building and dramatic play, rather than the strongly defined activities areas found in traditional schools. The furnishings are sturdy and well maintained.

In every nursery area there are shelves of the building blocks designed by the school's founder and now a staple in most nursery schools. The degree to which a school is progressive is almost measurable by the amount of space and time devoted to building with these blocks. More space and time are devoted to them here than in any school in the city.

City and Country has a smaller range of materials than many other schools, and they are simple, open-ended ones which the school believes will avoid overstimulation.

Commercial or adults' artwork is not displayed in the nursery rooms. Pinned to classroom walls are portfolios of each child's often vibrant and expressive art. Children do not take it home daily to show their parents; they are not doing it for parental approval. It is their work.

A large backyard play area augments the school's rooftop play area and rainy-day playroom. The gymnasium, used in the school's innovative rhythms program, has a high, wood-beamed ceiling.

In the outside play areas there are sturdy green crates, large enough to hold several children, lightweight aluminum hanging ladders for climbing into and out of, miniature sawhorses, planks for construction, and the large hollow blocks. With these materials, children construct their own play spaces.

Separation. The 2s, 3s, and 4s are visited by their teachers before school begins. Parents are requested to give whatever time they are able to the separation process, which may take anywhere from a week to four weeks. When school begins, children are brought into the class in small groups for short sessions. Parents remain with them in the classroom, withdrawing gradually to stand by in the foyer if needed.

Parent involvement. The school attracts families from all five boroughs and New Jersey. There's a broad range of parents whose professions range from the arts to the more traditional occupations of medicine, law, and investment banking. There are frequent parent/teacher get-togethers above and beyond the twice-yearly academic conferences. Evening lectures are held at which teachers explain their methods and work, or in which an outside professional speaks. The board of trustees is composed of alumni, parents, staff, and friends.

Financial. A deposit of $4,000 is due by February 15 or according to the contract date for those who enroll later. The balance of tuition and fees is payable in five installments. A 10-installment plan is available as well. Both plans begin April 1st. A $500 enrollment fee is required. Many parents make additional financial contributions to the school's Annual Fund.

Graduates. Have gone on to Art and Design, Bronx Science, Brearley, Brooklyn Friends, Calhoun, Dalton, Dwight, Elisabeth Irwin, Fieldston, Friends Seminary, Horace Mann, Marymount, Music and Art, Nightingale-Bamford, Riverdale, Saint Ann's, Spence, Stuyvesant, Trevor Day, Trinity, Regis, UNIS, as well as other schools.

Member. ERB, ISAAGNY, NAIS, NYSAIS.

Corlears School
Ages: 2.6–10 yrs (5th grade)

Nonsectarian Nursery and Elementary School

324 West 15th Street
(between 8th and
9th Avenues)
Zip: 10011
Tel: 741-2800
Fax: 807-1550
Website: www.corlearsschool.org
E-mail: office@corlearsschool.org

Established 1968
Thya Merz,
Head of School
Saphiatou N'Jie,
Director of Admissions
Nursery enrollment: 55
Total enrollment: 180

School year. Early-September through the second week in June. Summer program from mid-June through the end of July.

Ages	Hours	Days	Tuition
2s/3s	8:45–12:00/3:15	Mon–Fri	$20,035–$25,475
4s/5s	8:45–3:15	Mon–Fri	$27,525
6s–10s	8:45–3:15	Mon–Fri	$29,740

Extended hours. Early drop-off (8:00) and after-school care are available for children age 3 years and older at a modest fee. In addition, after school specialty classes for 4s and up include drama, chess, sports, and foreign language.

Program. Developmental/Progressive. The core curriculum consists of social studies and science. Preschoolers learn through direct observation and hands-on activity. Teachers pay close attention to socialization and emotional development. Language arts evolve through listening and responding to storybooks, dictating stories, verbal problem solving, and the writing process. Science is begun through cooking, daily observations about the weather, seasonal changes, planting seeds, water experiments. Observations, such as "What floats/What sinks," are recorded on wall charts. Math (one of this school's great strengths) begins as play with multi-colored Cuisenaire rods, which encourage abstract thinking and problem-solving and what the school calls "Big Ideas."

Children's varied artwork—figurative and abstract—has a free, exuberant look reflecting each child's unique style. Children write stories with illustrations. The school prides itself on its sense of community. Corlears is very much a neighborhood school.

Admissions. The application fee is $50. Interested families are encouraged to attend the autumn open house. Morning tours are given twice weekly during October and November. The application deadline is December 1st. ERB scores are not required. The director of admissions interviews parents. Children applying participate in small playgroups. Notifications are made according to ISAAGNY guidelines.

Class size. The twos and threes classes are limited to sixteen children. Other classes range from eighteen to twenty.

Staff. Each classroom has a head teacher and one assistant teacher, most are in graduate school. There are specialists in art, music, movement, physical education, science, library, and Spanish. There's also a learning specialist, reading specialist, and a consulting social worker.

Facilities. Completed in 2011, Corlears's building provides large, bright classrooms each with its own bathroom and kitchen area. Classrooms provide a large block space, a place for dramatic play, carpeted meeting and reading area, plus stations for cooking, washing-up, and science. All ages visit the 14,000 volume library, science lab, art studio, and gym. Every day, children spend time in the large back yard. Full-day children bring their lunch.

Summer program. Five-week program in natural science and technology for children ages 3 to 9 years; open to children from other schools.

Separation. "It's a gentle weaning," says the school's admissions director. Children begin the year with small groups and partial days. The younger children take a week or two to adjust. Parents leave the classroom when the children are ready.

Parent involvement. Parents serve on the school's board, and run initiatives and fundraisers such as the Spring Fair, Auction, the Diversity Committee, and more. Most of the parents give to the annual fund. Parent/teacher conferences are scheduled twice-yearly.

Financial. A tuition deposit of $6,000 is due upon enrollment. The balance is due in equal installments May 1 and September 1. Each family makes a non-interest bearing, one-time loan of $1,000 per child, payable in three installments. The annual building and equipment fee is $1,000, $600 for the second child, none for the 3rd child.

Twenty-five to thirty percent of students receive financial aid, ranging from 15 to 90 percent of tuition. A deposit of $200 is required for families receiving financial aid.

Graduates. Graduates have gone on to Allen-Stevenson, Berkeley-Carroll, Brooklyn Friends, Browning, Calhoun, Dalton, Ethical Culture, Fieldston, Friends Seminary, Hewitt, Little Red School House, Nightingale-Bamford, Packer-Collegiate, Poly Prep, St. Luke's, UNIS, and Village Community School.

Chartered. By the Board of Regents of the State University of New York.

Accredited: The New York Association of Independent Schools (NYAIS).

Member. ERB, ACS, NAEYC, ISAAGNY, NAIS, NAEYC, NYSAIS, Early Steps.

CP Kids

Ages: 3 months–5 yrs

Nonsectarian

The Field House at Chelsea Piers
  Pier 62
  23rd Street and Westside Hwy
Zip: 10011
Tel: 336-6500 ext. 6573
Fax: 336-6515
Website: www.chelseapiers.com/fh
E-mail: bistil@chelseapiers.com

Established 2004
Lindsay Bistis,
Director
Enrollment: 70

School year. September–June or year-round.

Age	Hours	Days	Tuition (monthly)
3 mons–5 years	8–6	5/4/3/2 days	$1,325–$1,795/ $1,075
3 mons–5 years	9–3:30	5/4/3/2 days	$1,090–$1,355/ $815

Program. Developmental. The guiding philosophy of the program at CP Kids is that optimal development takes place in an environment that gives balanced, attentive care to the whole child. The school works to support, nurture, and encourage children to grow in three basic areas: physically, through careful attention to the child's health, fitness, and nutrition; socially, by building strong relationships characterized by trust, respect, and love; and cognitively, through active learning, which forms the basis for all other activities.

Admissions. The application fee is $75. Parents can call anytime to arrange a tour of the preschool. Priority in admissions is given in the following order of affiliation: Chelsea Piers employees, tenants of Chelsea Piers, clients of Chelsea Piers, community members.

Class size. The class is made up of 9 to 15 children with two full-time teachers.

Staff. Lead teachers are New York State certified. Assistant teachers have previous experience in early childhood education and various levels of higher education.

Facilities. CP Kids is located in the Field House at Chelsea Piers. The school features a new, sunny, and spacious classroom. The school also has access to the facilities within the Field House and parks located nearby.

Summer program. The summer program runs during July and August. It follows the curriculum of the regular school year with more time devoted to outdoor activities.

Afterschool program. Parents may request additional hours at a rate of $14.00 per hour or may sign up for the extended day program that includes the hours from 8–9 A.M. and 3:30–6 P.M.

Separation.   Parents spend two full days in the classroom with the child, participating in activities and helping the child adjust to the new environment.

Tuition assistance.   Discounts are given to Chelsea Piers employees, Chelsea Piers tenants, and siblings.

Transportation.   Chelsea Piers is not far from the 23rd Street stop of the C and E subway lines. The M23 bus makes stops in the Chelsea Piers complex.

Downing Street Playgroup Cooperative
Ages: 2–4 yrs

32 Carmine Street
Zip: 10014
Tel: 924-2557
Website: www.downingstreetplaygroup.org
E-mail: info@downingstreetplaygroup

Nancy Mastrototaro,
Director
Enrollment: Approximately 25

School year.   Follows the New York City public school calendar.

Ages	Hours	Days	Tuition (monthly)
2s/young 3s*	9 A.M.–12 P.M.	Tues Thurs	$341
3s/4s	9 A.M.–12 P.M.	Mon Wed Fri	$435
3s/4s**	9 A.M.–2 P.M.	Mon Wed Fri	$565
3s/4s	9 A.M.–12 P.M.	Mon–Fri	$656
3s/4s	9 A.M.–2 P.M.	Mon–Fri	$803

*After attending the school for one semester, families may apply to be part of the "lunch bunch" program, which extends the day to 2 P.M.
**For returning families only.

Program.   The Downing Street Playgroup is a cooperative playgroup that was founded in 1969 by a group of parents. Parent participation is an integral part of the program and the school's success. The aim of the program is to foster a supportive learning environment where a love for learning is instilled in every child. Children learn to socialize and express themselves through creative activities.

There's an emphasis on helping children become active members in the school's community.

Classes are directed by a certified teacher who works with an assistant teacher and a rotating parent teacher.

Admissions. The application fee is $40. Applications can be downloaded from the school's website. The application fee is non-refundable. Applications are processed from Labor Day through mid-December. Applications received after the December deadline are placed in a second pool and families are notified if openings become available. Open house tours are held in the evening, usually in late October. In January through February, applicant families attend a tour/playdate during which parents and their children come to the school to explore the classroom and meet teachers in a small group. Priority is given to siblings and children of alumni. Admissions decisions are sent out in early March in accordance with ISAAGNY's calendar.

Class size. The 2s/3s group has a maximum of twelve students and the 3s/4s has a maximum of 15 students.

Facility. The school is located at 32 Carmine Street on the second floor above the Downing Street public playground.

Parent involvement. Since the school is a cooperative, parent involvement is mandatory. Parents serve as parent-teachers once a month and manage administrative and financial duties and are involved in just about every aspect of the school. Meetings are held for one hour in the evenings each month.

The Downtown Little School
Ages: 2–5 yrs

Nonsectarian Nursery School

15 Dutch Street

Zip: 10038

Tel: 791-1300

Website: www.downtownlittleschool.org

Established 1999

Kate Delacorte,

Co-Director

Meredith Gary,

Co-Director

Enrollment: 85

School year. September through mid-June.

Ages	Hours	Days	Tuition
2s	8:45–11:15 or 12:00–2:30	Mon–Thurs	$10,300
3s	8:45 – 11:45 or 1:00 – 4:00	Mon–Fri	$10,300
4s	9:00 – 12:00	Mon–Fri	$10,300
	9:00 – 2:30	2 days	$15,760
4s/5s	9:00 – 2:30	Mon–Fri	$15,760

Program. Major stated goals of the school are "to have the children feel comfortable in an educational setting, to stimulate their curiosity, to give them the opportunity to explore materials and social relationships." The school offers interrelated experiences that emphasize language skills, the exploration of feelings, dramatic play and block building, and include science, art, music, water play, and cooking.

Admissions. The application fee is $50. The school accepts applications right after Labor Day adheres to ISAAGNY guidelines, and has a lottery. A waiting list is maintained. Preference is given to siblings. The school seeks diversity.

Staff. Head teachers have completed or are close to completing a masters degree in early childhood education.

Facilities. There is one ground floor area with a rooftop playground.

Summer program. The summer program runs for six weeks.

Separation.   Twos have a 3-week phase-in period, threes have a 1-week phase-in.

Parent involvement.   Conferences are held twice a year and as requested by parents or teachers. Parents are welcome in the classroom.

Financial.   A tuition deposit of $1,000 is required when parents register. The balance is payable in three installments. Financial aid is available.

Graduates.   Have gone on to a wide range of public and private schools.

East Village Tots Childcare Center
Ages: 2–4 yrs

Nonsectarian

297 East 10th Street

Zip: 10009

Tel: 982-8701

Fax: 982-8701

Website: www.eastvillagetots.com

Established 1983

John Touhey,

Founder

Danyce Alonzo,

Director

Enrollment: 15

School year.   September through July.

Ages	Hours	Days	Tuition (monthly)
2–4	8:30–3:00	Mon–Fri	$1,100
2–4	8:30–3:00	3 or 4 days	$850–$950

Program.   Developmental. Play is seen as the child's work in a nurturing social and emotionally supportive environment. Social skills are stressed. Activities include block building, sand and water play, dramatic play, cooking, storytimes, play with puzzles, games, small play objects, as well as arts, crafts, and music.

Admissions.   There is no application fee. Inquiries are ongoing. Applications are accepted whenever positions are open. Parents will be asked to visit the center and meet the director. Children are observed in groups with the parents

309

present or they may join in school activities. Parents are notified of acceptance on an ongoing basis.

Class size.   There are five 2s, 3s, and 4s and three staff members; with a 5 to 1 student/teacher ratio.

Facilities.   The ground floor of a residential brownstone on the northern edge of Tompkins Square Park. Children us Tompkins Square Park for outdoor play. They bring their lunches.

Parent involvement.   Parent visits are welcome any time, and there are social get-togethers once or twice a year. Parents serve on the board of directors and help arrange social events. Families come from the East Village, and the parent body is extremely diverse.

Financial.   A deposit is required on signing the contract, payments follow a prescribed schedule. Tuition is payable on the first of every month. There is a charge of $10 if a child is picked up late. Financial aid is available.

Transportation.   No private bus service is available.

The Educational Alliance Preschool
Ages: 2–4 years

Jewish Nursery

197 East Broadway (between
Jefferson and Clinton Streets)
Zip: 10002
Tel: (646) 395-4250
Website: www.edalliance.org/preschool

Established 1970
Leslie Klein Pilder,
Director
Enrollment: 85

School year.   Early September through early June.

Ages	Hours	Days	Tuition
2–5	8:30–12:30	2, 3, 5 days	$4,955–$9,510
2–5	8:30–3:00	2, 3, 5 days	$6,930–$11,490
2s	2:00–4:00	Tues Thurs	$2,840

Early drop-off and extended day options (3–6 P.M.) are available for an additional $100 to $330/month.

Program. The Educational Alliance Preschool provides students with child-centered classrooms based on NAEYC (National Association for the Education of Young Children) guidelines. Each classroom offers children a mixture of individual, self-directed play, and group activities led by teachers. Every room has learning centers which provide children the opportunity to interact freely with the environment and each other, developing cognitive, social, emotional, and physical skills. Each classroom has a reading corner, a sand table, an art area, a dramatic play corner, and block center (as mandated by law). Teachers provide small group and whole class experiences for the children, engaging youngsters in activities not easily experienced on their own. Art, cooking, science, literacy, and cultural lessons often occur in group settings.

Based on interest, the Torah Tots classrooms direct simple Jewish blessings as part of the curriculum.

Admissions. The application fee is $150. Tours begin in mid-September and applications are due by December 30th. Parents should call to arrange to visit the school. Parents are notified in March. Children of all faiths are welcome.

Class size. In accordance with regulations of the New York City Department of Health; typically for 2s classes there are two teachers for ten children; three teachers for a class of 12. For 3s, there are two teachers for a class of 15.

Staff. All lead teachers have master's degrees in early childhood education. Assistant teachers are certified by the New York City Department of Health.

Facilities. The school is located within the Educational Alliance, a community center and settlement house. In addition to its large classrooms, the school has play roofs equipped with climbing apparatus. Children use the gym daily where there are tricycles, wagons, balls, and mats. Children bring their own lunches. Snacks are provided by the parents and the school. All shared food is Kosher.

Summer program. Weekly summer programs/sessions are available.

Parent involvement. There is an active Parent Association which raises money for the school, plans special activities (such as holiday parties), and helps create a state of the art preschool experience.

Parents are encouraged to share their talents both in and out of the classroom. Seminars for parents on topics of interest are offered. Teacher conferences are held twice yearly, and are available at any time upon request. Parents are encouraged to stay with their children during the early transition weeks.

Financial. A deposit equal to two months tuition is required upon contract. The remainder is payable monthly (Credit cards and electronic transfer are accepted.) Partial financial aid is available. There is a 10 percent discount for siblings and a special early bird discount of 5 percent of the tuition, excluding the registration fee if the entire tuition is paid when contracts are due.

Transportation. Most of the children come from the school's immediate neighborhood: the Lower East Side, Tribeca, Soho, and the Village. The school is close to public transportation.

Graduates. Have gone on to Beth Jacob, The Blue School, Little Missionary, Manhattan Day School, Mesivta Tifereth Jerusalem, Ramaz, St. James and St. Joseph's, The Town School, and Village Community, UNIS, as well as the Earth School, the Neighborhood School, NEST + M, P.S. 234, 130, and 110.

Affiliations. UJA Federation of New York, which also provides some of the school's scholarship money, JCC Association, United Neighborhood Houses.

Member. Downtown Early Childhood Association.

First Presbyterian Nursery School

Ages: 2.3–5 years

12 West 12th Street (between
Fifth and Sixth Avenues)
Zip: 10011
Tel: 691-3432
Website: www.fpcns.org
E-mail: info@fpcns.org

Established 1952
Ellen Ziman,
Director
Enrollment: 105

School year.   Monday after Labor Day through mid-June.

Ages	Hours	Days	Tuition
young 2s	9:00–11:30	Tues & Fri	$9,000
older 2s/young 3s	1:00–3:30	Mon Wed Thurs	$12,140
3s	8:45–11:45/1:00–3:30	Mon–Fri	$14,760
4/5s	8:45–11:45	Mon–Fri	$16,800
	8:45–2:15	Mon–Thurs,	$20,430
		Fri until 1:15	

Children need not be toilet-trained on entry.

Program.   Developmental Interaction. The school's philosophy is inspired by the Reggio Emilia Approach and is based on the principle that learning occurs best through interaction and relationships with peers and adults and also through hands-on involvement with carefully chosen materials in a responsive environment. Children are encouraged to make choices and solve problems and explore and discuss in a setting that includes a variety of work areas: blocks; sensory and art materials; music, movement, cooking, dramatic play; and caring for plants and animals. Language skills are developed through conversation, literature, and storytelling. Age-appropriate curriculum evolves from the children's interest both as a group and as individuals. Interests are pursued in the classroom through discussion, books, and investigations; and outside the classroom through trips in the building and neighborhood and city. Large motor activity takes place daily, on the roof playground or indoors during inclement weather. For the 4s, there is a twice-a-week after-school program offered in six-week segments and focusing on special interests such as printmaking, gardening, etc.

ERBs are administered on the premises.

Admissions.   The application fee is $45. Call between the Monday after Labor Day and the end of September to request an application. Returned applications are entered into an admissions lottery. Families whose applications are drawn from the lottery are invited to see the school for a tour/open house. Tours and open houses are held in October and November. There are 33 openings for 2s each year, at least 9 for 3s, and typically a few for 4/5s. Children's visits follow in January and February and consist of a 30-minute classroom playtime with a few other children. Parents remain with their children during the visit.

Admissions notifications are sent in accord with ISAAGNY guidelines, in early March. Early notification is given to siblings, church members, and children of former students. Early notification status does not guarantee admission.

Class size. Ten to twelve 2s, fifteen 3s, twenty or twenty-three 4/5s.

Staff. Each class has a head teacher and assistant teacher, an aide, student teachers, and specialists. Head teachers have a master's degree/certification in early childhood education; assistant teachers have a bachelor's or associate's degree in early childhood with professional experience. There are specialists for woodworking, music, and movement. A consulting psychologist visits the school every week.

Facilities. The school is located on the fourth floor of the church house. The school's, well-equipped facilities include four spacious classrooms with tall windows overlooking church garden and 12th Street, a circulating library of children's and adult books, a woodworking room, and a room set up for movement and indoor play in inclement weather. There is also a fenced-in, rubber-padded roof playground with a playhouse, climbing equipment, riding toys, big blocks, balls, etc. Children bring their own lunches; snacks are provided.

Separation. A parent meeting is held before the first day of school to explain the separation process which is gradual and may be adjusted to individual abilities and needs. For young 2s, a parent consultant assists parents through the phasing-in period, when schedules build incrementally from a shorter day with half groups to a full session with full groups. The goal is for children to be in school without their parents as soon as they are able to be in a group relying on the teachers for support.

Parent involvement. There are parent/teacher conferences twice a year as well as ongoing dialogue with parents about their children. The school holds an open school night to discuss curriculum and an ongoing schools night to help parents plan their search for their child's next school. In addition, the school offers occasional parenting workshops as well as a seminar series on parent issues such as communication, discipline, and siblings.

Parents participate in classes on school birthdays, act as trip chaperones, and share their talents, jobs, and stories with the children. They also volunteer in the parent-run library and in various fund-raising activities such as the bake sale, puppet show, and the annual auction. Parent fund-raising supports the scholarship fund.

Financial. A $1,000 deposit applicable toward tuition is required with the signed contract. The balance of tuition is paid in three installments; a monthly payment schedule can also be arranged; tuition assistance is available based on need and availability of funds.

Transportation. Children come from Greenwich Village, the East Village, Soho, Tribeca, Chelsea, Gramercy Park, Stuyvesant Town, and are brought by their parents or caregivers.

Graduates. Have gone on to Allen-Stevenson, Brearley, Brooklyn Friends, Buckley, Calhoun, Chapin, City and Country, Corlears, Dalton, Dwight, Ethical Culture, Epiphany, Friends Seminary, Grace Church, Little Red School House, Packer Collegiate, St. Ann's, St. Luke's, Spence, Trinity, UNIS, Village Community, as well as Hunter Elementary, the Lab School, PS 3, PS 41, PS 116 and other public schools.

Affiliations. First Presbyterian Church.

Member. Downtown Early Childhood Association, ERB, ISAAGNY, ATIS.

14th Street Y Preschool
(formerly known as "Gani")
Ages: 2.4–5 yrs

344 East 14th Street
Zip: 10003
Tel: (646) 395-4325/6/7
Website: www.14streety.org
E-mail: liz_hirsch@14.streety.org
zelda_warner@14streety.org

Established 1984
Liz Hirsch,
Director
Zelda Warner,
Admissions
Enrollment: 90

School year. Mid-September through beginning of June. Summer program available.

Ages	Hours	Days	Tuition*
2s/3s	9:00–1:00	3 days	$11,300–$12,850
2s/young 3s	1:45–4:45	3 days	$9,400–$10,600
3s/4s	9:00–1:00	5 days	$13,900–$15,400
3s/4s	9:00–3:00	5 days	$15,900–$17,450

*Members of the Y receive a discount.

Extended hours. Early drop off is available for an additional charge when there is sufficient interest.

Program. Developmental. The 14th Street Y's experienced early childhood staff provides a warm, nurturing environment, helping young children grow socially, emotionally, and educationally while gaining self-confidence and exploring new concepts. The school's philosophy is inspired by both the Reggio Emilia and Bank Street approaches. The curriculum includes a variety of activities, including imaginative play, language arts, block building, sand and water play, art, music, fine and gross motor activities, and storytelling. The program provides children with a thematic approach to learning. Topics of interest are chosen by the children in the class and are investigated in the classroom learning centers. Children always use manipulative materials when learning math and science. Jewish values are woven through the program in a variety of ways. Jewish holidays and Shabbat are observed and celebrated through stories, songs, dance, games, and cooking projects. There is physical activity on the outdoor rooftop playground and gym.

Admissions. The application fee is $50. Applications are available online after September 1st or parents may call to request an application. The school will contact parents to schedule a time to tour with the director/staff with their children.

Class size. Ranges from 12 in the 2s/young 3s class, to a maximum of 20 in the 4s with a minimum of two teachers in each class.

Staff. All teachers meet certification requirements of the Department of Health. The school provides staff with a range of professional development opportunities.

Facilities. The school occupies an entire floor of a four-story Jewish Community Center on 14th Street between First and Second Avenues. The floor has been divided into five extremely large classrooms. A large indoor gymnasium and a rooftop playground that provides excellent space for gross motor activities. There is a dedicated art room, movement studio, and an indoor pool for weekly swim instruction for the four-year-olds

Summer program. June through mid-August.

Separation. Gradual phase-in. Parents are asked to be available until the child adjusts.

Parent involvement. The 14th Street Y Preschool has an active Parents Association. The PA hosts several social fund-raising events during the year. The Parenting and Family Center offers classes and activities in all areas of family life: support, guidance, parenting tips and education including workshops and classes on parenthood, prenatal care, Mommy and Me, single parenting, working moms, Me and My Dad, and more. The combination of Parenting and Family Center with the 14th Street Y Preschool provides families with extensive and innovative educational, social, and cultural experiences.

Financial. A deposit of $2,500 is due on signing the contract; the balance is payable in six installments beginning July 1st and December 1st. Financial aid is available.

Transportation. No private bus service is available.

Graduates. Graduates have been accepted at many private schools including City and Country, Corlears, UNIS, Friends Seminary, Grace Church, Saint Ann's, the Abraham Joshua Heschel School, Little Red School House, Ramaz, Rodeph Shalom, Solomon Schecter, and Ethical Culture. Public schools include neighborhood schools, NEST + M, Hunter College Elementary School, and other gifted and talented programs.

Affiliations. The 14th Street Y is a program of the Educational Alliance.

Member. Downtown Early Childhood Association, ERB, BJE, Parents League.

Jack and Jill School
Ages: 2.6–5 yrs

Nonsectarian Nursery School

209 East 16th Street (between   Established 1949
  3rd Avenue and   Mrs. Jean Leshaw,
  Rutherford Place)   Director
Zip: 10003   Enrollment: 55
Tel: 475-0855
Website: jackandjillschool.com

School year. Mid-September through June 4.

Ages	Hours	Days	Tuition
young 3s	9:00–12:00	Mon–Fri	$12,160
	1:00–4:00	Mon–Thurs	$9,910
young 4s	8:45–12:15	Mon–Fri	$12,970
	8:45–2:30	Mon–Fri	$13,940
4s/5s	8:45–3:00	Mon–Fri	$14,190

Children must be 2½ when they enter and must be toilet-trained. Early morning drop-off at 8:15 A.M. may be arranged for a fee.

Program. Traditional. The school, though it eschews workbooks and worksheets and focuses strongly on social development, also includes a structured reading- and math-readiness program and many activities with a strong cognitive focus. Activities include

318

cooking, science, dramatic play, block building, carpentry, arts and crafts, storytime, and work with small play objects. The 3s focus on social adjustment and self-care, seasonal observations and celebrations, and simple concepts. The 4s and 5s have more defined study units and take many field trips. An integrated curriculum allows exploration through varied activities. Special classes are offered in Spanish and music/movement.

ERBs are given on the premises. Some ongoing school admissions directors visit to observe applicants in a classroom setting.

Admissions. The application fee is $75. Inquiries are from October on. The applications deadline is January 15th. Parents should call for an applications packet and ask for the date of the school's open house. Tours are given weekly in the fall. After submitting an application, parents arrange an interview with the director during November or December. The child is observed in January or early February. Notifications are sent by March. Preference is given to children of parish members and siblings.

Class size. There are two 3s classes of eleven, one young 4s class of twenty, and one 4s/5s class of twelve to fourteen children. The 3s classes have two teachers, the young 4s have three teachers and the 4s/5s class has a head teacher and an assistant.

Facilities. The school is located on the ground floor of St. George's Parish House. The entrance is down a flagstone-paved drive and off the church's tiny courtyard. There are three comfortable classrooms, two of which look out on the play yard facing 16th Street. The yard has an imaginative climbing structure. The classrooms are well equipped and divided into small activities centers for dramatic play, block building, woodworking, storytime, and so on. On rainy days, the school uses the flagstoned church chantry as a play space. Mats cover the floor. A hall in the church is used for weekly music and movement classes.

Summer program. Three weeks in June and a July camp.

Separation. Teachers visit children at home before school begins. Children are introduced in small groups for shortened sessions. Parents may remain in the classroom, especially the first week, but are encouraged to wait in the hall after that.

Parent involvement.   Parents are involved in raising funds. There are occasional evenings with outside experts speaking on child development, and breakfasts devoted to ongoing schools selection and the ERBs. Parents are welcome in the classroom. Conferences are held twice yearly.

Financial.   A registration fee of $1,500 is due on signing the contract. The balance is payable in two installments in June and November or in nine monthly payments, June through February. Some scholarship aid is available.

Graduates.   Have gone on to Allen-Stevenson, Birch Wathen, Brearley, Browning, Buckley, Chapin, Collegiate, Convent of the Sacred Heart, Corlears, Dalton, Epiphany, Ethical Culture, Family School, Friends Seminary, Grace Church, Greenwich Village Neighborhood, Heschel School, Hewitt, Horace Mann, Lenox, Little Red School House, Marymount, Nightingale-Bamford, Park East Eshi, Rudolf Steiner, St. Ann's, St. Bernard's, St. David's, St. Hilda's & St. Hugh's, St. Joseph's, St. Luke's, Spence, Town, Trinity, UNIS, and Village Community School.

Member.   ERB, Downtown Schools Association, ISAAGNY, NAEC, Parents League.

Jewish Community Project
Ages: 2.4-5 yrs

Early Childhood Center

146 Duane Street
Zip: 10013
Tel: 212-334-3533
Website: www.jcpdowntown.org
Associate Director
Marcia Marks Thaler,
Assistant Director, Preschool
Enrollment: 150

Established 2005
Sharon Sharofsky Mack,
Director
Wendy Gelsanliter,

Tuition. $6,500 (3 days, 3 hours)–$19,700 (5 days, 5 hours).

Program.   Developmental. The Preschool fosters growth of each child in nurturing environment that supports all areas of their development (including cognitive, social, and emotional) and encourages emerging independence. The school works with parents to form partnerships and to set appropriate goals for children. The importance of community is central to the program.

The curriculum provides multiple opportunities for children and families to explore Jewish heritage, holidays, and appreciation of Jewish life. Jewish values are integral to the philosophy of the program.

The Resource Collaboration Method, a system for using collaboration, observation, and context to best realize abilities in every student, has been pioneered at the JCP Early Childhood Center and is being presented as a model to early childhood educators statewide.

Summer program.   A summer camp is available.

Admissions.   The admissions fee is $70. All interested families are required to attend an information session before applying to the preschool. The program is explained in full, time for questions and answers, and a tour of the facility is given. After these meetings, applications are available for those who are interested. Group play visits are scheduled in January and notification letters are sent in accord with the ISAAGNY calendar.

Staff.   Each class has three teachers, a head teacher with a master's degree, an associate, and an assistant. There are specialists for movement, music, speech, parenting, and early childhood development. The teaching staff is routinely available.

Separation.   A home visit followed by a gentle phase-in schedule assists children in forming bonds of trust as they acclimate to classroom life.

Parent involvement.   A strong Parent Association assists in creating a cohesive sense of community. Conferences occur twice a year and parents are invited to visit the class several times throughout the year, including an opportunity to participate in the weekly in-class Shabbat celebration.

Financial.   Financial assistance is available.

Graduates. Graduates opt for a wide variety of ongoing schools, including public, private, downtown, uptown, Brooklyn, single sex, and coed.

Kid's Korner
Ages: 20 mos–5 yrs

247 West 24th Street   Established 1992
 (between Seventh and Eighth Avenues)   Yolanda Contrubis,
Zip: 10011   Director
Tel: 229-9340   Jennifer Denza,
Fax: 414-5745   Education Director
Website: www.thekidskornerpreschool.com   Enrollment: 38

School year. September through June. A July and August summer program is optional.

Ages	Hours	Days	Tuition
2s/3s	8:30–5:30	2 to 5 days	$8,581–$18,728
	8:30–4:00	2 to 5 days	$8,581–$12,790
	9:00–12:30 or 2:30–5:30	2 to 5 days	
4s/5s	8:30–5:30	3 to 5 days	$15,052–$18,728
	8:30–4:00	3 to 5 days	$14,111–$16,934

Further flexibility of schedule is available.

Program. Developmental. Kid's Korner strives to give children a warm, accepting environment where they will develop confidence, self-esteem, inner discipline, and increasing independence. The children explore and discover their world through structured and free-play activities, which enable each child to learn at his or her own pace.

Admissions. The application fee is $50. Applications are available on the website and must be submitted before a tour can be scheduled. There is a playdate for the child with a teacher and a small group of other children.

Class size.   There are three classes. The 2s have six children, the 3s and the 4s/5s have a maximum of twelve each.

Staff.   Each class has a full-time teacher and an assistant teacher. Music and Spanish are part of the curriculum. Yoga, dance, and piano are optional.

Facilities.   The school occupies two floors in a brownstone in Chelsea. Both the 3s and 4s/5s rooms are arranged into centers focusing on science, blocks and puzzles, art, music, and dramatic play.

Parent involvement.   Parents and teachers keep in touch about a child's development through informal and scheduled conferences. The school encourages parents to participate in as many school events as their busy schedules allow. Parents are often invited to speak about or show the children any special skills or interests. Parents also help to raise funds for the school so that teachers can attend educational conferences as well as meet other needs.

Financial.   One-quarter of the year's tuition is required upon enrollment. The balance is payable in three installments. Siblings receive a 5% discount.

Graduates.   Have gone on to City and Country, Corlears, Dalton, Epiphany, Hunter, Little Red School House, Our Lady of Pompeii, St. Luke's, UNIS and Village Community School, as well as The Anderson Program, Lower Lab, and public schools in the area.

Member.   NAEYC.

Third Street Music School Preschool

Ages: 2*–5 yrs

*Must be 2 by March 15th before school starts.

Nonsectarian

235 East 11th Street (between
  2nd and 3rd Avenues)
Zip: 10003
Tel: 777-3240
Fax: 477-1808
Website: www.thirdstreetmusicschool.org
E-mail: ryoung@thirdstreetmusicschool.org

Established 1979
Risa Young,
Director of Early Childhood Programs
Enrollment: 86

School year. September through mid-June.

Ages	Hours	Days	Tuition
2s	9:00–12:00 1:00–4:00	Mon–Fri	$12,400
3s	9:00–12:00/ 1:00–4:00	Mon–Fri	$12,200
4s–5s	9:00–3:00	Mon–Fri	$15,500

Program. Developmental. The Third Street Music School Settlement was founded in 1894, "to provide arts instruction to the children of the Lower East Side, regardless of their ability to pay." It is the oldest community music school in the country. LAM (Learning, the Arts and Me, now named The Third Street Music School Preschool), is the nursery program. It emphasizes fostering creativity and social development. Learning is through exploration. Music, art, creative movement, early language, and math are all part of the curriculum. Third Street was the prototype for settlement schools throughout the country and has provided artistic training for thousands of children.

There are many group projects which encourage children to cooperate, share ideas, and plan work together. The warm relationships teachers foster with the children creates a relaxed, respectful and cheerful tone which allows children to feel comfortable and truly express themselves. The arts are integrated into the math, language arts, science, and social studies curriculum. There's weekly Spanish class plus countless ways the school immerses the children in something Spanish daily.

Nearby resources, such as St. Mark's farmer's market are visited. In the fall, groups often choose to study apples or pumpkins, discovering how the produce got to the city, how it grows, and how it is harvested. Children walk to the market, interview farmers, look at all the different wares, and make purchases. After returning to school, children talk or create books about their experiences, and have cooking projects that have yielded apple crisp and apple sauce. One math activity has children taste-testing different color apples, red, green, and yellow, and graphing the results based on favorites.

Orff Instruments are introduced; children meet once a week with an Orff-trained music specialist as well as a creative movement specialist. Children learn with the music specialist. Every month children learn a new instrument. By the 4s, age appropriate instrumental classes are offered with a focus on violin and keyboard. There are also dance performances and concerts that classes may attend.

Admissions. The application fee is $40. Applications are available on the website in August. Tour reservations begin after Labor Day, and are scheduled from October through January. The application deadline is January 15th. A group play interview will be scheduled for the parent and child once an application has been received. Notifications are sent according to ISAAGNY guidelines.

Class size. Fours class is eighteen each, sixteen in the 3s class, with two teachers per class; 2s have twelve children and three teachers.

Staff. Teachers are fully certified, and have been at the school for 15 years. There is an active teacher development program, and all teachers have extensive experience in early childhood education, and hold a degree. Head teachers are all Orff trained and all are experienced music teachers. Assistant teachers hold bachelor's degrees.

Facilities. The recently renovated preschool classrooms of the Third Street Music School, include a 300-seat auditorium, and many studio/practice rooms equipped with pianos, a dance studio, and special classrooms. The school's music library houses over 10,000 records, books, libretti, and scores. The program has its own preschool library. There is music instruction for children and adults as well as 36 music education partnerships.

Summer program. A five-week Summer Arts Camp, relaxed program for children 3 to 6 years-old from the end of June though July. Children bring their own lunch and must be toilet-trained.

Separation. Separation is gradual and based on the individual needs of the child. The first day of school is a one-hour visit. School starts with a modified schedule that gradually builds up to a full schedule. Parents or caregivers may stay in the classroom until the child feels comfortable. Teachers work closely with parents and children to facilitate a smooth separation process.

Parent involvement. The Parents Association is composed of class representatives and other parent volunteers who assist in planning special events, the library, the annual fund-raiser, and projects. The school hosts a book fair, an art fair, and Curriculum Night potluck dinner each year.

Parent/teacher conferences are held twice a year, and parent discussion groups which focuses on child development, child rearing, and how children learn are offered throughout the year.

Financial. Parents submit a deposit along with a contract. Approximately fifteen percent of students receive financial aid.

Affiliations. The Third Street Music School Settlement is a member of the National Guild of Community Schools of the Arts, the Downtown Early Childhood Association (DECA), ERB, ISAAGNY, and the Parents League.

Graduates. Have gone on to Friends Seminary, Grace Church, Hannah Senesh, Special Music School, Village Community School, Little Red School House, St. Luke's, UNIS, as well as PS 41, PS 40, PS 3, PS 116, PS 234, PS 3, PS 110, Hunter, NEST + M, the Neighborhood School, Children's Workshop, Earth School, and the Lab school.

Sara Curry Preschool at
Little Missionary Day Nursery
Ages: 2–6 yrs

Nonsectarian

93 St. Mark's Place

Zip: 10009

Tel: 777-9774

Fax: 777-2655

Established 1896

Eileen Johnson,

Director

Enrollment: 39

School year. Beginning of September through end of June. A summer program is available.

Ages	Hours	Days	Tuition (monthly)
2s	8:30–3:00	Mon–Fri	$1,275
3s	8:30–3:00	Mon–Fri	$1,275
4s	8:30–6:00	Mon–Fri	$1,275
2s, 3s, 4s	*3:00–6:00	Mon–Fri	$25 per day
	*(afterschool program)(3–5-day option)		

Three- and four-day programs are also available at a prorated cost; after-school tuition varies based on the number of days and hours.

Program. Developmental. The goal of the program is for teachers to be in tune with each child's psychological development. Children learn how to express themselves and communicate and to be part of a social group. Play is used as a means for children to develop problem-solving strategies. The program is enriched with art, music, dance, and trips. Children go out daily to a playground or the library

Admissions. There is no application fee. The application process for the following September begins in January. Families must attend an open house, complete an application, and come in for an individual visit with their child. The school seeks to keep all its classrooms balanced in terms of gender, age, and to reflect to the diversity of the community.

Class size. In the 2s classroom there are twelve children with three teachers. The 3s classroom has fifteen children with three teachers and in the 4s program there are twelve children with three teachers.

The afterschool program has eight to twelve children with two to three teachers.

Facilities.   The school is located in the ground and first floors of a brownstone owned by the school; it has a front garden and a rear play yard. Outdoor play also takes place in Tompkins Square Park playgrounds and play spaces, other local parks, and the community garden at 6th Street and Avenue B. Children bring their own lunches, but healthy snacks (whole-grain crackers, fruits and vegetables, juice) are served at regular points during the day.

Summer program.   There is a summer program in July available for children two to six years of age.

Separation.   Separation is based on the needs of the individual child and family. Parents/caregivers are encouraged to stay until both they, and the child, feel comfortable at school and are welcome in the classrooms as long as their behavior is consistent with the program's aims.

Parent involvement.   Parents/caregivers serve on the board of directors and its related committees. Families are extremely active in fund-raising and construction projects. The school functions best by creating and developing a partnership between educators and families, one that takes into account and serves the needs of children and the people who care for them. Parent workshops are presented monthly in collaboration with The New York Psychoanalytic Society's Parent Child Center. These workshops provide a safe and open environment for parents to discuss parenting issues under the guidance of experienced professionals. This is a free service to parents.

Financial.   Tuition is due at the beginning of each month. Some financial assistance is available. ACS vouchers and other child care subsidies are accepted.

Graduates.   Generally go on to alternative public schools in District 1 and some private schools.

Little Star of Broome St. Day Care Center

Ages: 2–5 years

131–51 Broome Street
Zip: 10002
Tel: 673-2680
Fax: 777-7971

Mary Cheng,
Director
Early childhood enrollment: 65

School year: Open all year.

Hours: 8:00–6:00, depending on individual needs of families.

Facility: The school is located in a one-story building with four spacious classrooms, a large library, kitchen, and an outdoor playground with an area for gardening and apple trees for picking.

Financial: Licensed to take ACS vouchers.

Affiliation: Chinese-American Planning Council

Manhattan Kid's Club

Ages: 3 mos–5.8 yrs

Nonsectarian All-Day Care

21 East 13th Street
Zip: 10003
Tel: 741-3774
Fax: 989-7897

Established 1996
Beth Garcia,
Executive Director
Bouasavanh Rathamarry,
Educational Director

(Second Location)
629 East 14th Street
Zip: 10009
Tel: 533-1977
Fax: 533-1719

Beth Garcia,
Educational Director
Enrollment (13th Street): 89
Enrollment (14th Street): 136

(Third Location)
Opening in 2011–2012

School year. Year round.

Ages	Hours	Days	Tuition (monthly)
3 mos–9 mos	7:30–6:00	Mon–Fri	$1,700
10 mos–24 mos	7:30–6:00	Mon–Fri	$1,700
2–3.8 yrs	7:30–6:00	Mon–Fri	$1,700
3–5.8 yrs	7:30–6:00	Mon–Fri	$1,700

The monthly tuition is pro-rated for fewer days per week and includes snacks, lunch, and diapers.

Program.   The Manhattan Kid's Club is a full-time, child care center that encourages social interaction and exploratory play while nurturing positive self-esteem. The program is child-centered and activity-oriented, providing youngsters with a varied environment to explore at their own pace and according to their individual cognitive abilities. The school believes, "childhood should be a journey . . . not a race." All families are welcome; children can learn to recognize what they have in common while respecting and enjoying the diversity that makes each of them unique.

The daily activities include both individual and group time, free choice and structured activity, as well as quiet and active periods. The space is divided into areas offering creative art activities, dramatic play, books, cognitive games, and small- and large-muscle activities.

The most important goal of the curriculum is to help children become enthusiastic learners. This means encouraging them to be active, creative explorers who are not afraid to try out their ideas and think their own thoughts.

Admissions.   The registration fee is $150. Children may be enrolled at any time throughout the year. Tours are given by appointment only. If a class is at capacity, parents may place their child on a waiting list.

Class size.   The infants and 1s classes have eight children each with three teachers, the 2s have ten children each with two teachers, and the 3s, 4s, and 5s have eighteen children with two to three teachers in each class.

Facilities.   At the 15th Street location, there are eight classrooms, an indoor gymnasium, kitchen, staff area, and business office. The children use Washington Square and Union Square Parks for outside play time. At the 14th Street location, there are eleven classrooms, infant/toddler indoor play space, children's library room, and kitchen staff area. The children use the Stuyvesant Town playgrounds.

Separation.   Before entering, families and children are encouraged to visit for a few hours to become familiar with the teachers and students. Because each child is different, the staff works with the parents and child to make the transition as easy as possible.

Parent involvement.   Parents are welcome at all times to observe, visit, or eat lunch with their children, as well as to volunteer to help in the classroom (volunteers must have a PPD/Mantoux tuberculosis test yearly). All communication between the staff and the families is based on the concept that parents are and should be the principal influence in children's lives. Parents are invited to two parent/teacher conferences each year and are encouraged to speak with the staff about any concerns or questions they have about their child with regard to the program. Parents are asked to volunteer for school cleanings, held on two separate weekends, which enables the school to limit the days the school is closed.

Financial.   One month's tuition is required as a deposit. Tuition is paid monthly by the 5th of each month.

Transportation.   Most families live or work in the neighborhood and the children are brought by their parents or caregivers. No private bus service is available.

Manhattan Nursery School
Ages: 15 mos–5 yrs

Nursery School

38 West 32nd Street, Suite 306
   (between Fifth Avenue and Broadway)
Zip: 10001
Tel: 631-0543/0547
Fax: 244-8077
E-mail: contact@manhattannurseryschool.com

Established 1996
Sinok Park,
President
Kyeongsook Rim,
Director
Enrollment: 93

School year.   All year.

Ages	Hours	Days	Tuition (monthly)
15 mos–2 yrs	8:00–7:00	Mon–Fri	$1,410
2–3 yrs	8:00–7:00	Mon–Fri	$1,270
3–5 yrs	8:00–7:00	Mon–Fri	$1,210

Tuition is pro-rated for two-, three-, and four-day-a-week schedules. Flexible hours are available for all ages. A 5% sibling discount is available.

Program.   Developmental. The program offers various educational activities, which include art, dramatic play, table games, puppetry, read-alouds, songs, poems and musical games. Breakfast, lunch, and snack are provided.

Admissions.   Parents call for an appointment to tour the facility and are required to submit an application. The school maintains an active waiting list.

Class size.   There are seven classes. The toddler class has a maximum of twelve, the pre-K a maximum of sixteen.

Staff.   Each class has a head teacher and assistant teacher.

Facilities.   Classrooms are large, colorful, bright, and very cheerful. Various learning areas focus on library, reading, housekeeping, puzzles, blocks, drama, art and music, and computer. The school is fully air conditioned and carpeted and features a well-equipped indoor playground.

Parent involvement.   Parents are closely involved in the school's day to day activities. There are two parent/teacher conferences each year.

Financial.   A registration fee of $50 as well as a half-month's tuition deposit are required upon registration. In addition, a $10 materials fee is payable each month. The half-month tuition deposit is returned to the parent upon the child's departure from school.

Transportation.   Parents bring their children directly to the classrooms.

Mei Wah Preschool
Chinese Methodist Center Corporation

Ages: 3–5 yrs

Methodist All-Day Care

69 Madison Street
  (at Catherine Street)
Zip: 10002
Tel: 349-2703
Fax: 349-0702
E-mail: cmcc@cumc-nyc.org

Established 1975
Mey Joy Choy,
Director
Enrollment: 20

School year: All year.

Ages	Hours	Days	Tuition (monthly)
3–5 yrs	8:30–6:00	Mon–Fri	$475
3–5 yrs	8:30–12:30 or	Mon–Fri	$375
	3:00–6:00	Mon–Fri	$275

Children must be toilet-trained.

Program. Developmental. The program is bilingual and bicultural and offers an early childhood curriculum.

Admissions. There is no application fee. Parents may call at any time of year to see if vacancies are open and to arrange to visit the school. Children are accepted on a first-come basis. If no spaces are available, children will be put on a waiting list.

Class size. There is one group of 20 children with two staff members.

Facilities. The classroom is fully equipped and there is an indoor gym. Snack, lunch, and supper are homemade and provided daily.

Parent involvement. There is an orientation meeting in which the Center's regulations are discussed. Parents are involved in fundraising and assist at holidays and on field trips. Visits are by appointment only.

Financial. There is a $50 non-refundable registration fee. Tuition is payable monthly or in advance.

Transportation. No private transportation.

Graduates. Attend public and parochial schools.

Affiliation. Chinese United Methodist Church.

Montessori School of Manhattan
Beach Street Campus and Gold Street Campus
Ages: 2–6 yrs

Montessori School

54 Beach Street (between
  Hudson and Greenwich Streets)
Zip: 10013
Tel: 334-0400
Fax: 334-0483

2 Gold Street (between
  Maiden Lane and Platt Street)
Zip: 10038
Tel: 742-2830
Website: www.montessorimanhattan.com
E-mail: administration@montessorimanhattan.com

Established 2003
Mrs. Bridie L. Gauthier,
  Head of Schools
Ms. Kristin Ramey,
  Director of Education/Admissions
Ms. Sharahn McClung,
  Director of Administrative Affairs,
  Beach Street Campus
Ms. Cecelia Fernandez,
  Director of Administrative Affairs,
  Gold Street Campus
Enrollment:
  Beach Street:
  250 capacity
  Gold Street:
  300 capacity

School year. September–June

Ages	Hours	Days	Tuition
Toddlers (2s)	12:45–3:45	Tues Thurs	$10,750
Toddlers (2s)	12:45–3:45	Mon Wed Fri	$12,750
Toddlers (2s)	8:45–11:45	Mon–Fri	$16,750
Toddlers (2s)	12:45–3:45	Mon–Fri	$16,750
Toddlers (2s)	8:45–3:45	Mon–Fri	$21,750
Preschool (3–6 yrs)	9:00–12:00	Mon–Fri	$15,750
Preschool (3–6 yrs)	1:00–4:00	Mon–Fri	$15,750
Preschool (3–6 yrs)	9:00–4:00	Mon–Fri	$20,750

Program. Montessori. The environment and curriculum are designed to provide children ages 2 to 6 with a life-long love of learning. The Montessori-certified teachers are specially trained in using Montessori methods and materials to successfully guide each child in developing unique abilities within a carefully planned curriculum. Using learning materials designed to be responsive to a wide range of interests and skills, children are encouraged to explore a world of ideas, information, and creativity. The Montessori curriculum stresses an interdisciplinary approach to learning.

Supported by one-on-one guidance from teachers, students work both independently and in small groups with other children. Parents and community resources contribute to and enrich the learning partnership.

Admissions.   The application fee is $50. Parents should download the application from the school's website. When a completed application is received, the admissions department will contact the family to schedule a classroom observation. A parent interview and classroom observation are required. The admissions department reviews all applications. Parents receive a contract after children have been accepted. Admissions is complete when the school receives the signed contract and specified fees. Priority is given to siblings and alumni families.

Children applying for preschool must be toilet-trained; children applying for toddlers do not have to be toilet trained.

Class size. Toddlers: 10 children, two teachers; Preschool: 16 Children, two teachers.

Staff. Teachers are Montessori certified and have New York State

Department of Education certification. All teachers are CPR and first aid trained and certified.

Facilities. The Beach Street campus consists of three toddler classrooms and six preschool classrooms on three floors. The beautifully renovated facility is all natural wood, with natural lighting in each classroom. There is a playroom on each floor where students have music, yoga, drama, performing arts, and movement classes. There is an art studio where they have weekly art lessons.

The Gold Street campus consists of four toddler classrooms and five preschool classrooms on a single floor. This facility is also all natural wood, with natural lighting in each classroom, and a full gymnasium, art studio, and yoga studio. Students participate in music, yoga, drama, Spanish, movement, and art specialty classes in addition to the traditional Montessori curriculum.

Summer program. Part-time and full-time programs are available. The MSM Summer program follows the same daily schedule as the one followed during the academic year with a greater emphasis on cultural studies and physical development. During the summer the children spend more time enjoying swimming, on outdoor activities, music, yoga, Spanish, Tae Kwon Do, and arts and crafts projects.

After School. Optional after-school classes are offered at the Beach Street campus from 4:00–4:45 P.M. once per week. These classes include, but are not limited to: Spanish, ballet, cooking, Tae Kwon Do, and musical theater.

The Wall Street campus offers early drop-off and late pick-up for those families requiring an extended school day. Students in the Extended Hours Programs enjoy a variety of art, music, and group activities, as well as snack, storytime and free play. Children may be dropped off as early as 8:00 A.M. and picked up as late as 6:00 P.M. The Extended Hours Programs are available for both occasional and regular use.

Separation. New children take part in a gradual phase-in in which children first meet in smaller groups for a shortened schedule. During the phase-in days, parents should be prepared to remain at or close to the school. If a child shows a willingness to allow parents to leave the classroom they are encouraged to do so. Other children may experience greater difficulty in separating from parents and need them to remain in the classroom for a longer period of time. Each child's separation needs are addressed individually.

Parent involvement.   Parents are encouraged to join the Parents Association, take part in educational workshops, and volunteer for classroom activities. The Parents Association meets with the Head of Schools regularly throughout the school year. One of the major goals of this group is to provide activities and events that will enrich the lives of the student body. The PA sponsors, plans, and implements annual fundraisers and takes part in other enriching activities.

Workshops on a variety of topics are offered by staff two or three times each year and all MSM families are encouraged to participate in these events. Parents are also encouraged to be involved in their children's school life in a variety of ways, including, sharing their expertise and talents, and helping supervise on class trips.

Financial.   The Tribeca campus offers full and partial tuition assistance. Application forms are available upon request.

Transportation.   Tribeca Campus: 1, A, C, E trains; Wall Street Campus: 2/3, 4/5/6, N/R trains.

Graduates.   Have attended a variety of public and private schools, including Spence, Packard, Saint Ann's, Nightingale-Bamford, Horace Mann, St. Luke's, Friends Seminary, Lycée Francais, Little Red School House, The Anderson Program, Brooklyn Heights Montessori, Calhoun, and PS 234, 41 and 89.

Member.   AMS; ATIS.

Nazareth Nursery

Ages: 2–6 yrs

Catholic

214–16 West 15th Street
   (between 7th and 8th
   Avenues)
Zip: 10011-6501
Tel: 243-1881
Website: www.nazarethnursery.com

Established 1901
Sister Lucy Sabatini,
Director
Enrollment: 55

School year.   September through July.

Ages	Hours	Days	Tuition (monthly)
2–6	8:00–5:30	Mon–Fri	$830

°Child must be toilet-trained.

Program. Nazareth Nursery is a Montessori school with a Catholic emphasis. The day includes supervised play and work periods during which children can work with a variety of age appropriate Montessori materials.

Admissions. Inquiries are year round. Parents should call and arrange to visit the school. Children of all faiths are welcome.

Class size. There are three multi-age groups with three staff members in each group.

Facilities. The school has three comfortable classrooms and a backyard play area. Lunch, morning, and afternoon snacks are served.

Parent involvement. Four to six parents meetings each year are devoted to child safety and health, parenting, and child development. Parents are involved with fund-raising, as classroom aides, on school committees, and with special classroom projects and field trips.

Financial. Payments are made quarterly or monthly. There are some preliminary fees before a child is admitted. A loan of $175 is required per child, and a $265 per child payment to the building fund is required. The loan is refunded if all obligations have been fulfilled.

Transportation. The school does not provide transportation. The children come from Chelsea and Greenwich Village, from other Manhattan neighborhoods, and the outlying boroughs.

Graduates. Have gone on to Guardian Angel, St. Bernard's, St. Francis Xavier, St. Joseph's and P.S. 11, 41, and to public and parochial schools in Brooklyn, the Bronx, Staten Island, and New Jersey.

Affiliation. The school is affiliated with the Archdiocese of New York.

Member. North American Montessori Teachers Association.

Our Lady of Pompeii Elementary School

Ages: 3–13 yrs

Catholic

240 Bleecker Street
Zip: 10014
Tel: 242-4147
Fax: 691-2361
Website: www.LadyofPompeii.org

Established: 1931
Veronica Beato,
Principal

School year. September through June.

Ages	Hours	Days	Tuition (monthly)
3s	8:30–2:00	Tues Wed Thurs	$6,500
4s	8:30–2:00	Mon–Fri	$6,500
Kindergarten	7:50–2:30	Mon–Fri	$4,990

Enrollment. There are places for sixteen 3s, twenty 4s, and twenty-four kindergartners.

After-School Program: Is available.

Affiliation. Archdiocese of New York and Middle States Association of Schools and Colleges.

The Park Preschool

Ages: 2–5 yrs

Nonsectarian Nursery School

275 Greenwich Street
(one block south
of Chambers between
Greenwich and West
Broadway)
The Barclay School
Zip: 10007
Tel: 571-6191
Fax: 732-5256
Website: www.theparkpreschool.org

Established 1989
Ellen Offen
and Kevin Artale,
Directors
Enrollment: 73

School year.   September through June, and a summer camp from the end of June through early August.

Ages	Hours	Days	Tuition
All	8:30–5:30	2,3,5	$9,600–$20,900
All	8:45–3:30	2,3,5	$9,000–$19,400
All	8:45–1:00	2,3,5	$7,800–$16,500
2–3.5	8:45–11:45	2,3,5	$7,200–$15,100
All	1:00–4:00 or 5:30	2,3,5	$7,200–$16,500

There is an enrollment fee of $150 and a supply fee ranging from $175 to $300. Children need not be toilet-trained.

Program.   Progressive. The school has a relaxed, welcoming atmosphere. Teachers help children develop social skills, independence, and self-esteem. Learning is tailored to each child's developmental level and emotional needs. The school believes that children "think by doing." The program gives them opportunities to experiment, discover, and express their original ideas. "We give them freedom, let them try, let them fail, encourage them, let them succeed, and rejoice with them," says the director. Groups are mixed age: younger children model appropriate social and academic strategies by watching the older children; the older children reinforce concepts they have already learned by teaching the younger ones.

Each room has areas for science, math, language arts, art, manipulatives, and puzzles, with a library and listening center. Walls display the children's artwork.

Admissions.   Parents must call the school the Thursday after Labor Day to schedule a tour and get an application. Tours are held from October through January, take about an hour between 9:30 and 10:30 A.M.

Class size.   There are three mixed-age classrooms, including two 2s–3s classrooms with 12 students, two teachers, and one assistant teacher and one 3s–5s class with 18 students and two teachers.

Staff.   Music and movement specialists visit once a week.

Facilities.   Entry at street level takes you past the director's office and into a large room with wide storefront windows. The older children occupy this space. Downstairs, the two classrooms are windowless but brightly-lit with clean, off-white walls. Here, the 4s were observed with their movement specialist, dancing with colored scarves. Children use the playground of Washington Market Park, half a block away.

Summer program.　A summer program is offered from the end of June to early August.

Separation.　All students are phased in and it takes about a week, after which separation is tailored to the individual child's needs.

Parent involvement.　Parental involvement is encouraged. On occasion, parents teach a special class to the children, accompany children on field trips, or cook a special holiday treat.

Financial.　Deposits are due upon application to insure a spot and are non-returnable or transferable. Financial aid is not available.

Transportation.　Most families come from within walking distance in Battery Park City and Tribeca.

Graduates.　Have gone on to Allen-Stevenson, Berkeley Carroll, Brearley, Chapin, City and Country, Sacred Heart, Columbia Grammar, Packer Collegiate, Corlears, Grace Church, St. Luke's, UNIS, Village Community School, PS 3, 89, 150, 234, Early Childhood Center, Anderson, Hunter, NEST, and the Lab School.

Preschool of the Arts

Ages: 18 mos–5 yrs

121 West 19th Street (between 6th and 7th Avenues)
Zip: 10011
41 Cooper Square
Zip: 10003
Tel: 212-229-9075
Website: www.nycpreschool.org

Established 1999
Sarah Rotenstreich, Director
Jennifer Idelson, Admissions Director
Enrollment: 140

School year.　September through mid June.

Ages	Hours	Days	Tuition
18 mos–24 mos	9:00–11:30	Mon Wed Fri or Tues Thurs or Mon–Fri	$14,000–$19,000 (all ages)
2.0–3.0	9:00–12:00	Mon Wed Fri or Tues Thurs or Mon–Fri	
3.0–4.0	9:00–12/2:30	Mon–Fri	
4.0–5.0	9:00–2:30	Mon–Fri	

Ages	# of Children per class	# of Staff
18 mos–24 mos	8	2
2.0–3.0	10–12	2
3.0–4.0	12–15	2–3
4.0–5.0	14–20	3

Program.   Developmental/Reggio Emilia. Preschool of the Arts is a Jewish preschool which integrates an educational program with a Reggio Emilia curriculum. Preschool of the Arts is a vibrant and innovative learning community where child-focused exploration, creativity, and collaboration inspire the program.

The school draws its inspiration from the Reggio approach to education and developmentally-appropriate educational practices. Children learn science, math, social studies, literacy, the arts, Judaic studies, and moral values through an integrated approach to education. The goal is to nurture each child's personal journey towards social, emotional, and educational growth.

The cornerstone of the school is its arts program, hence the school's name. Since art is such an integral part of the program, there is an atelierista—an art director—who provides children with open-ended opportunities to create. They use a wide array of art media and create their works on diverse surfaces, and generate art in a host of settings including the beautiful art studio. The classrooms, an indoor garden, and an outdoor yard encourage the flow of creative energy in students. In addition to the visual arts program, children enjoy weekly music and movement as well as yoga classes taught by experts in these fields.

Children learn the customs, traditions, and moral values of Judaism. These lessons are woven naturally through the program so that they become both a meaningful and treasured part of each child's life. Children eagerly anticipate the Jewish holidays such as Rosh Hashanah, Chanukah, Purim, and Passover and understand how to meaningfully and joyfully participate in each holiday. The school regularly celebrates holidays with parents and members of the larger Chelsea community. The school carefully selects teachers who model and nurture Jewish values such as charity, friendship, tolerance, discipline, and respect for the environment and the rights of others.

Summer program. The Summer of the Arts program for pre-schoolers runs from June-July. The program integrates various creative arts and educational themes in a safe, multisensory, and Jewish-spirited setting. Each week the program offers children opportunities to experience music, yoga, art, baking, sports, gymnastics, and science through exciting, stimulating, hands-on activities. Children experience daily outdoor and water play and are taken on weekly trips throughout the neighborhood.

Parent involvement. The school wholeheartedly embraces and encourages parental involvement and understands how it enriches the program. Parents and grandparents are invited to become partners in their children's education by always welcoming them into the school, including them in celebrations, and encouraging them to visit classrooms to share their areas of special interests and expertise. The school cherishes the warm relationship it has with its parents through programs such as the parent social, family holiday and Shabbat events, Me and My Favorite Guy Day, Moms and Muffins, and more.

The Parent Link is a venture started by parents for parents. As the organization for parent participation in the school, the Parent Link encourages all parents to become involved and lend their talents, skills, and time to the school. The goal of Parent Link is to foster a sense of community and create opportunities for social interaction. The Parent Link co-chair and the school administrator work hand in hand to offer support to parents and enrich each family's experience at Preschool of the Arts. The Parent Link facilitates various family events and projects throughout the year, including concerts, workshops, carnivals, and charity projects.

Facilities. Preschool of the Arts has beautiful classrooms, an indoor garden, outdoor space, gym, social hall, and art gallery. Each classroom's airy architecture creates an inviting work and play space and provides many opportunities for children to explore and develop.

The classrooms are designed to facilitate center-base learning; centers typically include a dramatic play area, art center, block area, science and discovery table, writing center, and sensory table. Child-sized sinks allow children to practice self-care and hygiene and provide them with the opportunities to practice everyday skills such as washing paintbrushes. Many classrooms boast a cozy loft, a multipurpose space that serves as an oasis for small group activities and dramatic play.

The social hall is an expansive and beautiful multipurpose space that accommodates up to 250 people. The social hall is used to host parent curriculum meetings, children's athletic games, family Shabbat dinners, and other community-wide gatherings. Families that attend the preschool and other local families often use the space to host important events such as birthday parties or even a wedding. The social hall is also home to frequent upscale networking events hosted by Young Jewish Professionals. There is a separate office for ERB testing for the pre-K students.

Staff.   According to the director, "The early childhood program is led and inspired through collaboration between the school director, pedagogistsa, atelierista, and psychologists. The program is carried out by a team of licensed and experienced teachers. Their roles and visions continually evolve as they interact with and observe our children and reexamine our understanding of educational and psychological theory." The well credentialed staff creates activities that engage children's natural curiosities. In addition to the educational and visual arts program, children enjoy weekly art, movement, and music classes with instructors who possess expertise in these fields. Specialists on staff include yoga instructors, woodworking instructors, Super Soccer Stars coaches, and music teachers.

The on-staff school psychologist, Dr. Dana Levy, is also an Assistant Clinical Professor of Child and Adolescent Psychiatry at the NYU Child Study Center. Dr. Levy specializes in child and adolescent evaluations, school consultation, parent consultation, and treatment for a wide range of childhood disorders.

Director Sarah Rotenstreich brings many years of both teaching and administrative experience to Preschool of the Arts. As co-author of *Curriculum of the Arts*, a curriculum used by over 300 schools worldwide, Mrs. Rotenstreich has shown the benefits of integrating progressive teaching methodology with Jewish values in the preschool setting.

Admissions. The admissions fee is $75. Application packages are available through the website or by calling (212) 229-9075. All prospective parents must attend an open house and/or a morning school tour. After a completed application is received and parents have attended a school tour, the admissions office will contact parents to schedule a parent interview/child play date.

Separation. To ease the transition between home and school, teachers meet each child before school begins on their home visit. The first school event is a play date in the park where children get to meet their classmates and teacher in a fun and safe environment. The school offers workshops with an on-staff psychologist to share information regarding separation and how to best ease each individual child's transition into the school. The beginning of the year transition schedule, including a phase-in schedule during the first week of school, is planned to best accommodate students.

Member. ERB, BJE

The Quad Preschool Program at the Quad Manhattan

Ages: 2.5–5 yrs

Nonsectarian Inclusion Preschool

54 Reade Street (between Church and Broadway)
Zip: 10007
Tel: (212) 513-1840
Website: www.thequadmanhattan.
E-Mail: info@thequadmanhattan.com

Established 2011
Emily Andrews,
Preschool Director

School year. September through June. Optional vacation programs are available (including a Spring Break Program and Summer camp.)

Ages	Hours	Days	Tuition
2.5–3.4	9:00–11:30 or 12:00–2:30	Mon–Fri	$10,800–$22,750 (all ages)
3.6–5	8:45–2:45 (optional half days on Tues and Thurs)	Mon–Fri	

Program. Structured. The Quad Preschool has partnered with Tools of the Mind, a research-based curriculum that focuses on self-regulated learning. The central themes at this unique inclusion preschool, which is just one part of an extensive program, The Quad Manhattan, include the use of collaborative problem solving, social cognition, and self-directed learning through play. The Quad Manhattan also offers after-school and weekend programming, workshops, and family events tailored for its twice exceptional "2E" student and family population.

The play-based inclusion preschool supports the notion that all children deserve an individualized curriculum. With a 3:1 staff to student ratio, each child is able to pursue their unique passions and interests while also being a part of a preschool community that supports the development of executive functioning skills such as impulse control and emotional regulation. This program is tailored to serve children that may have some gifted abilities as well as learning disabilities or mild developmental delays. The preschool, and The Quad as a whole, strives to create a welcoming environment for all kinds of children and families.

Admissions. The application fee is $75. Applications are accepted starting on August 15th for the following school year. Acceptances are done on a rolling basis, pending availability and program fit. See the website for details regarding parent tours.

Class size. The Quad Preschool Program consists of three classrooms of 8–10 children. The three classrooms will be grouped based on age, developmental level, and achieving ideal group chemistry based on the children's needs and interests. The toddler group (2.5–3.4 years of age) consists of 6-8 children. The two mixed-age preschool rooms have 8–10 children.

Staff. The school has both general education and special education

346

early childhood professionals on staff. All lead teachers are certified by New York State and have master's degrees. All staff are trained in the Tools of the Mind technique and curriculum. Consulting therapists and specialists meet regularly with teachers to collaborate on curricular decisions and content.

Facilities. The Quad Preschool Program is located in Tribeca and is part of The Quad Manhattan. It is designed with children's unique sensory profiles in mind. The downtown clubhouse space includes a sensory gym, adaptable tech room, art space, and café.

Separation. There is a built-in separation-transition period during which parents are encouraged to stay in the classroom with their child. Once children are ready, parents are welcome to move to the café area.

Financial. Limited financial aid is available and is based on need. Priority in financial awards is determined to serve the overall mission and goals of the school and promote diversity of the student body.

Transportation. Nearest subway stations: Chambers Street 1, 2, or 3 lines and Brooklyn Bridge 4 or 5 lines.

Affiliations. The Director is a member of the NAEYC.

San José Day Nursery
Ages: 1–6 yrs

Catholic

432 West 20th Street
(between 9th and
10th Avenues)
Zip: 10011
Tel: 929-0839
Fax: 924-0891
E-mail: sanjoseday@yahoo.com

Established 1921
Sister Trinidad Fernandez,
Director
Enrollment: 57

School year. September through July. School is closed during the month of August. No summer program.

Ages	Hours	Days	Tuition
All	8:00–5:00°	Mon–Fri	$195 to $200 weekly

°Beginners need not be toilet-trained. Some students stay until 6:00 P.M.

Program.   The school blends Montessori and progressive methods. Religious activities are part of the curriculum.

Admissions.   The application fee is $175. Inquiries are year round. Call during the year for an application and to arrange a visit. Notifications are sent promptly, depending on when an application is filed.

Class size.   There are four classes which include eight 1s, thirteen 2s, seventeen 3s, and twenty 4s and 5s. Each group has two in staff. The majority of the staff are fluent in Spanish.

Facilities.   The school is located on three floors of a brownstone directly opposite General Theological Seminary. It has an outdoor playground equipped with climbing apparatus, and a spacious yard for outdoor meals in good weather.

Parent involvement.   One or two evening seminars are offered on child-rearing and developmental stages. Parents may visit any time. They arrange fund-raising events and help out during shows and holiday social events.

Financial.   A contract or deposit is not required. No financial aid is available. There is a supplies fee of $50.

Transportation.   About half the children live in the neighborhood; the rest have parents working close by. Bus service is not available.

Graduates.   Have gone on to Guardian Angel as well as independent and public schools.

Affiliations.   Archdiocese of New York, Catholic Charities of Greater New York.

TriBeCa Community School

Ages 2–5 yrs

22 Ericsson Place
Zip: 10013
Tel: 226-9070
Fax: 226-9073
Website: www.tribecacommunityschool.com
E-mail info@tribecacommunityschool.com

Established 2006
Ayala Marcktell,
CEO and Founder
Karen Kuller,
Director
Enrollment: TriBeCa
Community opened in 2006.

School year. September–June. A summer program is being developed.

Ages	Hours	Days	Tuition*
2–5	9–12 noon or 1–4 P.M.	5 days	$14,500
2–5	9–12 noon or 1–4 P.M.	4 days	$14,000
2–5	9–12 noon or 1–4 P.M.	3 days	$11,000
2–5	9–12 noon or 1–4 P.M.	2 days	$8,000

*Tuition can be paid monthly in August through May (10 payments).

Program. The TriBeCa Community School is inspired by the Reggio Emilia approach to early childhood education, which is based on nurturing a child's sense of self-esteem and competency. Children are engaged in experiences that are tailored to their natural curiosity about the world using such tools as music, art, theater, science, and the surrounding neighborhood. Programs are designed to cultivate students' cognitive, intellectual, and social skills through long-term inquiries based on the children's and teachers' interests. These investigations emphasize collaboration, documentation of the children's work, problem-solving, and the involvement of parents and the community. Emphasis is placed on open-ended materials and imaginative play is encouraged.

Admissions. Application fee is $50. Parents are asked to attend a one-hour introductory session and submit an application after deciding that the school is the appropriate choice for their family. Siblings of currently enrolled children and alumni have priority. Admission is ongoing until places are filled. TriBeCa Community School does not test children nor interview families.

Class size.   2 yrs: up to 10 children, with two collaborating teachers. 3 yrs: up to 15 children with two collaborating teachers. 4 yrs: up to 18 children with two collaborating teachers.

Staff.   Teachers are certified by New York State in early childhood education and participate in ongoing training throughout the year. Teachers work in teams.

Facilities.   The TriBeCa Community School is located in the newly-renovated Ice House building. It was designed with children in mind, affording ample opportunities for play and exploration. Classrooms offer lots of open space and are designed with familiar elements to create a home-like environment and foster a feeling of belonging. A central atelier (art studio) offers access to materials for inspiring and engaging children in creative projects.

Separation.   There is a separation-transition period during which parents are encouraged to stay in the classroom.

Parent involvement.   The school has an open door policy. Parents are viewed as partners in the educational experience and are encouraged to be involved in constructive ways. The school provides a parents' sitting area where parents can learn more about their children's activities and the school in a comfortable setting. Parents are also encouraged to attend parent workshops sponsored by the school.

Financial.   10% of tuition is due with the application and thereafter: 30% by March 1st, 30% by May 1st, 30% by July 1st. No financial aid is presently available.

Transportation.   Nearest subway stations: Franklin and Canal Streets, 1 and 9 lines.

Member.   NAEYC, NAREA (a Reggio Emilia organization).

Trinity Parish Preschool and Nursery

Ages: 6 mos–5 yrs

Episcopal Nursery School

68 Trinity Place (directly
behind Trinity Church)
Zip: 10006
Tel: 602-0829 or 0802
Fax: 602-9601
Website: www.trinitywallstreet.org

Established 1982
Linda Smith,
Director
Enrollment: 127

School year. All year.

Ages	Hours°	Days	Tuition (monthly)
6 mos–3 yrs	8:00–6:00 only	Mon–Fri	$2,562 to $2,667
3–5 yrs	8:00–6:00 only	Mon–Fri	$2,168°

°Part-time program available for a reduced cost.

Program.   Traditional. In addition to an emphasis on social skills and verbalizing, there is strong, individualized skills preparation in pre-reading, premath, science, music, art. The program provides an academic curriculum which stresses learning geared to individual growth. Children are encouraged to communicate, share their thoughts and ideas, and to respect the rights of others. The classroom environment is designed to enhance the development of each child physically, emotionally, socially, intellectually, and spiritually. Children attend a weekly chapel service. The school also holds an annual Christmas pageant.

Admissions.   No application fee.
Inquiries are at any time. Parents should arrange to visit the school. Children of all faiths are welcome.

Class size.   There are eight infants or ten toddlers and twelve to twenty preschool children and three staff members.

Staff.   Of the forty-four full- and part-time staff members, eleven are state-certified with degrees in early childhood education. The remainder either have degrees in childcare or are enrolled in college. A pediatrician and a consulting psychiatrist are available.

351

Facilities. The preschool and nursery occupies eleven large rooms on two floors of a large, well-maintained office building occupied by Trinity Church. The babies have a separate crib and toy-filled room and regularly use a nearby room and an adjoining, carpeted lounge that is climate controlled and air conditioned. Older children use the indoor gymnasium.

Separation. Parents are asked to pick up their child early during the first two weeks to ease the child's transition to school.

Parent involvement. Conferences are held three times a year and as parents request them. Families are invited to participate in a wide variety of programs sponsored by Trinity Church.

Financial. A non-refundable deposit of $250 is due for registration, and tuition is payable monthly.

Transportation. A large number of children live in lower Manhattan. No private bus service is available.

Graduates. Have gone on to many schools within New York City, including Brearley, Claremont, Chapin, Dalton, Grace Church, Hewitt, Packer, St. Ann's, St. Luke's, Trinity, and UNIS.

Affiliations. Trinity Episcopal Church.

Member. ERB, ISAAGNY, NAES.

University Plaza Nursery School, Inc.

Ages: 2–5 yrs

Nonsectarian Parent Cooperative

110 Bleecker Street (between
LaGuardia Place and
Mercer Street)
Zip: 10012
Tel: 677-3916
Fax: 471-1700
Website: www.universityplazanursery.org
E-mail: info@universityplazanursery.org

Established 1967
Loyan Beausoleil,
Director
Enrollment: 39

School year. Mid-September through mid-June.

Ages	Hours	Days	Tuition
2.0–5	9:00–2:00	Mon–Fri	$11,150

An afterschool program is available from 2:00-4:30 P.M. at an additional cost.

Program. Activities include free play, block building, art, cooking, outdoor play, yoga, gymnastics, writer's workshop, music, and nature study. Music and movement teachers visit weekly. Children bring their own lunch and parents take turns providing snacks.

Admissions. The application fee is $50. Applications are accepted September through November. Parent tours are given in November while school is in session. Notification is sent in March. Preference is given to the children of full-time faculty, staff, and students of New York University.

Class size. There are ten children in the 2s class, twelve children in the 3s class and seventeen children in the 4s/5s, each with two full-time teachers, and a third, part-time special education teacher or student teacher intern.

Staff. Each classroom has a certified teacher and an assistant. Student teacher interns come from the Borough of Manhattan Community College and New York University.

Facilities. Three well-equipped rooms in NYU's Silver Towers building with an adjoining playground, and use of the Key Park in Washington Square Village.

Summer program. A six-week summer program is available.

Separation. The school year begins with a transition schedule that includes home visits, shortened days, and smaller groups. Parents are encouraged to stay in the classroom until their child is comfortable.

Parent involvement. Parents help run the school. Each parent performs a job that requires approximately four hours of services each month. (They may buy exemption from these duties if they wish.) There are monthly board meetings and general meetings two times a year. Conferences are scheduled twice a year and as necessary.

Financial.   A non-refundable deposit is due on signing the contract. Tuition aid is available for eligible families.

Transportation.   Close to A C E, F/V, 4, 5, 6, N, R, Houston Street buses, Broadway buses.

Graduates.   Have gone on to private schools such as Friends Seminary, Grace Church, Little Red School House, St. Anthony's, St. Luke's, Village Community School, UNIS, City and Country, Brearley, as well as Hunter, The Anderson Program, PS 3, 11, 41, 89, 116, 234, and NEST + M, Saint Ann's, gifted and talented programs, The Neighborhood School, and The Earth School.

Member.   Downtown Early Childhood Association, NAEYC, ERB, Parents League, Parent Cooperative Preschools International.

Village Kids Nursery

Ages: 2–5 yrs for nursery school
(Parent-Child Classes for ages 12–24 mos.)

244 West 14th Street 2nd Floor
(near 8th Avenue)
Zip: 10011
Tel: 337-2587
Fax: 337-2588
Website: www.villagekidsnursery.com
E-mail: info@villagekidsnursery.com

Established June 2006
Molly Malone,
Director
Enrollment: 50

School year.   Mid-September through the end of May. There is also a six-week summer program for two weeks in June and four weeks in July.

Ages	Hours	Days	Tuition
Pre-separation (12–24 mos)	1 1/2	2	$8,700–$10,900
2s (1.11 yr–2.11)	3 hrs/day	2/3/5	$13,600
3s and 4s (2.11 yrs–5 yrs)°	4 hrs/day°	5	$15,600

°optional 1½ hr extension for 3s and 4s; optional after-school one hour Spanish $17,600.

Program.   The program of Village Kids Nursery is based on the premise that kids growing up in downtown Manhattan have rich lives full of various kinds of stimulation, unique in both quantity and quality. These children deserve a school experience that helps them make sense of their world.

The purpose of Village Kids Nursery is to provide a safe, stimulating, creative, respectful, and nurturing environment for students, families, and teaching staff. Children become part of a community and are encouraged to try new things, ask questions, explore ideas, and discover themselves.

Teachers with diverse styles are encouraged to bring their creativity to the classrooms and engage in a process of developing themselves through explorations with children. They are fostered like artists, not supervised like technicians. Children are encouraged to create, experiment, and explore their world. The overriding belief is that authority should be based on respect, not power. Compassion and acceptance are cornerstones of this philosophy. Diversity is encouraged within an individualized curriculum designed to accommodate children who fall outside the spectrum of typical development.

Admissions.   There is a $50 application fee. Families are given individual tours. Tours are generally for adults only but exceptions are made at the parents' request. Families may choose to apply before or after touring. (If the tour schedule becomes overbooked, applications are required before touring.) Applications are due in January. Small group play dates are scheduled for February. (Play dates are not used for admissions purposes.) Placement letters are sent in March.

There is also a January start program. Applications are taken year round and placement letters are sent out in November. Priority is given to siblings and students enrolled in the Pre-separation program. (No application is necessary for Pre-separation classes.)

Class size.   The 2s class has eight children and two teachers. The 3s has 10–12 children and 2–3 teachers. The 4s has 16 children and 2–3 teachers.

Staff.   Head teachers have New York State certification and are trained to work with their age group. Assistant teachers have bachelors degrees or significant experience with preschool age children. Specialists in music, art, and gymnastics have appropriate training.

Facilities. Features five classrooms located on the second floor. There is also an 800-square-foot gym.

Summer program. The program, which is mornings only, runs two weeks in June and four weeks in July. Mixed-age classes are generally composed of children who attend the regular school. Some new children are accepted as space allows.

After-school programs. Various specialty classes are offered in the afternoons. Classes for 3s and 4s run from 1:30–2:30 P.M. (Children in the 9–1 P.M. program have a short rest time between the morning and the after-school.) Classes are open to children from other schools as well. After-school classes are offered school-age children from 3:30–4:30 P.M.

Separation. Separation is very gradual. Teachers conduct home visits before school starts. Children begin in half groups with shortened days. Parents or caregivers remain in the classroom. Gradually the day becomes longer, the half groups merge, and parents move out of the classroom into the hall, down the hall, and eventually out of the school. The process is individualized for each family as needed.

Parent involvement. Parents have a voice in many of the decisions made in the school, and organize all the fund-raising (generally an annual auction which helps fund scholarships, capital improvements, and a professional development fund for teachers). Parents and teachers are encouraged to be in contact, providing mutual feedback, sharing observations, and learning from each other. The school works to build a community of learners among children, teachers, and parents, based on reflection and respect.

Tuition assistance. The school offers limited financial assistance based on financial need. It will also consider barter arrangements and individualized payment plans. Those seeking financial assistance are asked to submit a recent tax return and letter describing their financial circumstances.

Transportation. The school is located very near the A/C/E trains, the L train and 8th Avenue and 14th Street buses. The 1/2/3 trains and 7th Avenue buses are less than a block away.

Graduates. Many graduates have gone on to Village Community School, Little Red School House, Saint Ann's, City and Country, PS 3, PS 41, PS 234, and PS 89. Others attend Friends Seminary, St. Lukes, Grace Church, Corlears, Packer, Ethical Culture, Ideal, Hunter, and Anderson.

Member. Parents League.

Village Preschool Center

Ages: 2–5 yrs

Nonsectarian

136 West 10th Street
(between Greenwich Avenue
and Waverly Place)
Zip: 10014
Tel: 645-1238
Fax: 645-0129
Website: www.villagepreschoolcenter.com

Established 1977
Suzette Burdett,
Jeffrey Ramsay, and
Brunie Surget,
Co-Directors
Enrollment: 150

School year. September through June. Summer program, June to mid-August.

Ages	Hours	Days	Tuition
2s/3s	9:00–11:50 or 12:45–3:35	3–5 days	$10,000–$16,500
3s/4s/5s	9:00–2:10 or 12:45–4:15	3–5 days 3–5 days	$14,500–$24,000 $11,500–19,000

Program. Montessori, Reggio Emilia, and Bank Street–oriented. The school provides a warm, supportive, family atmosphere for a child's first separation from home where each child is special and where learning and play are integrated. There is a strong but unpressured academic component. Activities include indoor play in the sky-lit "playtrium." Montessori materials, art, cooking, dramatic play, stories, daily sing-a-longs with a guitar, puppetry, water play, and reading-readiness games, a Montessori reading program, 1 on 1, with a specialist, math readiness, phonics (from age 2 on), introduction of the alphabet, colors, shapes and numbers, hands-on science projects, including caring for pets. A small group activity is always available for the children to join, but children are never forced to join any activity. Social skills and relationships are stressed.

Twos are introduced to French through songs, stories, and common expressions; there are formal French lessons daily for the threes and fours. All programs include French.

The school is committed to charitable work, including support for a land mine removal, disaster relief, and a Haitian orphanage.

Admissions. There is no application fee. Admissions are ongoing, requests for visits may be scheduled through the school's website. There's a forty-five minute 1-on-1 interview with the child.

Class size. Five classrooms with up to 20 children per day. Student teacher ratio is 1 to 5.

Staff. All head teachers are licensed. Full-time staff members include specialists in reading, French, woodworking, science, drama, music, and puppetry.

Facilities. The school has five classrooms and a sky-lit "playtrium."

Separation. Parents or caregivers may stay until the child has successfully adjusted to school.

Parent involvement. The school encourages parent involvement. The directors are available day and night for parents and will help with any crisis. Parents often give lessons on special holidays such as Chinese and Indian New Year, on weekly themes, and talking about work, and play music as part of the Instrument of the Week program. Families participate in the charitable activities. Conferences are held once yearly and as necessary.

Financial. The school does not require a contract. There is a registration fee, not applicable towards tuition, and a deposit of the first and last months' tuition is due upon enrollment. Tuition is payable in four installments or monthly for special situations.

Graduates. Have gone on to Calhoun, City and Country, Collegiate, Chapin, Ethical Culture, Dalton, Friends Seminary, Grace Church, Little Red School House, Lycée Francais, Packer, Poly Prep, Saint

Ann's, St. Luke's, Trevor Day, Trinity, Village Community School, UNIS, as well as The Anderson Program, Lower Lab, Hunter, NEST, Spruce Street School, Special Music School, Midtown West, PS 3, PS 11, PS 41, PS 116, PS 234, PS 150.

Members & Affiliations. Parents League, ERB. DECA, American Association of Teachers of French, AMS, NAEYC.

The Washington Market School
Ages: 2.0–4.9 (Duane Street)
2.9–5.0 (Hudson Street)

Nonsectarian Montessori Affiliated Nursery School

55 Hudson Street	Established 1976
Zip: 10013	Ronnie Moskowitz,
134 Duane Street	Head of School
Zip: 10013	Ajanta Vora,
Tel: 406-7271 (Duane Street)	(Hudson Street) Site Director
Tel: 233-2176 (Hudson Street)	Joan McIntee,
Website: www.washingtonmarketschool.org	(Duane Street)
E-mail: administration@washingtonmarketschool.org	Site Director
	Aida Torres-Schneider,
	Administrator
	Enrollment: 330

School year. Mid-September through mid-June.

Ages	Hours	Days	Tuition
2–5 yrs*	9:00–12:00 or 1:00–4:00	Mon Tues, or Wed–Fri, or	$7,040–$14,800
		Mon–Fri full day	$20,720

*Tuition varies based on program and schedule.

Program. Montessori. Ronnie Moskowitz, head of school, founded the Washington Market School in 1976. Her first class of twelve children has grown considerably and the school is considered to be one the finest early childhood programs in Manhattan. She is the "often unseen eyes in every classroom," and knows every child. The

359

school is supported by local artists, entertainment industry executives, celebrities, and neighborhood pioneers and professionals and has become an integral part of the Tribeca community. The program aims to offer a creative educational experience within the structure of a Montessori framework and inspired by Reggio Emilia approach. Teachers encourage each child to fulfill his/her own developmental needs, encourage individual freedom, and provide social experiences using Montessori materials and age-appropriate activities. Washington Market is noted for its programs in science, art, and chess. The goals of the school are the development of each child's self-esteem, independence, and an inherent interest in learning and creativity in a non-racist, non-sexist, and non-elitist community.

Admissions. The application fee is $40. Inquiries are from September on. Applications may be cut off in January. Requests for tours are available on the school's website in early September. On tours, after observing in the classroom, parents meet with several other parents and the director for a question-and-answer period. Notifications are sent in March. Preference is given to siblings, and highly values diversity of all kinds.

Class size. The youngest half-day classes have ten children, with three in staff. The older groups have fifteen to twenty children, with three staff members each.

Staff. Twenty-nine of the 44 staff members have or will soon have masters degrees in early childhood education and related fields. Volunteers include teaching interns from NYU, Borough of Manhattan Community College, and Pace College's "City-as-School."

Facilities. *Duane Street*: the ground floor in a Tribeca co-op with a gym. *Hudson Street*: two floors in a Tribeca co-op with a gym/recreation area. Both schools have art and music rooms.

Summer program. A seven-week summer camp for 2s–6s is offered at the Hudson Street school, limited to enrolled students.

Separation. *Duane Street*: For the first two weeks, the youngest children meet in half classes for 90 minutes and parents are asked to stay for these shortened periods. *Hudson Street*: There is a four-day phase in period. Parents may stay in the classroom for about twenty minutes for several days.

Parent involvement. Parent seminars are given monthly by the school's development specialist. There is a monthly "Mug and Muffin" session where parents discuss parenting issues. Recent topics have included sleep disorders, aggression, limit-setting, and other developmental issues. Parents can choose to be involved in fund-raising: potluck suppers, the annual gala, bake sales, and the like; they also arrange social events and go on field trips. Conferences and classroom observations periods are scheduled twice yearly and upon request.

Financial. A non-refundable deposit is required on signing the contract. Tuition is payable in five installments. About 6 percent of students receive partial scholarships.

Transportation. No private bus service is available.

Graduates. Have gone on to Birch Wathen Lenox, Brearley, Chapin, Collegiate, Convent of the Sacred Heart, Dalton, Dwight, Friends Seminary, Grace Church, Hewitt, Little Red School House, Nightingale-Bamford, Packer Collegiate, Riverdale, Ross, Saint Ann's, St. Luke's, Stephen Gaynor, Trinity, UNIS, Village Community School, and to public schools, programs for the gifted and talented, Hunter, NEST, and Anderson, and PS 3, PS 11, PS 41, PS 124, and PS 234.

Chartered. By the Board of Regents of the State University of New York.

Member. AMS, Downtown Early Childhood Association, ERB, ISAAGNY, NAEYC, New York State Association of Independent Schools (NYSAIS), Early Childhood Council of NYC, Parents League, Child Care, Inc.

West Village Nursery School
Ages: 2.8–5 yrs

Nonsectarian Parent Cooperative

73 Horatio Street (between
   Greenwich and
   Washington Streets)
Zip: 10014
Tel: 243-5986
Fax: 243-6121
Website: www.westvillagenurseryschool.org
E-mail: admissions@westvillagenurseryschool.org

Established 1962
Tory Ruffolo,
   Director
Enrollment: 48

School year. Mid-September through early June. Summer program available in June and July.

Ages	Hours	Days	Tuition
2s	two afternoons	Mon Wed or Tues Thurs	$3,900
(with parent)	a week	for 27 weeks	
3s/4s	9:00–12:00	Mon–Fri	$11,100
4s	9:00–2:00	Mon–Fri°	$12,750

Children must be 2.8 in September for 3s group.
°Until noon on Fridays.

Program. Developmental with an emphasis on socialization. The school was founded in 1962 by a group of neighborhood parents; some taught at the school for many years. The program does not have an academic orientation. The curriculum includes arts and crafts, block building, dramatic play, music and movement, and cooking. Every year the maple tree in the school's backyard is tapped, the sap collected, and boiled down to make syrup. Based on children's interests and abilities, themes are developed that incorporate the skills that form a basis for reading and math.

Special programs. Parents/2s workshops begin a three-year sequence. These groups have a maximum of eight children and meet twice a week for 1½ hours.

Admissions. The application fee is $45 Inquiries are from September on. Open houses are held in the fall. Parents visit the school in December and January for individual interviews and informational tours given by members of the admissions committee. Brief group play sessions for children applying to the 3s and 4s classes are held with parents present. Notification is sent in early March; siblings and children of alumni are given preference. WVNS seeks diversity and encourages applications from families of all backgrounds.

Class size.   The 3s class consists of fifteen children, the 4s, of eighteen. At least three adults—the teacher, parent-teacher, and assistant teacher—staff each class. Occasional teaching interns assist. There is also a music specialist and a yoga instructor.

Staff.   Class meetings are held once a month to discuss how and what the children are learning. The teacher also meets twice a year, or more often if necessary, with parents for private conferences. Teachers' enrichment is available through workshops, seminars, and course work in early childhood.

Facilities.   The school occupies two floors of a West Village brownstone owned by the co-op. Its safety surfaced, backyard playground is well equipped for 3s and 4s and has a summer wading pool.

Summer program.   The summer program runs for five weeks in June and July (Monday through Friday from 9:00–1:00).

Separation.   Children in the 3s group are introduced in small groups for short periods with a parent present as needed. The process normally lasts from two to three weeks. Parents do not assist in the classroom for the first month of school.

Parent involvement.   The school is closely knit and family oriented. It is owned and operated by the parents and they are unusually and deeply involved in all aspects of the school. The staff has full responsibility for the educational program. Parents share all other tasks, contributing their professional skills and creative talents. Parents take on a variety of administrative tasks, including fund-raising. Many are on the board. They serve in the classroom on a rotating basis, averaging two times a month, and commit a half-day to refurbishing the classroom during the two weeks before school begins. Through parent/teacher workshops the school fosters a strong parent support program so families share the experience of raising children. Lifelong friendships are made among parents and children.

Financial.   The school does not have an endowment but they own the building that they are in, 73 Horatio Street, and also have some rental income. Interest from a reserve fund helps keep tuition rates low as well. A deposit of $1,000 is due on signing the contract, the balance is due in June, and in January. Partial tuition aid is available with priority given to families already in the school.

Transportation.   No private bus service is available. Children come predominantly from Greenwich Village, Chelsea, Tribeca, and Soho.

Graduates.   Have mainly gone on to City and Country, Corlears, Friends Seminary, Grace Church, Little Red School House, St. Luke's, Village Community, and PS 3 and 41.

Chartered.   By the New York State University Board of Regents of the State University of New York.

Member.   Downtown Early Childhood Association, NAEYC, ISAAGNY, Parents League.

World Class Learning Academy
Ages: 3–11 yrs

Nonsectarian Inclusion Preschool

44 East 2nd Street
Zip: 10003
Tel: (347) 225-6184
Website: www.wclacademy.org
E-Mail: info@wclacademy.org
ejurgensen@wclacademy.org

John Taylor,
Head of School
Elizabeth Jurgensen,
Director of Learning
Sarah Bottoms,
Admissions Director
Enrollment: 40

School year.   September through June.

Ages	Hours	Days	Tuition
3s	8:30–12:00	Mon–Fri	$14,000
3s	Full day	Mon–Fri	$22,500
4s (pre-K)	Full day	Mon–Fri	$25,500
5s (K)	Full day	Mon–Fri	$31,900

*Children must be 3 and toilet trained by September 1st.

Program.   Traditional. The school is part of a network of six schools located in the United States that started in Washington, DC in 2000. The program is structured and nurturing. Readiness lies at the heart of the school's philosophy. Classrooms are large and well ordered. Teachers focus on basic skills, encouraging creativity, with the goal that every day each child learns something new.

WCLA mainly follows the British system, incorporating the International Primary Curriculum including standardized tests for children in first grade and above. The dress code includes a purple golf shirt with pink letters among other options.

Admissions.   The application fee is $50. Applications are available either by phone or online. Photographs are requested along with a completed application. The Head of School and a member of the admissions team interview children along with their parents. ERBs are not required, siblings are given priority and admissions decisions are sent according to ISAAGNY guidelines.

Class size.   The nursery classes will have up to 16 children with one head teacher and one assistant.

Staff.   The Head of School, John Taylor, has spent over 30 years educating children all over the world. All teachers hold Honors degrees from the United Kingdom, and many have experience teaching at other WCLA schools in the US. All teachers are trained to teach the International Primary Curriculum. There are specialists for music and Spanish.

Facilities.   WCLA is housed in a newly renovated building located next to De La Salle Academy. There's a state-of-the-art new gym, bright spacious playroom with bikes and blocks, a library, a music and movement room, and beautiful, bright classrooms with interactive whiteboards.

Separation.   The separations process is handled gently. Parents walk their children into the playroom and are encouraged to engage them in an activity with teachers who sensitively build bonds with the children.

Parent Involvement.   Parents are invited into classrooms for special projects, to read stories or go on school trips. There are parent groups that support the school and help organize special days and events.

Financial.   Financial aid is available.

Affiliations.   ISAAGNY pending, International Primary Curriculum, The Parents League.

Your Kids "R" Our Kids
Clockwork Learning Centers

Ages: 3 mos–5 yrs

30 West 15th Street

Zip: 10011

Tel: 675-6226

Fax: 675-2094

Website: yourkidsourkids.com

E-mail: yourkids@clockworklearning.com

Established 1993

Dr. Suzie Shapiro,

Education Director

Total enrollment: 52

School year.   Year-round program.

Ages	Hours	Days	Tuition (monthly)
All	7:30–6:00 P.M.	5 days (full time only)	$1,595–$1,745

°Breakfast and afternoon snacks are provided.

Program.   Progressive/Developmental. Based on the Bank Street model, much attention is paid to individual growth. There is some structure and stability, and each group has a schedule, but there is flexibility. A typical day's schedule is well-organized; it includes free play (with puzzles and blocks), creative movement, art and singing as well as "learning time." Academic skills grow out of children's interests; math, reading, and language are a natural extensions of these interests.

Admissions.   Registration is open all year, but parents should apply at least three to six months in advance to secure a start date. To schedule a tour, call or visit the website. A registration fee and a one-month advance payment are required at time of enrollment. Fees are paid monthly.

Class size.   Infant/toddlers have a 4:1 teacher/child ratio; pre-schoolers, 7:1. Children move on to the next group depending on readiness, not chronological age.

Staff.   Each preschool class has a teacher with a BA or comparable early childhood education qualifications. There are also weekly specialists in music, art, and French.

Facilities.   An air-conditioned, clean, and freshly painted floor-through loft of the ground floor of a residential building off of Fifth Avenue, in the Flatiron District. Video cameras are the security at the main entrance. There's password released front doors that buzz people in. There are five play/classrooms with age appropriate equipment and furnishings. The bathrooms have child-sized fixtures. In good weather, children play in the Union Square playgrounds, a block and a half away, as well as visiting libraries and child-friendly shops.

Separation.   The majority of children at Your Kids have working parents and the school takes this into account by accommodating the individual needs of the child during the initial transition period. Children and parents visit the facility before the child begins school. The child starts with a shortened day; however, the staff build bonds with children quickly.

Parent involvement.   The doors are open to parents to observe without an appointment. Since the school is not a non-profit entity, parents don't have to fund-raise. There are parent/teacher group meetings (by classroom) at least three times a year. Individual parent/teacher conferences are made by request and progress reports are sent home twice yearly. Parents are encouraged to attend field trips.

Graduates. Have gone on to Friends Seminary, Grace, St. Joseph's, UNIS, Village Community School, and PS 41, among other schools.

Affiliations. Member, NAEYC. Proprietorship.

Additional Ongoing Schools with Nursery, Pre-Kindergarten and Kindergarten Programs

For families who have children in an ongoing school or are alumni, or legacies, an ongoing independent (private) school with a nursery program is a very attractive choice. It eliminates the onus of going through the admissions process for kindergarten when the competition for places is most fierce.

There are a number of ongoing schools that offer nursery programs beginning with pre-kindergarten in addition to their elementary and/or middle and high school programs, that are not included in this book, mainly because they do not have a focus on the education of younger children. A more complete description of these ongoing schools and their programs can be found in *The Manhattan Family Guide to Private Schools*, 6th edition, Soho Press.

Below are some ongoing schools that were not included in this book, but that offer pre-kindergarten and/or nursery programs. '

Children's Storefront

70 East 129th Street
New York, NY 10035
Tel: 427-7900
Fax: 289-3502
Website: www.thechildrensstorefront.org
Total enrollment: Approximately 175
    (Pre-kindergarten through 8th grade)

Ethical Culture

33 Central Park West
    (at 63rd Street)
New York, NY 10023
Tel: 712-6220 (main number)
Tel: 712-8451 (admissions)
Fax: 712-8444
Main Website: www.ecfs.org
Total enrollment: Approximately 500 (Pre-kindergarten 4s through 5th grade); Pre-K places: 36

Grace Church School

86 Fourth Avenue
 (at 14th Street)
New York, NY 10003
Tel: 475-5609
Fax: 475-5015
Website: www.gcschool.org
Total enrollment: 417 (Junior kindergarten 4s through 8th grade),
 Junior kindergarten places: 30

Little Red School House and
Elisabeth Irwin High School
LREI

Lower and Middle Divisions
272 Sixth Avenue (Bleecker Street)
New York, NY 10014
Tel: 477-5316
Fax: 677-9159
Website: www.lrei.org
Total enrollment: 575 (Pre-kindergarten 4s-12th grade),
 Pre-kindergarten places: 30

Manhattan Country School

7 East 96th Street
New York, NY 10128
Tel: 348-0952
Fax: 348-1621
Website: www.manhattancountryschool.org
Total enrollment: 190–195
 (4/5s Pre-kindergarten/kindergarten through 8th grade)
 4/5s places: 19

Saint David's School

12 East 89th Street
New York, NY 10128
Tel: 369-0058
Fax: 289-2796
Website: www.saintdavidschool.org
Total enrollment: 400 (Pre-kindergarten 4s through 8th grade)
    Pre-kindergarten places: 16; kindergarten places: 55

St. Luke's School

487 Hudson Street
New York, NY 10014
Tel: 924-5960
Fax: 924-1352
Website: www.stlukeschool.org
Total enrollment: 205 (Junior kindergarten 4s through 8th grade)
    Junior kindergarten places: 18; kindergarten places: 10–15

RESOURCES AND NURSERIES FOR CHILDREN WITH SPECIAL NEEDS AND LEARNING DISABILITIES

Nursery school directors can often identify children who have either a developmental lag, behavioral, and/or psychological issues, or learning disabilities as soon as they enter their first Mommy and Me class as toddlers. Early intervention really makes a difference. Parents no longer have to wait until their child is struggling in elementary school to seek the appropriate programs. Remediation, testing, evaluations, and counseling can be started when children are as young as two years old. Children who might not have been able to keep up in a normal classroom and would suffer from feelings of low self esteem can be taught how to overcome and deal with their learning issues in these specialized early childhood programs and then possibly move on to a mainstream school.

If you are concerned that your child may have a learning issue don't be afraid to ask the teacher if she thinks that it's a good idea to have your child evaluated; if the answer isn't satisfactory ask your nursery school director. Your child's school should be apprised of any testing you do outside, and provided with the results so it can best work with your child. It's best to test early and then re-test every three years (or as often as every year if necessary). Medication is sometimes prescribed for children with attention disorders to help them settle down and acclimate.

The Parents League can provide a complete listing of schools for children with developmental and learning disabilities with classes that are small in size and highly structured. They vary in size from about six to twelve students per class with a head teacher, an assistant and a variety of specialists who work with children one-on-one. Often, these schools will have mixed-age groupings of children because many learning disabled children learn at rates that do not correlate with their ages.

Here are some of the resources in the New York City area that educate children with learning disabilities and other issues. Many children with learning disabilities have gone on to wonderful colleges (including the Ivy League) and have successful careers and happy and productive lives.

Everyone Reading
Formerly, The New York Branch of the
International Dyslexia Association

71 West 23rd Street, Suite 514
Zip: 10010
Tel: 691-1930 ext. 12
Fax: 633-1620
Website: www.everyonereading.org
E-mail: info@everyonereading.org

Everyone Reading, formerly The New York branch of the International Dyslexia Association is a not-for-profit organization that provides information, referrals, training, and support to professionals and families with respect to the impact and treatment of people with dyslexia. It offers a free telephone referral service; as well as training and workshops for professionals and peer support groups for adults, parents, and teens. The agency also sponsors an annual conference on dyslexia and related topics. Annual memberships are available.

The Learning Disabilities Association of New York City Telephone Referral Service

Tel: 645-6730
Fax: 924-8896
Website: www.LDANYC.org
E-mail: info@LDANYC.org
Open weekdays from 9 A.M. to 5 P.M.

This nonprofit organization is an affiliate of the Learning Disabilities Association of America. Trained counselors will explain how to recognize symptoms, and offer referrals to community based agencies in the New York City area. The Learning Disabilities Association also provides printed material and conducts monthly workshops and adult support groups.

The Parents League of New York, Inc.

115 East 82nd Street
Zip: 10028
Tel: 737-7385
Website: www.parentsleague.org

The Parents League sponsors a workshop and provides information and referrals about learning disabilities to member parents. The Parents League has staff that are particularly knowledgeable about which schools specialize in which type of LD. Please refer to page XXX of this directory for more information about The Parents League of New York.

Resources for Children with Special Needs

116 East 16th Street
5th floor
Zip: 10003
Tel: 677-4650
Fax: 254-4070
Website: www.resourcesnyc.org

Resources for Children is a nonprofit information, referral, advocacy, training, and support center for programs and services for children (from birth to age twenty-six) with learning, developmental, emotional, or physical disabilities. They publish a camp directory.

Advocates for Children of New York, Inc.

151 West 30th Street, 5th floor
   (between 6th and 7th Avenues)
Zip: 10001
Tel: 947-9779
Fax: 947-9790
Website: www.advocatesforchildren.org
E-mail: info@advocatesforchildren.org

Advocates for Children works to protect and extend the rights of children with learning and/or developmental disabilities in public schools, in addition to various other information.

National Dissemination Center for Children with Disabilities

Ages: Birth to 22 yrs

1825 Connecticut Avenue NW
Suite 700
Washington, DC
Zip: 20009
Tel: (1-800) 695-0285 or (202) 884-8200
Fax: (202) 884-8441
Website: www.nichcy.org
E-mail: nichcy@aed.org

A special education information service.

The A.D.D. Resource Center, Inc.

215 West 75th Street
Zip: 10023
Tel: (646) 205-8080
Fax: (646) 205-8080
Website: www.addrc.org

Harold R. Meyer,
Executive Director and Founder

Established in 1989 by AD/ADHD guru as a volunteer resource center, the ADDRC has grown to offer a variety of programs and information on the topic. Seminars, courses, workshops, and services for parents and children that focus on ADD/ADHD Attention Deficit/Hyperactivity Disorder and related issues are available.

The National Center for Learning Disabilities

381 Park Avenue South, Suite 1401
Zip: 10016
Tel: 545-7510/toll free: 888-575-7373
Fax: 545-9665
Website: www.LD.org

NCLD is a voluntary, not-for-profit organization founded in 1977 by Carrie Rozelle. It operates a national information and referral service and is the nation's only central, computerized resource clearing-house committed solely to the issues of LD.

AMAC Children's House
2.6–5 years

25 W. 17th Street
Zip: 10011
Tel: 645-5005
Fax: 645-0170
Website: www.amac.org
E-mail (Available through the website)

Established 1961
Frederica Blausten,
Executive Director
Enrollment: Approximately 250

School year. All-year

Age	Hours	Days	Tuition
2–5	8:30–1:30	Mon–Fri	N/A

Program. The center uses the Applied Behavior Analysis (ABA) method, the only scientifically-based and state-approved treatment for autistic spectrum disorders. It seeks to eliminate the frustrating and time-consuming splintering of services that families of special-needs children often face. This method relies on intensive behavioral programming to teach targeted skills and behaviors.

The program looks at the family system as a whole, paying particular attention to the interaction of emotional, cognitive, and language development in the child. AMAC participates in the Universal Pre-K program. The organization also has a school serving children 5–21-years-old as well as after-school and weekend programs.

Admissions. Enrolled children have difficulties ranging from autism to emotional problems. Most children have average intelligence and potential for mainstream programs.

Applications are taken throughout the year, and the center urges parents to apply as soon as they identify a need.

Parents call, are screened, and an appointment is made for a full-team screening at the preschool. Acceptances are based on the

379

openings available. The center attempts to balance ages and abilities. Private and public funding is available.

Tests.   An evaluation from an outside source is helpful. If this has been done, it should be furnished, but is not required. The center has experts in specialized assessments.

Class size.   Children are placed in small mixed-age groups of six, eight, or ten children. Each group is assigned one special education teacher and at least two assistant teachers. In addition, the center has on staff two speech and language specialists, a part-time consulting staff including occupational therapists, a psychiatrist, and psychologists who work with and participate in team conferences with the children and their families.

Separation.   Teachers and a social worker will meet the family and child two or three times before school begins. When school begins, parents may remain until children are comfortable or as their schedules permit.

Parent involvement.   There are informal and formal gatherings with other parents and family members, as well as special school outings and holiday celebrations. The school encourages the entire family to visit. Seminars and classes are given on subjects of interest to the parents. Parents can visit at any time, and staff members are always available.

Transportation.   Children come from all over the metropolitan New York area, and are brought by parents or by NYC Department of Education buses.

Graduates.   Many of the children who graduate from the school can be mainstreamed into educational programs for normal children or less restrictive educational programs. Others go on to special education programs.

Affiliations.   Association for Metroarea Autistic Children.

The Early Childhood Center at the Stephen Gaynor School

3–6 years

148 West 90th Street
Zip: 10024
Tel: 787-7070
Website: www.stephengaynor.org
Email: dlogue@stephengaynor.org

Donna Logue,
Director
Enrollment 30

Full day: 8:30–2:30 $47,500
Half day: 8:45–11:45 $27,000

Program.   A program specially designed and dedicated to teaching children with learning disabilities the skills required to succeed in a mainstream educational environment. Special educators, occupational therapists and speech-language pathologists work together to create a dynamic curriculum that combines traditional early childhood experiences with effective methods in special education. The program also offers one-on-one instruction.

ADDITIONAL LISTINGS

The listings below are an incomplete number of programs that change frequently. Parents should call the Early Childhood Direction Center (see page 392) for guidance.

Child Development Center

Ages: 2–5 years

34 W. 139th Street

Marian Davidson-Amodeo,

Zip: 10039

Director

Tel: 690-7234

Website: www.jbfcs.org

Click on "Programs and Services,"

enter: Child Development Center

Serves approximately 40 children in the Therapeutic Nursery School

The center serves children with developmental, behavioral, emotional, or organic handicapping conditions. In the Therapeutic Nursery School, two teachers work with each group of eight children. Therapy is available for parents, as well as the programs for children that include OT, speech play therapy, and more. The center also includes an outpatient mental health clinic for children and/or families. The center also serves as a consultant to many day care centers and nursery schools. The center is a program of the Jewish Board of Family and Children's Services, Inc.

Upper Manhattan Mental Health Center

1727 Amsterdam Avenue

William Witherspoon,

Zip: 10031

Director

Tel: 694-9200

Website: bowencsc.org

East River Schools

577 Grand Street (between
   Madison Avenue and the
   FDR Drive)
Zip: 10002
Tel: 254-7300

Steve Berman,
Director

Preschool program for children with a full range of developmental disabilities, ages 2 to 5 years.

The Gillen Brewer School

410 East 92nd Street
Zip: 10128
Tel: 831-3667
Fax: 831-5254
Website: www.gillianbrewer.com
E-mail: info@gillenbrewer.com

Established: 1993
Donna Kennedy,
Head of School
School age enrollment: 70
Preschool enrollment: 16

The Gillen Brewer School began as an early childhood program and evaluation site, and now extends up through the elementary grades. Parents are very pleased with the school. The program serves children who have a wide variety of language-based and non-verbal learning disabilities.

The program spans a 12-month year that follows the New York State learning standards while meeting each student's needs individually. The preschool program serves children from just under 3-years old to 5-years-old. The school-age program serves children 5- to 10-years-old who are classified as either learning disabled, emotionally disturbed, speech, or health impaired.

Kennedy Child Study Center

151 East 67th Street
Zip: 10021
Tel: 988-9500
Fax: 327-2601
Website: www.kenchild.org
E-mail: info@kenchild.org

Meegan Schmidt,
Human Resources Director

The center serves hundreds of families annually, providing services for slowly developing and retarded children who may also have multiple handicaps. Services include diagnostic evaluations, educational assessments, infant and preschool special education, infant stimulation and therapeutic intervention, and family services, including education.

Northside Center for Child Development, Inc.

Early Childhood Center

1301 5th Avenue (at 110th Street)
Zip: 10029
Tel: 426-3400
Fax: 410-7561
Website: www.northsidecenter.org

Dr. Thelma Dye, Director
Dr. Roseann Harris, Director, Early Childhood Center

A therapeutic nursery for children with developmental difficulties.

Episcopal Social Services Therapeutic Nursery

Therapeutic Nursery School

2289 5th Avenue
Zip: 10037
Tel: 283-3100

United Cerebral Palsy of New York City
Manhattan Children's Center
Ages: 3–5 years

122 E. 23rd Street
Zip: 10010
Tel: 677-7400 ext. 400
Fax: 982-5268
Website: www.ucpnyc.org   Enrollment: 84

Multi-service center providing a special education preschool.

PARENTING and OTHER RESOURCES

Information Sources and Referral Agencies,
Advisors, Testers, Learning Specialists,
Parenting Centers and Parent–Toddler Programs,
Support Groups and Workshops and Seminars

INFORMATION SOURCES
AND REFERRAL AGENCIES

(ACS)

Telephone Service: 311
Website: www.nyc.gov
click: Administration for Children's Services, Head Start Info.

Formerly known as the Agency for Child Development, ACD, now the Agency for Child Services, ACS is responsible for funding and monitoring all public day care programs in New York City.

Parents may call ACS's 311 to obtain a listing of all licensed nursery schools and family or center-based day care programs in the metropolitan area. ACS counselors will provide limited information, including the names and addresses of several programs in the caller's residential or work neighborhood, ages of children served, cost of care, and hours of operation.

ACS partially or fully funds care for children whose parents meet its financial guidelines at participatory nursery schools and center-based or family day care programs. Parents wishing to take advantage of this financial aid must apply to the agency and be screened at one of its regional offices. ACS also administers the federally sponsored Head Start program which serves 3- to 5-year-olds.

Center for Children's Initiatives (CCI)

322 Eighth Avenue (at 26th St)   Nancy Kolben,
   4th Floor   Executive Director
New York, New York: 10001
General Telephone: (212) 929-7604
Parent Services: (212) 929-4999
Fax: (212) 929-5785
Website: www.centerforchildrensinitiatives.org

New York City's largest child care resource and referral agency, CCI is a nonprofit organization serving parents, early childhood professionals, early learning, and school age programs. Parent Services has trained counselors that provide telephone consultations and child care referrals to over 4,000 parents annually. Families can obtain information on finding early care as well as school age and summer programs for children age birth through twelve. The service also includes information on how to access child care subsidies, tax credits, and resources for children with special needs. Parent Service provides publications that are step-by-step guides for parents with respect to each child care option.

CCI also offers training to child care program staff and child care providers. A corporate membership program offers child care consultations, referrals, and workplace lunchtime seminars for employees.

New York City Association for the Education of Young Children

66 Leroy Street, St. Luke's Place
(near 7th Avenue
below Grove Street)
Zip: 10014
Tel: 807-0144
Fax: 807-1767
E-mail: office@nycaeyc.org
Website: www.nycaeyc.org

This is the largest membership group in New York City specifically concerned with the education of young children (from infancy to age eight). Through the state and national organizations, NYC-AEYC is part of a network of thousands of people actively working on programs, research, legislation, teacher training, and other issues affecting young children. The national organization, NAEYC, is located in Washington, DC (www.naeyc.org); in New York State, NYSAEYC is located in Albany (www.nysaeyc.org).

The New York City Department of Health, Division of Day Care

Website: www.nyc.gov

This city agency shares responsibility for all New York City child care with the Agency for Child Services (ACS). The division of day care licenses programs and provides training for new providers.

The agency will mail to inquirers an address and telephone listing of all currently licensed early childhood programs in the metropolitan area.

All programs listed in this directory are licensed, and each is inspected twice and sometimes three times a year. Each must be relicensed every two years and those caring for children under 2 years old must be relicensed every year. Licensing covers minimum standards for physical space, equipment, program/group size, teacher/child rations, staff credentials, health examinations and immunization schedules for staff and children, food service, and admissions policies.

Schools and centers are allowed to enroll two children per room above the number for which they are licensed, because attendance varies so greatly among preschoolers. Each classroom where there are children age 2 and older must have at least one state-certified teacher. Minimum child/staff rations require that there be one teacher and an assistant for 2s groups with six to ten children, 3s groups with 11 to 15 children, 4s groups with 13 to 20 children, and 5s groups with 16 to 25 children. All faculty and staff must be fingerprinted. Children must have health examinations yearly and at least 90 days before entering school. Infants and children under age 3 must be examined 30 days before and twice yearly. School and center personnel are forbidden to administer medication to children unless it is specifically labeled with adequate documentation. Each program must also receive approval from the Buildings and Fire departments.

Educational content and play equipment are not specified beyond the dictum that they be "appropriate and adequate."

To find licensed school listings online at the DOH website, go to www.nyc.gov. Under the "City Agencies" heading, click on "Health and Mental Hygiene," then "Search Bureau of Day Care." On the "Bureau of Day Care" page, click on "Research Group Day Care Facilities," click on "Manhattan" (or another borough), search listing alphabetically or by zip code. Listings include school name, address, and status of license.

Early Childhood Direction Center
New York Presbyterian Hospital

435 E. 70th Street #2A   Marilyn Rubinstein,
Zip: 10021   Director
Tel: 746-6175
E-mail: mrubinst@nyp.org
Website: http://www.p12.nysed.gov/specialed/techassist/ecdc/

Established in 1982. Provides free neutral information and referral to parents, professionals, and agencies looking for services for children with known or suspected special needs. Children must be between newborn and five years of age. Staff can provide information about evaluations, early intervention services, preschool special education services, child care, Head Start, summer programs, home care, respite programs, parent education, support groups, counseling, advocacy, financial, and legal assistance.

The center is funded by the New York State Education Department, and New York Presbyterian Hospital.

Early Childhood Resource and
Information Center
Division of New York Public Libraries

66 Leroy Street, St. Luke's Place
 (near 7th Avenue
 below Morton Street)
Zip: 10014
Tel: 929-0815
Website: www.nypl.org

The center is located on the second floor of the attractive old Carnegie building. Downstairs there is room for stowing strollers. Upstairs is the collection of materials that includes picture books and DVDs. Free workshops and seminars presented by educators cover a wide variety of topics related to early childhood. To receive a monthly schedule, send a self-addressed, stamped envelope.

Early Steps

540 E. 76th Street
(between York Avenue and
the FDR Drive)
Zip: 10021
Tel: 288-9684
Fax: 288-0461
Website: www.earlysteps.org

Jacqueline Y. Pelzer,
Executive Director

Early Steps provides counseling, guidance, and referral services to families of children of color as looking for and enrolled in city independent schools. Early Steps serves all families of color whether they need financial aid or not. It is not a scholarship program or a program for low income families.

THE ERB
The Educational Records Bureau

470 Park Avenue South
2nd floor, South tower
Zip: 10016
Tel: 672-9800
Fax: 370-4096
Website: www.erb.org

Although the ubiquitous "ERB," an IQ test and developmental scale that is required for admission to most of Manhattan's elite private kindergartens, is not supposed to be a measure of success, it is. If your child scores well, it's truly a good thing. When scores fall below above average, admission to the best private schools becomes an uphill battle, or impossible.

The ERB has been under contract with ISAAGNY (Independent Schools Admissions Association of Greater New York) for over fifty years. The ERB administers a variety of intelligence and developmental tests to children of all ages. According to the ERB, all of the examiners are at least master's level, many are doctoral level candidates, some are clinical psychologists or even PhD's. There are roughly fifty examiners employed at the ERB during the admissions season and they are all experienced. If your child's nursery school is a member of ISAAGNY then your child will probably be tested at his or her nursery school; if not you can bring your child to the ERB offices for testing.

Having a central testing agency administer one test for kindergarten admissions to all children is intended to "eliminate repetitive testing and thus minimize the strain on children and parents," attest many admissions directors. Prior to the selection of the ERB, parents used to take their children for formal testing at each ongoing school to which they applied. However, many ongoing schools still require up to an hour of their own "informal testing," so you can still expect your child to be thoroughly scrutinized everywhere he or she goes. It seems to parents that it is the strain on the ongoing schools and their admissions offices that has mostly been alleviated since they can now see many more than one child at a time.

Children are compared with others their age; there is no advantage in holding off testing with the idea that your child will "know more." In fact, children are expected to do more as they become older; in some cases the younger child might have a slight edge. More children are now being tested in spring; in many instances those tested early score higher. Also, the later in the year it is, the more likely your child may have a cold or other illness. If your nursery school director thinks that your child is ready and "your child is four-years-old by May 1st and, will separate readily," testing in the spring can often prove better. Each report is individually written, reviewed, and e-mailed in the order of the test date. Remember to schedule well in advance of school deadlines. It usually takes a few weeks to receive the ERB report.

At some nursery schools, the fall semester of the four-year-old group is like the "Princeton Review" for the ERB. Children are given worksheets for practicing matching skills, copying geometric shapes, and tracking mazes. They are drilled in their colors, taught to write their names, and play with parquetry blocks (for spatial relations). Some children even bring work home.

The cost is about $500 but there is an ISAAGNY Fee Waiver Program for families who require financial aid. Parents must fill out a form requesting that the test results be sent to the ongoing schools to which the parent has applied. There is a minimal additional charge for each school in excess of six. Be sure to follow up with the schools to make sure that they received the results. The test determines strengths and weaknesses and where along the developmental scale a child falls; it was not devised as an admissions test, it is an evaluation of a child's development in language and visual/motor skills. The test is composed of four verbal and four nonverbal (or performance) sections. Children do not have to read or write to take this test. Like all standardized tests, it is a snapshot of the child's development taken on one day.

Parents are sent a full copy of the confidential ERB report. You can discuss the results with your nursery school director or you may schedule a private consultation with the ERB, or both. It is common belief that some of the very selective ongoing schools admissions directors have a cut-off score below which they will not admit a candidate. This is simply not true, there are children with astronomical scores who have not been admitted and children with scattered scores who have been.

If you coach your child for this test, it might be discovered. One four-year old blurted out "I forgot it all," as he walked into the tester's office. However, sending a child into a testing situation cold isn't a good idea either. Check the ERB website for sample questions and instructions.

The testers are looking for how spontaneous a child is when responding to questions that have never been heard before, for their problem-solving strategies and other levels of information. Remember there's no substitute for experience, and a trip to a museum, a concert, a farm, the children's zoo, the bakery, and the grocery store can all be opportunities for learning and will increase your child's general knowledge.

Familiarity with test procedures also helps. It's a good idea to let your child know that they are going to do "special work" with a teacher who would like to see how much they know. Let them know that there will be some new things and that he'll get a chance to learn. It's important that your child knows that you'll be in the waiting room if you bring him or her to the ERB's offices; the child should be comfortable if he or she takes the test at a familiar nursery school. Some schools even have special rooms designated just for ERB testing. If your child has separation issues it may be best if your spouse or caregiver brings him or her to ERB's offices.

ERB will not test an unhappy or reluctant child; the anticipation of a pleasant experience is the best preparation for being tested and, of course, a little luck.

Head Start

Tel: 232-0966
Website: www.nyc.gov
City agencies, Department of Health and Mental Hygiene, Division of Day Care, research group day care facilities.

Independent Schools Admissions Association of Greater New York (ISAAGNY)

Website: www.isaagny.org

Founded in 1965, and composed of admissions directors and heads of early childhood programs, They are rotating heads composed of nursery school directors and the directors of admissions at the ongoing schools.

ISAAGNY meets on a regular basis to simplify and coordinate the admissions procedures among independent schools in the New York Metropolitan area. It is now composed of approximately 150 member schools. ISAAGNY contracted with the Education Records Bureau (ERB), see pages 393–395, to administer uniform admissions testing. In addition, ISAAGNY schools have the same admissions notification and parent reply dates. These guarantee that families have at least two weeks in which to decide what school to accept. The dates vary each year, depending on how weekends fall on the calendar.

Board of Regents of the State University of New York Office of Early Education and Reading Initiative

Tel: (518) 474-5807
Fax: (518) 486-7290
Website: www.nysed.gov

Above and beyond New York City's day care licensing, many nonpublic nursery schools and kindergartens are voluntarily registered by the Board of Regents of the State University of New York, which, through regulations set by the State Department of Education, has additional requirements than the city's. In addition to meeting the board's requirements for classroom size, location, construction, eating, rest, sanitary facilities, equipment, outdoor play space, and fire and safety regulations, the classrooms must include activities centers for block building, dramatic play, water play, creative arts, painting, clay, collage, science and nature study, cooking and music, as well as adequate books, pictures, puzzles, games, and small manipulatives. Outdoor play space must have 200 square feet per child, check for details.

Child/teacher ratios are at eight to one for 3s, ten to one for 4s (with a maximum of twenty children per class) and fifteen to one for 5s (with a maximum of twenty-two children per class). These class sizes are based on the availability of 35 square feet of indoor space per child.

Each school must show evidence of developmentally appropriate curriculum and early education programs adapted to ages, interests, and needs of the children. Children must also have the opportunity to choose and become involved in manipulation of various materials, objects, and textures, dramatic play activities, arts, large motor play, discussions and games, literature, music, science, and field trips. Schools must also show positive parent collaboration in the education of their children, including conferences, parent workshops, newsletters, and participation in program planning and decision making.

OTHER NYC GOVERNMENT-RUN REFERRAL ORGANIZATIONS

NYC Department of Health and Mental Hygiene

(Licenses Childcare Facilities)
Website: www.nyc.gov

Child Development Support Corp

Tel: (718) 398-6738
Website: www.cdscnyc.org

ADVISORY, TESTERS,
and OTHER RESOURCES

Aside from this book and the director of your nursery school, there are other useful resources in Manhattan to help you choose the right ongoing independent or nursery school for your family. Keep in mind that the best source of information is always from the school itself. Ask the school you are interested in if they offer spring tours. Perhaps you can rule it out or take a second look in the fall when you apply. Once the fall admissions process gets rolling at the ongoing schools, you will usually not be able to take another look until your child is accepted to the school. Advisory services or educational consultants help parents approach the independent school admissions process in an organized manner and provide reassurance and advice.

Parents, whether you choose to use a consultant or not, please be advised that some independent schools admissions officers have told me that they do not look kindly on applicants who use the services of consultants. So if you choose to use one, obviously be discreet.

All of the services listed below require a fee and the range, which is vast, is from about $200 to $5,000, or more.

1. Education First

Website: www.nyedu1st.com.
E-mail: maura@nyedu1st.com; victoria@nyedu2st.com

Victoria Goldman, author of this book, and Maura Wollner, an expert in education and child development, advise parents on how to optimize their admissions strategies, select schools, and explore New York City's extensive educational opportunities.

2. The Parents League of New York, Inc.

115 East 82nd Street   Patricia Girardi,
Zip: 10028   Executive Director
Tel: 737-7385
Website: www.parentsleague.org

Annual membership fee: $125 for one year or $300 for three years.

The Parents League was founded in 1913 and is a nonprofit organization of parents and independent schools. It offers a school advisory service for member parents who need advice about the process of applying to schools and information about the schools. Interested parents can call for an appointment. The advisors now have broad experience with respect to independent schools as educators, admissions directors, heads, financial aid officers, board members, and parents' association representatives.

The Parents League distributes the *New York Independent Schools Directory*, published by the Independent Schools Admissions Association of Greater New York (ISAAGNY). Anyone may purchase this book for an additional $20.00 at the office, $23.00 by mail or online. *Please be aware that the entries in this book are written by the schools themselves.*

The Parents League sponsors Independent School Day, held in the fall, at which parents can pick up printed material, including brochures and applications, from various city independent schools, that primarily serve grades K–12. Representatives from the independent schools are available to answer *brief* questions. Be prepared for a mob scene, but it will save you countless phone calls.

The Parents League sponsors forums on admissions, learning issues, and parenting, at which admissions directors, nursery school directors, learning specialists and others from five or six independent schools as well as others, speak and then answer questions from the audience about the admissions process. It offers a summer advisory service and a special education advisory service.

3. Penny Miskin, MS

167 East 82nd Street, Suite 1B
Zip: 10028
Tel: 396-1062

Ms. Mishkin has been in private practice for 15 years; her specialty is fine motor skills, visual-spacial perception, and occupational therapy.

4. Sharon H. Spotnitz, Ph.D.

444 East 86th Street
Zip: 10028
Tel: (212) 734-0095
E-mail: shsphd@mac.com

Dr. Spotnitz, former executive director of ERB, is a licensed psychologist and child and school psychologist with a specialty in testing children who have learning disabilities. She administers neuropsychological, psychological and psychoeducational evaluations in addition to providing educational consultations and comprehensive assessments. Dr. Spotnitz tests students of all ages and grade levels ranging from preschool through graduate school.

5. Lana F. Morrow, Ph.D.

350 Central Park West
Suite 1Q
Zip: 10025
Tel: (646) 338-7676

Dr. Morrow administers neuro-psychological evaluations and remediates children who have learning disabilities. She advises families as to which independent school will be best suited for their child and offers talks, referrals, and strategies on organization and cognitive, and academic planning.

6. Schools & You

328 Flatbush Avenue   Sarah D. Meredith
Suite 372
Brooklyn, New York
Zip: 11238
Tel: (718) 230-8971
Website: www.schoolsandyou.com

Ms. Meredith provides information and consultations on Manhattan and Brooklyn school choices from nursery through eighth grade for both public and private schools. She will consult by phone, Internet, or in your home, workplace, or another convenient location. Resource materials accompany every consultation.

7. Smart City Kids

1619 Third Avenue   Roxana Reid
(91st Street Between 2nd and 3rd Avenues)
Suite #1
Zip: 10019
Tel: 979-1829
Website: www.smartcitykids.com

Ms. Reid, a former kindergarten teacher with a master's in social work, specializes in nursery and kindergarten admissions. Smart City Kids holds workshops and private sessions that prepare parents and children for every aspect of the admissions process: how to handle interviews, testing, skill requirements, applications, and essays.

8. Robin Aronow, Ph.D

155 Riverside Drive
Suite 12C
Zip: 10024
Tel: 316-0186
E-mail: robin@schoolsearchnyc.com

Fees range, billing options are available.

Dr. Aronow, a social worker not a psychologist, works individually with families considering mainly public and private schools on all aspects of the admissions process from nursery school through upper grades.

9. Manhattan Private School Advisors

360 Central Park West   Amanda Uhry
Zip: 10025
Tel: 280-7777
Website: www.privateschooladvisors.com
E-mail: info@privateschooladvisors.com

Amanda Uhry, an alumna of Fieldston, University of Pennsylvania, and Columbia Graduate School of Journalism, owned a successful public relations firm for a decade before opening her advisory firm. MPSA works with families on every aspect of the admissions process for all grade levels.

10. Madden & Warwick, LLC

1112 Park Avenue   Mary Madden,
Zip: 10128   Jane Warwick
Tel: 831-3272
E-mail: Mam1750@aol.com; jwarwick25@aol.com

Mary Madden and Jane Warwick advise families about the private school admissions process from nursery through middle school. Rates vary according to need.

11. Hilton & Haves Association, LLC

300 East 59th Street
Suite 401
Zip: 10022
Tel: (917) 796-8238
E-mail: jhilton5@nyc.rr.com; ritahaves@aol.com

June Hilton and Rita Haves specialize in nursery and kindergarten admissions. June Hilton formerly Director of Admissions at Trinity School and Rita Haves who currently sits on the boards of both a nursery school and ongoing school have many years of experience in private school admissions combined. Fees vary according to parents' needs.

12. Child Mind Institute

445 Park Ave (at 56th Street)   Harold Koplewicz , MD,
Zip: 10022   President
Tel: 308-3118
Website: www.childmind.org

Comprehensive evaluations, testing and remedial services are offered to children of all ages.

---

13. Antoinette Lynn, PhD

350 Central Park West
Suite 1Q
Zip: 10025
Tel: (212) 666-3180
E-mail: ajlynn@aol.com

Dr. Lynn, a licensed clinical psychologist, specializes in evaluating children with learning issues for over twenty years.

PARENTING CENTERS AND CLUBS, PARENT-TODDLER PROGRAMS[*]

Free to Be Under Three
Ages 6 mos–32 mos

Nonsectarian Parent-Child Program
1157 Lexington Avenue
789 10th Ave (between 52nd and 53rd Streets)
Tel: 988-1708
Website: www.freetobeunderthree.com

Program: Singing, group activities, dance, and free play. According to the website, "language development and the respect for the individual spirit of a child are the commitment of the program."

Facilities: Held in the downstairs classrooms of All Souls; and a new West Side location on the second floor of a building

School Year. Late Sept–Mid May

Summer Program: 8 weeks June and July.

	Hours
Fall Spring (12 wks)	45 minute classes
	1 hr classes
	1 hr 15 min classes
Summer (8 wks)	45 minute class
	1 hr

Check website or call for tuition; there is usually a 6–month wait list for a spot.

---

[*] See also La Escuelita pre-school program, p. 168, supra, and Village Kids Nursery parent-child classes, p. 354, supra.

74th Street MAGIC
at Epiphany Community Nursery School
Ages: 6 mos–3 yrs

510 East 74th Street
(off York Avenue)
Zip: 10021
Tel: 737-2989
Website: www.74magic.com
E-mail: magicinfo@74magic.com

Tuition: Costs vary by choice of activity and number of classes.

Program. 74th Street MAGIC offers "on my own" classes for 2s/3s. Other classes available include music, art, gymnastics, science, cooking, and dance. Summer program for children 3 months to 8 years old; a variety of creative and recreational activities.

Class size. Sessions in music, art, cooking, and science (for 2s and 3s). Children ages 6 months to 3 years must be accompanied by a parent or caregiver who should be prepared to participate. For children ages three through fourteen years, there is no parent or caregiver participation. Check website for specific programs and class sizes.

ACT Programs at the Cathedral
of St. John the Divine
Toddler program ages: 18–36 mos
Nursery program ages: 2.3–4.5 yrs

Nonsectarian

Cathedral of St. John the Divine
1047 Amsterdam Avenue (at 112th Street)
Tel: 316-7530
Fax: 316-7569
Website: www.actprograms.org

Established 1971
Marie Del Tejo,
Director of Programs
José V. Torres,
Executive Director

Program. Encourages individuality through variety and choice in activities within a guided structure. There are two programs, one for children 18–36 months old and their caregivers, the other a two-day-per-week nursery for children ages 2.3–4.5 years. The toddler program features gym in a well-equipped indoor playground, singing, storytelling. Weather permitting, older toddlers play outside and garden on the cathedral campus.

The nursery curriculum concentrates on development of interactive skills, pre-reading activities, and enjoyment of learning. Instructors communicate daily with parents about children's progress and families are informed of program changes, concerns, and interesting events outside of ACT.

So Glad We Waited Network
Ages Infant–Elementary years

275 Central Park West
Doctor's Suite 1E
Zip: 10024
Tel: 866-5620
Website: www.sogladwewaited.com
E-mail: sogladwewaited@aol.com

Lois Nachamie,
Director

The director, Lois Nachamie, a board certified psychotherapist, and a parent educator since 1990, and an award winning author whose books include *Big Lessons for Little People: So Glad We Waited, A Hand Holding Guide for Over 35 Parents,* and *Big Lessons for Little People: Teaching Our Children Right from Wrong While Keeping Them Healthy* is often consulted as an authority on parenting after 35. The network offers ongoing support groups for older parents of infants through elementary school age children. Individual and couples' counseling is available along with long- and short-term counseling for parenting and other family issues.

Groups register in September, January, and June.

Discovery Programs/The Toddler Center

251 W. 100th Street
Tel: 749-8717
E-mail: info@discoveryprograms.com
Website: www.discoveryprograms.com

A variety of parent/toddler classes are offered for children between 12 and 36 months, including gym, pre-ballet, art, and music-dance-and-storytime. Classes are directed to the child's developmental needs. The classes change seasonally, so ask for a recent catalogue. In addition to parent/toddler classes, there are gradual separation classes for 2-year-olds, and classes for 3-year-olds and up without their parents.

Early Childhood Development Center

Ages: 4 wks–3 yrs

Nonsectarian Parent/Child Programs

1900 Second Avenue
(between 97th and 99th Streets)
9th floor
Tel: 360-7803
Fax: 348-7253
Website: cchphealthcare.org

Established 1969
Becky Thomas,
Director

Program hours.   Varied, September through July.

Program.   The center arranges a 20-week series of hour-long discussion groups of eight to ten parents (usually mothers) with their children and infants. Most parents who join with infants remain for the full three years and become a strong support system for one another. The groups are led by a professional in the child development field and a trained parents facilitator. Topics cover developmental issues, family relations, schooling, problems of city living, and so on.

Admissions.   Call to find out if a group is available. Acceptances are on a rolling basis.

Enrollment.   The center may have as many as 19 groups operating at once.

Cost. $500 for twenty sessions.

Facilities.   ECDC is a part of the CCHP located in the 9th floor of the Mental Health Building of the Metropolitan Hospital. The center consists of a playroom equipped with age-appropriate toys and trained play teachers. Across the hall is the meeting room where parent discussion groups take place.

Staff.   The staff includes a child psychiatrist, psychologist, specialists in child development, a social worker, and a pediatrician. There is also a program for individuals interested in child development and parent education training. The school's training consists of a nine-month course, including observation and analysis with a curriculum developed by the center.

Publications.   The center also publishes three books by Dr. Nina Lief, Dr. Mary Ellen Fahs, and Becky Thomas, the school's founding directors, that are available in book stores: *The First Year of Life, The Second Year of Life,* and *The Third Year of Life*.

Sackler Lefcourt Center for Child Development
Ages: Infancy–3 yrs
Parent/Child Programs

17 East 62nd Street
  (between Fifth and
  Madison Avenues)
Zip: 10065
Tel: 759-4022
Fax: 838-7205
Website: www.sacklerlefcourtcenter.com

Established: 1982
Ilene Sackler Lefcourt,
Director

Program year.   September through June

Ages	Hours	Tuition
Mother/Baby 2–12 mos	50 min/wk	see website
Mother/Toddler 13–18 mos	50 min/wk	or call
Mother/Prenursery 19–30 mos;	1 hr 2 days/wk	for tuition
Prenursery		

Programs.   The Center's programs include playgroups for children with discussion groups for mothers. Groups are designed to promote social-emotional development and to provide information to parents about early childhood and the evolving parent-child relationship.

The play groups enable babies, toddlers, and young children to learn through play. With mothers present, children play independently, join in group activities, and interact with peers. Activities include: manipulative toys, water and sand play, and symbolic play materials.

Mothers groups meet weekly at the same time children play. While observing and interacting with their children, mothers discuss parenting and early childhood development. There are six to eight children and their mothers in each group. All groups are led by two professionals trained in early child development.

Admissions.   Enrollment begins in the spring; groups begin in fall. Parents should call to arrange an individual visit. Waiting lists are maintained.

Facilities.   Located on the ground floor of a townhouse on a quiet street, the center's small offices are attractively designed and furnished. There are two playrooms, the director's office, and a waiting area. The sunny pre-nursery playroom looks out on a courtyard and adjoins a room where mothers' discussion groups are held. The rooms are well-equipped with age-appropriate materials.

The Parenting Center at the 92nd Street Y

1395 Lexington Ave.   Sally Tannen,
   (at 92nd Street)   Director
Zip: 10128
Tel: 415-5611
Website: www.92Y.org/parenting

The Parenting Center is entirely independent of the Y's nursery school. Parents should call for a seasonal catalogue or go to the website for class descriptions, and to register for classes. The center offers an extensive selection of 12–16-week courses for parents and children, newborn to age 4. These include courses for parents-to-be and activities for parents and children to share, such as cooking, art, science, and movement. There are also workshops and seminars on such matters as sleep, setting limits, separation, and other issues and aspects of the parent-child relationship.

The Parenting Center has recently added two year-long separation classes; "Twos Together," a two-mornings-a-week class for children 2.4 years old in September and a two-afternoon "Threes Together," for children 2.10 years old in September. Call Sally Tannen for more information.

PARENT CLUBS and MORE RESOURCES

Citibabes

52 Mercer Street
3rd floor
Zip: 10013
Tel: 334-5440
Website: www.citibabes.com

A lunch spot, gym, and play area in which parents may entertain themselves and their toddlers. Classes, guest speakers, books, and child minding are some offerings.

Divalysscious Moms

136 East 55th Street
Suite 6P
Website: www.divamoms.com
Tel: (917) 601-0068

An organization that encourages mothers' networks for a wide variety of activities from spa treatments to interesting speakers, supporting charities, school admissions, personal issues, dining, and entertainment.

Testing for Kindergarten
by Karen Quinn

Website: www.testingforkindergarten.com

A parent's guide to simple strategies to help children with various tests including the ERB, public school placement, and gifted programs.

Junior Kumon/Kumon Learning Centers

Website: www.kumon.com

A preschool enrichment program that emphasizes academic skills in math and reading.

SUPPORT GROUPS AND WORKSHOPS
AND SEMINARS

New York University School of Continuing Education Center for Career Education and Life Planning

7 East 12th Street
Zip: 10003
Tel: 998-7200
Website: www.scps.nyu.edu

A family care provider education program for people who want to start their own day care center.

Parent Guidance Workshops

180 Riverside Drive
Zip: 10024
Tel: 787-8883
Fax: 787-9029
Website: www.samalin.com
E-mail: samalin@aol.com

Nancy Samalin, M.S.,
Director

Introductory and advanced workshops for parents of toddlers through teens are offered. Nancy Samalin also gives lectures and seminars at schools and institutions locally and nationally.

St. Luke's-Roosevelt Parent Family Education

Roosevelt Hospital
1000 10th Avenue
Room 11-A–28
Zip: 10019
Tel: 523-6222
Website: www.wehealnewyork.org

Jo Leonard, R.N., M.A., FACEE,
Director

Offers more than 20 classes, including pre-conception and lamaze childbirth classes, and provides infant/child CPR, first aid instruction, classes in parenting of toddlers, sibling preparation, and other programs for children of all ages and parents.

YWCA of the City of New York

50 Broadway
13th Floor
Zip: 10004
Tel: 735-9708
Website: www.ywcanyc.org

Early childhood programs are available at various YMCA's in Manhattan. Check the website for specific information.

Index of Schools and Programs
Alphabetical Index

Index of All-Day Programs (with starting age)

Index of Parent-Toddler Programs

Index of Schools/Programs
for Children with Special Needs

Index of Websites

Child Development Center, *www.jbfcs.org*
Children's Aid Society/The Philip Coltoff Center at Greenwich Village, *www.childrensaidsociety.org*
Children's All Day School and Pre-Nursery, *www.childrensallday.org*
Children's Garden at General Theological Seminary, The, *www.gts.edu*
Children's Learning Center, *www.clc-nyc.org*
Children's Storefront, *www.thechildrensstorefront.org*
Christ Church Day School, *www.christchurchnyc.org*
Citibabes, *www.citibabes.com*
City and Country School, *www.cityandcountry.org*
Claremont Children's School, *www.claremontschool.org*
Columbia Greenhouse Nursery School, The, *www.columbiagreenhouse .com*
Columbus Park West Nursery School, *www.cpwn.org*
Columbus Preschool and Gym, *www.columbuspre-school.com*
Convent of the Sacred Heart, *www.cshnyc.org*
Corlears School, *www.corlearsschool.org*
CP Kids, *www.chelseapiers.com/fh*
Creative Playschool, *www.5as.org/sections/playschool.asp*
Discovery Programs/The Toddler Center, *www.discoveryprograms.com*
Divalysscious Moms, *www.divalyssciousmoms.com*
Downtown Little School, The, *www.downtownlittleschool.com*
Early Childhood Resource and Information Center, *www.nypl.org*
Educational Alliance Preschool, The, *www.edalliance.org*
Educational Records Bureau, The, (ERB), *www.erbtest.org*
Epiphany Community Nursery School, *www.74magic.com*
Ethical Culture, *www.ecfs.org*
Family Annex, *www.thefamilyannex.org*
First Presbyterian Church Nursery School, *www.fpcns.org*
43rd Street Kids Preschool, Inc., *www.43rdstreetkids.org*
Free to Be Under Three, *www.freetobeunderthree.com*
Garden House School of New York, *www.gardenhouseschool.org*
Gillen Brewer School. The, *www.gillianbrewer.com*
Grace Church School, *www.gcschool.org*
Head Start, *www.nyc.gov* click: Administration for Children's Services, Head Start Info or *www.nyc.gov*. city agencies, Health and Mental Hygiene, Bureau of Day Care
Hollingsworth Preschool of Teacher's College, Columbia University, *www.tc.columbia.edu*
Horace Mann School Nursery Division, *www.horacemann.org*
House of Little People, *www.thehouseoflittlepeople.com*

Independent Schools Admissions Association of Greater New York (ISAAGNY), *www.isaagny.org*

International Preschools, the, *www.ipsnyc.org*

Jack and Jill School, *www.jackandjillschool.com*

JCC in Manhattan, The Saul and Carole Zabar Nursery School, The, *www.jccmanhattan.org/nurseryschool*

Kid's Korner, *www.thekidskornerpreschool.com*

La Escuelita, *www.laescuelitanyc.org*

La Scuola d'Italia "G. Marconi," *www.lascuoladitalia.org*

Learning Disabilities Association of New York City Telephone Referral Service, The, *www.ldanyc.org*

Learning, the Arts, and Me Nursery of Third Street Music School Settlement, *www.thirdstreetmusicschool.org*

Le Jardin a L'Ouest, *www.lejardinalouest.com*

Little Dreamers of NYC, *www.littledreamersofnyc.com*

Little Red School House, *www.lrei.org*

Lycée Francais de New York, *www.lfny.org*

Lyceum Kennedy French International School, *www.lyceumkennedy.org*

Madison Avenue Presbyterian Day School, The, *www.mapc.com*

Mandell School, The, *www.mandellschool.org*

Manhattan Country School, *www.manhattancountryschool.org*

Manhattan Private School Advisors, *www.privateschooladvisors.com*

Marymount School of New York, *www.marymount.K12.ny.us*

Medical Center Nursery School, The, *www.mcns.org*

Metropolitan Montessori School, *www.mmsny.org*

Montessori School of Manhattan, *www.montessorimanhattan.com*

Montessori School of New York International, *www.montessorischoolny.com*

Morningside Montessori School, *www.morningsidemontessori.org*

National Center for Learning Disabilities, The, *www.NCLD.org*

National Dissemination Center for Children with Disabilities, *www.nichcy.org*

Nazareth Nursery, *www.nazarethnursery.com*

New York Branch of the International Dyslexia Association, The, *www.nybida.org*

New York City Association for the Education of Young Children, *www.nycaeyc.org*

New York City Department of Health, Division of Day Care, The, *www.nyc.gov*

New York University School of Continuing Education Center for Career Education and Life Planning, *www.scps.nyu.edu*

92nd Street YM-YWHA Nursery School, *www.92y.org*

Northside Center for Child Development, Inc., *www.northsidecenter.org*
Nursery School at Habonim, The, *www.habonim.net*
Our Lady of Pompeii Elementary School, *www.LadyofPompeii.org*
Parenting Center at the 92nd Street Y, The, *www.92y.org*
Parent Guidance Workshops, *www.samalin.com*
Parents League of New York, Inc., The, *www.parentsleague.org*
Park Avenue Synagogue Early Childhood Center, *www.pasyn.org*
Park Preschool, The, *www.theparkpreschool.org*
Philosophy Day School, *www.philosophyday.org*
Purple Circle Day School, *www.purple-circle.org*
Rabbi Arthur Schneier Park East Day School, *www.rasped.org*
Ramaz School, *www.ramaz.org*
Red Balloon Community Day Care Center, The,
      www.Redballoonlearningcenter.com
Resurrection Episcopal Day School, *www.redsny.org*
Rhinelander Nursery School, The, *www.rhinelandercenter.org*
River-Park Nursery School and Kindergarten,
      www.riverparknurseryschool.com
River School, The, *www.theriverschool.com*
Riverside Church Weekday School, *www.weekdayschool-nyc.org*
Riverside Montessori, *www.twinparks.org*
Rodeph Sholom School, The, *www.rodephsholomschool.org*
Roosevelt Island Day Nursery, *www.ridn.org*
Rudolf Steiner School, The, *www.steiner.edu*
St. Bartholomew Community Preschool, *www.stbarts.org*
St. Hilda's & St. Hugh's School, *www.sthildas.org*
St. Ignatius Loyola Day Nursery, *www.saintignatiusloyola.org*
St. Luke's-Roosevelt Parent Family Education, *www.wehealnewyork.org*
St. Luke's School, *www.stlukeschool.org*
Schools & You, *www.schoolsandyou.com*
74th Street MAGIC at Epiphany Community School, *www.74magic.com*
Smart City Kids, *www.smartcitykids.com*
So Glad We Waited Network, *www.sogladwewaited.com*
Stephen Wise Free Synagogue Early Childhood Center,
      www.swfs.org/ecc
Studio School, The, *www.studioschool.org*
Temple Emanu-el Nursery School, *www.emanuelnyc.org*
Temple Israel Early Childhood Learning Center,
      www.templeisraelnyc.org
Temple Shaaray Tefila Nursery, *www.shaaraytefilanyc.org*
Tender Care, *www.ymcanyc.org*
Town House International School, *www.townhouseinternationalschool.org*

Town School, The, *www.thetownschool.org*
Trevor Day School, *www.trevor.org*
TriBeCa Community School, *www.tribecacommunityschool.com*
Twin Parks Park West Montessori School, *www.twinparks.org*
Trinity Parish Preschool and Nursery, *www.trinitywallstreet.org*
United Cerebral Palsy of New York City Manhattan Children's Center,
   www.ucpnyc.org
University Plaza Nursery School, Inc., *www.universityplazanursery.com*
Vanderbilt YMCA, *www.ymcanyc.org*
Victoria Goldman, *www.victoriagoldman.net*
Village Kids Nursery, *www.villagekidsnursery.com*
Village Preschool Center, *www.villagepreschoolcenter.com*
Washington Heights and Inwood YM-YWHA, *www.ywaswhhts.org*
Washington Market School, The,*www.washingtonmarketschool.org*
West Side Family Preschool, *www.westsidefamilypreschool.org*
West Side Montessori School, *www.wsms.org*
West Village Nursery School, *www.westvillagenurseryschool.org*
William Woodward Jr. Nursery School, *www.woodwardns.org*
Yaldaynu Center, *www.anchechesed.org*
York Avenue Preschool, *www.yorkavenuepreschool.org*
Your Kids "R" Our Kids, *www.yourkidsourkids.com*